KINGSHIP AND POLITICS IN THE LATE NINTH CENTURY

This is the first major study in any language of the collapse of the pan-European Carolingian empire and the reign of its last ruler, Charles III 'the Fat' (876–88). The later decades of the empire are conventionally seen as a dismal period of decline and fall, scarred by internal feuding, unfettered aristocratic ambition and Viking onslaught. This book offers a fresh interpretation, arguing that previous generations of historians misunderstood the nature and causes of the end of the empire, and neglected many of the relatively numerous sources for this period. Topics covered include the significance of aristocratic power; political structures; the possibilities and limits of kingship; developments in royal ideology; the struggle with the Vikings; and the nature of regional political identities. In proposing new explanations for the empire's disintegration, this book has broader implications for our understanding of this formative period of European history more generally.

SIMON MACLEAN is Lecturer in History at the University of St Andrews, Scotland.

Cambridge Studies in Medieval Life and Thought
Fourth Series

General Editor:
D. E. LUSCOMBE
Research Professor of Medieval History, University of Sheffield

Advisory Editors:
CHRISTINE CARPENTER
Reader in Medieval English History, University of Cambridge, and Fellow of New Hall

ROSAMOND McKITTERICK
Professor of Medieval History, University of Cambridge, and Fellow of Newnham College

The series Cambridge Studies in Medieval Life and Thought was inaugurated by G. G. Coulton in 1921; Professor D. E. Luscombe now acts as General Editor of the Fourth Series, with Dr Christine Carpenter and Professor Rosamond McKitterick as Advisory Editors. The series brings together outstanding work by medieval scholars over a wide range of human endeavour extending from political economy to the history of ideas.

For a list of titles in the series, see end of book.

KINGSHIP AND POLITICS IN THE LATE NINTH CENTURY

Charles the Fat and the end of the Carolingian Empire

SIMON MACLEAN

PUBLISHED BY THE PRESS SYNDICATE OF THE UNIVERSITY OF CAMBRIDGE
The Pitt Building, Trumpington Street, Cambridge CB2 1RP, United Kingdom

CAMBRIDGE UNIVERSITY PRESS
The Edinburgh Building, Cambridge, CB2 2RU, UK
40 West 20th Street, New York, NY 10011–4211, USA
477 Williamstown Road, Port Melbourne, VIC 3207, Australia
Ruiz de Alarcón 13, 28014 Madrid, Spain
Dock House, The Waterfront, Cape Town 8001, South Africa

http://www.cambridge.org

© Simon MacLean 2003

This book is in copyright. Subject to statutory exception
and to the provisions of relevant collective licensing agreements,
no reproduction of any part may take place without
the written permission of Cambridge University Press.

First published 2003
Reprinted 2005

Printed in the United Kingdom at the University Press, Cambridge

Typeface Bembo 11/12 pt.   *System* LATEX 2$_\varepsilon$ [TB]

A catalogue record for this book is available from the British Library

Library of Congress Cataloguing in Publication data
MacLean, Simon.
Kingship and policy in the late ninth century : Charles the Fat and
the end of the Carolingian Empire / Simon MacLean.
p.   cm. – (Cambridge studies in medieval life and thought ; 4th ser., 57)
Includes bibliographical references and index.
ISBN 0-521-81945-8
1. Charles, le Gros, Emperor, 839–888.   2. France – Kings and rulers – Biography.
3. France – History – To 987.   4. Holy Roman Empire – History – 843–1273.   I. Title.
II. Series.
'.01 DC77.8M33   2003
944   '092 – dc21   2003043471

ISBN 0 521 81945 8 hardback

CONTENTS

List of maps and figures	*page* vii
Acknowledgements	viii
List of abbreviations	xi
Note on names, terminology and citations	xiv
Outline chronology	xv

1	INTRODUCTION	1
	The end of the Carolingian empire in modern historiography	1
	The shape of politics in the late ninth century	11
2	UN-FRANKISH ACTIVITIES: CHARLES THE FAT IN THE EYES OF CONTEMPORARY ANNALISTS	23
	The *Annals of Fulda*	24
	Bad advice	28
	The Vikings and the siege of Asselt	30
	Royal inactivity	37
	History and politics in the late ninth century	42
3	THE MEN WHO WOULD BE KINGS: THE 'SUPERMAGNATES' AND THE 'RISE OF THE ARISTOCRACY'	48
	The rise of Odo	49
	Politics and identity in Abbo's *Wars of the City of Paris*	55
	The supermagnates and the empire	64
	Conclusion	75
4	ROYAL POLITICS AND REGIONAL POWER IN THE LATE CAROLINGIAN EMPIRE	81
	Alemannia and Alsace	83
	Italy	91
	Franconia, Saxony and Bavaria	97
	West Francia	99
	The north Frankish circle	102
	Geilo of Langres	110

Contents

	Royal politics and aristocratic identity in late ninth-century west Francia	115
	Conclusion	120
5	THE END OF THE EMPIRE I: POLITICS AND IDEOLOGY AT THE EAST FRANKISH COURT	123
	The restoration of the empire, 884–5	124
	The attempted legitimation of Bernard, August–October 885	129
	The position of Arnulf, 876–85	134
	The revolt of Hugh, September 885, and the origins of 'German' royal consecration	144
6	THE END OF THE EMPIRE II: RESPONSE AND FAILURE	161
	Carolingian unity and the adoption of Louis of Provence, April–June 887	161
	The royal divorce, summer 887	169
	The career of Liutward	178
	The empress and the archchancellor	185
	The deposition of Charles the Fat, November 887	191
7	HISTORY, POLITICS AND THE END OF THE EMPIRE IN NOTKER'S *DEEDS OF CHARLEMAGNE*	199
	The date of the *Deeds of Charlemagne*	201
	Notker's bishops	204
	Contemporary references in the *Deeds of Charlemagne*	213
	Notker and the imperial succession	218
	Charles the Fat and Charles the Great	222
	Conclusion	227
8	CONCLUSION	230
	Bibliography	236
	Index	258

MAPS AND FIGURES

MAPS

1	The late Carolingian empire	*page* xviii
2	Alemannia	84
3	Landholding around Pavia	92
4	Northern Francia	105
5	Carinthia and Pannonia	137
6	Fiscal rights granted to Ötting in D CIII 128	140
7	Liutward's Italian interventions	181
8	Richgard's monastic empire	187

FIGURE

1	The Carolingian family	xvii

ACKNOWLEDGEMENTS

I have incurred many debts in the completion of this book, only a few of which can be acknowledged here. I am very fortunate to have had the opportunity to learn from some excellent teachers. In the first place I must thank Jinty Nelson, who supervised the PhD thesis of which this book is a revised version. Her encouragement and generosity with ideas and criticisms have improved both versions immeasurably. I have also learned much from Stuart Airlie, who not only inspired my interest in Carolingian history in the first place and suggested Charles the Fat as a suitable subject for research, but also commented helpfully on parts of my work. I am grateful to Rosamond McKitterick for acting so efficiently as my editor and making many valuable criticisms and corrections. Several other people were kind enough to read all or part of the original thesis, and forced me to think harder about my interpretations: in particular I should like to record my gratitude to my PhD examiners, Paul Fouracre and the late Tim Reuter, as well as to David Ganz, Matthew Innes, Paul Kershaw and Geoff West for their generous help. Naturally, I take full responsibility for the multitude of errors which doubtless remains. I have also benefited from conversations with many friends and colleagues: in particular, I am grateful to Guy Halsall and Alan Thacker for help and encouragement. Financially, I am fortunate to have been supported by two bodies without which my postgraduate study would have been impossible: the Student Awards Agency for Scotland (from which I held a Major Scottish Studentship) and the Institute of Historical Research (which granted me a Scouloudi Fellowship). Thanks are also due to the fellows of Trinity Hall in Cambridge, who elected me to a Research Fellowship which allowed me to begin writing this book. More recently, I am grateful to my colleagues in the Department of Mediaeval History in the University of St Andrews for making it possible for me to finish it. The staff of Cambridge University Press have been extremely helpful, especially Bill Davies. The cover picture for the book was supplied by Bildarchiv Foto Marburg. I am also indebted to my friends for moral support and keeping me sane, in particular Anne Jenkins, John Kyle,

Acknowledgements

Steve Marritt and the players and touring squad of Eskbank Thistle F. C., *propugnatores* to a man. Special thanks go to Claire Jones for support and encouragement. My greatest debt is to my family, in particular my parents. They have given me much more than I have ever thanked them for, and I would like to dedicate this book to them.

ABBREVIATIONS

AA	*Annales Alamannici*, ed. W. Lendi, *Untersuchungen zur frühalemannischen Annalistik. Die Murbacher Annalen, mit Edition* (Freiburg, 1971)
AB	*Annales Bertiniani*, eds. F. Grat, J. Vielliard, S. Clémencet and L. Levillain, *Annales de Saint-Bertin* (Paris, 1964)
AF	*Annales Fuldenses*, ed. F. Kurze, MGH SRG (Hanover, 1891)
AF(B)	*Annales Fuldenses*, Bavarian continuation
AF(M)	*Annales Fuldenses*, Mainz continuation
AH	*Annales Hildesheimenses*, ed. G. Waitz, MGH SRG (Hanover, 1878)
ARF	*Annales Regni Francorum*, ed. F. Kurze, MGH SRG (Hanover, 1895)
AS	*Annales Iuvavenses*, ed. H. Bresslau, MGH SS (vol. 30, Hanover, 1926), pp. 727–44
AV	*Annales Vedastini*, ed. B. von Simson, *Annales Xantenses et Annales Vedastini*, MGH SRG (Hanover, 1909)
AX	*Annales Xantenses*, ed. B. von Simson, *Annales Xantenses et Annales Vedastini*, MGH SRG (Hanover, 1909)
BM	J. F. Böhmer and E. Mühlbacher, *Regesta Imperii. Die Regesten des Kaiserreichs unter den Karolingern, 751–918* (Innsbruck, 1908)
CDL	G. Porro-Lambertenghi et al. (eds.), *Codex Diplomaticus Langobardiae* (Historiae Patriae Monumenta 13) (Turin, 1873)
D(D)	Diploma(s) of church/ruler (see bibliography for full details):
Bünd	*Bündner Urkundenbuch*
AC	Arnulf of Carinthia
BF	Berengar I of Friuli
C2	Carloman II
CB	Charles the Bald
CIII	Charles III the Fat
CS	Charles the Simple

List of abbreviations

Crem	Cremona
Frei	Freising
K	Karlmann of Bavaria
L	Lothar I
L2	Louis II of Italy
L3	Louis III of west Francia
LC	Louis the Child
LG	Louis the German
Lor	Lorsch
Loth2	Lothar II
LS	Louis the Stammerer
LY	Louis the Younger
OG	Otto I the Great
OP	Odo of Paris
RB	Rudolf of Burgundy
Reg	Regensburg
SG	St-Gall
Zur	Zurich
DA	*Deutsches Archiv für Erforschung des Mittelalters*
EME	*Early Medieval Europe*
FMSt	*Frühmittelalterliche Studien*
HZ	*Historische Zeitschrift*
JMH	*Journal of Medieval History*
MGH	Monumenta Germaniae Historica:
Capit	Capitularia regum Francorum, eds. A. Boretius and V. Krause, MGH Leges section III (2 vols., Hanover, 1883–97)
Epp	Epistolae (8 vols., Hanover, 1887–1939)
SRG	Scriptores rerum Germanicarum in usum scholarum separatim editi (Hanover, 1871–)
SRG NS	Scriptores rerum Germanicarum, nova series (Hanover, 1922–)
SRL	Scriptores rerum Langobardicarum, ed. G. Waitz (Hanover, 1878)
SS	Scriptores (32 vols., Hanover, 1826–1934)
NCMH2	R. McKitterick (ed.), *The New Cambridge Medieval History, volume II, c.700–c.900* (Cambridge, 1995)
Notker, *Continuatio*	Notker, *Erchanberti Breviarium Continuatio*, ed. G. H. Pertz, MGH SS (vol. 2, Hanover, 1829)
Notker, *Gesta*	Notker, *Gesta Karoli Magni*, ed. H. F. Haefele, *Notker der Stammler, Taten Kaiser Karls des Großen*, MGH SRG NS (Berlin, 1959)

xii

List of abbreviations

PL	*Patrologia Latina*, ed. J.-P. Migne (221 vols., Paris, 1841–66)
QFIAB	*Quellen und Forschung aus italienischen Archiven und Bibliotheken*
Regino, *Chronicon*	*Reginonis abbatis Prumiensis Chronicon cum continuatione Treverensi*, ed. F. Kurze, MGH SRG (Hanover, 1890)
Settimane	*Settimane di Studio del Centro italiano di studi sull'alto medioevo* (Spoleto, 1953–)
TRHS	*Transactions of the Royal Historical Society*
ZGO	*Zeitschrift für die Geschichte des Oberrheins*
ZSRG GA	*Zeitschrift der Savigny-Stiftung für Rechtsgeschichte, Germanistische Abteilung*

NOTE ON NAMES, TERMINOLOGY AND CITATIONS

Following conventional practice, I have anglicised and modernised names of people and places wherever possible. The one exception is Louis the German's eldest son, to whom I refer in the German spelling as Karlmann in order to distinguish him from the contemporary west Frankish ruler Carloman II. Kings are given their conventional nicknames for convenience, to help distinguish all the Louis and Charleses from each other. Monasteries are referred to in the form St-Martin (or S Cristina for Italian examples), saints themselves in the form St Verena. I have left some commonly used words in the original language where a translation would not adequately convey the full meaning: *fidelis/es* (faithful man in the sense of follower); *honor/es* (office held from the king); *regnum/a* (kingdom or part of a kingdom); *reguli* (petty kings or kinglets, as applied to post-888 rulers); *marchio/nes* (regional representative of the ruler); *Königsnähe* (nearness/access to the king).

Due to considerations of space, the footnotes are not intended to be comprehensively bibliographical. The bibliography itself is limited to the works cited in the footnotes. Charters are cited by edition, rather than page, number. I have used the unconventional abbreviations *AF(M)* and *AF(B)* for, respectively, the Mainz and Bavarian continuations of the *Annales Fuldenses*.

All excerpts from sources are translated into English, with the original given in Latin only if the interpretation of particular words is critical to the argument. Renderings of the most important narratives are taken directly from the excellent translations of J. L. Nelson, *The Annals of Saint-Bertin* (Manchester, 1991) and T. Reuter, *The Annals of Fulda* (Manchester, 1992), unless otherwise indicated. Quotations from Notker's *Deeds of Charlemagne* follow the less reliable but still useful translation of L. Thorpe, *Two Lives of Charlemagne* (London, 1969), with amendments where necessary.

OUTLINE CHRONOLOGY

839	Birth of Charles the Fat.
840	Death of Louis the Pious, followed by civil wars between his sons.
841	Battle of Fontenoy.
843	Treaty of Verdun: empire divided into east, west and middle kingdoms.
870	Treaty of Meersen: Lotharingia divided between east and west Francia.
875	Death of Louis II of Italy without heir, followed by extended struggle for power.
876	Death of Louis the German: east Francia divided between his sons (Karlmann of Bavaria, Louis the Younger of Franconia/Saxony, Charles the Fat of Alemannia and Alsace).
877	Death of Charles the Bald, succeeded by his son Louis the Stammerer.
879	Death of Louis the Stammerer and abdication of Karlmann after a stroke. Viking Great Army returns to Continent.
879–80	West Frankish succession dispute, kingdom divided between Louis III and Carloman II.
880	Remaining four Carolingians defeat usurper Boso of Vienne and come to sworn agreement at Vienne. Treaty provides for political cooperation, mutual succession and resolution of territorial disputes. Lotharingia reunited.
880–4	Deaths of three of the four parties to the Vienne agreement, all without heir: Louis the Younger (882), Louis III (882) and Carloman II (884). Charles the Fat inherits all of their kingdoms. He is also crowned emperor by the pope in 881.
882	Charles besieges Vikings at Asselt, and pays ransom.
882–5	Intense Viking activity, especially in northern Francia.
885	Emperor blinds and imprisons his cousin Hugh of Lotharingia, and attempts to limit the political power of his nephew Arnulf of Carinthia.

Outline chronology

885–6 Viking siege of Paris. Charles pays ransom to free the city.

886 Winter: Charles falls ill and retreats to Alsace.

887 Summer: emperor adopts Boso's son Louis of Provence and divorces his wife Richgard. November: Arnulf of Carinthia mounts a palace coup and deposes the emperor, taking over as king in east Francia.

888 January: Charles dies of natural causes. Kings are legitimately crowned from outwith the direct male Carolingian line (and outwith the dynasty) for the first time since 751: Odo of Paris (west Francia); Rudolf (Transjurane Burgundy); Guy of Spoleto (west Francia and then Italy); Berengar of Friuli (Italy).

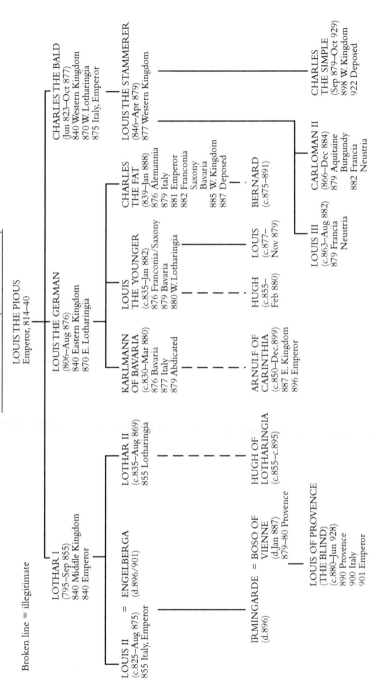

Figure 1. The Carolingian family

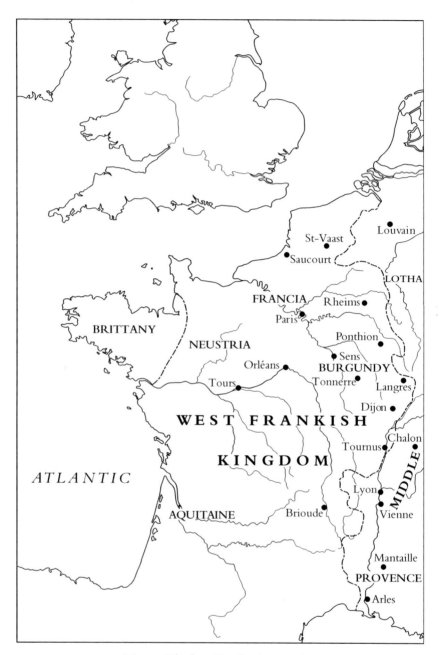

Map 1. The late Carolingian empire

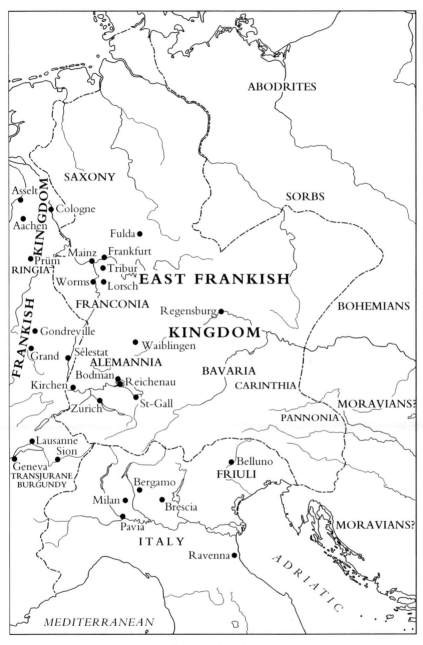

Map 1. (cont.)

Chapter 1

INTRODUCTION

THE END OF THE CAROLINGIAN EMPIRE IN MODERN HISTORIOGRAPHY

The dregs of the Carlovingian race no longer exhibited any symptoms of virtue or power, and the ridiculous epithets of the Bald, the Stammerer, the Fat, and the Simple, distinguished the tame and uniform features of a crowd of kings alike deserving of oblivion. By the failure of the collateral branches, the whole inheritance devolved to Charles the Fat, the last emperor of his family: his insanity authorised the desertion of Germany, Italy, and France ... The governors, the bishops and the lords usurped the fragments of the falling empire.[1]

This was how, in the late eighteenth century, the great Enlightenment historian Edward Gibbon passed verdict on the end of the Carolingian empire almost exactly 900 years earlier. To twenty-first-century eyes, the terms of this assessment may seem jarring. Gibbon's emphasis on the importance of virtue and his ideas about who or what was a deserving subject of historical study very much reflect the values of his age, the expectations of his audience and the intentions of his work.[2] However, if the timbre of his analysis now feels dated, its constituent elements have nonetheless survived into modern historiography. The conventional narrative of the end of the empire in the year 888 is still a story about the emergence of recognisable medieval kingdoms which would become modern nations – France, Germany and Italy; about the personal inadequacies of late ninth-century kings as rulers; and about their powerlessness in the face of an increasingly independent, acquisitive and assertive aristocracy. This book is an examination of the validity of these assumptions, and aims to retell the story of the end of the Carolingian empire through the prism of the reign of its last emperor, Charles III, 'the Fat'.

[1] E. Gibbon, *History of the Decline and Fall of the Roman Empire*, new edn (2 vols., Chicago, 1990), vol. 2, chap. 49, p. 213.
[2] See R. McKitterick and R. Quinault (eds.), *Edward Gibbon and Empire* (Cambridge, 1997), esp. R. McKitterick, 'Gibbon and the Early Middle Ages in Eighteenth-Century Europe', pp. 162–89.

I

Kingship and Politics in the Late Ninth Century

Charles the Fat (the nickname is convenient, but not contemporary[3]) was the great-grandson of the emperor Charlemagne, whose wars of conquest and cultural reforms had shaped the territory and character of the Frankish empire under the Carolingians in the late eighth and early ninth centuries. In 843 the empire was split, in traditional Frankish style, between the grandsons of Charlemagne, and despite Viking invasion and periods of internal conflict its constituent kingdoms remained in the Carolingians' hands for nearly five further decades. Charles the Fat is traditionally seen as the squanderer of this family inheritance. The end of his reign heralded the destruction both of the monopoly on legitimate royal power which the Carolingian dynasty had maintained since 751, and of the territorial coherence of the pan-European Frankish empire. At the time of his succession as king of Alemannia in 876 the Carolingian hegemony was very much intact, and Charles was but one king among several controlling the *regna* of the empire. However, within a decade he had become his dynasty's sole ruling representative. A bewildering mixture of illness and misadventure stripped the Carolingian house of all its other adult legitimate males, and delivered into Charles's hands first Italy (879), then Bavaria, Franconia and Saxony (882), and finally the west Frankish kingdom (885). This comprehensive agglomeration of territories amounted to a restoration, for the first time since 840, of the entire empire of Charlemagne, which extended over a million square kilometres. In 881 Charles added the imperial crown to his list of titles, a dignity which enhanced his status and moral authority, although it gave him no new powers. However, Charles's unparalleled success (or fortune) in the acquisition of Carolingian kingdoms during his reign was overshadowed by the abject failure of its conclusion, when, in November 887, he was deposed in a palace coup by his nephew Arnulf of Carinthia, before dying of natural causes a matter of weeks later. Because Charles remained heirless and Arnulf was a bastard, a legitimacy vacuum opened up at the top of Frankish politics. Although descendants of Charlemagne ruled at sporadic intervals in tenth-century France and Italy, the ending of the main Carolingian line's monopoly on legitimate royal power in the crisis of 887–8 meant that parts of the empire were made subject to rule by female-line and non-Carolingians for the first time since 751, and its territories were split apart once and for all. It is generally believed that Charles's loss of power reveals him to have been a failure, an unimaginative and personally weak do-nothing ruler in whose feeble grip the Carolingian

---

[3] The nickname 'Fat' was coined no earlier than the twelfth century: K. Nass, *Die Reichskronik des Annalista Saxo und die sächsische Geschichtsschreibung im 12. Jahrhundert* (Hanover, 1996), p. 49. The dimensions of Charles's girth are thus lamentably unknown. I am grateful to John Gillingham for this reference.

Introduction

empire, unprotected from internal conflict and Viking attack, was allowed to tear itself apart. The reign therefore symbolises the end of an era.

As a result of this, the issue of how the reign should be interpreted also has broader historiographical implications. The negative scholarly opinion which prevails about Charles the Fat is based less on critical study of the available evidence than on presuppositions about the course of Carolingian political history as a whole. The historiography of the end of the empire is suffused with ideas from three main strands of scholarly tradition. The first concerns the overall trajectory of Carolingian politics as a curve of rise until about 830, and then decline and fall. It is a commonplace that royal power declined in the later ninth century (according to a recent authority this is 'obvious').[4] While the landed power of the monarchy dwindled, the aristocracy 'rose', assuming ever more regalian rights, taking over defence against the Vikings and ultimately seizing power in 887–8 from a Carolingian dynasty which was drained of its economic and moral authority. The king–aristocracy relationship is characterised here as oppositional. Late ninth-century kings, and especially Charles the Fat, the ultimate victim of these processes, ruled not with, but rather in spite of the high nobility, who eventually rose up and seized power for themselves. The female-line, illegitimate and non-Carolingian kings who assumed the mantle of kingship in 888 (a contemporary called them *reguli*, 'kinglets') were members of the high aristocracy: therefore, the reasoning goes, any evidence for their activities prior to this date should be read as revealing stages in their 'rise' to kingship.[5]

This type of thinking still lies submerged in many of the standard works on the period: the 'rise of the aristocracy' has become an accepted and largely unquestioned historical reference point the authority of which can be invoked to explain other phenomena of the late ninth century.[6] The principal reason for this is historiographical: the model, as teleological as it is, fits very neatly into the traditional grand narratives of medieval European history. In particular, it is still often assumed that to explain the supposed emergence of 'feudalism', 'France' and 'Germany' in the tenth century, it is necessary to postulate a crisis of state power developing throughout the late ninth century and facilitating the shift from 'public' (royal) to 'private' (aristocratic) authority.[7] The work of the

---

[4] B. Arnold, *Medieval Germany, 500–1300. A Political Interpretation* (London, 1997), pp. 34, 82.

[5] *AF(B)* s.a. 888, p. 116.

[6] C. Lauranson-Rosaz, 'Le Roi et les grands dans l'Aquitaine carolingienne', in R. Le Jan (ed.), *La Royauté et les élites dans l'Europe carolingienne (début IXe siècle aux environs de 920)* (Lille, 1998), pp. 409–36, esp. p. 434, to cite one recent, randomly selected example.

[7] For apposite comments on the historiographical issues, see T. Reuter, 'The Origins of the German *Sonderweg*? The Empire and its Rulers in the High Middle Ages', in A. Duggan (ed.), *Kings and*

Kingship and Politics in the Late Ninth Century

Belgian author Jan Dhondt, whose 1948 book *Études sur la naissance des principautés teritoriales en France* is the classic account of the 'rise' thesis, remains the most coherent attempt to expound it systematically on the basis of analysis of the contemporary sources.[8] Dhondt argued that the ninth century saw a centrifugal redistribution of resources, and by implication power, from the Carolingian kings to a grasping aristocracy, speeded up by the exigencies of defence against the Vikings.[9] By the late ninth century, some aristocrats were acting as kings in all but name, allowing them to dispense with Carolingian authority. Dhondt's thesis remains hugely influential, and has become tacitly ratified by and crystallised in historical convention.

Secondly, intricately entwined with the 'rise of the aristocracy' model is the view that the later ninth century was an era of regional particularism and growing provincial desire to secede from the empire. Ultimately, these concerns go back to the nineteenth century and the dawn of professional history, the practitioners and patrons of which were often preoccupied with defining the character and origins of modern nation-states.[10] However, these early academic enterprises left an enduring legacy to modern historians, notably French but often followed by those writing in English. In the words of Pierre Riché, for instance, the Treaty of Verdun of 843, which divided the empire into three vertical strips, two of which resembled modern France and Germany in territorial extent, was 'the birth-certificate of Europe'.[11] In contrast, post-war German historians have become extremely cautious about ascribing modern nationalities to early medieval polities, anxious to avoid reproducing the chauvinistic and teleological perspectives of their predecessors. Recent work, exemplified by Carlrichard Brühl's enormous treatise on the subject, has

---

Kingship in Medieval Europe (London, 1993), pp. 179–211, at pp. 210–11; D. Barthélemy, 'Debate: the "Feudal Revolution" I', *Past and Present* 152 (1996), 196–205, at 199; S. Reynolds, 'The Historiography of the Medieval State', in M. Bentley (ed.), *Companion to Historiography* (London and New York, 1997), pp. 117–38, at pp. 124–5; D. Barthélemy, 'La chevalerie carolingienne: prélude au XIe siècle', in Le Jan (ed.), *La Royauté et les elites*, pp. 159–75, at p. 168.

[8] J. Dhondt, *Études sur la naissance des principautés territoriales en France (IXe–Xe siècle)* (Bruges, 1948). J. W. Thompson, *The Dissolution of the Carolingian Fisc in the Ninth Century* (Berkeley, 1935) was an earlier but even more flawed attempt.

[9] On the Viking aspect of the thesis, the most influential work has been F. Vercauteren, 'Comment s'est-on défendu, au IXe siècle dans l'empire Franc contre les invasions normandes', in *XXXe Congrès de la Fédération Archéologique de Belgique* (Brussels, 1936), pp. 117–32.

[10] See now P. Geary, *The Myth of Nations: the Medieval Origins of Europe* (Princeton, 2002). However, some nineteenth-century works remain valuable: in particular G. Waitz, *Deutsche Verfassungsgeschichte* (8 vols., Berlin, 1876–96); and E. Dümmler, *Geschichte des ostfränkischen Reiches*, 2nd edn (3 vols., Leipzig, 1887–8).

[11] P. Riché, *The Carolingians: a Family who Forged Europe* (Philadelphia, 1993), p. 168; C. Brühl, *Deutschland-Frankreich: Die Geburt zweier Völker* (Cologne and Vienna, 1990), pp. 7–82 comments perceptively on the historiographical issues.

Introduction

emphasised that there is no convincing evidence for recognisably French and German national identities before the eleventh century, until which time politics continued to be articulated in a resolutely Frankish idiom.[12] German scholarship has nevertheless continued to debate the emergence of regional political identities in the so-called principalities or 'younger stem-duchies' of the late ninth and tenth centuries. Traditionally these have been thought of as provincial solidarities within former Carolingian subkingdoms such as Bavaria, Saxony and Franconia, each one cemented by its own ethnic identity and led by a semi-autonomous duke (a 'risen' aristocrat) who represented his people and ruled them more or less in lieu of the king.[13] Although the duchies' ethnic basis has been questioned by Karl-Ferdinand Werner and his followers, who prefer to see them as direct successors to regnal structures created by the Carolingians, their emergence continues to be a primary focus for discussions of late ninth-century history.[14]

These historiographical concerns, the origins of nations and the rise of the aristocratic duchies, have cluttered up the political history of the ninth century with a considerable amount of unwelcome baggage. The exposition of these alleged processes has been prioritised over the observation of what actually happened. The search for origins encourages teleology, leading to the late ninth-century evidence being interpreted backwards, from the perspective of the known outcome. It has also led to the assumption that the high aristocratic families who went on to lead the post-Carolingian kingdoms and duchies did so as representatives of ethnic groups: the emergence of smaller political units after 888 is therefore linked in historiographical traditions to the model of the rise of

---

[12] Brühl, *Deutschland-Frankreich* (mysteriously, Brühl's book has exactly 843 pages); K. F. Werner, 'Völker und Regna', in C. Brühl and B. Schneidmüller (eds.), *Beiträge zur mittelalterlichen Reichs- und Nationsbildung in Deutschland und Frankreich* (Munich, 1997), pp. 15–43. Cf. the comments of S. Airlie, 'After Empire: Recent Work on the Emergence of Post-Carolingian Kingdoms', *EME* 2 (1993), 153–61 and Arnold, *Medieval Germany*, pp. 1–12.

[13] The enormous older bibliography on this subject is best accessed through the discussion of H.-W. Goetz, *Dux und Ducatus. Begriffs- und verfassungsgeschichtliche Untersuchungen zur Entstehung des sogenannten 'jüngeren' Stammesherzogtums an der Wende vom neunten zum zehnten Jahrhundert* (Bochum, 1977), pp. 11–91.

[14] K. F. Werner, *Structures politiques du monde franc (VIe–XIIe siècles)* (London, 1979); K. Brunner, 'Der fränkische Fürstentitel im neunten und zehnten Jahrhundert', in H. Wolfram (ed.), *Intitulatio II. Lateinische Herrscher- und Fürstentitel im neunten und zehnten Jahrhundert*, (Vienna, Cologne and Graz, 1973), pp. 179–340. See now R. Le Jan, 'Continuity and Change in the Tenth-Century Nobility', in A. Duggan (ed.), *Nobles and Nobility in Medieval Europe* (Woodbridge, 2000), pp. 53–68, esp. pp. 55–6. Goetz, *Dux und Ducatus* is an all-out assault on the concept of duchies which in its desire to demolish the over-legalistic approaches of previous scholars perhaps threw the baby out with the bathwater; see Brühl, *Deutschland-Frankreich*, pp. 303–29. M. Becher, *Rex, Dux und Gens. Untersuchungen zur Entstehung des sächsischen Herzogtums im 9. und 10. Jahrhundert* (Husum, 1996) is a sophisticated study showing how ethnic aspects can be built into a subtle understanding of the political processes at work.

Kingship and Politics in the Late Ninth Century

the aristocracy. Thus, when it comes to explaining the disintegration of the Carolingian empire, the concerns of post-war historians of the early Middle Ages have resulted in similar conclusions to those reached by the constitutional–legal historians of previous generations.[15] The way the story is told has changed, but the plot and the ending remain essentially the same.

The third theme which has dominated historians' thinking on the end of the empire brings these general issues to bear on a specific problem, namely the deposition and death of Charles the Fat in 887–8, the only part of the reign itself which has been studied in any detail. German historians of the twentieth century debated at length the significance of these events for medieval constitutional history (*Verfassungsgeschichte*). The best example of this is the well-known exchange between Gerd Tellenbach and Walter Schlesinger and some others in the 1930s, 1940s and 1950s. While Tellenbach took the view that Arnulf's revolt was essentially just another military coup of a type common enough in the brutal world of Frankish politics, Schlesinger insisted that his rise represented the establishment of a new kind of elective kingship brought about by the development of an increasingly independent and class-conscious aristocracy which began to impose institutional checks on the power of the monarchy.[16] The matters at stake were essentially whether or not 887–8 saw the creation of a kingdom of Germany, and whether king or *Volk* (the people) had the whiphand within it. The main reason for the spectacular divergence of views lies in the fact that the two continuations of our main narrative source, the *Annals of Fulda* (*Annales Fuldenses*), which inevitably exert great influence on the structure of modern accounts, present diametrically opposed versions of the events of 887. The twentieth-century disputants were thus readily able to find in the contemporary texts exactly what they wanted to find, and to construct contradictory hypotheses accordingly.

Despite this problem, and despite the fact that the concerns debated by Tellenbach and Schlesinger are no longer such hot issues as they were

---

[15] E.g., C. Brühl, *Fodrum, Gistum, Servitium Regis. Studien zu den wirtschaftlichen Grundlagen des Königtums im Frankenreich und in der fränkischen Nachfolgestaaten Deutschland, Frankreich und Italien vom 6. bis zur Mitte des 14. Jahrhunderts* (Cologne, 1968), pp. 35–6; J. Fried, 'The Frankish Kingdoms, 817–911: the East and Middle Kingdoms', in *NCMH2*, pp. 142–68, at p. 158.

[16] Most of the contributions are collected in H. Kämpf (ed.), *Die Entstehung des deutschen Reiches (Deutschland um 900)* (Darmstadt, 1956) and E. Hlawitschka (ed.), *Königswahl und Thronfolge in fränkisch-karolingischer Zeit* (Darmstadt, 1975). For useful commentaries see J. Freed, 'Reflections on the Medieval German Nobility', *American Historical Review* 91 (1986), 553–75, at 555; C. R. Bowlus, 'Imre Boba's Reconstructions of Moravia's Early History and Arnulf of Carinthia's *Ostpolitik* (887–892)', *Speculum* 62 (1987), 552–74, at 554–7, 573. T. Reuter, 'The Medieval Nobility in Twentieth-Century Historiography', in Bentley (ed.), *Companion to Historiography*, pp. 177–202, at p. 185, n. 28 notes a methodological aspect to the dispute.

Introduction

in Germany in the 1940s, the terms of the discussion about the balance between aristocracy and emperor established the paradigms for many further discussions of the rising of Arnulf and the end of the Carolingian empire.[17] Historians are still inclined to sidestep the thorny problem of how to reconcile the contrasting annalistic sources by selecting somewhat indiscriminately from each of them to create a single political narrative. The accepted history of the 880s has become a cut-and-paste catalogue of disasters: individual events are taken out of context from different sources in order to affirm an image of events running out of control. This amounts to a tacit declaration by posterity of Schlesinger as the victor in the debate over German *Verfassungsgeschichte*: the crisis of 887–8 is commonly held to be the direct outcome of momentous but nebulous historical processes, such as the 'rise of the aristocracy' and the 'decline of royal authority', which the course of contemporary events passively reveals, but does not affect.[18]

The discussion of these models over the decades has given expression to a starkly defined arc of Carolingian decline. Although the scholarship on which it originally depended is now old, this picture endures because of its neatness: it explains in a plausible and satisfying manner a wide range of aspects of the period c. 850–c. 950. As such, to challenge it is to question the framework in which Carolingian (and post-Carolingian) political history as a whole is understood. The traditional paradigm hinges in particular on the interpretation of the end of the empire. While the significance of this turn of events is widely recognised, its causes are seen as self-explanatory. The politics of the later 870s and 880s have therefore been in a sense dehistoricised. These years are still usually seen as dismal, dark and semi-detached from the main, implicitly more important, period of Carolingian rule. By turning the late ninth-century Carolingians, and Charles the Fat in particular, into victims of traditional historiographical villains like grasping aristocrats, and inexorable historical processes such as the rise of nations, they are effectively erased from history as political actors, and turned into unthinking ciphers whose fates confirm but do not influence the unstoppable tide of progress towards the high medieval future. As a result, since Ernst Dümmler's positivist survey of 1888, the reign of the last emperor has never been considered as requiring a major study in any language, and the handful of articles which have dealt with

---

[17] See for example E. M. Eibl, 'Zur Stellung Bayerns und Rheinfrankens im Reiche Arnulfs von Kärnten', *Jahrbuch für Geschichte des Feudalismus* 8 (1984), 73–113, at 75–6.

[18] W. Schlesinger, 'Die Auflösung des Karlsreiches', in W. Braunfels (ed.), *Karl der Grosse. Lebenswerk und Nachleben* (5 vols., Düsseldorf, 1965–7), vol. 1, pp. 792–857 is the classic statement; cf. more recently J. Fried, *Der Weg in die Geschichte. Die Ursprünge Deutschlands bis 1024* (Berlin, 1994), pp. 109, 447–8.

Kingship and Politics in the Late Ninth Century

the period focus almost without exception on the emperor's deposition.[19] To this extent, Gibbon's 'dregs' have indeed been left in the darkness he thought they deserved.

However, although these comments do serve to describe broad patterns and themes still current within the historiography, they should not be taken to imply that scholarship on the later ninth century has stood still since the Second World War, or that all historians subscribe to the views which have just been sketched out. On the contrary, recent work has advanced our understanding of later Carolingian politics considerably. The institutional–statist orthodoxies established in the mid-twentieth century by the generation of the illustrious Belgian historian François-Louis Ganshof are being gradually refined by more subtle understandings of how earlier medieval government worked.[20] As we shall see in the next section, political structures are not now measured by the standards of modern state hierarchies, with power defined and delegated from the top down, but instead are characterised as fluid networks of patronage and allegiance within the aristocracy, and between powerful aristocrats and the king.[21] These new perspectives have problematised older paradigms of political development. The traditional framework for understanding the relationship between king and aristocracy has thus changed. Consequently, since the 1980s, a wave of reassessment has swept over the historiography of ninth-century kingship and rehabilitated the historical reputations of Louis the Pious (814–40) and Charles the Bald (840–77).[22]

The present book is intended to build on such research and to apply some of its conclusions to the politics of the 870s and 880s, understanding of which remains encased in conventional orthodoxies. Roger Collins recently observed that it might be about time someone stood up for

[19] The best-known (and best) article is H. Keller, 'Zum Sturz Karls III. Uber die Rolle Liutwards von Vercelli und Liutberts von Mainz, Arnulfs von Kärnten und der ostfränkischen Großen bei der Absetzung des Kaisers', *DA* 34 (1966), 333–84. Dümmler, *Geschichte des ostfränkischen Reiches*, vol. 3, pp. 175–295.

[20] F. L. Ganshof, *Frankish Institutions Under Charlemagne* (Providence, 1968); F. L. Ganshof, *The Carolingians and the Frankish Monarchy* (London, 1971).

[21] For a full historiographical discussion, see M. Innes, *State and Society in the Early Middle Ages* (Cambridge, 2000), pp. 1–12. Among the most important works, see J. L. Nelson, *Charles the Bald* (London and New York, 1992); R. McKitterick (ed.), *The New Cambridge Medieval History vol. II c.700–c.900* (Cambridge, 1995); B. H. Rosenwein, *Negotiating Space: Power, Restraint and Privileges of Immunity in Early Medieval Europe* (Manchester, 1999); Innes, *State and Society*; S. Airlie, *Carolingian Politics* (forthcoming). G. Sergi, 'L'Europa carolingia e la sua dissoluzione', in N. Tranfaglia and M. Firpo (eds.), *La Storia. I grandi problemi dal Medioevo all'Età contemporanea* (10 vols., Turin, 1986), vol. 2, pp. 231–62 is a coherent overview and refutation of the traditional picture.

[22] See especially P. Godman and R. Collins (eds.), *Charlemagne's Heir: New Perspectives on the Reign of Louis the Pious, 814–840* (Oxford, 1990); Nelson, *Charles the Bald*. New work on Louis the German is also forthcoming from Eric J. Goldberg.

Introduction

Charles the Fat.[23] To some extent, what follows may be viewed as a case for the defence. However, its purpose is not primarily to rehabilitate Charles in order to turn him into a 'better' or 'good' king (although given the consistently bad press he has hitherto had, some such revisionism is inevitable). Nor is it strictly speaking a biography: little will be said, for example, about his earlier life, although much could. Rather, this book aims to use the reign as a window onto the political events and structures of the late Carolingian empire, and hence to reach new conclusions about the reasons for and nature of its disintegration. By thus evaluating the reign in a broader context, it is hoped that some light will also be cast on the workings of Carolingian politics more generally: in studying a political system at the point where it stopped working, as Stuart Airlie has pointed out, we can also reflect on what made it work in the first place.[24] To this end, the aim is to consider the sources in context, rather than subordinate their information to historiographical preconceptions about the 'rise of the aristocracy' or the inevitability of the empire's collapse. The conclusions reached suggest that late Carolingian imperial politics retained more vitality and viability than is usually acknowledged. The end of the empire, when it came, was not the inevitable result of unsustainable imbalances in a decaying system, but primarily the outcome of a royal succession dispute which resonated with some wider concerns within the political community of the time. Space does not permit comprehensive coverage of the events and structures of the period concerned. Detailed regional case-studies on the model of Matthew Innes's important study of the middle Rhine valley would, for example, add much to the book's 'top-down' perspective and help refine its conclusions.[25] Accordingly, the themes covered, although they contribute to a consistent set of overall conclusions, are focused on the areas where sources are in greatest supply. Moreover, the weight of the traditional historiographical concerns already outlined have an obvious influence on the themes chosen; for example, the nature of the relationships between kings and aristocrats, the ideas and practices of kingship, and the rise of the duchies.

Chapter 2 deals with the evidential basis for the traditional version of events, and argues that historians have been too heavily influenced by the agenda of one particular author, the Mainz continuator of the *Annals of Fulda*. The subsequent two chapters are concerned with political structures, in particular Charles's relationship with the high aristocracy.

---

[23] R. Collins, 'The Carolingians and the Ottonians in an Anglophone World', *JMH* 22 (1996), 97–114 at 109.

[24] S. Airlie, '*Semper fideles?* Loyauté envers les carolingiens comme constituant de l'identité aristocratique', in Le Jan (ed.), *La Royauté et les élites*, pp. 129–43.

[25] Innes, *State and Society*.

9

Kingship and Politics in the Late Ninth Century

Here we will assess the evidence for the argument that the period witnessed a decay of the structures of government and a consonant increase in aristocratic authority. Particular attention is paid to the position of the 'supermagnates', some of who would take over as kings after the emperor's death, but we will also address questions of loyalty and secessionism among the political communities of the empire's regions. Chapters 5 and 6 reconstruct the events of the period from 884 until 888, focusing on developments in the politics of the imperial succession and offering a new hypothesis as to the circumstances of Charles's deposition. Because this analysis is based on a contextualisation of the changing political positions of the main actors, it will also cast light on broader issues relating to Carolingian kingship and political structures. Finally, chapter 7 offers a new reading of one of the canonical texts of ninth-century historiography, Notker the Stammerer's biography of Charlemagne, which was written for Charles the Fat, and which will allow us to draw together many of the themes already discussed.

Perhaps surprisingly given the comparative dearth of secondary literature, there is a relatively large body of source material available for the reign, much of it neglected because of a scholarly over-reliance on the evidence of the Mainz version of the *Annals of Fulda*.[26] Among the alternative contemporaneous narratives, we are well served up to 882 by Archbishop Hincmar of Rheims's *Annals of St-Bertin* (*Annales Bertiniani*); after 882 by the Bavarian continuator of the *Annals of Fulda*; and for the whole period by the *Annals of St-Vaast* (*Annales Vedastini*) and Regino of Prüm's *Chronicon* (the latter written up in 908). The more literary material provided by Notker and the poem on the siege of Paris by Abbo of St-Germain-des-Prés brightly illuminate particular moments and events. Perhaps the most neglected of all the classes of evidence are Charles's royal diplomas, of which over 170 are included in the standard edition by Paul Kehr: this high number of charters from a reign lasting only eleven years makes Charles perhaps the best-documented of all the Carolingian kings.[27] These charters will be used extensively as sources of crucial detail on a variety of subjects which remain opaque to readers of the more (apparently) self-explanatory narrative sources. They are invaluable, most obviously, in reconstructing patterns of political patronage, and in discussing court ideologies. Further points will be elucidated from lesser chronicles, letters, and non-royal charters. It is hoped, therefore, that the

---

[26] See below, chap. 2.

[27] R.-H. Bautier, 'Les Poids de la Neustrie ou de la France du nord-ouest dans la monarchie carolingienne unitair d'après les diplômes de la chancellerie royale (751–840)', in H. Atsma (ed.), *La Neustrie. Les pays au nord de la Loire de 650 à 850* (2 vols., Sigmaringen, 1989), vol. 2, pp. 535–63 provides statistics.

Introduction

revised narrative presented in this book is based on a more comprehensive range of evidence than that customarily consulted by historians dealing with this period, and hence that its findings will have greater validity when brought to bear on broader historiographical issues concerning the collapse of the Carolingian empire.

THE SHAPE OF POLITICS IN THE LATE NINTH CENTURY

In order to provide some background to the rest of the book, and further introduction to some of its main themes, it is necessary first to outline briefly some of the most relevant features of society and politics in the Carolingian period as they are understood in current scholarship. Carolingian society was essentially rural and agricultural, dominated by rich monasteries and powerful landholders. Following the hugely influential work of the Belgian historian Henri Pirenne, who saw the absence of long-distance trade as crucial, the ninth century was for a long time interpreted as economically stagnant.[28] Occasionally this has even been brought to bear as a factor leading to the collapse of the empire.[29] Pirenne's pessimistic vision remains much debated, and is still echoed by modern authors.[30] However, despite the general dearth of evidence, historians are increasingly inclined to highlight the more positive economic aspects of the period. In the first place, close analysis of coin finds and estate surveys has shown that institutions like monasteries and royal palaces did not scrape by on a purely subsistence basis, but rather produced surpluses which stimulated local markets and economic activity on all levels.[31] Moreover, it has now become abundantly clear that neither long-distance trade nor urbanism were as stagnant as the Pirenne thesis made out. The decline in the mid-ninth century of the North Sea emporia like Dorestad, which acted as entry points for goods and silver from the North Sea, the Baltic and, indirectly, the Middle East, was offset by the rise of inland towns in their hinterland.[32] Powerful landholders could

---

[28] H. Pirenne, *Medieval Cities* (New York, 1925); H. Pirenne, *Mohammed and Charlemagne* (London, 1939). Pirenne was reacting to the more optimistic A. Dopsch, *Die Wirtschaftsentwicklung der Karolingerzeit*, 2nd edn (Weimar, 1921–2), which remains useful.

[29] Although principally by Marxist non-specialists.

[30] For example, R. Fossier, 'Les tendances de l'économie: stagnation ou croissance?', *Settimane* 27 (1981), 261–74.

[31] See especially J. P. Devroey, *Études sur le grand domaine carolingien* (Aldershot, 1993).

[32] The most sustained direct critique of Pirenne is R. Hodges and D. Whitehouse, *Mohammed, Charlemagne and the Origins of Europe. Archaeology and the Pirenne Thesis* (London, 1983). See also R. Hodges, *Dark Age Economics*, 2nd edn (London, 1989); P. Johanek, 'Der fränkische Handel der Karolingerzeit im Spiegel der Schriftquellen', in K. Düwel et al. (eds.), *Der Handel der Karolinger- und Wikingerzeit* (Göttingen, 1987), pp. 7–68; A. Verhulst, *The Rise of Cities in North-West Europe* (Cambridge, 1999); R. Hodges, *Towns and Trade in the Age of Charlemagne* (London, 2000);

Kingship and Politics in the Late Ninth Century

benefit from these developments. However, the ability of the Carolingian kings right up to the end of the ninth century to exert at least some influence on the directions of trade, and to profit from its proceeds through control of tolls and markets, cannot now be doubted.[33] The production of high-status objects such as luxury manuscripts and elaborate reliquaries testifies to the dynasty's continuing access to sources of wealth.

The Carolingians were, therefore, able to extract economic surpluses from resources beyond the land they controlled immediately, as landlords in their own right. However, this crown (or fiscal) land was important too, not only in sustaining the progress of the itinerant court around the realm, but also in maintaining the palaces and estates which stood as reminders of kings' authority even when they were absent. As we have seen, historians still view the fate of the royal fisc as an extremely important factor in the Carolingians' demise. Following the work of Dhondt in particular, it is frequently stated that the supposedly increasingly weak dynasty squandered its resources, giving away land, churches and regalian rights in an attempt to buy the support of aristocrats who, by the same process, became ever more powerful and independent. Although not all historians would still subscribe to the details of this model, the endurance of its conclusions demands that we pause to consider its general validity.

It should be re-emphasised that Dhondt's use of the sources was flawed, as Jane Martindale has convincingly demonstrated. He paid too little attention to the relative quality of grants made by the Carolingians to the aristocracy, and to the fact that comparatively few charters were actually issued for representatives of its higher echelons.[34] It is clear that fiscal lands distributed by ninth-century kings were not those belonging to the key estates on which their economic position was directly based, and that rulers actually maintained some influence over property after they had granted it out. Resources granted to aristocratic beneficiaries were not simply 'lost' to the fisc.[35] Likewise, the oft-mentioned tendency of the later ninth-century Carolingians to concede vital royal privileges such as minting, toll, judicial and market rights and control of monasteries to powerful nobles, especially bishops, has also been asserted without

---

M. McCormick, *Origins of the European Economy. Communications and Commerce, AD 300–900* (Cambridge, 2001); J. P. Devroey, 'The Economy', in R. McKitterick (ed.), *The Early Middle Ages* (Oxford, 2001), pp. 97–129; A. Verhulst, *The Carolingian Economy* (Cambridge, 2002).

[33] T. Endemann, *Markturkunde und Markt in Frankreich und Burgund vom 9. bis 11. Jahrhundert* (Constance and Stuttgart, 1964), pp. 105–61; Nelson, *Charles the Bald*, pp. 19–40.

[34] J. Martindale, 'The Kingdom of Aquitaine and the Dissolution of the Carolingian Fisc', *Francia* 11 (1985), 131–91; see also Nelson, *Charles the Bald*, pp. 54–5, 233.

[35] See most recently Innes, *State and Society*, p. 204; S. Airlie, 'The Palace of Memory: the Carolingian Court as Political Centre', in S. Rees-Jones, R. Marks and A. Minnis (eds.), *Courts and Regions in Medieval Europe* (Woodbridge, 2000), pp. 1–20, at p. 11.

Introduction

reference to the political circumstances of such grants.[36] The documents revealing such gifts cannot be isolated from their immediate political contexts and understood instead as facets of an amorphous 'historical process'. In any case, the detailed work of historians on the control of these rights points to the conclusion that their concentration in the hands of autonomous local power-brokers was primarily a phenomenon of the tenth century, or in some cases the eleventh.[37]

Furthermore, the 'self-privatisation' model of ninth-century politics is conceptually misconceived, as it rests on the idea that the most important, or even the only important, historically significant way that aristocrats relate to kings is materially. This assumption tends to ascribe to the aristocracy an anachronistic unity of purpose and over-simplistically suggests that royal power was only as enduring as its capacity to distribute material resources, thus underrating its less quantifiable charismatic or cultural elements. The king's power legitimised aristocratic power and gave shape to the idea of the kingdom as an entity. The traditional view also relies on a modern dichotomy between 'public' and 'private' power which did not apply in the early Middle Ages.[38] Strategic grants of rights and land to supporters were not necessarily a drain on royal resources because real, if historically less visible, political capital flowed back in the other direction. Although land was a fundamental element of early medieval political influence, its control cannot be seen as a zero-sum game fought out between mutually exclusive royal and aristocratic interests.[39] Similarly, it no longer seems as certain as it did to previous generations of historians that aristocratic families had corporate political identities which meant kings had to deal with their interests *en masse*. Instead, it is now clear that the creation of political affinities with powerful regional nobles was a crucial element of effective royal power which allowed kings

---

[36] For an example, see below, pp. 110–15.

[37] R. Kaiser, 'Münzpriviligien und bischöfliche Münzprägung in Frankreich, Deutschland und Burgund im 9.–12. Jahrhundert', *Vierteljahrschrift für Sozial- und Wirtschaftsgeschichte* 63 (1976), 289–338; R. Kaiser, '*Teloneum Episcopi*. Du tonlieu royal au tonlieu épiscopal dans les *civitates* de la Gaule (VIe–XIIe siècle)', in W. Paravicini and K. F. Werner (eds.), *Histoire comparée de l'administration (IVe–XVIIIe siècles)* (Munich, 1980), pp. 469–85; F. Hardt-Friedrichs, 'Markt, Münze und Zoll im ostfränkischen Reich bis zum End der Ottonen', *Blätter für deutsche Landesgeschichte* 116 (1980), 1–31; O. Guyotjeannin, *Episcopus et comes. Affirmation et déclin de la seigneurie épiscopale au nord du royaume de France* (Geneva, 1987), pp. 9–65; H. Hoffmann, 'Grafschaften in Bischofshand', *DA* 46 (1990), 374–480; A.-M. Helvétius, *Abbayes, évêques et laïques. Une politique du pouvoir en Hainaut au Moyen Age (VIIe–XIe siècle)* (Brussels, 1994), pp. 153–310; F. Bougard, *La Justice dans le royaume d'Italie de la fin du VIIIe siècle au début du XIe siècle* (Rome, 1995), pp. 253–69.

[38] J. L. Nelson, 'The Problematic in the Private', *Social History* 15 (1990), 355–64; Reynolds, 'Historiography of the Medieval State'.

[39] C. Wickham and T. Reuter, 'Introduction', in W. Davies and P. Fouracre (eds.), *Property and Power in the Early Middle Ages* (Cambridge, 1995), pp. 1–16.

Kingship and Politics in the Late Ninth Century

to influence local politics.[40] Far from being a weak-willed submission to the diminution of royal power, the very act of granting out privileges and immunities, one of the functions of which was to limit the activities of local royal representatives, was itself a statement of authority.[41] In the absence of formal state structures, the deployment of patronage was the very basis of Carolingian power, not its antithesis. It reinforced the noble elite's control over land, and provided the cultural glue which held the empire together.[42] To study these phenomena properly, rather than appealing to a generalised decline of 'state' power and property which swung the political balance in favour of the aristocracy, we must look at the individual documents which record this kind of patronage, and ask more specific questions about their contemporary meaning and political context.

All this is not to say that the aristocracy remained in stasis during the Carolingian period. For example, there is some evidence in the royal capitularies of later ninth-century Italy that kings were becoming anxious about the growing power of 'patrons', presumably large-scale landholders, over the freemen who lived within their spheres of influence.[43] This is not the place to go into these matters in detail. However, we ought to be wary of reading too much political significance into the existence of such figures in the later ninth century. This kind of powerful landlord could often be a useful royal ally in areas far from the centre of the king's authority, and as such were sometimes even deliberately created and empowered by rulers.[44] It is misguided to think of these lordships as inherently inimical to effective government. Even those freemen who did fall under their influence retained obligations to public duties, although this is not always immediately apparent from the sources.[45]

Moreover, the ethos of lordship and heritability of office did not, as has often been claimed, progressively infect the behaviour and diminish the effectiveness of ninth-century 'public officials', especially counts, the fundamental Carolingian royal representatives. We can no longer be

---

[40] As demonstrated by two important studies: B. H. Rosenwein 'The Family Politics of Berengar I, King of Italy (888–924)', *Speculum* 71 (1996), 247–89; Innes, *State and Society*.

[41] Rosenwein, *Negotiating Space*; see also P. Fouracre, 'Eternal Light and Earthly Needs: Practical Aspects of the Development of Frankish Immunities', in Davies and Fouracre (eds.), *Property and Power*, pp. 53–81.

[42] See Rosenwein, 'Family Politics of Berengar', p. 249; P. Fouracre, *The Age of Charles Martel* (Harlow, 2000), esp. pp. 18–27.

[43] G. Tabacco, *I Liberi del re nell'Italia carolingia e postcarolingia* (Spoleto, 1966), pp. 51–2, 72; G. Tabacco, *The Struggle for Power in Medieval Italy* (Cambridge, 1989), p. 130.

[44] See below, pp. 110–15.

[45] Tabacco, *I Liberi del re*, pp. 105–7; A. Castagnetti, 'Arimanni e signori dall'età postcarolingia alla prima età communale', in G. Dilcher and C. Violante (eds.), *Strutture e trasformazioni della signoria rurale nei secoli X–XII* (Bologna, 1996), pp. 169–285 at pp. 172–4.

Introduction

confident that counties became increasingly heritable as time passed (or even if they did, that this necessarily diminished their character as royal benefices). This assumption traditionally rested on a mistaken interpretation of the Capitulary of Quierzy (877).[46] It is true that members of the nobility often held *honores* in the same areas as their relatives, as time and tradition helped them build up claims.[47] However, this was a fundamental tendency of early medieval politics which was not simply confined to the late ninth century. As far back as our evidence goes, Frankish kings had always expected their representatives to be well-endowed in their localities: this is what made them useful and effective in the first place.[48] Equally, leading aristocrats always expected *honores*, and maximising the political benefit of their distribution was one of the basic aims of kingship. There were certainly many endemic tensions within the system, but these often took the form of conflicts over the control of royal offices themselves.[49] The evidence does not allow us to conclude (as many have) that the end of the empire was caused by the bastardisation of royal service with 'proto-feudal' ties which took counts out of the 'public' sphere and removed them from the king's control.[50] The king's power depended on the power of the aristocracy. Counts continued to think of themselves as performing royal service right through the century. Aristocratic lordship and royal power always coexisted in the Frankish polity.

These problems with the traditional view are partly derived from their basis in a maximalist reading of the capitularies (broadly speaking legislative documents structured as the proceedings of assemblies), from which it has been concluded that Carolingian rule was underpinned by a fixed hierarchy of royal representatives who became increasingly independent and hard to control. This is not a measure which we can reasonably apply to ninth-century politics.[51] Capitularies may have prescribed a kind of hierarchy in theory, but that does not mean one existed in practice. Early medieval kingship was never about parcelling up morsels of sovereign or 'state' power and delegating them to carefully chosen subordinates. Counts and other key royal representatives like *missi dominici* (the king's inspectors) were not a type of removable official in the modern sense.

---

[46] See Nelson, *Charles the Bald*, pp. 248–9; S. Airlie, 'The Aristocracy', in *NCMH2*, pp. 431–50 at p. 444.

[47] For an example see D. Jackman, 'Rorgonid Right: Two Scenarios', *Francia* 28 (1999), 129–53, at 129–38.

[48] Fouracre, *Age of Charles Martel*, pp. 13–15.

[49] For one conspicuous example, a dispute over the county of Autun, see *AB* s.a. 864, p. 114; 866, p. 126. On tension, see Airlie, '*Semper fideles?*'.

[50] S. Reynolds, *Fiefs and Vassals. The Medieval Evidence Reinterpreted* (Oxford, 1994), esp. pp. 111–14.

[51] See P. Fouracre, 'Carolingian Justice: the Rhetoric of Improvement and Contexts of Abuse', *Settimane* 42 (1995), 771–803.

Kingship and Politics in the Late Ninth Century

Rather, they were members of already powerful regional families who were persuaded to align themselves with the Carolingian polity by redefining their power in terms of royal service.[52] There is no overwhelming evidence that, as a rule, royal representatives, such as counts, became more locally embedded as time passed, or that late ninth-century kings had more difficulties than their predecessors in trying to remove them.[53] Deposing a count or bishop was always tricky. Throughout the Carolingian period rebellious aristocrats who had their offices confiscated often reappeared back in position after a period of time. Few Carolingians felt secure enough to have one of their leading aristocrats executed or permanently exiled, except in extreme circumstances. These people and their families were wealthy and influential independently of the ruling dynasty: the Carolingians did not create their aristocracy, but emerged from it.[54] As a result, they could not afford to deal too high-handedly with the nobility. Important noble families did have dynastic consciousness and strong group identity.[55] However, these factors do not *per se* mean that such families were politically obstructive. Aristocratic family identity, group-consciousness and domination of local offices were not peculiarities of the late Carolingian period, but rather ubiquitous features of the early medieval European nobility.

Carolingian government was thus a loosely constructed entity which depended on a series of alliances and relationships with regional power-brokers, constantly nurtured by the judicious deployment of patronage and also sustained by royal ideology. One conspicuous sign that aristocratic lords remained part of this system in the late ninth century is that kings managed to form effective armies right up until the end of the dynasty's hegemony in 888.[56] Lordship was the very basis of military

---

[52] J. Hannig, 'Zentralle Kontrolle und regionale Machtbalance. Beobachtungen zum System der karolingischen Königsboten am Beispiel des Mittelrheingebietes', *Archiv für Kulturgeschichte* 66 (1984), 1–46; J. Hannig, 'Zur Funktion der karolingischen *missi dominici* in Bayern und in den südöstlichen Grenzgebieten', *ZSRG GA* 101 (1984), 256–300; Innes, *State and Society*, pp. 188–95.

[53] A. Krah, *Absetzungsverfahren als Spiegelbild von Königsmacht. Untersuchungen zum Kräfteverhältnis zwischen Königtum und Adel im Karolingerreich und seinen Nachfolgestaaten* (Aalen, 1987), pp. 379–401 provides a handlist of cases. See also Airlie, 'The Aristocracy'. The central issues could be further illuminated by research on more specific cases.

[54] K. F. Werner, 'Important Noble Families in the Kingdom of Charlemagne – a Prosopographical Study of the Relationship Between King and Nobility in the Early Middle Ages', in T. Reuter (ed.), *The Medieval Nobility. Studies on the Ruling Classes of France and Germany from the Sixth to the Twelfth Century* (Amsterdam, New York and Oxford, 1979), pp. 137–202; originally published with appendices as 'Bedeutende Adelsfamilien im Reich Karls des Grossen. Ein personengeschichtlicher Beitrag zum Verhältnis von Königtum und Adel im frühen Mittelalter', in Braunfels (ed.), *Karl der Grosse*, vol. 1, pp. 83–142.

[55] See now R. Le Jan, *Famille et pouvoir dans le monde franc (VIIe–Xe siècle). Essai d'anthropologie sociale* (Paris, 1995). See also below, pp. 54–5.

[56] See below, pp. 58, 121.

Introduction

service in the period, providing the structures by means of which the army was summoned.[57] However, the Vikings, against whom most of these armies were assembled, have also been identified as having had a cataclysmic effect on Carolingian rule. Certainly the end of the empire coincided with the most intense period so far of Scandinavian raiding on the Continent. Having been effectively forced out of Francia by the defensive measures of Charles the Bald in the mid-860s, the Vikings began to concentrate their energies on the Anglo-Saxon kingdoms instead. The relative respite enjoyed by the Franks endured until 879, when the so-called Viking Great Army (the term is contemporary) returned to take advantage of the political confusion which attended the death of King Louis the Stammerer.[58] Although Viking warbands were loosely organised, and could break apart and reform at will, the Great Army was particularly well coordinated, and posed significant problems for the Carolingian kings. Before famine forced it to leave in 892, parts of the Army overwintered in and ransacked areas from Normandy to Burgundy, and in 885–6 besieged Paris and extracted a large ransom, a success which disturbed several contemporary commentators.

Historians generally stop short of ascribing to the Vikings direct agency in the end of the Carolingian empire. Current views of their activity stress their role as an integral part of European political culture rather than an alien and disruptive force.[59] Although their impact was massive, their aim was not to bring down the empire, but rather to participate in it. Nevertheless, the Scandinavians have been made indirectly culpable for the empire's fate. In the first place, they have been held partly responsible for the deposition of Charles the Fat in 887, the event which heralded the *de facto* dissolution of his dynasty's royal monopoly. The emperor's inability to fight off the invaders, especially at Asselt in 882 and Paris in 886, has been cited as a cause of contemporaries' loss of confidence in him, and thus of his removal from office.[60] Secondly, the Vikings have been given an important role in the posited rise of aristocratic power, in that the increase in raids supposedly caused a localisation of defence which

---

[57] T. Reuter, 'Plunder and Tribute in the Carolingian Empire', *TRHS*, 5th series, 35 (1985), 75–94; T. Reuter, 'The End of Carolingian Military Expansion', in Godman and Collins (eds.), *Charlemagne's Heir*, pp. 391–405; G. Halsall, *Warfare and Society in the Barbarian West* (London, forthcoming), chap. 4. Cf. R. Abels, *Lordship and Military Obligation in Anglo-Saxon England* (London, 1988).

[58] For an accessible general discussion see S. Coupland, 'The Vikings in Francia and Anglo-Saxon England to 911', in *NCMH2*, pp. 190–201.

[59] N. Lund, 'Allies of God or Man? The Viking Expansion in a European Perspective', *Viator* 20 (1989), 45–59; cf. P. Heather, 'State Formation in Europe in the First Millennium AD', in B. Crawford (ed.), *Scotland in Dark Age Europe* (St Andrews, 1994), pp. 47–70.

[60] For references see S. MacLean, 'Charles the Fat and the Viking Great Army: the Military Explanation for the End of the Carolingian Empire', *War Studies Journal* 3 (1998), 74–95.

both damaged royal prestige and increased the power of regional leaders who effectively took over as rulers of their areas. We will consider these claims more fully in later chapters.[61] It is undeniable that the Scandinavian presence put a serious strain on the relationship between the king and his regional commanders, upon which the structures of the empire depended. However, it is worth re-emphasising here that the traditional model tends to misconceptualise the problem. It decontextualises the political significance of the evidence by assuming an anachronistic unity of consciousness and behaviour among the aristocracy. In fact, local and royal organisation of defence cannot be seen as mutually exclusive. The king's authority was effective because of powerful regional leaders, not in spite of them. Participation in warfare was always central to the identity of the Carolingian aristocracy.[62] Although the sources are not always explicit about this, war was usually carried out in the king's name. Central elements of the thesis, such as the appearance of proto-castles as focal points for the newly localised and militarised nobility, rest on broad and unsustainable generalisations from individual sources (in this case a clause in the 864 Edict of Pîtres).[63] Far from being agencies of division, the army and warfare were important forums for the building of a common political identity even when, as for most of the ninth century, the type of war engaged in was defensive.

The constant presence of the Vikings must have normalised the duties of defence and of service under the king. This habituation rested on a broader cultural conformity across the empire, the nobility of which instinctively looked, in the ninth century, to the Frankish (Carolingian) kings for leadership. When considering the relationship between aristocracy and king in this period, we must bear in mind that they shared the same thought–world. The Carolingians were essentially an aristocratic family themselves, and as such had had to work very hard to distance and distinguish their power from that of the nobility from which they emerged.[64] Royal consecration and similar rituals enabled them to assert

---

[61] See below, Chaps. 3–4.

[62] See K. Leyser, 'Early Medieval Canon Law and the Beginnings of Knighthood', in L. Fenske et al. (eds.), *Institutionen, Kultur und Gesellschaft im Mittelalter. Festschrift J. Fleckenstein* (Sigmaringen, 1984), pp. 549–66; Barthélemy, 'La chevalerie'.

[63] C. Coulson, 'Fortresses and Social Responsibility in Late Carolingian France', *Zeitschrift für Archäologie des Mittelalters* 4 (1976), 29–36 discusses the broad concept of the duty to defend the homeland. See also MacLean, 'Viking Great Army', pp. 82–3. A. Renoux (ed.), *Palais médiévaux (France-Belgique)* (Le Mans, 1994), provides a survey of such structures in the most affected areas, which uncovers little archaeological evidence for late ninth-century aristocratic forts. See also A. Renoux (ed.), *Palais royaux et princiers au Moyen Age* (Le Mans, 1996).

[64] Airlie, '*Semper fideles?*'; S. Airlie, 'Narratives of Triumph and Rituals of Submission: Charlemagne's Mastering of Bavaria', *TRHS*, 6th series, 9 (1999), 93–119.

Introduction

and reinforce their royal authority. However, court rituals and less formal pastimes such as hunting helped to build corporate identities which bonded kings and nobles.[65] Aristocratic children were often brought up at royal courts, which provided springboards for successful political and ecclesiastical careers.[66] Monasteries and nunneries where royal and aristocratic patrons and oblates came into contact and were commemorated together also formed nodes of interaction.[67] Common cultural values were also defined and transmitted through collections of histories which celebrated the divinely ordained success of the Frankish people.[68] The existence of these values reminds us that any explanation of politics which rests on the assumption of innate antagonisms between nobility and ruling dynasty must be questioned.

Finally we must return to the political centre and its tools of power. In terms of what we might call the formal structures of government, it is difficult to measure the directions of change in the ninth century. In particular, the tailing off of capitularies in the kingdoms west of the Rhine and south of the Alps after around 840, and their total absence in the east Frankish kingdom, has often been taken as a symptom of governmental weakness. Nevertheless, we continue to encounter active royal representatives like counts and *missi* ('sent men') in local charters right through the ninth century. Clearly, their functioning was not dependent on political structures whose existence was revealed and regulated exclusively by means of capitularies. There is little direct evidence for the practical use of these documents, for example as reference points in resolving disputes, and even an attempt to codify the capitularies at the height of their production at the court of Louis the Pious apparently failed to turn up more than a fraction of those which had been so far compiled.[69]

---

[65] J. L. Nelson, 'The Lord's Anointed and the People's Choice: Carolingian Royal Ritual', in J. L. Nelson, *The Frankish World, 750–900* (London and Rio Grande, 1996), pp. 99–130.

[66] M. Innes, '*A Place of Discipline*: Aristocratic Youth and Carolingian Courts', in C. Cubitt (ed.), *Court Culture in the Early Middle Ages* (forthcoming).

[67] For example, see H. Becher, 'Das königliche Frauenkloster San Salvatore/Santa Giulia in Brescia im Spiegel seiner Memorialüberlieferung', *FMSt* 17 (1983), 299–392; on oblates see M. de Jong, *In Samuel's Image: Child Oblation in the Early Medieval West* (Leiden, New York and Cologne, 1996).

[68] From a growing bibliography on the subject, see R. McKitterick, 'The Audience for Carolingian Historiography', in A. Scharer and G. Scheibelreiter (eds.), *Historiographie im frühen Mittelalter* (Vienna and Munich 1994), pp. 96–114; R. McKitterick, 'Political Ideology in Carolingian Historiography', in Y. Hen and M. Innes (eds.), *The Uses of the Past in the Early Middle Ages* (Cambridge, 2000), pp. 162–74; H. Reimitz, 'Ein fränkisches Geschichtsbuch aus Saint-Amand', in C. Egger and H. Weigl (eds.), *Text-Schrift-Codex. Quellenkundliche Arbeiten aus dem Institut für österreichische Geschichtsforschung* (Vienna, 1999), pp. 34–90.

[69] H. Mordek, 'Karolingische Kapitularien', in H. Mordek (ed.), *Überlieferung und Geltung normativer Texte des frühen und hohen Mittelalters* (Sigmaringen, 1986), pp. 25–50; though cf. R. McKitterick, 'Zur Herstellung von Kapitularien: Die Arbeit des Leges-Skriptoriums', *Mitteilungen des Instituts für Österreichische Geschichtsforschung* 101 (1993), 3–16.

Kingship and Politics in the Late Ninth Century

Capitularies seem, in any case, to have functioned less as formal legislation than as 'instruments of power' proclaiming Carolingian authority and empowering regional agents to act upon it.[70] The progressive increase in royal charters during the ninth century suggests that in some senses they had replaced capitularies as tools for building the power of royal agents. Like capitularies, charters were intensely royal objects, the presence of which imparted something of the king's presence even when he himself was absent.[71] Possession of the documents and the grants of lands and rights they sanctioned enabled royal representatives to assert themselves on behalf of the ruler.[72] There are hints in the narrative sources that late ninth-century east Frankish kings did issue capitularies which have not survived.[73] However, the abiding impression is that things were done differently east of the Rhine, where the conduct of politics was less reliant on the written word, but where royal authority was nevertheless at least as secure as elsewhere.[74] For example, we learn from an annalistic source that Charles the Fat met with his men in May 884 'and sent guardians of his frontiers against the Northmen'.[75] This report of what was probably an oral decision could nevertheless serve as a concise paraphrase of the type of defensive arrangement recorded in written capitularies of the early ninth century. Similarly, we have evidence for Charles regulating the conditions of military service in 887 in a royal charter.[76] The political aims of both these acts are consonant with the intentions of the early Carolingian capitularies, even if the medium of delivery was different.[77]

The stability of all these structures of rule was frequently unbalanced during the ninth century by conflicts within the Carolingian dynasty. Power struggles between fathers and sons, a prominent feature of Frankish politics since at least the sixth century, took on extra complexity with the division of the empire in 843, which created the circumstances for in-house conflicts which cut across the family tree horizontally and diagonally as well as vertically.[78] Once uncles and cousins (not to mention Vikings and Slavs) became potential allies for disaffected sons, the possibilities of trouble were exponentially increased. Particularly potent

---

[70] Innes, *State and Society*, pp. 253–4. The coincidence of the high point of capitulary output and the most energetic court sponsorship of reform was presumably no accident.

[71] Airlie, 'Palace of Memory', p. 11.

[72] For the example of Geilo of Langres, see below, pp. 110–15.

[73] *AF* s.a. 852, pp. 42–3 (on which see T. Reuter, *Germany in the Early Middle Ages, c.800–1056* (London and New York, 1991), pp. 84–9); less definitely *AF(M)* s.a. 882, p. 99.

[74] Reuter, 'Plunder and Tribute'; Reuter, *Germany in the Early Middle Ages*, pp. 84–94.

[75] *AF(M)* s.a. 884, p. 101.   [76] D CIII 158; MacLean, 'Viking Great Army', pp. 83–5.

[77] These comments are intended to be general: this is an area in need of much further research.

[78] See now the exhaustive study of B. Kasten, *Königssöhne und Königsherrschaft. Untersuchungen zur Teilhabe am Reich in der Merowinger- und Karolingerzeit* (Hanover, 1997).

Introduction

outbreaks of rebellion could threaten the positions of even very powerful rulers, as they did those of Louis the Pious in the early 830s and Charles the Bald in the late 850s. Paradoxically, however, this kind of in-house revolt, although dangerous to individual kings, helped to reinforce the hegemony of the Carolingian dynasty as a whole. Every rebellion of the ninth century except one was fronted by a member of the dynasty. This pattern testifies to the success of the Carolingians in nurturing the idea that only they could be kings, and that one king could only be replaced by another from the same family.[79] Rebellions of this kind provided outlets for the frustrations and ambitions of the aristocracy, while simultaneously reaffirming the normality of Carolingian royal legitimacy. Naturally, this mechanism could only work as long as there was a sufficient number of royal family members. As we shall see, in the circumstances of the mid-880s, when the stock of adult male Carolingians had been drastically reduced by illness and accident, the system could swiftly turn against the dynasty.

There is no obvious upwards trend in the intensity of conflict within the ruling house in the later decades of the ninth century. There was no generalised phenomenon of unrest in response to increasingly effete kingship. Such conflict was endemic, and the simple fact of its existence cannot explain the collapse, or even the weakening, of the empire. However, the single ninth-century usurpation attempt led by a non-Carolingian, that of Count Boso of Vienne in 879–80, posed more serious problems.[80] Boso's attempt to seize the throne of west Francia was made in response to the power vacuum created by the dispute over the succession to Louis the Stammerer (d. 10 April 879). Successions were often times of high tension which prompted manoeuvring and realignment within the political community, and the fast turnover of kings in the 870s and 880s did make this an unusually turbulent period of Carolingian history. Because Boso was an outsider (despite his wife being Carolingian), his initial success in having himself crowned and anointed as king in Provence represented a challenge to the very basis of Carolingian hegemony.[81] If Boso succeeded in showing that non-Carolingians could become kings, the dynasty's monopoly on royal legitimacy would collapse, along with the empire it supported. In the event, this is not how it turned out. The four Carolingians ruling at the time were spurred to common action by the rebellion, sending several armies to defeat Boso militarily, and then coming

---

[79] Airlie, 'Semper fideles?'

[80] For the following paragraph see S. MacLean, 'The Carolingian Response to the Revolt of Boso, 879–87', EME 10 (2001), 21–48.

[81] Airlie, 'Semper fideles?', pp. 139–41; S. Airlie, 'The Nearly Men: Boso of Vienne and Arnulf of Bavaria', in Duggan (ed.), Nobles and Nobility, pp. 25–41.

Kingship and Politics in the Late Ninth Century

together to decide a political alliance which would prevent such a figure emerging in the future. The sworn settlement which they sealed at Vienne in 880 tidied up a number of outstanding territorial disputes. However, it also included a family arrangement which provided for the mutual succession to each other of the four kings, all of whom were heirless. Not only did this work out in practice more or less as planned, but the evidence also suggests that the kings continued to cooperate politically. The rising of Boso, as dangerous as it was, therefore actually brought about a rare period of accord within the Carolingian house. The dynasty's real problems only surfaced in subsequent years when, as we will see, the early deaths of the rulers who were party to the Vienne agreement brought about a new and different kind of succession crisis which was not so easily resolved.

One aim of this very selective and highly compressed preliminary survey of pertinent themes is to highlight the extent to which this book's conclusions build on the findings of recent research by other historians. This research demonstrates in general terms that almost all of the concepts and arguments on which the traditional 'decline and fall' model of the end of the empire rests have been effectively dismantled. Many of the phenomena traditionally thought to have catalysed late Carolingian stagnation, such as intra-dynastic conflict and aristocratic power, were in fact fundamental elements of the early Middle Ages as a whole. This is not the same thing as saying that nothing changed over the period: the dynamic nature of early medieval culture and politics is becoming increasingly apparent. Rather, the point is that explanations of the end of the empire can no longer be allowed to rest on broad assumptions about 'historical processes' such as the rise of the aristocracy or the declining strength of the Carolingian kings. Such assertions do not stand up to detailed scrutiny, and need to be replaced with explanations which interpret all the sources in their political contexts, rather than using them selectively to illustrate a story whose plot and ending are pre-determined by historiographical convention. The fact that this kind of analysis has never been fully applied to the events of the late 870s and 880s testifies to the strength of these conventions, whose axioms have become part of the grain of historiographical tradition, and remain central to the master narratives of the course of Carolingian history as a whole. With these conclusions in mind, we now turn to an analysis of the reign of Charles the Fat, in the hope of understanding the end of the Carolingian empire in a clearer light.

Chapter 2

UN-FRANKISH ACTIVITIES: CHARLES THE FAT IN THE EYES OF CONTEMPORARY ANNALISTS

From the reams of pages which have been devoted by historians to the practice of Carolingian kingship, perhaps only Charles the Fat has emerged with the reputation of a 'failed king'.[1] This judgement is all the more striking in the similarity of the terms in which it has been postulated. The uniformity of opinion has proved remarkably impervious to changes in time, fashion and historiographical genre. Thus while the tone of William Stubbs's rather extreme judgement, that Charles was 'dangerous and unmanageable; a diseased, idiotic raving madman... who was probably put out of the way for his own good' could easily be put down to Victorian sensibilities and ideas about the asylum, it is significant that judgements of Charles even in vastly more subtle and sophisticated recent studies have been expressed using a similar idiom.[2] Likewise, specialised articles on the reign are no less likely to comment negatively on Charles's personality and abilities than textbook summaries of the period.[3]

This generally held belief in the personal inadequacy of Charles to fulfil the office of king is expressed in terms of three quite specific major criticisms which are met again and again in the modern historiography. These are: firstly, that he was dominated by his advisers, especially his archchancellor Liutward of Vercelli; secondly, that he was incapable in his dealings with the Vikings; and thirdly, that he was sickly, inactive and immobile, a do-nothing king.[4] What evidence is there for these claims? In this chapter it will be argued that each of these three main criticisms is

---

[1] G. Tellenbach, 'From the Carolingian Imperial Nobility to the German Estate of Imperial Princes', in Reuter (ed.), *The Medieval Nobility*, pp. 203–42, at p. 209; R. Schieffer, 'Karl III. und Arnolf', in K. R. Schnith and R. Pauler (eds.), *Festschrift für Eduard Hlawitschka zum 65. Geburtstag* (Kallmünz, 1993), pp. 133–49, at p. 134.

[2] W. Stubbs, *Germany in the Early Middle Ages 476–1250* (London, 1908), p. 65; Fried, *Der Weg in die Geschichte*, p. 423.

[3] Cf., for instance, J. Dunbabin, *France in the Making, 843–1180* (Oxford, 1985), p. 15; Riché, *The Carolingians*, p. 217; Schieffer, 'Karl III. und Arnolf', p. 134.

[4] E.g. Keller, 'Zum Sturz Karls III.', p. 338; C. P. Wormald, 'Viking Studies: Whence and Whither?', in R. T. Farrell (ed.), *The Vikings* (London and Chichester, 1982), pp. 128–53, at p. 140; C. R. Bowlus, *Franks, Moravians and Magyars. The Struggle for the Middle Danube, 788–907* (Philadelphia, 1995), p. 209.

Kingship and Politics in the Late Ninth Century

drawn almost exclusively from a single source, the Mainz continuation of the so-called *Annals of Fulda*; and, moreover, that this source must be read with much more scepticism than has generally been allowed by previous commentators.

The continuing uniformity of opinion is in large part simply a result of the fact that Charles the Fat has been much less studied than most other Carolingian kings: the absence of new research arguing the contrary case means that historians have tended to accept prevailing historiographical opinions. It is also, however, testimony to the influence which traditional historical paradigms can persistently exert over scholars generations after they were first conceived. The purpose of this chapter is therefore not simply to rehabilitate the historical reputation of Charles the Fat, although that will emerge as one aspect of the argument. As outlined in chapter 1, there is also a broader issue at stake. The judgement of Charles as a failure rests in part on a teleological assumption: the fact that his reign ended in his own deposition and the collapse of the Carolingian empire is taken to demonstrate that he was a weak king. This in turn feeds into and supports the longstanding historiographical models which underpin the conventional negative interpretation of the late Carolingian empire as a whole: most notably, that the aristocracy 'rose', that France and Germany 'emerged', and that murderous conflict within the royal house escalated. The existence of these processes is easier to assert if it is assumed that Charles the Fat, the man who was ultimately their victim, was personally weak, and thus powerless to resist the inevitable tide of history: his reign was the empire's acid test, its 'failure' the final proof of Carolingian decline. In subsequent chapters we will examine these assertions in a wider historical context. First, however, it is necessary to demonstrate that they rest in large measure on the Mainz continuator of the Fulda annals, whose perspective has dominated modern accounts of Charles the Fat's reign and shaped its interpretation. By doing so, we will be able not only to knock away one of the main blocks on which conventional understanding of the collapse of the empire rests, but also to reach a better understanding of the text itself within the context of late ninth-century historiography.

THE *ANNALS OF FULDA*

The composite work known for convenience to historians as the *Annals of Fulda* is our principal source for east Frankish history in the second half of the ninth century, and as such necessarily provides the framework for all discussions of the kingdom's politics in the period. Although the textual history of the annals remains debatable, we can say for certain

Charles the Fat in the eyes of contemporary annalists

that it is independent of other known sources from the 830s onwards, and that from about the mid-860s the version we have was being written up contemporaneously in the circle of Archbishop Liutbert of Mainz (863–89).[5] The manuscripts diverge in 882. One manuscript group contains a direct continuation of the Mainz annals, likewise produced under the supervision of Liutbert, which went on until the year 887; while another group, whose text extends to 901, provides an alternative perspective clearly written from a Bavarian viewpoint. Both continuations appear to have been written up contemporaneously, on a year-by-year basis.[6]

Liutbert was archchaplain at the court of Louis the German from 870–6, and retained this position, which amounted to that of the king's chief adviser, under Louis the Younger (876–82), in whose kingdom Mainz lay. Accordingly, the text up until 882 is partisan to those rulers, vilifying or suppressing mention of their main rivals (including, in the case of Louis the Younger, Charles the Fat) while promoting their own aspirations.[7] However, the work was not strictly speaking a 'court' or 'official' record; rather, it reflected the viewpoint of the archbishop himself. In its consistent opposition to the divorce plans of Lothar II in the 860s, for example, the text sometimes diverged from the attitude of Louis the German, who shifted position in accordance with his desire to achieve maximum political benefit from the complicated scandal.[8]

This is an important point to bear in mind when considering the annals composed by the Mainz continuator in 882–7. On the death of Louis the Younger in January 882, his brother Charles the Fat inherited his Franconian–Bavarian kingdom and, because he already had an

---

[5] T. Reuter, *The Annals of Fulda: Ninth-Century Histories, vol. 2* (Manchester and New York, 1992), pp. 1–14 is the best guide to the detailed debates concerning the *AF*'s origins and authorship. See also now R. Corradini, *Die Wiener Handschrift Cvp 430. Ein Beitrag zur Historiographie in Fulda im frühen 9. Jahrhundert* (Frankfurt, 2000).

[6] This will be assumed except where indicated. I also assume, for convenience and on the basis of probability, that the authors were male.

[7] An example is provided by Charles the Fat's involvement in the politics of the succession to Louis II (*AB* s.a. 871, p. 183; 874, pp. 196–7; 875, p. 198; Andreas of Bergamo, *Historia*, MGH SRL (Hanover, 1878), p. 230) which is completely ignored by the *Annals of Fulda*.

[8] C. J. Carroll, 'The Archbishops and Church Councils of Mainz and Cologne During the Carolingian Period, 751–911', PhD thesis, University of Cambridge (1998), pp. 5–6. J. L. Nelson, 'The *Annals of St-Bertin*', in M. T. Gibson and J. L. Nelson (eds.), *Charles the Bald: Court and Kingdom*, 2nd edn (Aldershot, 1990), pp. 23–40 shows that similar conclusions can be drawn about the relationship between Hincmar of Rheims and Charles the Bald from the former's *Annals of St-Bertin*; cf. J. L. Nelson, 'History-Writing at the Courts of Louis the Pious and Charles the Bald', in Scharer and Scheibelreiter (eds.), *Historiographie im frühen Mittelalter*, pp. 435–42. On Louis the German, Charles the Bald and Lothar's divorce, see now S. Airlie, 'Private Bodies and the Body Politic in the Divorce Case of Lothar II', *Past and Present* 161 (1998), 3–38.

archchancellor in Bishop Liutward of Vercelli, Liutbert lost the high position at the east Frankish court which he had enjoyed for so long. We know that Liutbert was extremely unhappy at this development and was reluctant to accept his demotion: a charter drafted in November 882 in the monastery of Weißenburg, where he was abbot, insisted on referring to him as archchaplain, an epithet which rightfully belonged to Liutward under the new regime.[9] This bitterness heavily informs the standpoint of the Mainz annalist in all his reports between 882 and mid-887, which are consistently and pointedly hostile towards both Liutward and Charles. It should be stressed, however, that the text is emphatically not anti-Carolingian. In fact, its one note of praise for the emperor is sounded for his defeat and blinding of the royal pretender Hugh of Lotharingia, a bastard son of Lothar II.[10] The author's agendas were personal, not directed at the failings of an effete dynasty.

The Bavarian continuator, on the other hand, displays all the traits one would expect from a medieval provincial chronicler. His annals concentrate on Bavarian matters, and he has no obvious axe to grind either way in his reports about goings-on at court: this text is no more an 'official' court history along the lines of the *Royal Frankish Annals* (*Annales Regni Francarum*) than is its Mainz counterpart. Indeed, Charles the Fat himself tends to vanish from sight when he is not in Bavaria or nearby in the east Frankish kingdom. The viewpoints of both sources change in the middle of 887, at which point the emperor deposed Liutward and replaced him with Liutbert.[11] As a result, the Mainz annalist is for the short remainder of his work sympathetic to Charles (although not, of course, to the disgraced Liutward), while the Bavarian continuator suddenly becomes *parti pris* and turns hostile to justify (probably retrospectively) the coup of Arnulf of Carinthia.[12]

Although all these circumstances are well enough known to historians, they are in fact rarely incorporated into accounts of the period. Despite the fact that the Mainz continuator's version is, for the bulk of the reign, clearly the more driven by a specific political agenda (opposition to Liutbert's exclusion from court), it has been generally accepted by scholars as the more reliable source, and even as an objective record of events. Historians frequently interpret the Mainz annalist

---

[9] D CIII 63.

[10] *AF(M)* s.a. 885, p. 103. The criticism in the same annal of Charles's attempt to designate his own bastard son as heir also provides back-handed testimony to the endurance of Carolingian views on dynastic legitimacy.

[11] On which see below, pp. 178–90.

[12] Bowlus, 'Arnulf of Carinthia's *Ostpolitik*', p. 557 is a good exposition of the change in tone of both authors.

Charles the Fat in the eyes of contemporary annalists

as reflecting a general contemporary disquiet with Charles, while ad-judging the less critical Bavarian continuator to be an apologist for the emperor.[13] Another common approach is to follow the hostile Mainz author until the deposition of Liutward in mid-887, and then to switch to the Bavarian annalist's justification of Arnulf's coup, in which the ex-tent and nature of the opposition to Charles is exaggerated for polemical reasons.[14] Evidence from quite different sources (which are only placed together in scholarly convention thanks to an accident of archival his-tory) is therefore blended without discussion or even acknowledgement of the different agendas of their authors. Often, the section critical of the emperor is accepted unproblematically as evidence for widespread dissatisfaction with Charles without acknowledging even the existence of alternative versions of events (from the Bavarian annalist as well as from Abbo of St-Germain-des-Prés, Regino of Prüm and Notker the Stammerer).[15]

Inconvenient differences in contemporary opinion are thus suppressed in order to provide a neat unified narrative which fits the conventional paradigm of a decline in royal power in the late ninth century.[16] It is a principal contention of this book that by taking all the sources from the reign together and reading them in their contemporary context, one can draw a quite different picture. Accordingly, the rest of this chapter is an attempt to remove the Mainz continuation of the *Annals of Fulda* from the privileged position it enjoys in the eyes of historians of the period and to show that it does not always deserve to be prioritised over the account of the Bavarian annalist. An examination of the rhetorical strategies of the Mainz annalist in relation to some of his major set-pieces will establish that his work's polemic is much more pointed, carefully constructed and unreliable than has been hitherto appreciated, and that it is the central source for the negative image of Charles in the modern historiography.[17]

---

[13] Keller, 'Zum Sturz Karls III.', after acknowledging the respective positions of the annalists, ul-timately follows the Mainz author. R. Collins, *Early Medieval Europe, 300–1000* (London, 1991), p. 288 asserts that the Mainz text was written by a partisan of Charles the Fat. G. Bührer-Thierry, 'Le conseiller du roi: les écrivans carolingiens et la tradition biblique', *Médiévales* 12 (1987), 111–23, at 112 describes it as 'official'. J. M. Wallace-Hadrill, *The Frankish Church* (Oxford, 1983), p. 330, characterises the Mainz annals as unpolitical. These authors imply that even Charles's allies lamented his alleged incompetence.

[14] E.g. Riché, *The Carolingians*, pp. 117–9, though without acknowledging of the existence of the Bavarian continuation.

[15] Fried, 'The Frankish Kingdoms', pp. 158–60. See below, pp. 55–64 (Abbo), pp. 191–2 (Regino), pp. 199–229 (Notker).

[16] The key text is the Bavarian continuator's tendentious 887 annal, which justifies Arnulf's coup by speaking of a realm-wide conspiracy against Charles the Fat: see above, p. 6 for discussion.

[17] That the text was polemical is acknowledged by Reuter, 'Plunder and Tribute', p. 75.

BAD ADVICE

This image, as noted above, has three main parts. Firstly, was Charles dominated by his advisers? There are only two substantial pieces of evidence for this. One is that Liutward was mentioned more than any other individual as intervenor in the texts of royal charters. Certainly, this shows us that he was exceptionally influential at court, but this is no more than we would expect from a man who was both archchaplain and archchancellor, the two most prominent court positions. Moreover, Liutward actually intervened in a comparatively limited geographical area.[18] This evidence only acquires the sinister quality of domination when considered in the light of our second source of evidence, namely the long set-piece on Liutward by the Mainz annalist in his entry for 887, on the occasion of the archchancellor's deposition.[19] This invective includes a number of charges: low birth, heresy, attacking the king's relative, the *marchio* Berengar of Friuli, and usurpation of royal rights. Liutward, we are told, surpassed even the Old Testament villain Haman because he was 'greater than the emperor and was honoured and feared by all more than the emperor'. In addition, he was depicted as the emperor's only counsellor.[20] Almost all these accusations are unique to this source.[21] However, the fact that bitterness towards Liutward, Liutbert's rival, was one of the text's *raisons d'être* should immediately arouse our suspicion. In any case, the claims are mostly demonstrably false. Liutward was not of low birth, but belonged to a significant Alemannic family associated with the royal monastery of Reichenau which had enjoyed *Königsnähe* at least since Charles the Fat's installation in the region in the late 850s.[22] Nor, most likely, was he a heretic: the Christological deviation of which he is accused (belief in Christ as one in unity of substance with God, but not in person) is garbled.[23] Likewise, despite his high position, he was far from being the emperor's only counsellor, and we can identify many more such men.[24] The feud with Berengar was based on the allegation that Liutward had kidnapped the *marchio*'s niece from the major imperial

---

[18] The intervention evidence is discussed fully below, pp. 178–85.

[19] *AF(M)* s.a. 887, pp. 105–6.

[20] This is implicit in the 887 annal, and explicit in *AF(M)* s.a. 882, p. 98.

[21] The allegation that Liutward was Charles's 'unique counsellor' is the exception, having been made also by Regino, *Chronicon*, s.a. 887, p. 127. However, Regino also had an axe to grind with Liutward, and this stock accusation was an obvious way of expressing it: see below, p. 176.

[22] J. Fleckenstein, *Die Hofkapelle der deutschen Könige. I. Teil: Grundlegung. Die karolingische Hofkapelle* (Stuttgart, 1959), pp. 190–1.

[23] Although some regional theological traditions did hold similar beliefs in the Carolingian period: see J. Cavadini, *The Last Christology of the West. Adoptionism in Spain and Gaul, 785–820* (Philadelphia, 1993).

[24] Several of whom are discussed below in chaps. 3, 4 and 6.

Charles the Fat in the eyes of contemporary annalists

nunnery of St-Salvatore in Brescia in order to marry her off to one of his relatives. However, this version of events may well be an invention of the Mainz annalist: it is quite likely that Liutward here acted not in spite of imperial authority, but rather with Charles's permission and even with the acquiescence of the nuns. As implied by the Bavarian annalist, who had no vested interest in the matter, Berengar, and not Liutward, was the aggressor.[25]

This last complaint is adduced by the Mainz author as the evidence for his assertion that Liutward was the real power behind the throne: if he could dictate noble marriages to further his own interests, and do so at the expense of a relative of the emperor and of an important imperial nunnery, by implication there was nothing he could not do. However, the fact that the annalist distorts the course of the feud in order to make this polemical accusation should alert us to the fact that his narrative is politically charged. This becomes even clearer when it is recognised that all the attacks on Liutward are couched in heavily stereotyped terms, using stock themes drawn from Carolingian history and biblical models. Each stereotype, however, achieves its specific impact only in the context of the dispute between Liutward and Liutbert. Low birth was a standard criticism (equated by members of the status-conscious upper echelons of Frankish society with moral poverty), used famously as the most potent accusation of which Thegan could think to belittle Ebo of Rheims in his *Deeds of Louis the Pious*.[26] As a heretic, moreover, Liutward was unfit to lead the royal chapel: the allegation was carefully chosen to imply that he was unfit to do his job as archchaplain (which Liutbert coveted).[27] The 'unique counsellor' was a classic Carolingian demonisation applied to kings' favourites by their enemies.[28] It was a notion which inverted the norms of Carolingian political culture, the rhetoric (if not always the reality) of which was based on ideas of broad discussion and consensus which drew their authority from biblical precedent.[29] In Liutward's case, he was given to influence the emperor 'without the knowledge of the other counsellors who had been accustomed to assist the emperor's

---

[25] *AF(B)* s.a. 886, p. 114 and s.a. 887, p. 115. Here I am in agreement with K. Schmid, 'Liutbert von Mainz und Liutward von Vercelli im Winter 879/80 in Italien. Zur Erschließung bisher unbeachteter Gedenkbucheinträge aus S. Giulia in Brescia', in E. Hassinger, J. H. Müller and H. Ott (eds.), *Geschichte, Wirtschaft, Gesellschaft. Festschrift Clemens Bauer zum 75. Geburtstag* (Berlin, 1974), pp. 41–60, at pp. 42–8.

[26] Thegan, *Gesta Hludowici imperatoris*, ed. E. Tremp, MGH SRG (Hanover, 1995), chap. 44, p. 232.

[27] Bührer-Thierry, 'Le conseiller du roi', pp. 118–19. The same message comes from *AF(M)* s.a. 882, p. 98, where Liutward is referred to as 'pseudoepiscopus'.

[28] Bührer-Thierry, 'Le conseiller du roi', pp. 119–21.

[29] On consensus see J. L. Nelson, 'Kingship and Empire in the Carolingian World', in R. McKitterick (ed.), *Carolingian Culture: Emulation and Innovation* (Cambridge, 1994), pp. 52–87.

Kingship and Politics in the Late Ninth Century

father'.[30] This last comment we may read as a direct reference to Liutward and his circle: if Liutward was the antithesis of consensus, the archbishop and his associates were its personification. Finally, as Geneviève Bührer-Thierry has stressed, there are significant affinities between the Mainz annalist's characterisation of Liutward and the Book of Esther. The annalist makes an explicit reference to this text when he states that Liutward 'surpassed both in rank and dignity that Haman who is mentioned in the Book of Esther. For Haman was second after King Ahasuerus; but Liutward was greater than the emperor and was honoured and feared by all more than the emperor.' To the educated ninth-century reader or listener, the parallels would have been striking: Haman was not only his king's second-in-command, he also carried his seal ring, a possible reference to Liutward's position as archchancellor. Haman, moreover, ultimately overreached his position and was replaced, with God's help, by his arch-enemy Mordechai.[31] If Liutward was Haman, then Liutbert, of course, was Mordechai.

All this demonstrates that, far from being a reliable description of the relationship between Liutward of Vercelli and Charles the Fat, the Mainz annal for 887 is an extremely pointed and polemical piece of writing. It deploys standard and well-known themes to show how Liutward, as opposed to Liutbert, was unfit to be archchaplain and archchancellor on a number of carefully chosen grounds: it is a portrait of an archetypally bad adviser, a collage of stereotypes tailored to fit contemporary conventions, and not, as historians have read it, a dispassionate history of the bishop of Vercelli's character and career. It is important to stress, moreover, that the context within which all its accusations acquire meaning is the rivalry between Liutward and the annalist's patron, Liutbert of Mainz: this is at the centre of each of its claims and allusions. The fact that this political rivalry so clearly informs the Mainz annalist's depiction of Liutward therefore calls into question its value as evidence for the archchancellor's domination of the emperor.

THE VIKINGS AND THE SIEGE OF ASSELT

The same rhetorical device, the setting up of stereotypes, is employed by the Mainz annalist in his discussion of Charles's dealings with the Vikings, which constitutes the second major element of the emperor's negative reputation. In this case, although other texts discussing the subject are available, it is the Mainz continuator's depiction of the siege of Asselt in 882 which dominates historians' accounts and colours their

---

[30] *AF(M)* s.a. 882, p. 98.   [31] Bührer-Thierry, 'Le conseiller du roi', pp. 116–17.

Charles the Fat in the eyes of contemporary annalists

representation of the other sources. The full text is worth reproducing here, broken up into sections to make the subsequent argument easier to follow:

[1] 'There came from various provinces innumerable men, an army to be feared by any enemy, if it had had a suitable leader and one it agreed on. There were Franks, Bavarians, Alemans, Thuringians and Saxons; and they set out with one accord against the Northmen, wanting to fight them. When they got there, they laid siege to the Northmen's fortification, which is called Asselt.

[2] When the fortress was about to fall, and those within were struck with fear and despaired of escaping death,

[3] one of the emperor's counsellors, a false bishop called Liutward, without knowledge of the other counsellors who had been accustomed to assist the emperor's father, got together with the most treacherous count Wigbert and went to the emperor and persuaded him not to attack the enemy, having been bribed to do so, and presented the enemy *dux* Godafrid to the emperor.

[4] Like Ahab, the emperor received him as if he were a friend and made peace with him; and hostages were exchanged.

[5] The Northmen took this as a good sign, and so that it might not be doubted that they would observe the peace, they hoisted a shield on high after their fashion and threw open the doors of their fortress. Our men, knowing nothing of their treacherousness, went into the fortress, some to trade, some to look around the fortifications. The Northmen reverted to their usual treacherousness by hauling down the shield of peace and closing the gates: all our men inside were either killed or bound in chains and kept for later ransoming.

[6] But the emperor ignored the shame inflicted on his army, raised the afore-mentioned Godafrid from the baptismal font, and made the man who before had been the greatest enemy and traitor to his kingdom into a co-ruler over it. For the counties and benefices which the Northman Roric, a faithful man of the Frankish kings, had held in Kennemerland, he gave to that same enemy and his men to live in.

[7] What was still more of a crime, he did not blush to pay tribute to a man from whom he ought to have taken hostages and exacted tribute, doing this on the advice of evil men and against the custom of his ancestors the kings of the Franks. He took away the churches' treasures, which had been hidden for fear of the enemy, and to his own shame and that of all the army which followed him, gave to those same enemies 2,412 pounds of purest gold and silver.

[8] Moreover, he ordered that anyone in his army who should, moved by divine zeal in defence of Holy Church, kill a Northman who was trying to break into the camp, should either be strangled or blinded.

[9] The army was greatly saddened by this, and regretted that such a prince had come to rule over them, one who favoured the enemy and had snatched victory over the enemy,

[10] and they returned to their homes greatly confused.[32]

[32] *Confusi* (rendered by Reuter as 'shamed').

Kingship and Politics in the Late Ninth Century

[11] The Northmen, however, sent ships back to their country, loaded with treasure and captives two hundred in number; they themselves remained in a safe place, waiting until there should again be a suitable opportunity for plundering.'[33]

On the surface, this is a damning assessment. Yet the annalist's literary strategy here is more subtle than it appears at first sight. His criticism of Charles is not simply the one commonly levelled against kings by the ecclesiastical authors of the ninth century, that the outcome of the siege was disastrous because there was no outright military victory and tribute had to be paid. His objection is much more pointed: it is that this is exactly the opposite of what Charles should have done.

Indeed, the whole report of the siege is carefully constructed as a series of norms and oppositions. This is clear from a comparison of sections 1 and 2. The Frankish army is described as 'an army to be feared by any enemy, if it had had a suitable leader and one it agreed on . . . they set out with one accord against the Northmen, wanting to fight them'. Heavy stress is laid, therefore, on the size, capacity to inspire fear, and eagerness of the army. However, the deal for peace was made by the emperor 'when the fortress was about to fall, and those within were struck with fear and despaired of escaping death'. Peace was agreed, in other words, just as the army was poised to fulfil its function: it should be feared, and it was; it wanted to fight, and it was guaranteed of victory. Inspiring fear, a willingness to fight and performing as a good leader are here presented as criteria for judging royal behaviour: the norms are established in section 1, then shown unfulfilled in section 2. The outcome (section 9) was the regret of the army and their dissatisfaction with Charles, who was personally to blame for snatching defeat from the jaws of victory.[34]

The same device is evident in the descriptions of the terms of the treaty struck by Charles with the Vikings. In sponsoring the baptism of their leader Godafrid (section 6), he made a man who had been the kingdom's 'greatest enemy' into a 'co-ruler' (*consors regni*), a term normally only applied to members of the royal family. Godafrid was raised from one extreme to the other. Moreover (section 7), Charles paid tribute and gave hostages to a man from whom he ought to have taken them: this was done against Frankish royal tradition. The tribute he paid to Godafrid was church treasure which had previously been hidden to prevent exactly this eventuality. Charles's behaviour was not simply wrong: it was both un-kingly and un-Frankish.[35]

---

[33] *AF(M)* s.a. 882, pp. 98–9.

[34] The inspiration of fear as a kingly quality was also stressed by Notker, *Gesta Karoli Magni*, ed. H. F. Haefele, *Notker der Stammler, Taten Kaiser Karls des Großen*, MGH SRG NS (Berlin, 1959), 1.5, p. 8; 1.18, p. 25; 2.15, pp. 79–80; 2.17, p. 84.

[35] See also Reuter, 'Plunder and Tribute', p. 75.

Charles the Fat in the eyes of contemporary annalists

If his actions therefore inverted those which were normally expected of a Frankish king, the Mainz annalist also made it clear that they were a direct breach of the will of God. In section 4, Charles is compared to Ahab, the Old Testament ruler who had made peace against the manifest wishes of God.[36] In section 8, it is reported how he then went further, ordering his men not to kill any Northmen on fear of death, even though they might be 'moved by divine zeal in defence of Holy Church'. Ahab was also, however, a king deceived by false prophets, and the Mainz annalist is not slow to identify to whom he was referring at the siege of Asselt. Section 3 relates how the deal for peace was brokered by 'a false bishop called Liutward, without knowledge of the other counsellors who had been accustomed to assist the emperor's father'. This is another oppositional passage, and one which provides the key for understanding the account as a whole. Liutward, acting only with the consent of the 'most treacherous count' Wigbert, is contrasted to the multiple counsellors who ought to have been consulted; as noted above, this was contrary to the principles propounded by the idealised rhetoric of Carolingian consensus. He is also, however, set off against the former counsellors of Louis the German: in other words, Liutbert of Mainz and his associates. Everything that took place at Asselt was exactly as it should not be, but this was the most important point. The implication is that if Liutward had not been in a position to act as a false prophet to Charles the Fat, and the emperor had had Liutbert at his side instead, the outcome would have been very different. Once again, the specific political gripe of the Mainz annals can be located right at the heart of one of its major set-pieces.

The Mainz annalist's version of the siege of Asselt is therefore built around a number of carefully chosen themes of normal and appropriate behaviour, which constitute a pointed attack on the emperor for doing just what he ought not to have done. Like an anti-king, against the will of his army and of God, he allowed defeat when victory was all but achieved and reached a peace which broke all the norms which should govern the actions of a Frankish king. Again, the touchstones of his judgement were rooted not only in biblical typology, but also in Frankish tradition, explicitly and implicitly. Einhard's biography of Charlemagne, a benchmark for commentators on rulership in the ninth century and beyond, had stressed the royal virtue of steadfastness (*constantia*) as crucial to the emperor's success.[37] At Asselt, we are presented with its antithesis. It was quite normal for Carolingian authors to stereotype and stylise the

---

[36] 3 Kings 20–22.

[37] Einhard, *Vita Karoli*, ed. O. Holder-Egger, MGH SRG (Hanover, 1911), chap. 7, p. 10; chap. 8, p. 11; chap. 18, p. 21. On Einhard's influence see e.g. B. Schneidmüller, *Karolingische Tradition und frühes französisches Königtum. Untersuchungen zur Herrschaftslegitimation der westfränkisch-französischen*

Kingship and Politics in the Late Ninth Century

behaviour of their enemies, especially the Vikings.[38] The Mainz author, however, applies this technique to the actions of Charles the Fat and Liutward of Vercelli in 882 as well, presenting us with a looking-glass world in which everything is out of place and nothing is as it ought to be. This is explicit in his conclusion: the army, forced to return home without a victory, did so 'greatly confused'.[39]

The political agenda of this account is therefore amplified by the pointed rhetorical strategies its author uses; it is more an ideological commentary on kingship than reportage. It is hence suspect as a passive barometer of contemporary opinion. However, this analysis of his literary strategies does not necessarily negate the information offered by the annalist: it is always possible that the author chose stereotypes to fit reality as he saw it. To answer this objection we must now turn to the equivalent report in the Bavarian continuation. This text, which, as noted above, is usually dismissed by historians as a pro-Charles polemic, in fact shows every sign of being a *more* objective version of events than that of the Mainz author. The Bavarian account, which is approximately the same length as that of its Mainz counterpart, begins with a detailed description of the army's advance up the Rhine, split into two contingents.[40] Treachery foiled an attempt at a surprise attack, necessitating a siege. The account of the siege takes up the bulk of the report, before a brief summary of the terms of the peace treaty.

Several points must be stressed about this source. Its information on the arrangement of the army and the siege is detailed and convincing. The division of the army into two contingents either side of the Rhine is consistent with what is known about other Carolingian campaigns which often moved in a pincer movement (and along river banks) towards their goals. Arnulf of Carinthia and the royal general Henry are depicted

---

Monarchie im 10. Jahrhundert (Wiesbaden, 1979); M. Innes, '"He never even allowed his white teeth to be bared in laughter." The Politics of Laughter in the Carolingian Renaissance', in G. Halsall (ed.), *Humour, History and Politics in Late Antiquity and the Early Middle Ages* (Cambridge, 2002), pp. 131–56.

[38] See for instance S. Coupland, 'The Rod of God's Wrath or the People of God's Wrath? The Carolingians' Theology of the Viking Invasions', *Journal of Ecclesiastical History* 42 (1991), 535–54. The 882 Mainz annal also makes archetypes of the Northmen. Section 5 reads like a microcosm of the 'traders or raiders' debate: they do exactly the opposite of what they seem to be doing when they drop their trading flag and slaughter the Franks. The annalist's use of the terms 'their customary treacherousness' and 'after their fashion' reveals that he has clear and categorical notions as to what constitutes normal Viking behaviour (this is essentially reduced to a desire for plunder).

[39] For another example of the polemical accusation of 'un-Frankish' behaviour, see *AF* s.a. 876, p. 86, which ridicules Charles the Bald's imperial stylings: 'despising all the customs of the Frankish kings, he held the glories of the Greeks to be the best.' The polemical nature of this passage *is* usually recognised by historians, in contrast to the report of the siege of Asselt. See now in general P. Buc, 'Ritual and Interpretation: the Early Medieval Case', *EME* 9 (2000), 183–210.

[40] Citations will be from *AF(B)* s.a. 882, pp. 107–9.

Charles the Fat in the eyes of contemporary annalists

as leading the Bavarian and Frankish contingents in the advance party. Not only were these leaders appropriate to armies from these *regna*, but the sending ahead of an advance party under Henry was a tactic used by Charles on at least one other occasion.[41] There is also a wealth of incidental detail about the siege included in the report. Precise dates, times of day, lengths of time and distances pepper the text, and we are given a vivid description of the unpleasant physical conditions of the siege and of the weather. Moreover, no fewer than four Viking leaders are identified by name.

This detail serves no obvious purpose within the logic of the text: it is not, for instance, in any way marshalled to provide a coherent apologia for the emperor or for the inconclusive outcome of the conflict. The account is also anomalous within the Bavarian continuation as a whole: most Viking raids, including all those of 883–5, went completely unmentioned by the author, and even the siege of Paris in 885–6 roused him to barely more than passing comment.[42] Moreover, it is worth noting the frequent use of the first person plural in the text, such as 'our men', 'hostages having been given by us', 'our hostages having been sent back'; and that the annals only resume their normal rhythm 'after the Bavarians had returned home'. In view of this it is quite possible, therefore, either that the author of this work was present at the siege of Asselt, or that he had access to an eyewitness report. The incidental detail of the Bavarian account is even more striking when compared with the dearth of similar material in the Mainz version which, despite its length, moves directly from the gathering of the army to the circumstances and terms of the peace treaty, the events which had the most importance for its author's polemical purpose. In other words, it is the Bavarian continuator who appears to be by far the more reliable witness to the actual events of the 882 siege.

With this in mind, two main conclusions may be drawn. Firstly, some central elements of the Mainz account can be regarded as highly suspect. The accusation of treachery which is levelled against Liutward by the Mainz author looks unlikely. The Bavarian annalist blames treachery for the failure of the initial surprise attack, not for a premature decision on the emperor's part to come to terms with the enemy. Moreover, he is clear that the fault lay in the advance party, 'among the Franks [i.e. Franconians]': Liutward was not a Frank but an Aleman with an Italian

---

[41] *AV* s.a. 886, p. 61; *AF(M)* s.a. 886, p. 105. Cf. Louis the Younger's use of Henry in this capacity against Boso in *AV* s.a. 880, p. 47.

[42] *AF(B)* s.a. 886, p. 114. Cf. *AF(M)* s.a. 883–5, pp. 100–3. Some of these raids were in distant Saxony, but the Bavarian continuator was certainly aware of events in that region: e.g. *AF(B)* s.a. 882, p. 109; 883, p. 110.

Kingship and Politics in the Late Ninth Century

bishopric, and in any case, as archchancellor, would presumably have been with Charles in the main body of the army. The Bavarian annalist (or his source) must have known what he was talking about, since the Bavarian contingent had been together with the Frankish 'traitors' in the advance party. This is probably why he recorded the names of the leaders of only these two groups. Similarly, the Mainz author's assertion that the terms of the peace deal were contrary to Frankish custom is demonstrably false: the policy of paying off invaders and setting them to defend lands at river mouths was by no means a new or untested measure, and on other occasions the Mainz annalist was conspicuously unopposed to such strategies.[43]

Secondly, the tone of the Bavarian account is instructive. It is by no means particularly pro-Charles: his initial attack is a failure, and the ensuing siege is long, nasty and inconclusive. However, it is significant that the annalist does not particularly criticise the emperor for this. The decision to come to terms with the enemy is attributed primarily to the illness spreading through both camps as a result of the summer heat and the number of corpses lying around unburied. Moreover, the annalist's sigh of relief is almost audible when he ends his account with the report that Charles 'graciously allowed his army leave to go home'. The generally neutral attitude of the Bavarian continuator is largely shared by other contemporary sources. The annalist of St-Vaast, ever-interested in the doings of the Vikings, enumerated their depredations before concluding with palpable satisfaction that Charles 'forced the Northmen to leave the kingdom'.[44] Hincmar and Regino, our other sources, offer more negative readings, but nevertheless nothing beyond the typical inclination of ecclesiastical authors to berate kings who used church resources to buy off their enemies and to read the attacks of the Vikings as manifestations of God's disapproval.[45] Indeed, it is interesting that the author closest to the siege itself, the Bavarian continuator, is also the most sympathetic to the emperor. Exactly the same phenomenon is discernible in the accounts of the Viking siege of Paris, where the only eyewitness report, that of Abbo of St-Germain-des-Prés, is also the sole text actually to praise the actions of the emperor.[46] Only writers more distant from events, as were Hincmar and Regino in 882, manipulated them in order to make points

---

[43] See now S. Coupland, 'From Poachers to Gamekeepers: Scandinavian Warlords and Carolingian Kings', *EME* 7 (1998), 85–114; S. Coupland, 'The Frankish Tribute Payments to the Vikings and their Consequences', *Francia* 26 (1999), 57–75 shows that tribute was usually an effective solution. Cf. *AF* s.a. 850, pp. 39–40; 873, pp. 80–1.

[44] *AV* s.a. 882, pp. 51–2.

[45] *AB* s.a. 882, pp. 248–9; Regino, *Chronicon*, s.a. 882, p. 119. On ecclesiastical attitudes see Coupland, 'Rod of God's Wrath'.

[46] See below, pp. 55–64.

Charles the Fat in the eyes of contemporary annalists

of personal import to them, such as (in Hincmar's case) the condemnation of royal use of ecclesiastical lands and (in Regino's) the interpretation of Viking attacks as evidence for God's displeasure at the sins of the Franks.

In the context of all the sources, the polemic of the Mainz annalist stands at one extreme of a spectrum of opinion. Its account of the siege of Asselt is anomalous, not representative. Historians have been wrong, therefore, to take the Mainz text as the key source for the events of 882 and to conclude that the ending of the siege was 'to the disappointment of all':[47] the work's extreme polemic is to be explained by its political agenda concerning Charles's exclusion of Liutbert from court. This type of misrepresentation (or at least exaggeration) is common enough in Carolingian historical writing. Annalists' reports of kings' dealings with Vikings were often conditioned by the state of their relationship with the ruler in question. Thus Hincmar's depiction of Louis III's widely celebrated victory over the Vikings at Saucourt in 881 as a defeat was motivated by the archbishop's dissatisfaction at being left out of high position at the young king's court.[48] In this sense it is a very similar text to the Mainz version of the siege of Asselt. However, while historians rightly take Hincmar's view of Saucourt with more than a pinch of salt, the Mainz continuator's view of Asselt has become fixed in historiographical convention. The idea of Charles the Fat as a king peculiarly inept in his dealings with Vikings is largely drawn from this text: once read in its context, this source loses its primacy and Charles appears no worse (or, it must be said, better) than any other king in the way contemporaries perceived his attempts to deal with the invaders.

ROYAL INACTIVITY

The third element of Charles the Fat's reputation as a failed king is that he was immobile and inactive, a 'do-nothing king'. For this idea, too, historians have drawn almost exclusively on the Mainz continuator of the Fulda annals. One subtle but telling way in which the author attempts to induce his audience to draw this conclusion is by his sparse reporting of the emperor's itinerary on major liturgical feast days. In the five full years of his reign when he is the sole royal subject of the annals, the Mainz author reports Charles's whereabouts only twice: the Purification of the Virgin in 884 and Christmas in 885. By contrast, the Bavarian continuation gives us Christmas of 882, 884 and 885, Easter in 883, 886

---

[47] Riché, *The Carolingians*, p. 217; Coupland, 'Poachers to Gamekeepers', p. 109.

[48] *AB* s.a. 881, pp. 244–5; Cf. *AV* s.a. 881, p. 50; *AF* s.a. 881, p. 96; for comments see P. Fouracre, 'The Context of the OHG *Ludwigslied*', *Medium Aevum* 54 (1985), 87–103. On the general point see Nelson, 'The *Annals of St-Bertin*', pp. 37–8.

37

Kingship and Politics in the Late Ninth Century

and 887, and Epiphany in 885. Similarly, in the Mainz annals between 870 and 881 we are told the location of Louis the German and then Louis the Younger on no less than twenty major festivals. In particular, from 872, with only one exception (876, the year in which Louis's three sons succeeded him), all the reported royal itineraries contain references to Christmas or Easter, or both. The Mainz continuator is therefore anomalous. This pattern is no accident. The mentioning of the king's whereabouts on feast days was not a simple matter of generic convention: as the Carolingians saw it, it was part of the grand narrative of Christian historiography. The Carolingian king was thought of (at least by himself and his friends) as *vicarius dei*, the representative of God on earth. His progress round the kingdom was intrinsically linked to the circular progress of the liturgical year and the ceremonies associated with it in both literature and reality. His presence at major churches on major festivals was a reflection of the relationship between God and the legitimate king. The omission of this information by the Mainz continuator is glaring, and has the effect of producing an image of an inactive and implicitly illegitimate ruler.[49]

In addition to this, the text juxtaposes Charles's inactivity with the vigour of its own heroes, whom it portrays also in a stereotyped way carrying out functions which should have been the king's. A report in the annal for 883 is instructive here: 'The Northmen came up the Rhine and burned many places lately rebuilt, taking not a little plunder. Archbishop Liutbert of Mainz came against them with a few men; but he killed not a few of them and took back the plunder. Cologne was rebuilt apart from its churches and monasteries and its walls were provided with gates, bars and locks.'[50] This is a palindromic entry: Liutbert has 'a few men', but he kills 'not a few'. He takes back the plunder seized by the raiders, and their work of destruction is undone by the rebuilding of Cologne. In other words, the actions of Liutbert negate those of the Vikings exactly. The subtext is that this is correct behaviour: in 882, by contrast, Charles the Fat did not negate the aims of the Northmen, but actually facilitated the realisation of their aims.

It is striking that throughout the Mainz continuation the same criteria of judgement are deployed by the author as had been used in the account of Asselt: inspiration of fear in the enemy, prevention of plunder, and evidence of God's favour, everything that had marked Charles out as a failure in 882. Liutbert's victory of 883, therefore, was measured partly by his success in retaking the attackers' booty. In 884, two victories of the *dux*

---

[49] Cf. P. Buc, *The Dangers of Ritual. Between Early Medieval Texts and Social Scientific Theory* (Princeton and Oxford, 2001), pp. 58–9.
[50] *AF(M)* s.a. 883, p. 100.

Charles the Fat in the eyes of contemporary annalists

Henry over the Northmen, one achieved while Charles sat talking with his men at Colmar, were explicit evidence of God's favour. Moreover, Henry's success is specifically in preventing the enemy's plundering (he kills them 'wherever they wanted to go to plunder'), and in creating fear in the minds of the Danes.[51] The Vikings who had been harrying the kingdom of Carloman II overwintered in the Hesbaye in 884–5, 'as if there were none to resist them'. Henry and Liutbert surprised them and showed them the error of their ways, killing some and, crucially, removing what they had foraged (plunder): again, the enemy was frightened and fled by night.[52] Godafrid was next to demonstrate (in the Mainz author's view) a typically Viking lack of faith, attempting to move up the Rhine until stopped by Henry, with God's help. After retreating, they were beaten again by Saxons and Frisians, collectively and pointedly referred to as 'christiani', who also recovered their plunder with interest.[53] As a final example, the siege of Paris in 885–6 is also assessed on these criteria. The Vikings here were, quite properly, scared of the Frankish army until the death of its local leaders, Hugh the Abbot and Gauzlin of St-Denis, upon which they emerged and 'took possession of the whole region, and were able to hunt and sport with no one to prevent them'.[54] Charles's failure at Paris is summed up by the annalist in exactly these terms: after Henry was also killed, the emperor was actually scared himself; he endorsed plundering and he paid tribute.[55]

The opposition between the inactivity of Charles and the vigour of other leaders (especially the figures traditionally closest to the east Frankish kings, namely Henry and Liutbert himself) is thus a firmly established and consistent substratum in the Mainz text.[56] However, the independence from royal impetus of this kind of aristocratic resistance to the Vikings may often have been more apparent than real. For example, the Mainz annals present the Viking-Frankish confrontations in the Hesbaye in 885 as if Henry and Liutbert were the only protagonists: it is only by consulting the annalist of St-Vaast, writing much nearer the scene of the action, that we learn of Charles's direct involvement in organising the campaign.[57]

One final element of Charles's reputation as a do-nothing king, namely his illness, figures in several sources. The evidence for the emperor's

---

[51] *AF(M)* s.a. 884, pp. 100–1.   [52] *AF(M)* s.a. 885, p. 102.   [53] *AF(M)* s.a. 885, pp. 102–3.

[54] *AF(M)* s.a. 886, p. 104. Note the interesting equation made here between hunting and lordship.

[55] *AF(M)* s.a. 886, p. 105.

[56] On another level, Liutbert's emergence as a war leader in frontier regions in the 880s may have been a consequence of his exclusion from the political centre.

[57] *AF(M)* s.a. 885, p. 102; *AV* s.a. 885, p. 56. For the similar examples of Gauzlin and Hugh, see below, pp. 102–10. *AF(M)* s.a. 884, p. 101 also refers to Charles's organisation of frontier defences.

Kingship and Politics in the Late Ninth Century

much-vaunted sickliness (or insanity, as Gibbon and Stubbs had it) amounts to: the widely reported 'fit' he suffered at Frankfurt in 873;[58] Hincmar's description of him as 'infirmus' in 876;[59] a charter of 883 in which the emperor made a gift to the church of Bergamo in thanks to St Alexander, 'to whose threshold we had refuge and by whose intercessions the Lord restored us to health from a grave sickness of the body';[60] two annalistic references reporting a sickness in the winter of 886–7;[61] and the Bavarian continuator's account that in 887 Charles 'underwent a cutting for a pain of the head'.[62] The most striking piece of evidence, the latter, has conventionally been taken to mean that Charles was trepanned in order to cure a tumour, epilepsy or some form of mental illness. However, Hans Oesterle has rightly pointed out that the text is best read as signifying a letting of blood to cure a headache, not an incision *of* the head itself, and that standard ninth-century medical wisdom would not have advised a trepanning for either head pains or for epilepsy.[63] Moreover if, as Oesterle plausibly argues, Carolingian medical knowledge incorporated the eighth-century tract 'De minutione sanguinis sive de phleotomia' attributed to Bede, it is highly significant that this text advises the opening of the 'vena cephalica' to relieve head pains on the nones (5th) of April, as we know that Charles was at Bodman, where the operation was performed, in March and April.[64] In other words, the blood-letting was carried out at this point not because of the mounting gravity of Charles's illness, as the Bavarian annalist, at this time anxious to justify Arnulf's usurpation, would like us to believe, but rather in accordance with the specifications of received medical wisdom.

The contexts of the other references allow us to play down their significance also. The spasm of 873 bears the hallmarks more of a literary set-piece than of a dispassionate medical report: Charles's attempts to strip away the trappings of secular life do not read like an epileptic fit, and may

---

[58] *AF* s.a. 873, pp. 77–8; *AB* s.a. 873, pp. 190–2; *AX* s.a. 873, pp. 31–2.

[59] *AB* s.a. 876, p. 210.

[60] D CIII 89. This evidence has not hitherto been taken into account.

[61] *AF(M)* s.a. 886, p. 105; *AF(B)* s.a. 887, p. 115.

[62] *AF(B)* s.a. 887, p. 115: 'pro dolore capitis incisionem accepit'.

[63] H. J. Oesterle, 'Die sogenannte Kopfoperation Karls III. 887', *Archiv für Kulturgeschichte* 61 (1979), 445–51.

[64] D CIII 157 shows him at Rottweil in mid-February, and *AF(B)* s.a. 887, p. 115 has him at Bodman before leaving for an assembly at Waiblingen after Easter, which fell on 16 April. The first diploma issued at Waiblingen was D 158 of 7 May, but we know that Pope Stephen was invited to the assembly for 30 April; *Fragmenta Registri Stephani V. Papae*, ed. E. Casper, MGH Epp 7 (Berlin, 1928), pp. 334–53, no. 14.

Charles the Fat in the eyes of contemporary annalists

rather reflect a personal crisis brought on by the young prince's internalisation of the church's teachings on worldly renunciation.[65] In any case, Louis the German allowed his son to take charge of important diplomatic and judicial hearings immediately afterwards.[66] Hincmar's 876 reference is isolated, and precedes by a matter of days the formal *divisio* of the eastern kingdom agreed to by Charles's brothers, a political event of the highest importance. The reference to the cure by St Alexander was presumably of the same disease (malaria?) which affected many people in Italy in the summer of 883, and had a habit of laying low visiting Franks from north of the Alps throughout the ninth century and later.[67] There is no evidence that this was anything more than a one-off fever. The illness of winter 886–7, which was probably a stroke, an affliction to which the east Frankish royal family seems to have been susceptible, was more serious, as Charles did not leave Alemannia at all during the following year, a highly unusual state of affairs.[68] Even this, however, was followed by intense diplomatic activity on Charles's part aimed largely at resolving the succession issue.[69] None of this evidence, therefore, permits the conclusion that Charles was seriously politically incapacitated by illness at any point in his reign before 887. Any royal illness was big news, and liable to be recorded. However, it is not justifiable to string these individual examples together to support a claim that Charles was in general a 'weak' or 'sickly' individual.[70]

We may conclude, therefore, that the sources do not support the dominant historiographical view of Charles as a sick and inactive character. Here again, the Mainz author is an anomalous witness. The siege of Paris will be discussed more fully in a later chapter,[71] but even a cursory reading of Abbo's *Wars of the City of Paris* reveals a judgement of the emperor's actions which is diametrically opposed to the image given by the Mainz annals. Moreover, in reality Charles's itinerary distinguishes him as one of the most mobile Carolingians of them all. During a short reign, he made six visits to Italy and two to the west Frankish kingdom, to say nothing of his journeys to the Rhineland, Lotharingia, Bavaria and the eastern marches. Charles's unusual mobility has been recognised by those historians who have worked on his charters.[72] In wider historical

---

[65] J. L. Nelson, 'Monks, Secular Men and Masculinity, c.900', in D. M. Hadley (ed.), *Masculinity in Medieval Europe* (Harlow, 1999), pp. 121–42.

[66] *AF* s.a. 873, p. 78.   [67] *AF(B)* s.a. 883, p. 110. Lothar II was a notable victim.

[68] I owe this suggested diagnosis to Tim Reuter. See also Oesterle, 'Kopfoperation'.

[69] On which see below, chap. 6.

[70] W. Hartmann, *Ludwig der Deutsche* (Darmstadt, 2002), p. 67 argues the contrary case.

[71] See below, pp. 55–64.   [72] E.g. P. Kehr, *Die Kanzlei Karls III.* (Berlin, 1936), pp. 5–6.

Kingship and Politics in the Late Ninth Century

convention, however, which relies on the canon of accusations emanating from Mainz, he remains a lazy and inactive ruler.

HISTORY AND POLITICS IN THE LATE NINTH CENTURY

In its consistent categorisation of the activities of the king and the magnates who populate its pages, the Mainz continuation of the *Annals of Fulda* constitutes not a dispassionate description of events, but rather a political commentary on them. Its schematisation of political behaviour into distinct types reveal it, to some extent, as a dialogue between good and bad, right and wrong. The attributions of fear, treachery, and so on can be seen as literary motifs deployed to create particular images. For instance, plunder, taken or prevented, provided a ready-made and stable metaphor with which to define victory and judge the outcome of battles. The consistent use of these motifs, moreover, is especially conspicuous given that they rarely figure in earlier sections of the Mainz annals. Tribute and plunder, for example, are only intermittently associated with Viking objectives and defeats in the annals before 882.[73] Similarly, divine favour or wrath is only invoked twice in the annals between 840 and 882 in relation to Viking raids, of which approximately seventeen are recorded.[74] The picture is very much the same with regard to the numerous reports of battles and campaigns against the Slavs, the enemies *par excellence* of the eastern Franks: on only four of these occasions had God's will been read into the outcome.[75] It is quite otherwise with the Mainz continuation after 882 which frequently mobilises divine judgement as a gloss on the outcome of encounters with Vikings, negatively in the case of Charles, positively in the case of other Frankish combatants. This is another very clear indication of the degree of care and artifice which went into the construction of the image of the emperor presented by the Mainz annalist. By denying him divine approval, the annalist presented Charles as an implicitly illegitimate ruler.[76]

This rhetorical use of divine approval shows how closely the message was intertwined with the medium. We have also seen how the annalist's

[73] *AF* s.a. 873, pp. 80–1; 876, p. 86 are exceptional. Cf. Nelson, 'The *Annals of St-Bertin*', pp. 37–8 on the inconsistency of even the highly opinionated Hincmar on such matters as tribute in relation to his judgements on Charles the Bald.

[74] *AF* s.a. 854, pp. 44–5 (actually a Danish civil war); 873, pp. 80–1 (a Frisian victory). Even Louis III's famous victory at Saucourt did not inspire a divine interpretation: *AF* s.a. 881, p. 96; similarly *AV* s.a. 881, pp. 50–1.

[75] *AF* s.a. 844, p. 35; 870, p. 70; 872, p. 76; 880, pp. 94–5.

[76] In general on this theme: K. F. Werner, 'Gott, Herrscher und Historiograph. Der Geschichtsschreiber als Interpret des Wirken Gottes in der Welt und Ratgeber der Könige (4. bis 12. Jahrhundert)', in E.-D. Hehl et al., *Deus qui mutat tempora. Menschen und Institutionen im Wandel des Mittelalters* (Sigmaringen, 1987), pp. 1–31.

Charles the Fat in the eyes of contemporary annalists

judgements were full of comparisons, explicit and implicit, with the traditional benchmarks of Carolingian kingship, Frankish tradition and biblical archetypes. The text's engagement in a dialogue with the industrious Carolingian past, especially the now semi-mythological reign of Charlemagne, added extra barbs to its attack. Charlemagne's formidable posthumous reputation was often the spectre at the late Carolingian royal feast: the representation of his descendants could be made to suffer from his dynasty's spectacular capacity for self-mythologising. The themes of the work also drew on the stock of ideas provided by one of the staple sources of Carolingian political thought, the Irish tract 'On the Twelve Abuses of the World' by an anonymous author known as Pseudo-Cyprian.[77] The ninth abuse listed by Pseudo-Cyprian, the unjust king, defines the duties of the ruler as, among other things, the prevention of theft, the defence of churches and the poor, the employment of good counsellors, and fighting the enemies of his realm.[78] Failures on exactly these counts were imputed by the Mainz annalist to Charles the Fat. However, one of the consequences for kings who failed to behave according to these rules was that the natural order was upset, causing plagues, famines and ecological disasters.[79] This kind of cosmic disturbance is, accordingly, catalogued by the Mainz author in association with Charles's limp performances against the Vikings, as mountains fell down, rivers burst their banks and plague wiped out the cattle and sheep of Francia.[80] Although Pseudo-Cyprian was certainly not the only source of these sorts of ideas, the text was known in the later ninth century: it was used, for example, by Hincmar of Rheims in a letter to Charles the Fat himself.[81] The Mainz annalist's deployment of Pseudo-Cyprianic prescriptions, whether or not they were drawn from the tract first-hand, adds to our sense of his work as a multi-layered endeavour. Its dialectic with the traditional norms of Carolingian political thought sharpened its attack and made it more cutting to a contemporary audience.

The author does not purely invent – we cannot doubt that Charles the Fat did pay tribute to the Vikings at Asselt or that Liutbert of Mainz did

---

[77] Pseudo-Cyprian, *De XII abusivis saeculi*, ed. S. Hellmann, in *Texte und Untersuchungen zur Geschichte der altchristlichen Literatur*, 3rd series, 4 (1909), 1–60. On the text see H. H. Anton, 'Pseudo-Cyprian. De duodecim abusivis saeculi und sein Einfluß auf den Kontinent, insbesondere auf die karolingischen Fürstenspiegel', in H. Löwe (ed.), *Die Iren und Europa im früheren Mittelalter* (Stuttgart, 1982), pp. 568–617.

[78] Pseudo-Cyprian, *De XII abusivis saeculi*, pp. 51–3.

[79] My remarks here rest on the work of R. Meens, 'Politics, Mirrors of Princes and the Bible: Sins, Kings and the Well-Being of the Realm', *EME* 7 (1998), 345–57.

[80] *AF(M)*, s.a. 883, p. 100; 886, pp. 104–5; 887, p. 105. Though cf. *AF(B)*, s.a. 886, pp. 114–15.

[81] Hincmar, *Ad Carolum III imperatorem*, *PL* 125, cols. 991–2; see Meens, 'Politics, Mirrors of Princes and the Bible', pp. 353–5.

Kingship and Politics in the Late Ninth Century

defeat them after the sack of Cologne – but he does attempt to interpret those events on his audience's behalf according to his own agenda. Therefore, this work does not simply *tell* us that Charles the Fat was 'a useless king' (*rex inutilis*), as Einhard tells us of the last Merovingian Childeric III: it *shows* us the effects of bad kingship in action. The author presented very clear criteria for assessing good kingship, and then showed Charles failing to fulfil each one in turn. His representation, in other words, was of a ruler who had by definition failed in the practice of Frankish kingship. The account is systematic, an exposition of Charles as the archetypally failed king (in contrast to the vigorous activities of Henry and Liutbert). This text is a commentary on political ideas: we may describe it as almost a parody or caricature of kingship.[82]

At every juncture of the continuation we encounter the antagonism between Liutward and Liutbert. Liutward is the archetypally bad archchancellor and he is culpable in the outcome of the siege of Asselt; while Liutbert vigorously fills the role against the Vikings which should have been Charles's responsibility. This agenda informs almost the entire text and motivates its criticisms. The work is therefore best interpreted as a 'private history', a justificatory manifesto for the opposition of Liutbert of Mainz, his circle and his Franconian supporters to the regime of Charles the Fat, an Aleman whose succession had turned Mainz into a politically peripheral region and marginalised the political community centred on the archbishop.[83] It contained more than the frank critical opinion which kings might occasionally expect to hear from their close advisers;[84] it was surely meant only for the eyes of the archbishop and his entourage. History of this kind could help give identity to a group by lending coherence to its aims and self-perception.[85] To write history, especially in the ninth century, was to engage in debates about real power. To successfully impose one's version of the past and present on others, and hence to suppress alternative interpretations, is a powerful way of legitimising a particular political position.[86] Liutbert and his circle were engaged in precisely this sort of endeavour. His exclusion from the political centre was expressed

---

[82] On this subject in general see now J. L. Nelson, 'Bad Kingship in the Earlier Middle Ages', *Haskins Society Journal* 8 (1996), 1–26.

[83] Cf. J. L. Nelson, 'Public *Histories* and Private History in the Work of Nithard', *Speculum* 60 (1985), 251–93.

[84] See Nelson, 'History-Writing', pp. 441–2 for possible examples of this.

[85] M. Innes and R. McKitterick, 'The Writing of History', in McKitterick (ed.), *Carolingian Culture*, pp. 193–220, at p. 203 discuss polemic as a self-justifying genre. In general see Hen and Innes (eds.), *Uses of the Past*.

[86] See Airlie, 'Narratives of Triumph'; R. McKitterick, 'Constructing the Past in the Early Middle Ages: The Case of the Royal Frankish Annals', *TRHS* 6th series, 7 (1997), 101–30.

in a way which not only gave voice to his frustrations with the king, but also bestowed upon his formerly influential network of Franconian supporters a sense of togetherness based on a common perception of being hard done by. The archbishop's position was similar to that of numerous aristocrats of the Carolingian period who lost out, often temporarily, in the scramble for royal favour; the difference was that his outrage registered on and survived in the written record. This reflected an unavoidable and normally tolerable situation within Carolingian politics: there was never enough *Königsnähe* to keep all the nobles happy all of the time. As long as competition for favour was alive, there would be winners (like Liutward) as well as losers (like Liutbert): real problems arose when resentment of the type expressed in the Mainz annals resonated with and amplified disputes within the ruling house.

As a rare window onto the self-perception and identity of an excluded political group, the Mainz annals are extremely valuable. However, from a historiographical perspective, it is unfortunate that this has been the main source for historians' judgements on Charles the Fat's abilities: they have taken on board the tone of the Mainz author as well as the information he provides.[87] As comparison with other contemporary sources shows, however, the text is certainly not to be accepted wholesale. The fact that historians have usually been keen to do just that reveals the authority which the 'decline and fall' paradigm of Carolingian history still exerts over the historiography. The Mainz continuation and the conventional historiographical view of the late Carolingian empire are mutually reinforcing. The text's weak king, beset by Vikings and barely propped up by the vigour of the high aristocracy, fits perfectly with the modern belief in a dwindling of royal power in the years leading up to 888. Moreover, that very belief encourages its proponents to prioritise the Mainz annals as the key source for this process.

Furthermore, we should beware of reading the chronicles of this period as continuations of the tradition of 'official' Carolingian histories begun by the *Royal Frankish Annals*. On the contrary, the Mainz and Bavarian annals reflect the diffusion of historiography away from the court in the post-Charlemagne period, and the emergence of writers whose agendas were personal, and could easily bring them into conflict with kings.[88]

---

[87] A parallel with Aethelred II of England, whose reign is traditionally assessed exclusively using the hostile *Anglo-Saxon Chronicle*, suggests itself: see S. Keynes, 'A Tale of Two Kings: Alfred the Great and Aethelred the Unready', *TRHS* 36 (1986), 195–217.

[88] Arguments which help dissolve the distinction between 'private' monastic and 'official' dynastic history are offered by G. Althoff, 'Gandersheim und Quedlinburg. Ottonische Frauenklöster als Herrschafts- und Überlieferungszentren', *FMSt* 25 (1991), 123–44.

Kingship and Politics in the Late Ninth Century

These authors, based in the provinces, were the children of the Carolingian Renaissance. They belonged to an intellectual milieu in which kings had lost their monopoly over historical writing and in which the recycling and reuse of Frankish history had become a prominent feature.[89] The late Carolingian period had a strong sense of its past, and arguments raged as to how it should be understood.[90] By contrast, early Carolingian writers based at court had tried to impose a 'party line' on the interpretation of history, and to a great extent succeeded.[91] However, after the division of the empire in 843 it became clear that it was impossible for one author or king to 'saturate the discourse' of politics.[92] Political disputes between and within kingdoms were fought out at the level of texts as well as at the level of events.[93] The (geographical) dispersal of royal power and the experience of intra-Carolingian political struggle were reflected in the emergence of a multiplicity of historical viewpoints. Consequently, there was more criticism of kings: but this cannot be read off straightforwardly as an indication that there was more to be critical about. Nor was there any direct equation between political geography and historiography: we should not simply read the *Annals of St-Bertin* as a 'west Frankish' chronicle, or the Fulda annals as a product of the east Frankish court. Rather, these texts are witnesses to lively debates within as well as between kingdoms, only some of whose protagonists will have committed their views to writing.

Once read in this context, the 'officialness' and historical veracity of the Mainz text are called into question, and one side-effect of this is to undermine the source-base for the traditional view of Charles's reign. In short, the Mainz continuation is not a good enough source to prove either that Charles the Fat was a 'failed king', or that he ultimately fell victim to an inevitable decline in Carolingian authority. In reality, we cannot confidently say anything about the personalities of Charles, Liutward or Liutbert: too often ascriptions of personality traits to such remote figures are the result of circular reasoning, inferred from the same events and

---

[89] McKitterick, 'Audience for Carolingian Historiography'; McKitterick, 'Political Ideology in Carolingian Historiography'. For the diffusion of learning in the later ninth century see J. L. Nelson, 'Charles le Chauve et les utilisations du savoir', in D. Iogna-Prat et al. (eds.), *L'École carolingienne d'Auxerre* (Paris, 1991), pp. 37–54.

[90] See for instance D. Ganz, 'Humour as History in Notker's *Gesta Karoli Magni*', in E. King, J. Schaefer and W. Wadley (eds.), *Monks, Nuns and Friars in Mediaeval Society* (Sewanee, 1989), pp. 171–83; M. Innes, 'Teutons or Trojans? The Carolingians and the Germanic Past', in Hen and Innes (eds.), *Uses of the Past*, pp. 227–49.

[91] Airlie, 'Narratives of Triumph'; R. McKitterick, 'The Illusion of Royal Power in the Carolingian Annals', *English Historical Review* 105 (2000), 1–20.

[92] Airlie, 'Private Bodies', p. 38.   [93] As highlighted by Buc, *Dangers of Ritual*, p. 58.

Charles the Fat in the eyes of contemporary annalists

actions which they are then used to explain. A satisfactory explanation of the end of the Carolingian empire cannot reduce the issues to the actions of 'strong' or 'weak' personalities, or magnify them into the workings of nebulous historical processes. Instead, we must seek to contextualise the sources to see what can be learned at the level of political events and political structures. It is to the latter which we now turn, as the focus for the next two chapters.

Chapter 3

THE MEN WHO WOULD BE KINGS: THE 'SUPERMAGNATES' AND THE 'RISE OF THE ARISTOCRACY'

In the year 880, the four surviving Carolingian rulers met at Vienne to draw a line under the revolt of Boso and to seal a succession and division treaty which led to a period of renewed concord in the royal dynasty.[1] One of their more specific goals was to make kingship more accessible to the nobility of Lotharingia, the symbolically and strategically important central Frankish realm which had been thrown into renewed turmoil by the events of 879. In this aim, the Vienne treaty was broadly similar to most other Carolingian family settlements. The point of subkingship, for example, was not only to keep junior members of the royal house happy by allowing them a tangible share in power, but also to give provincial aristocracies their 'own' king, who would often be married into a local family of note.[2] A nearby royal court was less a hindrance than a potential source of opportunity for regional aristocrats, serving as a source of offices which would help them entrench their local standing, and as a doorway leading onto the grander stage of imperial politics.[3] Equally, the Carolingians, lacking the institutions of the decayed Roman state, needed members of the aristocracy, whose power was rooted in control of land, to act as the means of transposing their authority from the palace to the localities. Those with access to royal ears, moreover, were less likely to join rebellions: inclusiveness, not keeping the magnates at arm's length, was the essential (if difficult) task of ninth-century kingship. In other words, Carolingian kingship was, from the very beginning, predicated on a close alliance between royal and aristocratic power: the relationship between the two was symbiotic.[4]

This perspective on the workings of Carolingian politics is now becoming the orthodoxy among historians of the period. However, as outlined

---

[1] See above, pp. 21–2.　　[2] See now Kasten, *Königssöhne und Königsherrschaft*.
[3] Airlie, 'The Palace of Memory'.
[4] As stressed many years ago by K. F. Werner: 'Untersuchungen zur Frühzeit des französischen Fürstentums (9.–10. Jahrhundert)', *Die Welt als Geschichte* 18 (1958), 256–89 (parts I–III); 19 (1959), 146–93 (part IV); 20 (1960), 87–119 (parts V–VI), esp. I; and also his 'Important Noble Families in the Kingdom of Charlemagne'.

48

The 'supermagnates' and the 'rise of the aristocracy'

in chapter 1, the end of the empire is still characterised in terms of the rising power and independence of the aristocracy and the associated growth of regional secessionism. It is supposed that during the 880s these trends came to a head and gave impetus to the emergence of a number of 'supermagnates', extremely powerful members of high-profile aristocratic families whose power eclipsed and undermined that of the Carolingians. Their presence gave a focus to the simmering discontent within the empire, enabling them to emerge as regional leaders and, in 888, as kings.

This chapter will provide a critique of this model of the Carolingian collapse, initially by means of a case study examining the relationship between Charles and Count Odo of Paris, the noble who succeeded to the west Frankish throne in 888. Given that he was to become one of the *reguli*, this relationship can be used as a litmus test for the issues surrounding the high aristocracy's role in the demise of Carolingian power. Moreover, the case of west Francia is ideal for studying the historiographical issues and the contemporary political dynamics. For one thing, it is usually supposed to have been the *regnum* whose aristocratic community was most eager to withdraw from Carolingian rule, dismayed by Viking attack and disillusioned with its new ruler based far away across the Rhine.[5] In addition, some French historians have recently reinforced the traditional paradigm, inspired by the work of Walther Kienast, whose argument that German-style duchies (self-conscious regional political communities) existed west of the Rhine, along with all the implications of that claim, has been taken on board without reflection on the refinements made by subsequent writers.[6] Once we have considered Odo and texts associated with him as windows on the political world of late ninth-century west Francia, his career can be used to illuminate the situation in the other parts of the empire where the families of the future kings of Europe were rising to power.

THE RISE OF ODO

As well as being count of Paris, Odo was the son of Robert the Strong, the progenitor of the celebrated Capetian dynasty, assuring him a special

[5] For example, Reuter, *Germany in the Early Middle Ages*, p. 119.
[6] W. Kienast, *Studien über die französischen Volksstämme des Frühmittelalters* (Stuttgart, 1968); W. Kienast, *Der Herzogstitel in Frankreich und Deutschland (9. bis 12. Jahrhundert)* (Munich and Vienna, 1968); O. Guillot, 'Les étapes de l'accession d'Eudes au pouvoir royal', in *Media in Francia. Recueil de mélanges offert à Karl Ferdinand Werner* (Maulévrier, 1989), pp. 199–223; O. Guillot, 'Formes, fondements et limites de l'organisation en France au Xe siècle', *Settimane* 38 (1991), 57–124; more implicitly, J. P. Brunterc'h, 'Naissance et affirmation des principautés au temps du roi Eudes: l'exemple de l'Aquitaine', in O. Guillot and R. Favreau (eds.), *Pays de Loire et Aquitaine de Robert le Fort aux premiers Capétiens* (Poitiers, 1997), pp. 69–116.

Kingship and Politics in the Late Ninth Century

status in medieval French history. However, regardless of the illustrious posthumous reputation enjoyed by him and his ancestors, the relative profusion of texts associated with his earlier career allows us to trace his considerable influence in western Francia before the death of Charles the Fat. Odo's political career effectively began in late 882, when he became count of Paris, and in 885–6 he led a heroic defence of the city against Viking siege. As a reward, Charles the Fat granted him the *honores* formerly held by his father on the lower Loire. These, centred on the county of Orléans and the monastery of St-Martin in Tours, enabled him to coordinate defence against the Vikings, making him the most powerful figure in Neustria and one of the most important in the whole kingdom.[7] Olivier Guillot, in a closely argued and illuminating article, has recently re-examined Odo's early career, claiming that the count was exercising royal prerogatives in Neustria during 886 and 887.[8] This is a suggestion with remarkable implications and one of the boldest restatements of traditional views about the late ninth century, and it is worth examining Guillot's arguments as a means of approaching the evidence for Odo's early career.

Firstly he claims that a late ninth-century Neustrian letter collection, which is mostly concerned with the ecclesiastical affairs of the church of Orléans, reveals a support network centred on Odo and extending from western Neustria to as far away as Sens (in Burgundy), and that this is politically significant.[9] The crucial text for this view is a letter, probably written in 887, from the widow of the lay abbot of St-Symphorien, Orléans, to Archbishop Walter of Sens, complaining that 'our relative Count Odo', along with Count Hucbald of Senlis, has usurped some of her land.[10] However, it is clear that the properties seized by Odo, and hence in his sphere of influence, are in the Orléannais, where he was count, rather than in the environs of Sens.[11] In fact, their seizure seems to have been directly connected by the widow with the imperial gift to Odo in 886 of the *honores* of his father in Neustria, specifically the county of Orléans: she complains that Odo committed the offence 'after he obtained, as you know, the superior authority in our area'.[12] The appeal to the distant archbishop Walter as a patron was relevant not because he was a close ally of Odo but rather because his uncle was Bishop Walter of Orléans, in whose diocese the disputed lands lay. His family ties,

---

[7] Refer to Map 1 for the locations mentioned in this chapter.

[8] Guillot, 'Les étapes de l'accession d'Eudes', p. 203; Guillot, 'Formes, fondements et limites', pp. 61–2.

[9] Guillot, 'Les étapes de l'accession d'Eudes', pp. 203–4.

[10] B. Bischoff (ed.), *Anecdota Novissima: Texte des vierten bis sechzehnten Jahrhunderts* (Stuttgart, 1984), pp. 131–2.

[11] *Ibid.*, p. 131, n. 1.   [12] *Ibid.*, p. 132. *AV* s.a. 886, p. 62 for Charles's grant to Odo.

The 'supermagnates' and the 'rise of the aristocracy'

not his political connections, made him useful to the widow. Certainly, Walter of Sens was a political ally of Odo in 888, when he crowned him king, but this does not prove that Odo had authority in the Sens area in 887. The real value of this letter is the rare glimpse it affords the reader of the situation under the surface of a change of authority in a region, showing that there were losers as well as winners. We should not have to think that such flaunting of newly acquired powers was unusual or a politically significant challenge to royal authority, simply because it does not quite tally with the impression of smooth handovers of *honores* implied by the dry formulas of charters. Indeed, the fact that the widow associated Odo's actions with his assumption of the countship in Orléans shows that he was able to carry out these acts exactly *because* of the commission he received on royal authority, and not in spite of it.

Secondly, Guillot makes a case for the exercise of royal power by members of the Neustrian aristocracy based on epithets given them in these letters.[13] He stresses in particular an introductory note written by Walter of Orléans for a monk en route to Italy, which asks the reader to offer prayers for a list of dead *seniores*, emperors, kings and various churchmen.[14] Guillot claims that Hugh the Abbot, Odo's predecessor in Neustria, is listed among the kings, but the wording is ambiguous enough to permit serious doubt on this. The text reads: 'Karoli scilicet imperatoris augusti, Hludovici ac Hludovici et Karlomanni regum, Hugonis excellentissimi abbatis adiugentes his Ottranni quondam Viennensis archiepiscopi, Evrardi Sennonensis, Gauzlini Parisiaci necnon Airbaldi...'[15] The phrase 'adiugentes his' ('in addition to these') could easily refer to all those, including Hugh, listed after the closing word 'regum' ('kings'). In addition, the term 'most excellent' used for Hugh here, and 'sublimatus' (lofty) applied to Odo elsewhere, thought by Guillot to be indications of their holding 'a quasi-royal pre-eminence', are being used in untechnical and subjective contexts, designed to show a degree of humility appropriate in the composition of a request for patronage.[16] In any case, such laudatory epithets were entirely appropriate in the late ninth century for application to lay abbots, who held a peculiarly exalted position in aristocratic society, and were by no means a sign of a usurpation of a royal prerogative.[17]

---

[13] Guillot, 'Les étapes de l'accession d'Eudes', p. 204.

[14] Bischoff (ed.), *Anecdota Novissima*, pp. 128–9.

[15] *Ibid.*, p. 129. The point would be lost if the passage were translated.

[16] *Ibid.*, p. 132; Guillot, 'Les étapes de l'accession d'Eudes', p. 204.

[17] G. Koziol, *Begging Pardon and Favour. Ritual and Political Order in Early Medieval France* (Ithaca and London, 1992), pp. 27–8, 38–9. On lay abbots in general the standard work is F. J. Felten, *Äbte und Laienäbte im Frankenreich. Studien zum Verhältnis von Staat und Kirche im frühen Mittelalter* (Stuttgart, 1980).

Kingship and Politics in the Late Ninth Century

Thirdly and most strikingly, Guillot suggests that Odo can be shown to have been regally distributing *honores* in the west while Charles the Fat still theoretically ruled.[18] A letter directed to the church of Auxerre by Walter of Orléans urges the clergy there to ignore the imperial candidate for the current episcopal vacancy, one Teutbertus, dismissing him as a compliant bureaucrat, and to choose instead a good man for themselves.[19] They appear to have taken heed: Charles's attempted appointment, which flouted a concession of free election made to Auxerre by Carloman II, seems, on the evidence of the *Deeds of the Bishops of Auxerre*, to have been obstructed, since that text lists a man called Herifridus as the successor to the late Bishop Wibaldus.[20] The *Deeds* relates all this as having taken place during the reign of an emperor Charles, but also says that it was a king (*rex*) who sent Herifridus to be invested after taking *consilium*.[21] Guillot's case, then, is that since Charles the Fat, *imperator*, had tried to impose Teutbertus, Herifridus must have been selected by Odo, who is to be identified with the unnamed *rex* of the *Deeds*. Obviously, such an epithet would be highly significant for our view of the politics of the 880s if it can be assumed to apply to Odo of Paris; Herifridus was a relative of Walter of Orléans and Walter of Sens (who invested him), and hence plugged into Odo's network of connections in the Neustrian aristocracy. However, we should not rely too heavily on a literal reading of the *Deeds of the Bishops*, which may be inaccurate. In the first place, doubt is cast on the distinction between Charles *imperator* and Odo *rex* by the various chronological and terminological errors of the text, which is consistently vague on events outside Auxerre and its properties.[22] The section of the work concerning events after 872 was not composed until the mid-930s, almost half a century after our case; this is a good reason to doubt its veracity for the events of the 880s, and its consistency in applying titles. In any case, the *Deeds* does not explicitly mention any dispute over the appointment.

In short, the *Deeds of the Bishops of Auxerre* is too rickety a foundation on which to build as precise an argument as Guillot's for the use of the word *rex* applying to Odo of Paris during the reign of Charles the Fat. This leaves us with the fact that Charles's attempted appointment of

---

[18] Guillot, 'Les étapes de l'accession d'Eudes', pp. 204–6.

[19] Bischoff (ed.), *Anecdota Novissima*, pp. 129–30.

[20] D C2 71. *Gesta Pontificum Autissiodorensium*, ed. L. M. Duru, *Bibliothèque historique de l'Yonne* I (1859), pp. 309–509, at p. 360.

[21] *Ibid.*, pp. 360–1.

[22] For example, Bishop Heribald (d. 857) is wrongly referred to as archchaplain: W. Wattenbach, W. Levison and H. Löwe, *Deutschlands Geschichtsquellen im Mittelalter* (6 vols., Weimar, 1973), vol. 5, pp. 569–70. For further observations on the work's sources and inaccuracies, see P. Janin, 'Heiric d'Auxerre et les *Gesta Pontificum Autissiodorensium*', *Francia* 4 (1976), 89–105.

The 'supermagnates' and the 'rise of the aristocracy'

Teutbertus was opposed, and that Herifridus, a man with connections to the Neustrian circle of Odo, seems to have succeeded. The significance of this observation, however, depends very much on the assumptions with which the observer approaches it. Odo, we know, was shortly to become king, and hence the power which Guillot sees him exercising is with hindsight considered to be at the expense of Charles's. However, even if Odo was involved in the process, it must have been on Charles's terms: given that Bishop Wibaldus had expired on 12 May 887 and Herifridus was invested on 29 August, it is surely eminently possible that the solution was reached amicably when Odo, clearly still in favour, appeared at the imperial court in mid-June.[23] All that the evidence reveals, therefore, is a senior bishop objecting to royal interference in an election which one of the king's predecessors had promised would be free, and urging the clergy to re-stage it. These texts give us a glimpse into the underbelly of Carolingian politics, where there were losers, like Teutbertus and the widow of the lay abbot, as well as winners. We catch a flavour of the difficulties experienced by kings who tried to micro-manage local disputes: but this was part of the normal workings of early medieval kingship, whose regional basis was always negotiated and sometimes contested.

We are fortunate to have, in addition to the Neustrian letters, two charters which give us some insight into the count of Paris's (public) self-perception during the 880s. One was issued by the imperial chancery, the other by the count.[24] The imperial document, issued in June 887 for Odo's monastery of St-Martin in Tours, confirms a return to the community of properties, which had presumably become absorbed into the abbatial holdings, in the count's charter of two months previously. The contents of the comital charter were clearly known to the imperial scribes. Interestingly, however, only parts of the count's text are reused in the royal diploma. Significantly, the shared elements are in the prayer clauses. Charles confirmed the grant for the sake of the souls of Odo and his parents, specifically Robert the Strong. This is an almost unique provision in any known charter of Charles the Fat, in which living magnates are not usually associated, even as here indirectly, with the spiritual benefits of the confirmation or grant. The archchancellor Liutward, another court figure whose power has been seen as eclipsing that of the emperor, is the only parallel.[25] In allowing this sentiment to be formalised, the

---

[23] DD CIII 160, 161. D 145 shows Charles the Fat's influence in Auxerre in late 886.
[24] D OP 55 and D CIII 160, both of which are modern copies of originals. The vocabulary of two other charters, DD OP 57 and 58, were taken as evidence for Odo's kingly aspirations at this time by Brunner, 'Der fränkische Fürstentitel', pp. 274–6. However, the charters' editor established that one is a forgery and the other heavily and anachronistically interpolated.
[25] D CIII 92. Cf. D 145 mentioning Hugh the Abbot, but posthumously.

Kingship and Politics in the Late Ninth Century

chancery thus associated Odo's name with a position normally reserved for the royal family, and one which was intimately bound up with prayers for the longevity of the dynasty and the *stabilitas regni*.[26] This and the extraordinarily high value of the penalty clause (600 lbs. of gold) testify to Odo's closeness to Charles at this point.

If Charles was keen to endorse such pious actions performed by Odo, the fact that Odo came all the way from Tours to Kirchen in Alemannia to obtain this confirmation is also significant. His self-perception as revealed in the Tours charter backs this up. He returns the properties for the good of his own soul and that of his father. As some historians have stressed, this document reveals a strong family consciousness on the part of Odo; by referring to his late father Robert as 'domnus' (lord), he adopts a rarefied vocabulary which indicates a clear dynastic identity.[27] However, Odo also, and firstly, requests benefits for the eternal life of Charles the Fat, 'our lord and master, chosen emperor by God'. Masses are to be said for Charles in which 'we wish to participate', and only then for Odo himself. In a world dominated by concepts of kin and honour, Odo's expression of such feeling is neither surprising nor new. The Carolingians may have monopolised kingship, but they were not the only family interested in dynasticism.[28] Odo may also have been trying to legitimise his own newly acquired position in Neustria by association with that of his father, whose heroic deeds against the Vikings were still celebrated at the end of the ninth century.[29] In any case, it is clear that neither the count nor the emperor considered family loyalty to be at odds with loyalty to one's lord.[30] Despite the presumed opposition of Odo to Charles, it is not surprising to find such politically correct sentiments in public documents like these.[31] If we read these sources in the context of

[26] Cf. D CIII 146, in which Odo is associated very closely with the emperor's gift: 'deprecante Odone comite in nostra elemosina ac sua'. For comments on the analogous position of Boso in some of Charles the Bald's charters, see S. Airlie, 'The Political Behaviour of Secular Magnates in Francia, 829–79', D.Phil thesis, University of Oxford (1985), pp. 220–2.

[27] S. Airlie, '*Semper fideles?*', pp. 141–2; K. F. Werner, 'Les premiers Robertiens et les premiers Anjou (IXe–Xe siècle)', in Guillot and Favreau (eds.), *Pays de Loire*, pp. 9–67, at pp. 31–2; building on R. Le Jan, '*Domnus, illuster, nobilis*. Les mutations du pouvoir au Xe siècle', in M. Sot (ed.), *Haut Moyen-Age. Culture, education et société. Études offertes à Pierre Riché* (Paris, 1990), pp. 439–48.

[28] For another example see H.-W. Goetz, 'Typus einer Adelsherrschaft im späteren 9. Jahrhundert: der Linzgaugraf Udalrich', *St Galler Kultur und Geschichte* 11 (1981), 131–73. Recent research has stressed the significance of the nuclear family: see Airlie, 'The Aristocracy', pp. 440–1; Le Jan, *Famille et pouvoir*, pp. 331–79.

[29] Regino, *Chronicon*, s.a. 867, pp. 92–3, which was written up in c. 908.

[30] Neither did Dhuoda, whose *Liber Manualis*, ed. P. Riché (Paris, 1975) is perhaps our best text on aristocratic family consciousness in this period. See M. A. Claussen, 'God and Man in Dhuoda's *Liber Manualis*', *Studies in Church History* 27 (1990), 43–52; Airlie, 'The Aristocracy', p. 436.

[31] E. Favre, *Eudes. Comte de Paris et roi de France (882–898)* (Paris, 1893), p. 73 thought that Odo's apparent deference to Charles must have been sarcastic.

The 'supermagnates' and the 'rise of the aristocracy'

the mid-880s, and disregard our own foreknowledge that the count was soon to become a king, there is no good evidence for the case that Odo and Charles were political rivals whose antagonism was a contributory factor in the disintegration of the Carolingian empire.

POLITICS AND IDENTITY IN ABBO'S *WARS OF THE CITY OF PARIS*

With reference to historians of the fall of another empire, Walter Goffart persuasively argued: 'Events, when treated seriatim, with due attention to the very limited consequences of each one, neither explain the growth nor the decline of empires... In investigating questions such as the rise and fall of empires, the subject of inquiry should be what contemporaries thought, not only what they did.'[32] To address more fully the question of contemporary perceptions of late Carolingian politics in northwest Francia, we are fortunate to have the poem *Bella Parisiacae Urbis* (*Wars of the City of Paris*) written by Abbo, a prolix monk of the suburban monastery of St-Germain-des-Prés and eye-witness of the Viking sieges of the city in 885–6.[33] This is a somewhat unusual text, glossed by its author and composed in two phases (the first draft c. 890, with brief additions covering later political developments made in the mid-890s), and explicitly intended both as a scholarly exercise and as a warning to others who would in future face Viking attack.[34] Although it is customary to insult Abbo's work for its deliberately obscure Grecisms and pretentious style, recent studies of its literary aspects have been more positive, seeing it as an example or even parody of the 'hermeneutic style' in vogue among contemporary poets.[35] Moreover, if the poem's laboured artiness is overlooked, its generic characteristics and philosophical outlook place it squarely within the mainstream of ninth- and tenth-century moralistic works concerning Christian encounters with

---

[32] W. Goffart, 'Zosimus, the First Historian of Rome's Fall', in W. Goffart, *Rome's Fall and After* (London and Ronceverte, 1989), pp. 81–110, at p. 107.

[33] Abbo, *Bella Parisiacae Urbis*, ed. H. Waquet, *Abbon. Le Siège de Paris par les Normands* (Paris, 1942), I, 24–6, p. 14 for his own place in events. Although it omits book III, which is not concerned with Paris, Waquet's edition will be the one cited here (by book, verse and page). The full text is edited by P. von Winterfeld in MGH Poetae 4 (Berlin, 1899), pp. 72–122. U. Önnefors, *Abbo von Saint-Germain-des-Prés. 22 Predigten. Kritische Aufgabe und Kommentar* (Frankfurt, Berne, New York and Nancy, 1985), pp. 16–18 gathers together scattered information on Abbo's life.

[34] Abbo, *Bella*, preface, 2, p. 4. Wattenbach, Levison, Löwe, *Geschichtsquellen*, pp. 581–2 for the dating.

[35] M. Lapidge, 'The Hermeneutic Style in Tenth-Century Anglo-Latin Literature', *Anglo-Saxon England* 4 (1975), 67–111, esp. 71–6, 101–3; P. Lendinara, 'The Third Book of the *Bella Parisiacae Urbis* by Abbo of Saint-Germain-des-Prés and its Old English Gloss', *Anglo-Saxon England* 15 (1986), 73–89. Modern readers' scorn is usually raised most by book III, which was nevertheless the most popular section in the Middle Ages.

Kingship and Politics in the Late Ninth Century

Vikings.[36] Despite its wealth of detail, however, its value to the political historian of the 880s and 890s has not been fully exploited.

Historians often ascribe dramatic significance to the siege of Paris. The Viking Great Army was active on the Continent between 879 and 892 after being defeated by Alfred of Wessex at Edington and attracted by the political turmoil following Louis the Stammerer's death, and it presented the Franks with military problems on a scale they had not encountered for two decades.[37] The Danes' attempt to move up the Seine towards Burgundy in 885 was one of the most threatening and coordinated raids of the ninth century, and even conservative estimates of the numbers involved exceed the probable number of defenders on the nine hectares of the Ile-de-la-Cité, the fortified centre of ninth-century Paris.[38] Unsurprisingly, contemporary writers were worried. In sentiments later echoed by Abbo, Archbishop Fulk of Rheims wrote to Charles the Fat pointing out the strategic significance of the town and warning him that 'if it was captured, it would be at the cost of the suffering of the whole kingdom'.[39] Although the siege lasted for over a year, it was well into 886 before the emperor heeded the archbishop's advice, arriving with a large army and ransoming the town, allowing the Vikings to pass up the river to overwinter in Burgundy providing they left Paris unmolested. Historians have been uniformly scathing about Charles's handling of the situation, taking it as a sign that Carolingian power was militarily effete, relating this to presumed west Frankish disillusionment with the dynasty, and citing it as a factor in the emperor's deposition almost exactly a year after the end of the siege.[40]

The emperor's handling of the Viking problem will be discussed further in the next chapter. For now, however, it should be stressed that beyond the habitual griping of the ecclesiastical chroniclers whose churches

---

[36] P. Szarmach, 'The (Sub-) Genre of the Battle of Maldon', in J. Cooper (ed.), *The Battle of Maldon. Fiction and Fact* (London and Rio Grande, 1993), pp. 43–61; in general see Coupland, 'Rod of God's Wrath'.

[37] *AV* s.a. 879, p. 44. For a blow-by-blow account see W. Vogel, *Die Normannen und das fränkische Reich bis zur Gründung der Normandie (799–911)* (Heidelberg, 1906), pp. 260–359.

[38] C. Gillmor, 'War on the Rivers: Viking Numbers and Mobility on the Seine and Loire, 841–886', *Viator* 19 (1988), 79–109, at 86–90; C. Brühl, *Palatium und Civitas. Studien zur Profantopographie spätantiker Civitates vom 3. bis 13. Jahrhundert* (2 vols., Cologne and Vienna, 1975), vol. 1, p. 11, n. 54.

[39] Flodoard, *Historia Remensis Ecclesiae*, eds. I. Heller and G. Waitz, MGH SS 13 (Hanover, 1881), 4.5, p. 563; Abbo, *Bella*, 1, 48–52, p. 18.

[40] For example: L. Musset, *Les Invasions. Le Second Assaut contre l'Europe chrétienne (VIIe–XIe siècles)* (Paris, 1965), p. 161; R. Schieffer, *Die Karolinger* (Stuttgart, Berlin and Cologne, 1992), p. 184. Vercauteren, 'Comment s'est-on défendu', and R.-H. Bautier, 'Le règne d'Eudes (888–898) à la lumière des diplômes expédiés par sa chancellerie', *Comptes rendus de l'académie des inscriptions et belles-lettres* (1961), 140–57 were strong influences on this thesis. Reuter, *Germany in the Early Middle Ages*, p. 120 is a rare exception.

The 'supermagnates' and the 'rise of the aristocracy'

had to foot the bill for the pay-off, there is little contemporary evidence for the siege having had a calamitous effect on Charles's reputation. Abbo's verse is usually cited in this context as an exposition of the great courage and bravery of Odo, and hence an explanation for his rise and for west Frankish disenchantment with Charles the Fat.[41] Given that Abbo wrote shortly after Odo's ascent to kingship, such politically correct disenchantment would not be surprising, and the new king clearly occupies centre stage. He is, for instance, distinguished by Abbo not simply due to his actions, but according to his superior moral rank, when he repeatedly refers to him as the 'future king', such as on his first appearance in the poem: 'He was venerated as consul and future king. He was the defender of the town and would become nourisher of the realm.'[42] The poet spells out in his introduction that the main players in his tale will be Odo and his own patron St Germanus, and at one point he lists the names of the defenders of the town with the observation: 'but Odo was the noblest'.[43] When he concludes his work it is 'although' Odo still lives, implying that the natural endpoint would in fact be the king's death.[44] And although other men, notably Bishop Gauzlin, Abbot Ebolus and Bishop Askericus come to the forefront to receive Abbo's praise, these men were not just Odo's brothers-in-arms, but also his later political allies in the time of the poem's composition, the latter two both serving under him as archchancellor.[45] It is plausible that Abbo started writing as a commission from Odo in the early years of his reign, or at least that the king read or heard the poem, especially given the close manuscript links between texts associated with his elevation to kingship and writings surrounding the cult of St Germanus.[46] With this in mind it is revealing that the poem does make an implicit point about the legitimacy of Odo by stressing his place as immediate successor to the deceased Charles the Fat.[47]

In stressing this 'official' view of Odo and of his succession, Abbo comes across to us as something like the new king's Einhard. His view

---

[41] For example P. E. Dutton, *Carolingian Civilization. A Reader* (Ontario, 1993), pp. 483–5, especially the selective translation. A conspicuous exception to the prevailing reading is J. M. Wallace-Hadrill, 'The Franks and the English in the Ninth Century: Some Common Historical Interests', in his *Early Medieval History* (London, 1975), pp. 201–16, at p. 208.

[42] Abbo, *Bella*, 1, 45–6, p. 18. See also 1, 94–113, pp. 22–4; 1, 245–8, p. 34; 1, 487–90, p. 52; 11, 163–5, p. 78.

[43] *Ibid.*, preface, 3, pp. 4–6; 1, 246, p. 34.   [44] *Ibid.*, 11, 615–6, p. 112.

[45] For Gauzlin see K. F. Werner, 'Gauzlin von Saint-Denis und die westfränkische Reichsteilung von Amiens (März 880). Ein Beitrag zur Vorgeschichte von Odos Königtum', *DA* 35 (1979), 395–462, reprinted in his *Vom Frankenreich zur Entfaltung Deutschlands und Frankreichs. Ursprünge-Strukturen-Beziehungen. Ausgewählte Beiträge. Festgabe zu seinem sechzigsten Geburtstag* (Sigmaringen, 1984). For Ebolus and Askericus see R.-H. Bautier's introduction to DD OP, pp. xxi–xxix.

[46] Werner, 'Gauzlin von Saint-Denis', p. 459, n. 214.

[47] Abbo, *Bella*, 11, 442–8, pp. 98–100; Guillot, 'Les étapes de l'accession d'Eudes', p. 218.

Kingship and Politics in the Late Ninth Century

of Odo may not be as skilful or as charged with polemic as Einhard's of Charlemagne, but he remains a politically correct apologist for a new dynasty. He writes with enthusiasm for Odo's qualities in the earliest section, to be dated during the period of the first realisation of the new king's authority.[48] His disappointment in the final few pages of book 2, which are part of the later additions, serves only to heighten our sense of Abbo's earlier belief in Odo's king-worthiness. In this context, his representation of Odo's relationship with the man he replaced as king is of great interest.

However, far from being the weak-willed incompetent depicted in the historiography, Charles the Fat comes into the picture in control as the legitimate emperor. Where Odo is 'rex futurus', Abbo makes Bishop Gauzlin say: 'The city was entrusted to us by the emperor Charles, by whose power almost the whole world is ruled in accordance with the Lord, the King and Ruler of the powerful, that the realm should not suffer destruction through it, but rather that through the city it is saved and will remain at peace.'[49] The emperor is here described in the highest terms, given his orthodox Carolingian place behind God in the rulership of the world and, explicitly, as the man from whom Gauzlin, Odo and their colleagues claim to derive their own authority. Later, when things got uncomfortable, it was to Charles, emperor of the Franks ('basileus Francorum'), that Odo went for reinforcements.[50] There is no hint of reproach for Charles's late appearance on the scene; he came when he was asked and the arrival of his troops was greeted with profound happiness in Paris.[51] His army reflects the extent of his authority – he arrives 'surrounded by an army of all peoples... a huge company of people of diverse tongues' – and it immediately inflicts a heavy defeat on the enemy.[52] Finally, Abbo did not see the deal struck by Charles allowing the Vikings to stay in Burgundy until spring as a compromise. Without any disapproval for the king, the poet instead turns on the Burgundians, whom he considers thus well repaid for their failure to provide military aid for Paris.[53] In practical terms, it also appears from the witness of this text that the Vikings did actually observe the deal struck to keep them out of Paris.[54]

[48] Wattenbach, Levison, Löwe, *Geschichtsquellen*, p. 581.
[49] Abbo, *Bella*, 1, 48–52, p. 18. The translation is from Szarmach, '(Sub-) Genre of the Battle of Maldon', p. 50.
[50] Abbo, *Bella*, 11, 163–5, p. 78.
[51] *Ibid.*, 11, 200, p. 80; Odo is not mentioned again until Charles's death at 11, 442, p. 98.
[52] *Ibid.*, 11, 315–34, pp. 88–90, with quote at 330–3.   [53] *Ibid.*, 11, 343–6, pp. 90–2.
[54] The broken treaty mentioned in the poem seems to refer not to Charles's deal but to a second agreement made by the inhabitants of Paris to prevent the Vikings ravaging the Meaux area, where Odo and Askericus both had interests (*ibid.*, pp. 96–8). The troubles incurred in Paris when the

The 'supermagnates' and the 'rise of the aristocracy'

Another striking contrast in the later stages of the poem is between the author's approving references to Charles the *basileus* and his admonitory address to Francia, for its pride and in misusing the purple 'to keep warm'.[55] By the time of writing this section, it is the present which lacks glory and honour for Abbo, the fading abilities of King Odo, not the good old days of the 880s. Such is the strength of this sentiment in the text that Édouard Favre was moved to suggest implausibly that these sections must have been composed before Charles's death, with the passages referring to Odo as future king interpolated later.[56] If we free ourselves from Favre's assumptions, it is clear that his analysis was more teleological than that of Abbo. It is not so surprising that the poet expressed grief at the death of Charles the Fat.[57] On this point, then, in the depiction of the dynastic predecessor of his king, Abbo clearly parts company with Einhard. Abbo's Charles III is very different from Einhard's Childeric III, a 'useless king': the poet was an apologist for a new regime, but he did not, as he might well have, denigrate the old one in the process.

Aside from providing this unambiguous and politically orthodox picture of the relationship between the emperor and the count, Abbo is also a useful witness to the existence or otherwise of the west Frankish particularism often invoked as a reason for the empire's disintegration. His poem reads very clearly as the work of a partisan eyewitness, being replete with patriotic and civic pride for his homeland and for the hero (Odo) who kept the enemy from the city gates. First and foremost, Abbo was a Neustrian and a servant of St Germanus. Book I closes with the poet addressing Neustria directly, mourning the ravages it has suffered at the hands of its invaders, and calling it 'the most noble of all the regions of the world'.[58] Neustria personified replies defiantly, and calls Abbo 'my offspring', which the author glosses: 'for this poet was of the Neustrian people'.[59] Moreover, the monastery of St-Germain-des-Prés, which lay on the Seine's left bank, was 'the most noble of all those which Neustria nourished at her great bosom'.[60] After his relics were moved for protection into fortified Paris, Germanus also became the patron and protector of the city, defending its inhabitants and providing martial and medicinal

---

invaders passed through must have been on the way south, as part of Charles's treaty, rather than en route north in violation of it, since Askericus, who is mentioned by Abbo, would have been at the imperial court at the time of the Danes' return (May 887): *ibid.*, pp. 94–6; *AV* s.a. 887, pp. 63–4. Bearing in mind the chronological confusion of the latter part of Abbo's work, I would suggest that it is the report of the largely peaceful encampment which refers to the Viking return down the Seine; Abbo, *Bella*, II, 347–87, pp. 92–4. Cf. Asser, *De Rebus Gestis AElfredi*, ed. W. H. Stevenson (Oxford, 1959), chap. 84, p. 71.

[55] Abbo, *Bella*, II, 606, p. 112. [56] Favre, *Eudes*, p. vi. [57] Abbo, *Bella*, II, 442–3, p. 98.
[58] *Ibid.*, I, 618, p. 60. [59] *Ibid.*, I, 624, p. 62, with n. *e.* [60] *Ibid.*, I, 465–6, p. 50.

Kingship and Politics in the Late Ninth Century

miracles to sustain them.[61] The town took on the same inviolable status as the saint's own sanctuary, which was also immune from attack due to Germanus's miracles.[62] In his collection of sermons, compiled some thirty years after the *Bella*, Abbo recalled that Germanus was 'the defender of Paris from enemy siege'.[63] Paris, whose focus lay on the right bank of the Seine, was more properly a Frankish than a Neustrian town. However, here we can see that the poet's strong civic loyalty (he described the town as 'sparkling like a queen over all cities') was fused with his veneration for the saint and for his Neustrian monastery.[64] These priorities came together in his claims that those who fell defending the town had the status of martyrs, an early expression of proto-Crusading doctrines.[65]

These sentiments do not, however, translate into a generalised west Frankish political consciousness. Indeed, the main targets for Abbo's distaste, other than the invaders, are the Aquitanians and Burgundians. The former were characterised as cunning and sharp-tongued, the latter as cowardly and predisposed to flight, and both were contrasted with the proud and noble 'Francigeni'.[66] Far from lamenting Charles's decision to allow the Danes passage up the Seine towards Burgundy, Abbo castigates instead the Burgundians, judging them to be thus aptly treated: 'You still didn't know the names of those by whose swords you then suffered, o warshy Burgundy. You didn't know them in the measure that Neustria, which adorned the marriage bed of the daughters of your nobility, could easily have told you. But you certainly know them now.'[67] In part, Abbo's ire was raised by the problems encountered by Odo in attempting to impose his royal authority in these regions in the time he was writing, after 888.[68] However, his comments also fit into a long tradition of similarly prejudicial northern characterisations of the inhabitants of southern west Francia.[69] In fact, the charter evidence proves that there *was* a considerable Burgundian presence at the siege of Paris, something which Abbo clearly chose to overlook.[70] When Odo did unite the west Frankish kingdoms under him after Charles's death, in the poet's view he did so emphatically

---

[61] *Ibid.*, I, 393–437, pp. 44–8; I, 467, p. 50; II, 127–62, pp. 76–8; II, 267–314, pp. 86–8; II, 347–87, pp. 92–4.

[62] *Ibid.*, I, 484–523, p. 52.   [63] Önnefors, *Abbo von Saint-Germain-des-Prés*, p. 63.

[64] Abbo, *Bella*, I, 12, p. 12; cf. also prefatory verse, p. 10; and I, 48–52, p. 18.

[65] *Ibid.*, I, 562–4, p. 56. Also Abbo, *Sermo adversus raptores bonorum alienorum*, ed. Önnefors, *Abbo von Saint-Germain-des-Prés*, p. 98, which may have been composed in the late ninth century (see Önnefors's comments at pp. 233–4 and 239–42).

[66] Abbo, *Bella*, II, 470–1, pp. 100–2.   [67] *Ibid.*, II, 343–6, pp. 90–2.

[68] Wattenbach, Levison, Löwe, *Geschichtsquellen*, p. 582.

[69] Lauranson-Rosaz, *L'Auvergne et ses marges* pp. 42–3.

[70] DD CIII 137–8, 140, 143, 145, 147; see also below, p. 101.

The 'supermagnates' and the 'rise of the aristocracy'

as a Neustrian.[71] There is no sign here of anything like a west Frankish independence movement.

Nor should Abbo's trenchant Neustrianness be taken as evidence for the kind of duchy-based secessionary tendencies which Kienast thought he detected west of the Rhine in the late ninth century. All the east Frankish leaders who feature in the poem are described in laudatory, not distant, terms. Henry, the imperial general, is a 'strong and powerful Saxon', whose death is narrated in heroic terms, while even Arnulf of Carinthia, who had come to power in the east in 887, was 'the lofty emperor'.[72] As we have already seen, Charles himself was 'basileus Francorum'.[73] This phrase is telling, as it shows that Abbo understood the term 'emperor (or king) of the Franks' in its traditional Carolingian sense, as referring to rule over the whole Frankish people and empire. With its derivatives, 'Franci' was a malleable term which could apply either to people inhabiting specific *regna* (Francia 'proper' east of the Seine, or Franconia around the Rhine-Main confluence), or to subjects of the entire empire. In the latter sense it was a legitimist term, used to lay claim to traditions of rightful Frankish kingship.[74] Abbo did use 'Francia' regularly to mean Francia 'proper', the region in which Paris lay.[75] Very occasionally he deployed the term to mean west Francia as a whole.[76] He was also, however, no stranger to the 'political' usage. In particular, he refers to Charles the Fat and his men as 'of the Frankish people' (*Francigeni*) in the same breath as recording that the emperor 'was surrounded by the arms of every people' and had 'a following of numerous people of diverse tongues'.[77] This was no exaggeration, as the charter evidence reveals that Charles was supported at Paris by contingents from almost every *regnum* of the empire.[78] Not least among them were parties from Neustria.[79] The 'Francigeni', then, were the people of the empire, including those from Neustria. In Abbo's view there was no contradiction in being, like him, *Neustrigenus* and *Francigenus* at the same time. His identity as revealed in the *Bella* was layered, rippling out in concentric circles from his home: he was a man

[71] Abbo, *Bella*, II, 442–50, pp. 98–100.

[72] *Ibid.*, II, 3–40, pp. 66–8; II, 217–18, p. 82; II, 578, p. 110. On Henry, who was actually a Thuringian, cf. *AV* s.a. 886, p. 61.

[73] Abbo, *Bella*, II, 164, p. 78.

[74] M. Lugge, *"Gallia" und "Francia" im Mittelalter. Untersuchungen über den Zusammenhang zwischen geographischer-historischer Terminologie und politischem Denken vom 6.–15. Jahrhundert* (Bonn, 1960), pp. 82–92; Brühl, *Deutschland-Frankreich*, pp. 83–130.

[75] Abbo, *Bella*, I, 10–1, p. 12; I, 440, p. 48; II, 390, p. 94; II, 447, p. 100; II, 453, p. 100; Abbo, *Sermo*, ed. Önnefors, *Abbo von Saint-Germain-des-Prés*, p. 94.

[76] Abbo, *Bella*, I, 188–98, p. 30, which mentions the Alps, is the only clear example.

[77] *Ibid.*, II, 315–21, p. 88 with the glosses at nn. *b*, *f*, *g*, *b*; II, 330–3, p. 90.

[78] DD CIII 137–51.   [79] DD CIII 139, 143.

of St Germanus, a Parisian, a Neustrian and a Frank. His *bêtes-noires* were other west Franks, not the emperor and his eastern followers. Abbo's perspective, which reflects that of Odo's circle, does not support the idea that regnal or regional secession was encouraged among the west Franks after the siege of Paris; quite the contrary, as a final example shows. It is very striking that on each occasion Abbo labels Odo 'the future king', it is in the context of the count's association with Paris and with St Germanus.[80] Here we catch a glimpse of the monk's own teleological agenda: it was not Odo's bravery, west-Frankishness or disappointment in the emperor which led him to kingship, but rather his relationship with the saint and the city protected by his relics.

This interpretation of west Frankish political consciousness at the end of the ninth century resonates with the writings of similar authors resident elsewhere in the empire. The anonymous annalist of St-Vaast, writing at the sharp end of Viking hostilities about 100 miles north of Paris in Arras, expressed a view of the imperial landscape which accorded very much with Abbo's, if delivered in a much more deadpan style. This author, who was writing contemporaneously, was very aware of the 'regnality' of the empire, its character as an agglomeration of political units, and hence seems to have been quite accepting of the emperor's absenteeism: his reports of the Viking raids against Rouen and Paris in 885 are reported with some sadness but without reproach for Charles, whose ultimate success in forcing the Danes back across the Seine is gladly recorded.[81] Like Abbo, the annalist portrayed Odo and Bishop Gauzlin, the military and moral champions of Paris, as working with and under Charles, and his high praise for their exploits makes the lack of criticism of the emperor even more striking. It seems clear that the annalist considered imperial authority to be present already at the siege, in the shape of these two men. When Charles fell, it was due to the 'eastern Franks'; he was betrayed 'by his own men', not by those like the annalist of St-Vaast who believed him to have taken his place in heaven.[82] This text, written in a community which suffered more than most at the hands of the Vikings, shows no evidence that their predations had turned west Frankish sentiment against the emperor.

Works from south of the Alps and east of the Rhine exhibit analogous outlooks. Andreas of Bergamo's *Historia*, composed not long after 877, is

[80] Abbo, *Bella*, I, 45–6, p. 18 (Odo as 'urbis tutor'); I, 487–90, p. 52 (Odo displays relics of Germanus from the city ramparts); II, 163–5, p. 78 (Odo represents Paris before the emperor). Note that Abbo, *Sermo de supradicto evangelio*, ed. Önnefors, *Abbo von Saint-Germain-des-Prés*, pp. 188–9 laments regnal division.

[81] *AV* s.a. 885, pp. 56–8; 886, pp. 60–3; cf. J. Ehlers, 'Die Anfänge der französischen Geschichte', *HZ* 240 (1985), 1–44, at 27–8.

[82] *AV* s.a. 887, p. 64.

The 'supermagnates' and the 'rise of the aristocracy'

designed as a continuation of Paul the Deacon's *History of the Lombards*, yet unproblematically blends events in Lombardy with a story which is essentially focused on the Carolingians. Andreas's inconsistent use of ethnic labels suggests that he saw himself as a man of Bergamo, a Lombard and a Frank: these categories were not mutually exclusive.[83] Similarly, on the evidence of his *Deeds of Charlemagne*, Notker the Stammerer identified himself first and foremost as a servant of the monastery of St-Gall, but also, and simultaneously, as an Aleman and a Frank, a point often missed by historians combing the text for evidence of an early German or east Frankish identity.[84] Even from Saxony, the most recently integrated *regnum* of the empire, we have an anonymous poem, based on Einhard's biography of Charlemagne and the *Royal Frankish Annals*, praising the virtues of the emperor who had conquered the Saxons in a prolonged and bloody war. The poet, who began his work in the reign of Charles the Fat and completed it in that of Arnulf, saw the Franks and Saxons as a single people united by Christianity, thus anticipating by several decades the well-known sentiments expressed by Widukind of Corvey.[85] The contrast between these texts and a work like Erchempert of Monte Cassino's *History of the Lombards and Beneventans*, written c. 889 in a region of southern Italy which had never been fully incorporated into the empire, is telling.[86] In this narrative the Franks and their rulers are only peripheral figures, pushed out of the spotlight by the dukes of Spoleto, the Arabs, the Byzantines and, of course, the eponymous Beneventans. Although not much more geographically remote from the main centres of Carolingian power than the likes of the Saxon Poet, the distance in Erchempert's political outlook is vast.

The identities of Abbo and his contemporaries were therefore multiple and fluid. The monk of St-Germain-des-Prés was very strongly Neustrian, and the Saxon Poet was decidedly Saxon; yet neither held this to preclude their full and willing membership of the *regnum Francorum*. Political solidarities were not set in stone, and their expression could be deliberately changed in times of trouble: therefore the eastern

---

[83] Andreas, *Historia*, pp. 220–31. This is especially clear in encounters with the Arabs and Beneventans: chap. 14, p. 227.

[84] As stressed by H.-W. Goetz, *Strukturen der spätkarolingischen Epoche im Spiegel der Vorstellungen eines zeitgenössischen Mönchs. Ein Interpretation der Gesta Karoli Notkers von Sankt Gallen* (Bonn, 1981), pp. 10–21. On Notker see below, chap. 7.

[85] Poeta Saxo, *Annalium de Gestis Caroli Magni Imperatoris Libri Quinque*, ed. P. von Winterfeld, MGH Poetae IV, pp. 1–71. Becher, *Rex, Dux und Gens*, pp. 17, 42–3; and pp. 50–66 on Widukind.

[86] Erchempert, *Historia Langobardorum et Beneventanorum*, MGH SRL, pp. 231–64; see now W. Pohl, 'History in Fragments: Motecassino's Politics of Memory', *EME* 10 (2001), 343–74. On Carolingian influence in the region, see G. West, 'Charlemagne's Involvement in Central and Southern Italy: Power and the Limits of Authority', *EME* 8 (1999), 341–67.

Kingship and Politics in the Late Ninth Century

Franks who rebelled against Charlemagne in the 780s articulated their opposition in terms of Thuringianness, while court sources continued to insist they were Franks.[87] In the same way, the languages of Neustrian, Frankish 'proper' or west Frankish separatism were available to men like Abbo and Odo in the mid to late 880s if they wanted to withdraw from the imperial 'Frankish' hegemony of the Carolingian dynasty; but they chose not to adopt such a vocabulary. These men continued to dress themselves in Frankish and Carolingian clothing right up until 888, and even beyond. Thirteen decades of the dynasty's rule were not cast aside lightly: Carolingian royal power was part of the inbred mental landscape of the aristocratic community. Kienast and the many other historians who have subscribed to the belief that powerful regional identities were a major factor in the disintegration of the empire therefore find little support in these sources. The west Frankish *regna* may well have been just as self-conscious as those in the east, but the expression of this consciousness was contingent and open to manipulation. Ethnic or regnal identity did not determine politics: politics, power and identity interacted much more subtly than that.[88] As long as Odo and the other high magnates of the 880s were loyal to the Carolingian emperor, their consciousness of themselves as regional representatives would remain submerged in their adherence to the *regnum Francorum*.

THE SUPERMAGNATES AND THE EMPIRE

The foregoing discussions should have made clear that despite the prevailing historiographical orthodoxy, the contemporary evidence points to the conclusion that Odo was not in opposition to Charles the Fat, and that regional loyalty remained intact during and after the siege of Paris. What, then, of the roles of the other 'supermagnates' during the 880s? These men originated from families of considerable landed wealth and political influence, the unarguable fact from which the 'rise of the aristocracy' model proceeds. Having said something about the contemporary perceptions of these people, how best to characterise the active relationship between their regional power bases and the court in the twilight of the Carolingian empire? Were they, as is frequently claimed, territorial

---

[87] K. Brunner, *Oppositionelle Gruppen im Karolingerreich* (Vienna, Cologne and Graz, 1979), pp. 48–53; M. Innes, 'Kings, Monks and Patrons: Political Identities and the Abbey of Lorsch', in Le Jan (ed.), *La Royauté et les élites*, pp. 301–24, at pp. 313–14.

[88] Becher, *Rex, Dux und Gens*, pp. 92–100 discusses related issues from Saxon examples; Brühl, *Deutschland-Frankreich*, pp. 264–7 suggests a more neutral way of comparing the situations either side of the Rhine.

The 'supermagnates' and the 'rise of the aristocracy'

lords whose power was a symptom of a political system in the final stages of dissolution?

As a starting point it is worth stressing that the siege of Paris, far from alienating Odo from Charles, actually brought them together. The last thing the emperor did before leaving the city in 886 was to distribute *honores* to those who had impressed him: 'a bishop by the name of Askericus was appointed to the town, and Count Odo was granted the lands of his father Robert [the Strong]'.[89] The lands to which the St-Vaast annalist here referred lay in Neustria, focused on the *honores* which Robert the Strong had received from Charles the Bald along the Loire after arriving in the mid-ninth century from his native Rhineland, to enable him to coordinate defence along the river. To the core counties of Tours, Angers and Orléans, which contained some of the best-fortified towns in west Francia, Robert added further *honores*, most notably the lay abbacy of St-Martin in Tours, prior to his death in 866.[90] The Carolingians were wary of referring to such blocks using the most appropriate vocabulary of dukes and duchies, which smacked too much of the semi-autonomous eighth-century lordships they had had to overcome on their way to power.[91] However, after the 860s there was a definite cohesion to this agglomeration of properties which, focused on St-Martin, formed the main defensive organisation against the Bretons and the Loire Vikings.

Nevertheless, while the annalist's words imply that Odo was Robert's direct successor twenty years after his death, the family situation is in fact not so self-explanatory. Robert's career under Charles the Bald was actually a typically unstable one, including an extended period of rebellion and a significant amount of time during which he ceded his Neustrian power base to the subkingship of Louis the Stammerer and moved to Burgundy.[92] Robert was eventually succeeded in the Breton march not by his sons but by one of his local rivals, Hugh the Abbot. His career was similarly patchy, including a spell out of Charles the Bald's patronage in the

---

[89] *AV* s.a. 886, p. 62.

[90] The complicated details are worked out by Werner, 'Untersuchungen IV'; K. F. Werner, 'Les Robertiens', in M. Parisse and X. Barral I Altet (eds.), *Le Roi de France et son royaume autour de l'an mil* (Paris, 1992), pp. 15–26; Werner, 'Les premiers Robertiens', pp. 10–37; P. Bauduin, 'La frontière normande aux Xe–XIe siècles: origine et maitrise politique de la frontière sur les confins de la haute Normandie (911–1087)', Thèse de doctorat, University of Caen (1998), vol. I, pp. 117–56. I am grateful to David Bates for this reference. On the fortifications see R. Kaiser, 'Les évêques neustriens du Xe siècle dans l'exercise de leur pouvoir temporel d'après l'historiographie médiévale', in Guillot and Favreau (eds.), *Pays de Loire*, pp. 117–43.

[91] Although see Regino, *Chronicon*, s.a. 861, p. 79; cf. Werner, 'Les Robertiens', p. 19. Nelson, *Charles the Bald*, pp. 166–7 sounds a note of caution. On the eighth-century duchies, see Fouracre, *Age of Charles Martel*, pp. 79–120.

[92] See Favre, *Eudes*, pp. 1–6; Nelson, *Charles the Bald*, pp. 183–7, 194–7, 209–10.

middle kingdom as would-be archbishop of Cologne.[93] The point is that, despite the presence of certain key *honores* in the possession of Robert, Hugh and Odo at various points in their lives, the Neustrian offices do not constitute a continuous core in the build-up of an entrenched territorial power. Under Charles the Bald it was the will of the king that sent Robert from Neustria to Burgundy, and likewise transferred his *honores* to Hugh. If Charles the Bald created territorial commands, he also unmade them and reallocated them. Likewise, in 886 it was the king, Charles the Fat, who decided that Hugh's position should revert to Robert's son Odo (although his relationship to Robert was clearly the basis of his claim). This, along with continuity in *honores* or properties, is an important link between the political careers of Robert, Hugh and Odo. Continuity of holding does not in any case say anything about how a magnate might choose to use such power; Hugh, for instance, spent many of his later years away from Neustria at the side of Carloman II in his Burgundian/Aquitanian kingdom. Odo's rise in 886, then, was not as neatly in succession to his father as implied by the terse report of the annalist of St-Vaast, but rather a direct result of his closeness to the emperor.[94] It also owed a lot to timing: the deaths of Hugh the Abbot and the war leader Henry left a vacuum in west Frankish military leadership which Odo's presence before the emperor in 886 placed him ideally to fill.[95] The problem is one of characterisation: any account which neglects the aspects of the count's career affected by *Königsnähe* must be inadequate.

We have already seen that Odo's dominance of Neustria allowed him great influence over the local balance of power. He acted not, however, as a territorial lord, but rather as the most powerful and best-connected magnate in the region. As such, his power had an impact on the positions of lesser aristocrats like the widow of the lay abbot of St-Symphorien in Orléans. It also enabled him to act as the emperor's middle man in Neustria, a *regnum* which was distant from the political centres of Charles the Fat's reign. This aspect of his position clearly influenced much of Odo's political activity. In 886, he handed over lands to the canons of St-Martin and St-Maurice in Tours, whose lay abbot he had just become, and these gifts were included in two general charters of confirmation issued by Charles the Fat.[96] The count also brought to Charles's attention

---

[93] On various aspects of his career, see Favre, *Eudes*, pp. 7–11; Werner, 'Gauzlin von Saint-Denis', passim; Nelson, *Charles the Bald*, pp. 177–9, 190–1; Y. Sassier, *Recherches sur le pouvoir comtal en Auxerrois du Xe au début du XIIIe siècle* (Auxerre, 1980), pp. 3–9.

[94] DD CIII 143 and 161 show that Odo acknowledged Hugh as a predecessor as well as Robert.

[95] Henry had a generalised military responsibility which included Neustria: *AF(B)* s.a. 886, p. 114; Regino, *Chronicon*, s.a. 887, p. 126; Brunner, 'Der fränkische Fürstentitel', pp. 275, 305–6, 309; Werner, 'Les Robertiens', p. 21.

[96] DD CIII 139, 146.

The 'supermagnates' and the 'rise of the aristocracy'

and acquired approval for a precarial grant in the Orléannais made by Archbishop Adalald of Tours and Bishop Raino of Angers to Abbot Hugh of St-Aignan.[97] In these charters we see Odo seeking imperial support and approval for activities and transactions being carried out at the heart of his personal political networks in Neustria, and mediating between the emperor and important members of the local aristocracy.

The development of the Neustrian march shows that birth was no guarantee of political success: even the *honores* of the great Robert the Strong did not become directly heritable. Men like Odo, who moved in the upper echelons of the imperial aristocracy, expected office. However, birth only got them to the starting gate in the race for *honores*: claims to lands and offices were often contested between families, and kings still had a say in the outcome.[98] The political significance of this can be discussed by reference to other, less well documented, of the big men of Europe in Charles's reign. We will focus on three figures, the only men given the significant title *marchio* ('margrave' is a very rough translation) in the charters of Charles the Fat. By the later ninth century, and from the 880s onwards in particular, this term referred to an intermediate power-broker holding delegated authority over a plurality of counts in one area, a count over counts.[99] That it was no longer a designation appropriate to the holder of a frontier marcher command is self-evident from the sphere of influence of our first *marchio* Rudolf, namely Transjurane Burgundy.[100] This was the mountainous region of present-day Switzerland around Geneva, Lausanne and Sion, where Rudolf was to become king in 888. During the earlier 870s, Rudolf had emerged in succession to his father Conrad as the main aristocratic player in the area, which was theoretically subject to the king of Italy but was in reality disputed. He had very probably become a close ally of Charles the Fat after the latter began to gain influence locally, perhaps as early as 871.[101] We ought not therefore to be surprised when we find Rudolf in attendance at the emperor's Lotharingian accession ceremony in 885, and again at the Metz war council on the way to relieve the siege of Paris in 886.[102] We also meet

---

[97] D CIII 143.

[98] D. Jackman, 'Rorgonid Right: Two Scenarios', *Francia* 28 (1999), 129–53, demonstrates this situation in earlier Carolingian Neustria.

[99] Brunner, 'Der fränkische Fürstentitel', pp. 207–11; K. F. Werner, 'Missus-Marchio-Comes. Entre l'administration centrale et l'administration locale de l'empire carolingien', in W. Paravicini and Werner (eds.), *Histoire comparée de l'administration (IVe–XVIIIe siècles)* (Munich and Zurich, 1980), pp. 191–239, at pp. 213–8 (reprinted in Werner, *Vom Frankenreich zur Entfaltung Deutschlands*).

[100] D CIII 112.

[101] See MacLean, 'Carolingian Response to the Revolt of Boso', pp. 41–2. On Rudolf's rise see introduction to DD RB, pp. 5–8.

[102] *AF(M)* s.a. 886, p. 105 for the assembly. See below, p. 126 for identification of Rudolf and discussion of the Lotharingian ceremony.

67

Kingship and Politics in the Late Ninth Century

the *marchio's fidelis* Vodelgis, and by implication possibly Rudolf himself, in the imperial entourage in Italy in February 885, facilitating Charles's journey to assume the west Frankish kingship.[103] A party from the transjurane abbey of Moutier-Grandval and Count Liutfrid, representative of the powerful Alsatian-Burgundian family known to historians as the Etichonids, who had previously dominated the region, were also in attendance at the outset of this Italian expedition.[104] The presence of Liutfrid as petitioner on behalf of the abbey suggests that, despite its eclipse in the 870s and 880s, his family retained its connections to Moutier-Grandval under Rudolf, and that Liutfrid himself was one of the counts subordinate to the *marchio*.[105] The outlines of the imperial power structures in the region can therefore be discerned: Charles championed the position of the relative newcomer Rudolf over that of more established local families such as that of Liutfrid, who nevertheless continued to obey the imperial summons. We can also identify two other of the *marchio's* counts by name, Turimbert and Manasses.[106] Rudolf may have been calling the shots in local affairs, but he did so with royal support and approval: moreover, the position of Liutfrid shows that the *marchio's* men were also the king's men.

Rudolf himself depicted his own position in exactly the same terms used for him by the king in the royal charters. When he underwrote the gift of lands north of Lake Geneva to the church of Lausanne by his man Reginold later in 885, he did so as Charles's *comes* (count) and *marchio*.[107] This royal connection can only have strengthened his regional authority. As a supporter of Charles, it was presumably Rudolf who prevented the bishops of Geneva and Sion from participating in the election to kingship of the anti-Carolingian rebel Boso at Mantaille in 879, and cooperated in dealing with the collaborator who had sat in the see of Lausanne.[108] Therefore, whereas the rise of the family of Conrad and Rudolf in Transjurane Burgundy was a result of their grasping of the

---

[103] D CIII 112. Most of the goods confirmed in his possession are in the heart of the Swiss Jura. See below, pp. 125–6.

[104] D CIII 108. On the Etichonids see F. Vollmer, 'Die Etichonen. Ein Beitrag zur Frage der Kontinuität früher Adelsfamilien', in G. Tellenbach (ed.), *Studien und Vorarbeiten zur Geschichte des grossfränkischen und frühdeutschen Adels* (Freiburg, 1957), pp. 137–84; M. Borgolte, 'Die Geschichte der Grafengewalt im Elsaß von Dagobert I. bis Otto dem Großen', *ZGO* 131 (1983), 3–54.

[105] Cf. R. Poupardin, *Le Royaume de Bourgogne (888–1038). Étude sur les origines du royaume d'Arles* (Paris, 1907), p. 79; H. Büttner, *Geschichte des Elsaß I. Politische Geschichte des Landes von der Landnahmezeit bis zum Tod Ottos III. und ausgewählte Beiträge zur Geschichtes Elsaß im Früh- und Hochmittelalter* (Sigmaringen, 1991), pp. 319–21.

[106] DD RB 2, 7.

[107] D RB 19 ('Signum Rodulfi gloriosi comitis . . . imperante donno nostro Karolo tercio'), and 2 ('Rodulfus comes nec non etiam inclitus marchius').

[108] R. Poupardin, *Le Royaume de Provence sous les carolingiens (855–933?)* (Paris, 1901), pp. 109–10.

The 'supermagnates' and the 'rise of the aristocracy'

opportunities available in the confused politics of the middle kingdom in the 860s, the clear implication is that in the 880s Charles the Fat used the existing configuration of their power to establish his own effective delegated authority by recognising Rudolf as a *marchio* supervising other royal officials in the area.[109] He was able to do this because of his personal relationship with Rudolf, not with the wide-reaching landed might of his clan. The respective positions of king and *marchio* relied on each other, and both put down deeper roots because of this, not in spite of it. Rudolf, like Odo, almost certainly waited until his lord was dead before proclaiming his own kingship in 888.[110]

The second of Charles's *marchiones*, Bernard Plantevelue (meaning 'Hairy-feet'), did not become one of the *reguli*, but did found a famous Aquitanian ducal line. Traditionally he has been depicted as exercising all the practical authority of a king without assuming a title which would attract the wrath of the Carolingians, and his career is discussed in terms of the 'rise' of his house to its ultimate ducal eminence.[111] Like Rudolf, his involvement in the high politics of the 860s and 870s was the key to his building up a large block of lands and *honores* in eastern Aquitaine, the Auvergne and western Burgundy.[112] Despite the lack of narrative source evidence for Bernard in the 880s, there is enough to suggest that, like Rudolf and Odo, he was a representative of Charles, in command of royal officials in the territories around his own power base in southern France. He had been a conspicuous participator on the Carolingian side in the campaigns against Boso, and thereafter charters from the monastery of St-Julien, Brioude, with which he had very close links, were dated after the imperial rule of Charles rather than after the regnal years of the local king Carloman II, indicating his alliance with the emperor already in the early 880s.[113] The abbey dated charters according to Charles the Fat's regnal years even after his own and the king's death.[114] It was in Boso's old

---

[109] Louis II also played a role in the rise of Conrad in the 860s: Poupardin, *Provence*, pp. 57–8; Andreas, *Historia*, chap. 9, pp. 226–7.

[110] Poupardin, *Le Royaume de Bourgogne*, p. 10, n. 1; DD RB, Introduction, p. 6, n. 4.

[111] Dhondt, *Études sur la naissance*, pp. 241–2; L. Auzias, *L'Aquitaine carolingienne (778–987)* (Toulouse and Paris, 1937), p. 423; D CIII 123 for Bernard as 'illustrissimus marchio', one of only two uses of this superlative by Charles's chancery. This term indicates a peculiarly superior position: Werner, 'Les premiers Robertiens', pp. 32–3. See also Kienast, *Herzogstitel*, pp. 166–8; Brunner, 'Der fränkische Fürstentitel', pp. 225–7.

[112] Auzias, *L'Aquitaine carolingienne*, pp. 389–99; Lauranson-Rosaz, *L'Auvergne*, pp. 52–8; Lauranson-Rosaz, 'Le Roi et les grands dans l'Aquitaine carolingienne', in Le Jan (ed.), *La Royauté et les élites*, pp. 409–36, at pp. 418–21.

[113] H. Doniol (ed.), *Cartulaire de Brioude* (Clermont and Paris, 1863), nos. 197, 260 and 263. At Conques, on the other hand, charters *were* dated after Carloman's reign. Further details provided by *AB* s.a. 880, p. 243; J. L. Nelson, *The Annals of St-Bertin: Ninth-Century Histories* (vol. 1, Manchester and New York, 1991), p. 221, n. 9.

[114] Auzias, *L'Aquitaine carolingienne*, pp. 418, 541–8.

Kingship and Politics in the Late Ninth Century

power base that Bernard intervened as *marchio* on behalf of the church of Lyon in June 885 along with the archchancellor Liutward, an association which places him at the heart of the newly-expanded imperial court.[115] Clearly, his support for the Carolingians in 879–80 had allowed him to extend his authority into some of the areas which had previously been Boso's domain, and to establish himself as one of Charles the Fat's key supporters west of the Rhine.

Finally, the case of the third *marchio*, Berengar of Friuli, can help us cast a clearer light on the way these big men operated in their localities in relation to the king.[116] In northern Italian political terminology, the term *marchio* had an even longer history as an appellation for a leading royal representative than it did north of the Alps.[117] There is ample evidence to make concrete the connection between Berengar and the king. He is to be found at the side of Charles in Italy as early as 875, when Louis the German sent his son across the Alps in a failed attempt to secure an east Frankish succession to Louis II against Charles the Bald, and was later the instrument of the emperor's attempts to establish his rule in Spoleto.[118] He is listed immediately after the king in a catalogue of witnesses and adjudicators to a royal judgement in 881, he was in a position to obtain royal favours for his followers, and he was closely associated with the archchancellor early in 882.[119] The strong links forged between Berengar and the kingdoms of the north, which were to stand him in good stead during his struggle for the Italian throne with Guy of Spoleto after 888, can only have been made stronger by his connections with Charles the Fat, and vice versa.[120] The evidence of this, and a demonstration of how king, *marchiones*, and counts related to each other before and after 888, is provided by a glance at the careers of certain Lombard aristocrats in the 880s, the period during which they fell under Berengar's influence, first as *marchio* and then as king. The count Berardus, for example, who came from Italy to help Charles the Fat and his Carolingian allies clean up the aftermath of the rebellion of Boso in 882 seems to have been also a man of Berengar, later supplying him with 300 men in the struggle with Guy.[121]

---

[115] D CIII 123.

[116] DD CIII 31 and 48 call him 'marchio'. D 37 calls him 'Berengarius dux et affinitate nobis coniunctum'. All three charters date from 881–2.

[117] Brunner, 'Der fränkische Fürstentitel', p. 324.

[118] Andreas, *Historia*, pp. 229–30. *AF(B)* s.a. 883, p. 110; cf. below, pp. 181–4. *AF(B)* s.a. 887, p. 115 implies he was out of favour for a short time at the start of that year.

[119] DD CIII 31, 37, 48.

[120] E. Hlawitschka, *Franken, Alemannen, Bayern und Burgunder in Oberitalien (774–962). Zum Verständnis der fränkischen Königsherrschaft in Italien* (Freiburg, 1960), pp. 77–8.

[121] *AV* s.a. 882, p. 52; *Gesta Berengarii imperatoris*, p. 376; Hlawitschka, *Franken, Alemannen, Bayern und Burgunder*, pp. 147–8.

The 'supermagnates' and the 'rise of the aristocracy'

Berengar's brother-in-law and ally Count Adalgisus II of Piacenza was a comital appointee of Charles the Fat.[122] Charles's *missus* Count Adalroch was listed among the *fideles* of Berengar's father and predecessor Eberhard of Friuli in the latter's will.[123] Count Erardus was in Charles's entourage in 881, and in Berengar's in 888.[124] The celebrated Suppo II, Adalgisus's father, also had well-documented links to both king and *marchio* before he died in 883.[125] Finally, Count Waltfred of Verona was a major supporter of Berengar as king, his 'highest counsellor' and successor in Friuli.[126] In the 880s, this connection was already clear, as was his place in the high favour of the emperor, who called him and Berengar his 'beloved faithful men and counsellors'.[127] The political circles of emperor and *marchio* intersected and overlapped at several points.

A charter of 884–5 issued by Bishop Haimo of Belluno, a town lying on the western fringes of Friuli, affords us a glimpse of how Berengar's authority was perceived by the aristocracy of his march.[128] Haimo, in a classic piece of early medieval episcopal rhetoric, relates how on acceding to his see he discovered it to be in a state of destitution, and describes the problems this situation had created for the poverty-stricken canons of his church. He goes on to paraphrase a confirmation charter issued by the emperor (Charles the Fat) which had happily eased his troubles. Most importantly for our purposes, however, is the role played by Berengar ('our *marchio*') in gaining this imperial favour: he is said to have first authorised Haimo's request himself, and then to have acquired the emperor's approval. His reward was to be commemorated in the regular masses offered by the grateful canons for the souls of 'the lord emperor' and his 'most illustrious count'. This document thus provides an explicit example of how a *marchio* could act as a middleman, mediating and channelling the relationship between the emperor and regionally important political figures like Haimo. At the same time, however, Charles could intervene directly, with Berengar's approval.[129] Berengar's relationship with the Carolingians and his function as a recognised regional power-broker

---

[122] Hlawitschka, *Franken, Alemannen, Bayern und Burgunder*, p. 112 and n. 4.

[123] D CIII 25; P. E. Schramm and F. Mütherich, *Denkmale der deutschen Könige und Kaiser*, 2nd edn (Munich, 1981), pp. 93–4; Hlawitschka, *Franken, Alemannen, Bayern und Burgunder*, p. 113.

[124] D CIII 35; *Gesta Berengarii imperatoris*, p. 379; Hlawitschka, *Franken, Alemannen, Bayern und Burgunder*, pp. 175–6.

[125] E.g. D CIII 25; Hlawitschka, *Franken, Alemannen, Bayern und Burgunder*, pp. 269–72.

[126] DD BF 4, 6, 8; Hlawitschka, *Franken, Alemannen, Bayern und Burgunder*, pp. 279–81.

[127] D CIII 32. See also D 31. For the significance of the appellation 'consiliarius' see below, pp. 182–5.

[128] P. Hirsch, *Die Erhebung Berengars von Friaul zum König in Italien* (Strasbourg, 1910), pp. 185–7.

[129] DD CIII 48–9. In D 48, Berengar intervened for Haimo.

Kingship and Politics in the Late Ninth Century

also permitted him to act as a player on a grander stage: in the after-math of the death of Louis II the *marchio* was the acknowledged leader of a substantial section of the north Italian aristocracy which was crucial in determining the political alignments of the subsequent period.[130] He retained this status during the reign of Charles the Fat, against whose enemies he led substantial military forces.[131]

These pieces of evidence give some substance to the notion of the *marchio* as a royal representative governing a multiplicity of lesser counts. In Berengar's case we can name several of these counts, observe their allegiance and value to both *marchio* and king, and take note of the fact that some of them are reported to have led large numbers of men, in the case of Adalgisus 1500, into battle on their lord's behalf. The fact that these men remained consistently loyal to Berengar after 888 is surely testament partly to the strength of the bonds he established with them as a result of being named *marchio* by Charles in the 880s; offices were attractive to aristocrats precisely because the prestige they conferred could bolster their local position in this way.

Odo was not referred to as *marchio* in any charter of Charles the Fat, but should certainly be counted in the same category as the other three. The terms *marchio* and *comes* could be interchanged. However, a more substantial point is that, unlike the other supermagnates, Odo seems to have controlled a series of counties directly rather than holding authority over a number of subordinate counts. In addition, he *was* given the epi-thet 'abbas'.[132] This is significant because it highlighted Odo's control of St-Martin, which dominated the Neustrian command. Similarly, Rudolf controlled St-Maurice-d'Agaune, the chief monastery of Transjurane Burgundy, while Bernard, although not officially lay abbot, effectively ran St-Julien at Brioude, the major house in the Auvergne.[133] The office of lay abbot was, despite its unpopularity with some churchmen, deployed by kings in this period as a valuable form of patronage: holders had access to the landed and military resources of their abbey, part of which was set aside specifically for this purpose, and remained free of the liturgical obli-gations required of regular abbots.[134] Equally, however, huge monasteries like these dominated their localities economically and socially. Brioude, for instance, was the resting place of the west Roman Emperor Avitus,

---

[130] *Registrum Johannes VIII. Papae*, ed. E. Caspar, MGH Epp. 7 (Berlin, 1928), nos. 74, 109, 241; P. Delogu, 'Vescovi, conti e sovrani nella crisi del regno Italico (ricerche sull'aristocrazia Carolingia in Italia III)', *Annali della scuola speciale per archivisti e bibliotecari dell'Università di Roma* 8 (1968), 3–72.

[131] *AF(B)* s.a. 883, p. 110.   [132] DD CIII 160, 161.

[133] Lauranson-Rosaz, *L'Auvergne*, pp. 54–5.

[134] Felten, *Äbte und Laienäbte* is the standard work, but is thin on the late ninth century. Cf. Werner, 'Les premiers Robertiens', pp. 29–30; Nelson, *Charles the Bald*, p. 234.

The 'supermagnates' and the 'rise of the aristocracy'

and control of this significant site had been important for those wishing to exercise authority in Aquitaine since Late Antiquity.[135] The strategic position, sacred status and political traditions of St-Martin in Tours and St-Maurice-d'Agaune put them on the same level. This kind of prestige drew enormous landed endowments, and as a result major abbeys constituted the focal point of local political networks and served as portals through which rulers could access and influence regional politics.[136] Charles's relationship with Odo and St-Martin was therefore the tip of an iceberg: using their *honores* as clout, the count and the other *marchiones* were able to act as intermediaries brokering local influence on behalf of the emperor. Charles's involvement in the circuits of Neustrian power is evident from the charters he issued for Odo or at his request, mediating and confirming deals done between the count's allies, and reorganising the relationship between Odo and his monasteries.[137] This type of deal, which is also apparent in the imperial charters for Bernard, Rudolf and Berengar, was characteristic of kingship in the large political units of the 880s and 890s, when rulers were unable to enter the minutiae of regional politics and so had to regulate local patronage networks via intermediaries like the *marchiones* and their monasteries.[138] As well as the role of the abbeys which supported these structures, we should also note the emergence of the viscount. It is no accident that some of our earliest evidence for viscounts in the Auvergne and Neustria comes from exactly this period.[139] As the name suggests, these men were deployed by counts to get on with day-to-day comital business in their place: like the office of lay abbot, viscounts freed the *marchiones* to bring their considerable comital, abbatial and political resources to bear on regional and imperial politics on behalf of the emperor.

The phenomenon of the lay abbacy is normally associated in the ninth century with the realms north of the Alps and west of the Rhine. Berengar's domination of Friuli sat instead within a long tradition of semi-autonomous Italian territorial duchies going back to the Lombard period, and also within the more recent context of his own family's power in the region.[140] However, neither Berengar nor the others can be characterised

---

[135] Brunterc'h, 'Naissance et affirmation des principautés', pp. 84–9.

[136] Innes, *State and Society* is a superb study of these dynamics, focused on Lorsch and Fulda.

[137] DD CIII 139, 143, 146, 160.

[138] DD CIII 48, 112, 123; Innes, *State and Society*, pp. 223–4.

[139] Lauranson-Rosaz, *L'Auvergne*, pp. 332–4; Werner, 'Les premiers Robertiens', pp. 29–30; cf. Werner, 'Les Robertiens', p. 22.

[140] See now C. La Rocca and L. Provero, 'The Dead and their Gifts. The Will of Eberhard, Count of Friuli, and his Wife Gisela, Daughter of Louis the Pious (863–864)', in F. Theuws and J. L. Nelson (eds.), *Rituals of Power from Late Antiquity to the Early Middle Ages* (Leiden, Boston and Cologne, 2000), pp. 225–80, esp. pp. 263–5.

Kingship and Politics in the Late Ninth Century

as territorial lords. Lordship was not defined in such terms in the ninth century. The direct, 'lordly', authority of such men encompassed not a block but a patchwork of properties, people and churches.[141] The *marchiones* were not all-powerful in their regions, nor were their commands hermetically sealed. Rather than using a loaded phrase like 'territorial aristocrats', it is better to think of these men as the chief royal representatives within more or less well-defined areas.[142] They required *honores* to enhance their status, influence and ability to pursue their own, as well as the ruler's, interests. We have already seen from the Auxerre case that Odo was not empowered to appoint bishops, although he may have had some influence on the choice.[143] Likewise, when the bishop of Nantes fled before the Vikings, it was the emperor who organised refuge for him; and it was also Charles who re-appointed Adalhelm to the see of Sées after a spell in Viking captivity.[144] Bernard Plantevelue, meanwhile, had a much less comfortable relationship with his local pontiffs. Most spectacularly, he fell out with Archbishop Frotar of Bourges over the control of St-Julien. Indeed, Frotar's high-profile career, which saw a series of important bishoprics and *honores* pass through his hands, suggests that Charles the Bald intended him to be a counterweight to Bernard's power in the 870s, despite the fact that both were conspicuous beneficiaries of royal favour.[145] Nor was Bernard's the only influential lay aristocratic family in the region; the counts of Toulouse, for instance, from whose misfortunes he had profited in the 870s, regained some of their old holdings at the expense of the *marchio's* son after Bernard died in 886.[146] This is a salient reminder that it is wrong to regard men like the *marchiones* as representing a type of removable royal official controlling a fixed area in an administrative hierarchy: it was by applying this anachronistic standard that a previous generation of historians concluded that late Carolingian government was stagnant. Nor were they territorial lords of units which had their own ethnic identities, whether we call these 'duchies' or *regna*. Odo did not embody and represent Neustria: he was simply the most significant political figure there, in part because of his association with the emperor and the

---

[141] Useful discussions are provided by Tabacco, *Struggle for Power*, pp. 131–6 and G. Sergi, 'Anscarici, Arduinici, Aleramici: elementi per una comparazione fra dinastie marchionali', in G. Andenna et al. (eds.), *Formazione e strutture dei ceti dominanti nel medioevo: marchesi, conti e visconti nel regno italico (secc. IX–XII)* (Rome, 1988), pp. 11–28.

[142] B. Arnold, *Princes and Territories in Medieval Germany* (Cambridge, 1991), pp. 61–73 reflects usefully on the concepts.

[143] See above, pp. 52–3.

[144] R. Merlet (ed.), *La Chronique de Nantes*, Collection de textes pour servir à l'Étude et à l'Enseignement de l'Histoire (vol. 19, Paris, 1896), chap. 21, pp. 66–8; *Miracula S. Opportunae*, in *Acta Sanctorum Aprilis III* (Antwerp, 1675), chaps. 2 and 6, pp. 68–9.

[145] Lauranson-Rosaz, *L'Auvergne*, pp. 54–5.   [146] Kienast, *Herzogstitel*, p. 168.

The 'supermagnates' and the 'rise of the aristocracy'

group of *honores* he had thus obtained. Rather, regional power struggles among men of considerable influence were unavoidable. The local basis of royal power was always contestable.[147] Kingship was about establishing mutually beneficial alliances with local potentates through whose mediation royal authority could be projected into regions far from the court; and whose own provincial power was legitimised by association with the ruler. Although kings increasingly sought to define their relationships with these men in terms of office-holding and hierarchy, such magnates were never part of a bureaucratic-style structure. Where rulers did sometimes succeed in disinheriting powerful counts, as Charles the Bald did to the sons of Robert the Strong, this was based not on the exercise of a specific royal prerogative, but rather on opportunist intervention in the configuration of regional politics when circumstances allowed. The shape of Carolingian politics was not a neat hierarchy, but a fragile structure of intersecting relationships whose balance had to be constantly adjusted and renegotiated.

CONCLUSION

Here, then, is one answer to the question of how Charles the Fat tried to govern the sprawling accumulation of *regna* which he began acquiring after 880. These four imperial aristocrats, Odo, Rudolf, Bernard and Berengar, were the major power-brokers in various coherent regions of the empire, and they fulfilled a role perhaps analogous to non-royal sub-kings. The chosen men were already members of families with land and power in these areas, and the centres of their authority were traditional, the heartlands of areas defined by geography and the outcome of more or less recent political history: Friuli, St-Martin in Tours, Transjurane Burgundy, Lyon and the Auvergne. But what also mattered was their personal relationship with the emperor: if the aristocracy as a whole was not a monolith, then equally nor were individual families like Rudolf's Welfs or Berengar's Unruochings. The *marchiones* did not somehow represent these families as elements of a 'rising aristocracy', nor did they personify their *regna* as ethnic or secessionary units. Indeed, although it was rooted in control of land, their power under Charles was legitimate and expressed by all parties in a legitimist idiom of delegation: this was how Carolingian politics worked.[148] Kings of this period did

---

[147] Innes, *State and Society*, pp. 195–210.
[148] On the success of the Carolingians in persuading already powerful regional aristocrats to adopt this idiom see Hannig, 'Zentralle Kontrolle und regionale Machtbalance'; Innes, *State and Society*, pp. 188–95.

Kingship and Politics in the Late Ninth Century

not act as motors of politics, selecting, appointing and deposing. Rather, their importance was sociologically constructed, and lay in their ability to legitimise the wider political community.[149] Accordingly, a description of the growth of important noble families' lands throughout the eighth and ninth centuries is insufficient to explain the nature of their position in the 880s: landed power may have put families in the pool of potential office-holders, but it did not automatically bring *Königsnähe* to their members. Their rise was in each case the outcome of a complex interaction between royal and local politics, and cannot be reduced to a simple story of inexorable ascent. Moreover, as shown by the disinheritance of Robert the Strong's sons in the 860s, and Bernard Plantevelue's in the 880s, the stock of these so-called 'principalities' and their rulers could fall as well as rise. Competition for power in the empire was not a zero-sum game: power was not a single and finite commodity competed for by mutually antagonistic groups. Royal and 'local' power formed parts of a negotiated system, and their mutual reliance is not diminished by the kind of latitude we have observed in its exercise in the case of Odo, who was not afraid to step on the toes of lesser aristocratic figures in his area. The emperor could not regularly intervene directly below the level of the high aristocracy. The solution was to shrink the number of key royal supporters and draw them closer to the court politically. The outcome was by no means free of tension, but it seems to have worked as well as Carolingian politics ever did. The *marchiones* did, as we have seen, travel long distances to appear at court and contribute to imperial ceremonies and campaigns throughout the reign. The west Franks did not choose a king from among their own number after the death of the heirless Carloman II in 884, as well they might, but instinctively turned east to look for another Carolingian. The Carolingianness of the empire was intact.

It would be misleading to suggest that Charles neatly blanketed his empire with a patchwork of such commands, although there are some analogous examples from Brittany and Frisia.[150] This model of Carolingian authority was by no means new or anomalous. In some ways, the Frankish empire lent itself to this sort of structuring, as a more or less loose agglomeration of *regna*.[151] To give but one clear example, the Neustrian

---

[149] Reuter, 'Origins of the German *Sonderweg?*', esp. pp. 204–5.

[150] J. M. H. Smith, *Province and Empire. Brittany and the Carolingians* (Cambridge, 1992), pp. 192–3; Coupland, 'From Poachers to Gamekeepers'. William the Pious eventually succeeded his father Bernard in some capacities: Lauranson-Rosaz, *L'Auvergne*, pp. 60–75; Guillot, 'Formes, fondements et limites', pp. 64–74.

[151] The work of Werner is the most significant here: see his *Structures politiques du monde franc* and, most recently, 'Völker und Regna'.

The 'supermagnates' and the 'rise of the aristocracy'

command formed a quite coherent body of *honores* which could easily be assigned to a single overseer, a position filled at various times in the second half of the ninth century by Robert the Strong, Louis the Stammerer, Hugh the Abbot, Odo of Paris, and finally Odo's brother Robert.[152] Moreover, it was able to rest on the substrata of local aristocracies which remained substantially stable over relatively long periods of time.[153] Charles the Bald governed the west Frankish kingdom by establishing a similar type of magnate command to that we have been discussing, and *marchiones* like Bernard were direct heirs to structures established in his reign.[154] Charles the Simple, in turn, did the same.[155] The evidence for the governmental practices of earlier kings such as Charlemagne and Louis the Pious points in a similar direction: these rulers dealt directly with only one or two important counts in a locality, or with a *missus dominicus* (a local power-broker favoured by the Carolingians) who would then mediate orders and information for their fellows and subordinates.[156] The position of the *marchio* Gerold in the 790s is instructive: he was simultaneously Charlemagne's appointed representative in Bavaria and a leading member of the Agilolfing dynasty which had controlled that *regnum* during its independence in the eighth century.[157] There was no contradiction here: the interplay of local influence and central appointment was crucial to the effectiveness of men like Gerold, and central to the structures of early medieval politics in general.[158] Another concrete example of the phenomenon comes from Saxony, where Wala seems to have been preeminent under his cousin Charlemagne.[159] It is no accident that these individuals were established in regions distant from the centres of early Carolingian power, just as the *marchiones* of Charles the Fat's reign controlled lands far from the emperor's home realm of Alemannia.

In other words, Carolingian kings and emperors had always been accustomed to dealing with powerful aristocratic individuals, and not

---

[152] As stressed by Werner, 'Les premiers Robertiens', p. 27.

[153] Werner, 'Untersuchungen IV'; Airlie, 'The Aristocracy', p. 435.

[154] Airlie, 'The Aristocracy', pp. 448–9.

[155] Ehlers, 'Die Anfänge der französischen Geschichte', pp. 22–3; K. F. Werner, 'Westfranken-Frankreich unter den Spätkarolinger und frühen Kapetingern (888–1060)', in Werner, *Vom Frankenreich zur Entfaltung Deutschlands*, pp. 725–77, at pp. 738–40.

[156] Hannig, 'Zentrale Kontrolle und regionale Machtbalance'; Hannig, 'Zur Funktion der karolingischen *missi dominici* in Bayern'; Innes, *State and Society*, pp. 193–4.

[157] Werner, 'Important Noble Families in the Kingdom of Charlemagne', p. 166.

[158] A similar process is evident in tenth-century England under Athelstan, who reduced the number of ealdormen and enlarged their territorial responsibilities as a response to the challenges of ruling a newly-expanded realm: see, for instance, J. Campbell (ed), *The Anglo-Saxons* (London, 1982), p. 172.

[159] G. Tellenbach, *Königtum und Stämme in der Werdezeit des Deutschen Reiches* (Weimar, 1939), p. 13; Kienast, *Herzogstitel*, p. 445.

Kingship and Politics in the Late Ninth Century

with the 'aristocracy' (or individual aristocratic families) as a monolithic entity. The key role of kings in this regard was thus to appoint men they thought they could trust to govern these regions in the name of Carolingian authority. In this sense, the dynasty's authority had always had a 'supervisory', rather than bureaucratic, character.[160] The real glue of Carolingian power, as Stuart Airlie has shown, was the dynasty's construction and maintenance of the 'political myth' that they alone could be kings:[161] this idea could only be enhanced by the exercise of power in the localities by men who claimed to be wielding it in the name of the king. Association with the king helped these men entrench their regional power, and gave them access to the higher platform of imperial politics. We should not dismiss late Carolingian political structures as fragile and fragmented: this was the nature of the dynasty's authority all along.

However, this is not to say that the outcome was an unqualified success. All things being equal, the system worked; but all things frequently were not. Charles's main problem stemmed from the succession situation. With the proliferation of kings after about 875, when a new and populous generation of Carolingians began to take on the task of ruling the empire, the *regna* became much more intensively governed than previously. Being entrusted with smaller areas of responsibility, kings were able to intervene more directly in the local patronage networks which ran through the aristocracy. For the aristocrats, this was an opportunity to enhance their standing by making best use of this new *Königsnähe*. However, as the Carolingians of this generation one by one met their early deaths and the kingdoms of the empire fell into the hands of Charles the Fat, the trend was reversed, and once more access to the royal ear became limited, available only to those with the favour of an often distant emperor.[162] The retreat of *Königsnähe* from the traditional heartlands of the empire was exacerbated by Charles's lack of a legitimate heir whom he could set up as a subking. The role of the *marchiones* therefore became especially significant in representing imperial authority, and their position was put under extra strain by the activity of the Northmen. This state of affairs did not undermine Charles's position *per se*, but the shrivelling of access to the court created tensions which would grow as time passed. The resolution of the succession issue thus came to be of paramount importance. As long as the identity of the empire's next ruler remained uncertain, anxiety would develop in the minds of the members of the

---

[160] Rosenwein, 'Family Politics of Berengar', p. 249.
[161] Airlie, '*Semper fideles?*'.   [162] Innes, *State and Society*, pp. 223–4.

The 'supermagnates' and the 'rise of the aristocracy'

aristocratic community, who needed reassurances as to where the source of *Königsnähe* would lie in future. Ultimately, it was this conjunction of circumstances which gave Arnulf his constituency for support in the coup of 887.

These matters will be discussed at greater length in chapters 5 and 6. However, it is important to stress in conclusion to this chapter that the reign of Charles the Fat clearly did not witness a definitive shift in the balance of power away from the king and in favour of the aristocracy. The formulation of the issue in these terms is misconceived. Even rebellious aristocrats were not attempting to opt out of the Carolingian system, but rather to acquire *more Königsnähe*. All the evidence points to the fact that the relationship between the two remained cast in a mould which had been more or less the same throughout the ninth century. In reality, the so-called 'territorial aristocracy' did not 'rise'. Aristocratic families had always been a powerful force in Frankish politics of which rulers had always taken account and made use. Charles the Fat's authority may not have been absolute or omnipresent, but then neither was Charles the Great's.

Charles had organised something on the basis of expediency. It was only his premature downfall at a time when there was no adult male Carolingian to assume his position that crystallised this contingent organisation into the tenth-century political map of duchies and principalities, not the inevitable build-up of aristocratic house properties over 100 or more years. The key factor was not a long process, but a single event. In fact, a measure of the king's success lies exactly in the fact that these property accumulations formed the cores of the post-888 *regna* within the territorial extent of the empire, Dhondt's criterion of failure. Regino's much-quoted statement that the post-888 kings were 'drawn from the bowels of their kingdoms' has been overinterpreted; they represented neither independent ethnic identities nor long-entrenched corporate aristocratic power.[163] Both Odo and Rudolf, for example, were relative newcomers who only became established in their power bases in the 870s and 880s, coinciding with Charles's own first attempts to exert influence in their regions. Capetian royal power, when it eventually emerged, would be based on the connection between Paris and Neustria which had been united in the new dynasty's hands by Charles's 886 grant to Odo. The careers of Odo, Rudolf and the other *reguli* were either created, endorsed or strengthened by Charles, and their post-888 position can only be explained fully in the light of their pre-888 relationship to the emperor.

---

[163] Regino, *Chronicon*, s.a. 888, p. 129.

Kingship and Politics in the Late Ninth Century

The underlying structures of his empire endured, and under the same men.[164] In this sense, the court of Charles the Fat propelled the dynastic lines of Rudolf, Berengar, Bernard and Odo towards their royal and ducal destinies.[165]

[164] See also K. F. Werner, 'La genèse des duchés en France et en Allemagne', *Settimane* 27 (1981), 175–207 (reprinted in Werner, *Vom Frankenreich zur Entfaltung Deutschlands*); Airlie, 'The Aristocracy', p. 449. My comments here are intended only to point out a general pattern relating to the Carolingian roots of tenth-century political units, and not necessarily as an endorsement of Werner's vision of much longer-term continuities.

[165] J. Fried, *Könige Ludwig der Jüngere in seiner Zeit* (Lorsch, 1984), pp. 12–13 makes similar claims for the court of Louis the Younger.

Chapter 4

ROYAL POLITICS AND REGIONAL POWER IN THE LATE CAROLINGIAN EMPIRE

In the last chapter the case was made that Charles the Fat ruled the empire in much the same way as had his predecessors. However, this observation cannot hide the fact that there was one major difference between the empire of Charlemagne and that of his great-grandson: its political geography. For generations the mental landscape of the Frankish elite had been dominated by political centres in Francia, the middle Rhine, northern Italy and eastern Bavaria, those regions where the Carolingians were best endowed with palaces and estates. Under Charles the Fat, thanks to a series of dynastic accidents, the traditional order of things was turned on its head. His home *regnum* of Alemannia was very much a political backwater in Carolingian terms. Although other fringe zones such as Provence and Aquitaine had historically hosted resident royal courts, that had been in times of Carolingian numerical strength. Charles never visited Aachen, the old seat of Charlemagne and Louis the Pious, and ruled from Alemannia during a period of dwindling numbers of kings: after 884, it became, along with northern Italy, *the* centre of the empire. The *marchio*, a type of regional middle-man who under Charlemagne had been mainly deployed in less-visited frontier regions such as Bavaria, now became a key player in what had previously been the heart of the empire. The political core had become peripheral, and the periphery had become the core.[1]

These developments inevitably had an effect on patterns of power within the aristocracy, upon whose cooperation early medieval kings were ultimately reliant. The Carolingian empire was not directly equivalent to entities like the British empire in the sense of having a fixed political centre whose operation was geared to managing and exploiting the peripheral colonies. Rather, it was made up of an agglomeration of *regna*, each with its own self-conscious political communities and local traditions. Members of all these communities, especially those whose families held

---

[1] The pioneering study of central and peripheral zones in early medieval kingdoms was E. Müller-Mertens, *Die Reichsstruktur im Spiegel der Herrschaftspraxis Ottos der Großen* (Berlin, 1980).

land and influence in more than one region, shared in the leadership of the Frankish polity. This widespread elite is conventionally known by the term 'imperial aristocracy'. The political centre could move, both in the sense of the itinerancy of the ruler, and in the way that different rulers had different power bases. Nevertheless, some groups of aristocrats were more used to being closely involved at court than others. By the 880s almost every region of the empire had had some experience of having access to its 'own' king. The political landscape of the 860s and 870s was well populated with legitimate Carolingians, and these decades witnessed the high-water mark in the diffusion of Carolingian *Königsnähe*. The generation of the imperial aristocracy which was in place during the reign of Charles the Fat was therefore accustomed to accessible kingship, which was an essential commodity in the furthering of any top-level aristocratic career, lay or ecclesiastical. As Charles's relatives died one by one, eventually leaving him in sole charge, the royal court as observed from traditional political centres like Paris and Mainz receded from view over the horizon.

In the absence of sons of his own to set up as subkings, one of Charles's responses was mobility: even a casual glance at his itinerary shows him to have been among the fastest moving of his line.[2] Another was the constant distribution and renegotiation of patronage, a kind of rule by remote control: it is no coincidence that Charles seems to have issued more charters per year than any of his predecessors.[3] Even local royal representatives like counts, embedded in regional society, were not automatically loyal: their support had to be nurtured. It is clear that the emperor's shadow did not fall in equal measure over all the territories under his dominion. As we have seen, the *regna* of the empire were not merely administrative units, but rather coherent imagined communities with their own leaders and focal points. Many had been semi-autonomous units before the eighth century, and would become so again in the tenth. Their strong regional identities did not evaporate while under the Carolingian umbrella but, as we saw from the work of Abbo, coexisted with a wider Frankish–imperial allegiance which the dynasty worked hard to maintain. Indeed, the Carolingian period even witnessed the creation of a brand new geo-political identity in Lotharingia.[4] Given motive and opportunity these identities

---

[2] See the maps in Brühl, *Fodrum, Gistum, Servitium Regis*.

[3] This is a rough calculation based on the standard editions. Figures are given by F. Bougard in his review of K. Wanner, *Die Urkunden Ludwigs II, Francia* 24 (1997), 211–13.

[4] B. Schneidmüller, 'Regnum und Ducatus. Identität und Integration in der lothringischen Geschichte des 9. bis 11. Jahrhunderts', *Rheinische Vierteljahrsblätter* 51 (1987), 81–114. Lotharingia is not discussed specifically in this chapter: see MacLean, 'The Carolingian Response to the Revolt of Boso', pp. 30–8.

Royal politics and regional power in the Late Carolingian Empire

could quite conceivably have asserted themselves against Carolingian authority rather than falling into line behind it. It is therefore striking that this does not seem to have happened during the empire's final years. We have already examined the stake that the supermagnates had in the Carolingian hegemony. In order to pursue these issues at a lower level, in this chapter we will ask how and with what intensity Charles the Fat was successful in forming stable alliances with the wider political communities of the various regions of the empire during the last decade of its existence. We will deal with the *regna* in the order that the emperor inherited them. By its very nature, this enquiry cannot hope to be at all comprehensive, and the coverage will be uneven due to the varying availability of evidence. Understanding of all the regions discussed would benefit from further research. Nevertheless, the evidence we have does enable us to reflect on the bigger picture of royal–aristocratic relationships and the networks of power which made Carolingian politics tick.

ALEMANNIA AND ALSACE

Alemannia, sometimes called Swabia, comprised the south-western part of modern Germany plus the eastern segment of Switzerland. It was not an area where the Frankish kings were traditionally well endowed, and had only really been systematically integrated into the empire from the reign of Louis the Pious, whose second wife, Judith, came from a prominent family based around Lake Constance.[5] Carolingian landholdings in the region were not extensive, but Louis's efforts to establish counties, build relationships with powerful local abbeys like Reichenau and St-Gall, and establish palaces such as Bodman and Ulm made it a viable enough royal heartland for him to consider using it to endow his fourth son, Charles the Bald, in 829.[6] A second major phase of organisation of royal resources was undertaken by Louis the German during the 850s, as he attempted to bring his authority more directly to bear in the south-west of the east Frankish kingdom. His strategies included the foundation of the nunnery of SS Felix and Regula in Zurich, a focus for royal prestige and patronage which was placed in the hands of his daughters.[7]

---

[5] J. Fleckenstein, 'Über die Herkunft der Welfen und ihre Anfänge in Süddeutschen Raum', in Tellenbach (ed.), *Studien und Vorarbeiten*, pp. 71–136.

[6] M. Borgolte, *Geschichte der Grafschaften Alemanniens in fränkischer Zeit* (Sigmaringen, 1984); T. Zotz, 'Grundlagen und Zentren der Königsherrschaft im deutschen Südwesten in karolingischer und ottonischer Zeit', in H. Nuber et al. (eds.), *Archäologie und Geschichte des ersten Jahrtausends in Südwestdeutschland* (Sigmaringen, 1990), pp. 275–93.

[7] D. Geuenich, 'Aus den Anfängen der Fraumünsterabtei in Zürich', in U. Brunold and L. Deplazes (eds.), *Geschichte und Kultur Churrätiens. Festschrift für Pater Iso Müller OSB zu seinem 85. Geburtstag* (Disentis,1986), pp. 211–31.

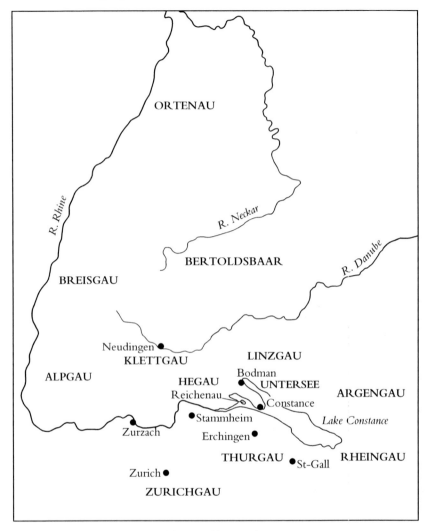

Map 2. Alemannia

For his sons he had other plans. The youngest, Charles the Fat, was established as *rector* of Alemannia, where he had been born in 839, while his brothers received similar commands in Franconia/Saxony and Carinthia.[8] The powers enjoyed by each of the sons were closely defined: writing

---

[8] M. Borgolte, 'Karl III. und Neudingen. Zum Problem der Nachfolgeregelung Ludwigs des Deutschen', *ZGO* 125 (1977), 21–55. See *AA* s.a. 839, p. 178 for Charles's birth. It is relatively unusual for the year of a king's birth to be reported explicitly in a ninth-century chronicle,

Royal politics and regional power in the Late Carolingian Empire

at St-Gall in 881, Notker the Stammerer tells us that they were allowed to determine minor judicial cases, while decisions regarding bishops, monasteries and counts, as well as the public fisc and all major judgements, were reserved for their father.[9] This information is corroborated by other sources.[10] In the early 860s, in order to entrench his sons in their positions, Louis had each of them married to prominent members of the aristocracy in their regions. Charles's bride was Richgard, daughter of one of the leading counts of northern Alsace, a region in which Louis had been canvassing support for several years and which had recently been officially ceded to him by his nephew Lothar II.[11]

Louis, perhaps mindful of the troubles his own rebellions had caused for his father during the 830s and wary of the dangers of usurpation, broke with Frankish tradition by refusing to allow his sons to call themselves kings while he still lived. Nevertheless, the sons did exercise powers which were quite appropriate to the dignity of Carolingian subkings.[12] Leadership of armies raised from their *regna* came under their remit, especially for Louis and Karlmann, who had marcher responsibilities, but also for Charles, who commanded forces in Moravian territory in 869 and in Italy in 875.[13] As the principal intermediate authority in their *regna*, the sons were also called in by their father to subscribe those royal charters which pertained to their regions.[14] Accordingly, they seem to have been just as capable of building up networks of association within the aristocracy as were sons of other Carolingian rulers, something which Louis the German presumably intended. Traces of these alliances can sometimes be detected: when Charles attempted to impose one of his clerics on the vacant see of Lausanne in 877, his choice was partly guided by the hospitality which the candidate had shown towards him while he was still a 'young man'.[15] Likewise, many of the men

---

and so it is significant that our information comes from a region with which Charles would have very strong associations throughout his life. See also Hartmann, *Ludwig der Deutsche*, pp. 66–76.

[9] Notker, *Continuatio*, p. 329.

[10] *AF* s.a. 873, p. 78 shows these provisions in action. D Frei 898 shows Karlmann's similar responsibilities.

[11] D LG 108; Borgolte, 'Karl III. und Neudingen', pp. 36–9; See M. Borgolte, *Die Grafen Alemanniens im merowingischer und karolingischer Zeit. Eine Prosopgraphie* (Sigmaringen, 1986), pp. 106–8 on his identity.

[12] As Kasten, *Königssöhne und Königsherrschaft*, pp. 220–37 has recently emphasised, subkingship was defined less in titular/institutional than in familial terms.

[13] For example, *AF* s.a. 858, p. 49; 870, p. 70 (Karlmann); *AF* s.a. 854, p. 44; 869, pp. 68–9 (Louis); *AF* s.a. 869, pp. 68–9; *AB* s.a. 875, p. 198 (Charles). *AB* s.a. 872, p. 186 is instructive, revealing the significance of Louis's and Charles's armies by their absence.

[14] DD LG 82–3, 105, 110, 116, 119, 145, 161, 163–5. See Borgolte, 'Karl III. und Neudingen', pp. 23–35.

[15] *Collectio Sangallensis*, ed. K. Zeumer, MGH Formulae Merowingici et Karolini Aevi (Hanover, 1886), pp. 390–437, no. 26.

Kingship and Politics in the Late Ninth Century

who came to populate Charles's court were Alemans who had begun their careers in the entourage of the future king before 876.[16] Louis the Younger enjoyed a similar degree of association with his men: when a fight threatened to break out between the Franks and Saxons at a royal assembly held in 875 at Tribur, it was he and not his father who intervened to keep the peace.[17] Evidently, the sons were already beginning to exert strong influence in their delegated commands before their father's death. As the eulogistic terminology of a poem composed for an *adventus* (reception ceremony) of Charles the Fat to the monastery of St-Gall reveals, while the sons may ordinarily have avoided having themselves addressed as kings, they eschewed few of the other trappings of kingship.[18]

Charles, then, was very much an Aleman. This has, however, been seen as causing him problems, not only by marginalising more distant nobles in Italy and west Francia, but also by inverting the political traditions of the east Frankish realm itself, the last three kings of which had ruled in large part from, and with men drawn from, Bavaria and Franconia. For Charles's predecessors, indeed, Alemannia had effectively been an intermediate zone, a stop-off point on the road between Frankfurt and Regensburg.[19] The resentment caused by the change in priorities is evident from the invective of the Mainz annalist on behalf of Archbishop Liutbert, one of those who lost out by this new situation.[20] The question remains of how Charles's methods of imposing himself in Alemannia differed from those applied in *regna* like Bavaria, and from strategies employed by previous kings. His more direct involvement in the governance of 'his' kingdom, which reflected his background, can be illustrated with reference to three different modes of royal authority.

Firstly, Charles maintained a high personal presence in Alemannia, staying there more often than in other *regna*. The region served as a central junction point on his wide-ranging itinerary, offering access to Bavaria, Italy, Franconia and Lotharingia. Favoured palaces like Bodman on the shores of Lake Constance not only provided hospitality for the

---

[16] Fleckenstein, *Die Hofkapelle der deutschen Könige*, pp. 189–98.

[17] *AF* s.a. 875, p. 83. See Bowlus, *Franks, Moravians and Magyars*, pp. 119–28 for Karlmann and the aristocracy of the south-west.

[18] W. Bulst, '*Susceptacula regum*. Zur Kunde deutscher Reichsaltertümer', in W. Bulst, *Lateinisches Mittelalter: Gesammelte Beiträge* (Heidelberg, 1984), pp. 130–68, at pp. 135–8. Charles had himself commemorated at Remiremont as *rex*, probably while in rebellion against his father in 872: G. Tellenbach, 'Liturgische Gedenkbücher als historische Quellen', in *Mélanges Eugène Tisserant* (Vatican, 1964), vol. 5, pp. 389–400, at pp. 396–9.

[19] E. Goldberg, 'Creating a Medieval Kingdom: Carolingian Kingship, Court Culture and Aristocratic Society under Louis of East Francia (840–76)', PhD thesis, University of Virginia (1998), pp. 281–351.

[20] See above, chap. 2.

Royal politics and regional power in the Late Carolingian Empire

imperial entourage, but also served as permanent representations of royal power while the ruler was absent.[21] Charles actively worked to define the political geography of Alemannia, and to intervene in local politics in a way he could not elsewhere. This effort is visible in at least one case, for which we are fortunate to have good evidence. Michael Borgolte has shown that land focused on the estate centre at Neudingen, between the sources of the Danube and the Neckar, was of special significance to the emperor.[22] Gifts in this area were made to the custodian of the royal chapel Ruodbert on two occasions, and the court scrutiny established by these grants was enhanced in 883 by a swap of adjacent lands with the abbey of St-Gall.[23] Charters from 882 and 887 record in their dating clauses that Ruodbert was seen as '*missus* of the emperor in place of the count' and '*vicarius*' in the region, revealing that this was a place administered with peculiarly close attention from the royal court.[24] Charles the Fat had spent some of his pre-kingship days in control of this particular locality; and it is no coincidence that it was Neudingen to which he retreated after being dislodged by the coup in 887.[25] It is possible, then, to characterise the maintenance of the Neudingen area free of outside influences as part of a personal politics pursued by Charles the Fat in this part of Alemannia throughout his reign. In view of this, it is significant that the charter which transferred control of some of this region to Ruodbert was interceded for by his two closest allies: the archchancellor Liutward, an Aleman himself, and the empress Richgard.[26]

Secondly, Charles also seems to have maintained particularly close links with the monasteries of St-Gall and Reichenau, both powerful landholders in Alemannia and the main academies for the recruitment of his court personnel. His gift of the estate of Stammheim in late 879 to St Otmar, one of the two major relic cults centred at St-Gall, represented a kind of symbolic atonement for the persecutions visited on Otmar by the

---

[21] See now Airlie, 'Palace of Memory'.

[22] Borgolte, 'Karl III. und Neudingen', pp. 39–49; Borgolte, *Die Grafen Alemanniens*, p. 164. See Map 2.

[23] See DD CIII 19, 38 and 68 respectively.   [24] DD SG 620 and 657.

[25] D SG 551 reveals his presence as *rector* in 870. Hermann of Reichenau, *Chronicon*, ed. G. H. Pertz, MGH SS 5 (Hanover, 1844), p. 109 for the retreat. The Neudingen area formed the kernel of the tenth-century Alemannic duchy, which testifies to the endurance of this power-structure established by Charles the Fat: see Borgolte, 'Karl III. und Neudingen', pp. 47–8; Zotz, 'Grundlagen und Zentren', p. 292.

[26] D CIII 38. Two other elements of the grant mark it out. Firstly, it was to revert after Ruodbert's death 'ad regiam potestatem', and secondly it was enacted in Pavia, making it exceptional as a document issued outside the *regnum* with which it was concerned; both of these facets highlight the political importance of the transaction in the eyes of the court. Neither of the other royal charters in question name a petitioner. It is interesting to note in passing that D 38 is one of only two charters of Charles the Fat known to survive in the form of twin original copies (D 65 is the other). On Liutward and Richgard, see below, pp. 185–91.

Kingship and Politics in the Late Ninth Century

king's predecessors at that site in the mid-eighth century.[27] Up until 879 Charles appears, on the evidence of the house historian Ekkehard, to have ordered that a feast should be provided for the brothers of St-Gall out of the income from his Stammheim property during the festival of Otmar, a celebration in which the king himself was in the habit of participating as 'frater conscriptus' (a temporary lay brother). The transfer of this land in that year was intended to put this arrangement on a firmer footing, setting out that it was to be used to support eight men in the permanent service of Otmar, and to pray daily for the king. From now on Charles, increasingly distracted by the affairs of the newly acquired Italian kingdom, was usually only represented in the festal period by royal legates.[28] He thus established a close affinity with St Otmar, to whom Notker referred as 'your [Charles's] patron', creating a solemn and permanent bond between the cult and the commemoration of his own kingship.[29] The gift of Stammheim not only strengthened Charles's relationship with Otmar, but also symbolically reached back across the whole Carolingian era to the beginnings of the dynasty's influence in Alemannia, connecting the king to local political traditions and legitimising his authority.

Something similar took place at nearby Reichenau, Alemannia's other major religious centre. An annual commemoration feast for Charles was established there in the mid-880s by Bishop Chadolt of Novara, the archchancellor's brother, to be provisioned from the estate of Erchingen which the bishop had received from the emperor.[30] The archchancellor's subsequent imperially approved acquisition of a cell 'within the monastery' was likely designed as a means of supervising the commemoration of Charles's rule in that abbey.[31] Here again we encounter Liutward at the heart of the personal politics of the king in Alemannia. St-Gall and Reichenau were among the most significant spiritual powerhouses of the kingdom, places where Carolingian charisma was actively nurtured.[32]

---

[27] D CIII 13. A. Borst, 'Die Pfalz Bodman', in H. Berner (ed.), *Bodman. Dorf, Kaiserpfalz, Adel* (Sigmaringen, 1977), pp. 169–230, at p. 200 presents all the evidence.

[28] Ekkehard, *Casus S. Galli*, ed. H. F. Haefele, *St Galler Klostergeschichten* (vol. 10, Darmstadt, 1980), chap. 6, p. 28. This paragraph follows K. Schmid, 'Brüderschaften mit den Mönchen aus der Sicht des Kaiserbesuchs im Galluskloster vom Jahre 883', in H. Maurer (ed.), *Churrätisches und st. gallisches Mittelalter. Festschrift für Otto P. Clavadetscher zu seinem fünfundsechzigsten Geburtstag* (Sigmaringen, 1984), pp. 173–94; and Zotz, 'Grundlagen und Zentren', p. 290. In general see K. Schmid, 'Von den "Fratres conscripti" in Ekkeharts st. galler Klostergeschichten', *FMSt* 25 (1991), 109–22.

[29] Notker, *Gesta*, 2.8, p. 61.

[30] J. Mabillon, *Vetera Analecta*, 2nd edn (Paris, 1723), p. 427. Its veracity is confirmed by a reference to it in D AC 35. Cf. below, pp. 145–6.

[31] D CIII 92; Schmid, 'Brüderschaften mit den Mönchen', pp. 185–7.

[32] Airlie, *Carolingian Politics* discusses the mechanics of this.

Royal politics and regional power in the Late Carolingian Empire

By fostering his relationship with them, in classic Carolingian fashion, Charles bought into the stock of charismatic religious authority which would help sustain his power throughout the empire.

A third means used by Charles to promote his authority in his home *regnum* is visible in his relationship with local counts. At the palace of Bodman on 1 May 879, a certain Palding passed on land which he had received from Louis the German to the monastery of St-Gall for the *memoria* of that king.[33] Three counts, Adalbert, Udalrich and Hildebold, were present, and the transaction was carried out 'by leave of the lord king Charles'. The use of the royal palace as the venue for the proceedings, and the subsidiary condition that the fisc would reclaim the land should the memorial provisions fall short of requirements, were among the reasons why Charles the Fat's name was invoked in the charter.[34] The charter also highlights how royal palaces like Bodman and monasteries like St-Gall acted as interfaces between kings and local aristocrats. We should not regard these as exceptional circumstances. Already in 876, the same Count Adalbert had acted as Charles's representative in a swap of lands involving the abbey of Rheinau, in which the king had rights.[35] A charter of 878 identifies him as a royal *missus*, while another of 884 endows him with the exalted title of *dilectus comes* ('distinguished count').[36] Hildebold was named as royal *missus* on another occasion under Charles the Fat, and also served Louis the German and Arnulf in this capacity.[37] Udalrich was associated with him in the charter of Louis the German just cited, and was later referred to by Charles as 'our most faithful relative (*nepos*)'.[38] A letter of Bishop Salomon II of Constance surviving from the late 870s refers to a journey he was about to undertake to the see of Strasbourg in the company of Count Udalrich and the abbot of Reichenau.[39] It is not specified that this was a royal mission; the letter is only a rather brisk missive to a lesser functionary. However, the high status of the legates suggest that it was; and we also know that Salomon had had cause to depend on the bishop of Strasbourg's hospitality while on the king's business on at least one other occasion.[40] The three men present as

---

[33] D SG vol. 3 Anhang 8. See Map 2 for the following.

[34] Borst, 'Die Pfalz Bodman', p. 199; H. G. Walther, 'Der Fiskus Bodman', in Berner (ed.) *Bodman*, pp. 231–75, at pp. 255–6; Airlie, 'Palace of Memory', pp. 11–12.

[35] D CIII 1; see K. Schmid, 'Königtum, Adel und Klöster zwischen Bodensee und Schwarzwald (8.–12. Jahrhundert)', in Tellenbach (ed.), *Studien und Vorarbeiten*, pp. 225–334, esp. pp. 231–2, 260–3.

[36] D Zur 132; D CIII 101. Borgolte, *Die Grafen Alemanniens*, p. 27 expresses some doubts about this identification.

[37] D SG 656 (Charles); D SG 557 and D LG 124 (Louis); D Zur 159 (Arnulf). For commentary see Borgolte, *Die Grafen Alemanniens*, p. 143.

[38] D CIII 57; see Borgolte, *Die Grafen Alemanniens*, pp. 255–66.

[39] *Collectio Sangallensis*, ed. Zeumer, no. 36.   [40] *Ibid.*, no. 33.

Kingship and Politics in the Late Ninth Century

royal representatives at Bodman in May 879 were thus close allies of the king.

Men such as these were holders of multiple counties in the Alemannic *regnum*. Udalrich, for instance, as count of the Linzgau, Rheingau and Argengau (this list is not exhaustive) had interests spreading right across the south of the region.[41] Large configurations of *honores* such as these are sometimes considered by scholars, when encountered in the late Carolingian period, to have existed as obstacles to the effective exercise of royal power.[42] However, the decision to empower these aristocrats in this way was taken by a strong king, Louis the German, as part of his drive to intensify royal government in the region during the 850s.[43] The strengthening of comital power was part and parcel of strengthening royal power. Royal fiscal lands passed into comital control not because the aristocracy channelled their acquisitiveness and aggression into anti-royal activities, but because the Carolingians perceived this as a more effective way of exercising authority than dealing directly with the running of estates scattered throughout the *regnum*.[44] Similarly, the fisc near Lake Constance at Untersee was placed in the hands of Count Adalbert during the reign proper of Charles the Fat.[45] Men like Adalbert and Udalrich were not inherently obstructive, but rather represented the emperor in his home kingdom in a manner analogous to that of other powerful local figures like Odo in Neustria. Aristocratic and royal power and control of land were not mutually exclusive. In Alsace, the personal politics pursued by Charles were channelled instead through abbeys controlled by his wife Richgard. Key lands which traditionally belonged to her natal family were employed by the emperor to reward his followers in the region, and to build a new imperial palace at Sélestat (Schlettstadt).[46] Here, as indeed at Stammheim, monastic, royal and aristocratic interests could have a common focus; they did not necessarily cancel each other out.[47]

Charles the Fat's political influence in Alemannia and Alsace was thus conspicuous and personal, articulated through close relatives and advisers

---

[41] Borgolte, *Die Grafen Alemanniens*, pp. 255–66 is the most convenient summary; this is Borgolte's Udalrich IV.

[42] Borgolte, *Geschichte der Grafschaften Alemanniens*, pp. 204–7, 256–8 implies this, as does Borst, 'Die Pfalz Bodman', p. 200.

[43] Borgolte, *Geschichte der Grafschaften Alemanniens*, pp. 245–58 for his findings in summary form.

[44] See *ibid.*, pp. 93–6 for an example of how a fisc could be transferred more or less intact to form a new count's *ex officio* holdings, in this case in the Zurichgau.

[45] D SG 96.

[46] See further below, pp. 186–9; S. MacLean, 'Queenship, Nunneries and Royal Widowhood in Carolingian Europe', *Past and Present* (forthcoming).

[47] See G. Althoff, 'Breisach- ein Refugium für Rebellen im frühen Mittelalter?', in Nuber et al. (eds.), *Archäologie und Geschichte*, pp. 457–72, at p. 469 on Stammheim.

Royal politics and regional power in the Late Carolingian Empire

like Richgard, Udalrich and Liutward.[48] Even the most powerful of the multi-beneficed Alemannic counts invoked royal authority when engaged in pursuing their own affairs. Charles's authority was articulated through more or less the same channels which had been opened up by the more distant figures of Louis the Pious and Louis the German: counts, palaces and royal monasteries. We must now attempt to place these conclusions in a wider political context. Did this make him 'too much' of an Aleman? Could he impose his presence with the same intensity elsewhere in the empire? And if not, what effect did this have on the outcome of his reign?

ITALY

Most of our evidence for Charles the Fat's activities in Alemannia predates 880, something which must be linked to his acquisition of his second kingdom, Italy, after the abdication of his stroke-afflicted brother Karlmann in autumn 879. We have already commented on the role played by Berengar in Friuli, and how this role enabled him to wield influence throughout the Italian kingdom (which comprised only the northern 40 per cent of the peninsula). In chapter 6 we will also discuss the importance of the archchancellor Liutward in mediating royal patronage in the north-west of the *regnum Italiae*. In addition to these arrangements, however, Charles made six trips to Italy himself, spending around half of his reign after 879 in the peninsula and issuing approximately half his charters for Italian recipients. To almost the same extent as Alemannia, Italy was 'his' kingdom.

Nonetheless, his roots did not go very deep. A king who was present half the time was an improvement on the largely absentee transalpine Italian rulers Charles the Bald (875–7) and Karlmann (877–9), but was not a patch on the ever-present Louis II (840–75) whose long reign, still fresh in the memory, had allowed certain members of the Italian aristocracy to build very close connections with the court.[49] The massive wealth of the Italian crown, moreover, was not totally assured. In particular, the conflicts among the aristocracy which characterised the period 875–9 drove kings to buy support more actively. The powerful bishops of the north Italian cities were the most conspicuous beneficiaries. Absentee rulers gave royal sanction to the *de facto* extension of bishops' jurisdiction

---

[48] Note also the case of Gozbert II, named in 886 as an imperial *missus* (D SG 656), for whom Charles intervened to consolidate his position as count around Rheinau: Schmid, 'Königtum, Adel und Klöster', p. 278; Borgolte, *Geschichte der Grafschaften Alemanniens*, p. 255.

[49] F. Bougard, 'La cour et le gouvernement de Louis II (840–875)', in Le Jan (ed.), *La Royauté et les élites*, pp. 249–67.

91

Kingship and Politics in the Late Ninth Century

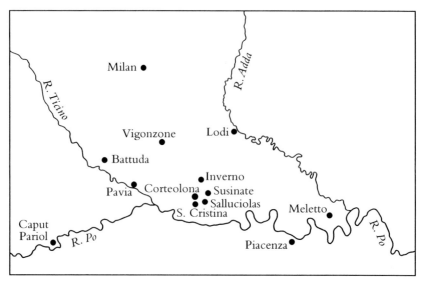

Map 3. Landholding around Pavia

and authority beyond the walls of their cities beginning with a grant to Wibod of Parma by Karlmann and continuing, albeit at a slow rate, into the tenth century.[50] Accordingly, kings began to voice concern that the demands of powerful (especially ecclesiastical) lords were beginning to encroach on the duties traditionally owed by the free to the crown.[51] In addition, many key fiscal estates had come into the control of the widowed empress Engelberga.[52] In the context of these subtle changes to the Italian political landscape, and for a king who was often absent, the maintenance of good relations with key power-brokers like Engelberga, Wibod and Berengar, who were leaders of important political factions in the 870s, was essential to the wielding of effective royal power in Italy. We may read their position as emblematic of Italian political structures in the 880s.

Charles the Fat issued several charters for each of these individuals and their followers, showing that he actively sought to create and renew

---

[50] D K 24; D CIII 78; Bougard, *La Justice*, pp. 198–203, 253–69. Note that, as Bougard shows, the grants of *districtio*, although originating in the late Carolingian period, only developed into a significant problem for kings in the post-Carolingian era.

[51] DD CIII 49–53; MGH Capit, vol. 2, no. 224, chaps. 3, 5 (Guy of Spoleto); Tabacco, *I Liberi del re*, pp. 51–2, 72.

[52] See D Crem 20; C. La Rocca, 'Les cadeaux nuptiaux de la famille royale en Italie' (forthcoming). I am grateful to Professor La Rocca for sending me a copy of this article in advance of publication.

Royal politics and regional power in the Late Carolingian Empire

alliances with them.[53] One context for understanding how these bonds were maintained on a less formal basis lies in the pattern of landholdings around the city of Pavia, the former Lombard capital.[54] Although under the Carolingians the city was still the most frequently utilised royal centre, members of the dynasty were more inclined than their Lombard predecessors to stay at rural estates and palaces. Pavia lost its exclusivity, and it was the venue for not a single Carolingian inauguration ceremony or funeral.[55] In the eyes of Charles the Fat, however, the town seems once again to have regained something of its former status. Pavia was the planned setting for his royal coronation, although in the end he had to settle for Ravenna.[56] It was also by far his favourite residence: he stayed there ten times, almost as often as Louis II did during his much longer reign, and five times as often as his next most frequented city.[57] Pavia was also given the epithet 'palatium' no less than five times in Charles's charters, more often than any other place in his empire, and the only such in Italy. This term was used figuratively in Carolingian political discourse, and in this context denoted a place of special royal significance rather than an actual building.[58] Finally, under Charles the administration of royal justice, which was focused on Pavia, appears to have been overhauled.[59] By taking an active role in the prominent legal life of the realm, Charles conformed to the traditions of kingship expected in the *regnum Italiae*.

We can illustrate the emperor's political interests by focusing on a set of properties in the vicinity of Olona (today Corteolona), the rural palace lying about 15 km east of Pavia, which can be closely associated with Charles's alliance-building. Corteolona was one of the emperor's favourite residences, and he used it as rural retreat while staying at Pavia. It lay in good hunting country, and was also the centre of one of the most extensive royal fiscs in the kingdom, stretching east from Pavia as far as the River Adda.[60] The royal monastery of S Cristina, which lay adjacent to

---

[53] DD CIII 15, 22, 32, 33, 36, 37, 56, 115, 126, 156, 166, 171.

[54] For the following, see Map 3.

[55] For details see G. Arnaldi, 'Pavia e il *Regnum Italiae* dal 774 al 1024', *Atti del 4 congresso internazionale di studi sull'alto medioevo* (Spoleto, 1969), pp. 175–87; C. Brühl, 'Das Palatium von Pavia und die *Honorantiae civitatis Papiae*', *Atti del 4 congresso*, pp. 189–220; Brühl, *Fodrum, Gistum, Servitium Regis*, pp. 369–425; F. Bougard, 'Palais princiers, royaux et imperiaux de l'Italie carolingienne et ottonienne', in Renoux (ed.), *Palais royaux et princiers*, pp. 181–94.

[56] *Registrum*, ed. Caspar, nos. 233–4.

[57] Brühl, *Fodrum, Gistum, Serbitium Regis*, pp. 401–6 gives statistics for each reign.

[58] T. Zotz, '*Palatium et curtis*. Aspects de la terminologie palatiale au moyen age', in Renoux (ed.), *Palais royaux et princiers*, pp. 7–15.

[59] Bougard, *La Justice*, pp. 275–96, 312–14.

[60] P. Darmstädter, *Das Reichsgut in der Lombardei und Piemont (568–1250)* (Strasbourg, 1896), pp. 189–90.

the central royal *villa* at Olona, is reported to have been a focus for royal patronage throughout the ninth century, but the first surviving charter in its favour was issued by Karlmann in 879.[61] Early in 880, Charles the Fat confirmed the monastery's rights and properties and made provision in return for the monks to pray for him, his family and his realm.[62] Just over a year later, he gave three holdings in a place called Susinate near Olona, which was associated with a royal forest, to a certain chaplain called Peter, who was an important figure in the entourage of Berengar of Friuli: after 888 he would serve as archchancellor and bishop of Padua, but he was acting as his lord's chaplain already in the early 880s.[63] Interestingly, this grant was made out of the lands of S Cristina, and indeed probably from the same property given to the monastery by Karlmann two years earlier.

This charter provides a good example of how kings were able to exploit royal monasteries, using their properties (especially those which had been granted from the fisc) as a fund of potential largesse with which to reward supporters. Such lands were therefore not simply 'lost' to the crown once they became part of ecclesiastical patrimonies. A second grant of this kind was made by Charles from the lands of S Cristina; this time part of the estates of Caput Pariol and Salluciolas were given to Bishop Wibod of Parma.[64] Salluciolas was an extensive property about 5 km from Corteolona, right next door to Susinate where Berengar's chaplain was endowed. Although the exact date of the lost charter relating this grant is unknown, we do know that less than a fortnight before Peter received his houses in Susinate Wibod was also granted three *mansi* in the estate of Vigonzone, which pertained to the royal palace at Corteolona, and lay about 14 km north of the palace.[65] Only 4 km north of Olona lay Inverno, an estate which was held by the empress Engelberga.[66] Finally in this complex of estates there lay the forest of Meletto, which was granted to Engelberga's proprietary foundation of S Sisto in Piacenza by Karlmann, in association with papal legates, shortly before his abdication in 879.[67] Meletto, although around 30 km east of the palace, was an appurtenance of Salluciolas, Wibod's property.[68]

The proximity to and interrelationships of these lands with each other, and with the important royal palace and church at Corteolona, are no

---

[61] D K 21.   [62] D CIII 20.   [63] D CIII 37.

[64] J. Lechner, 'Verlorene Urkunden', in J. F. Böhmer and E. Mühlbacher, *Regesta Imperii. Die Regesten des Kaiserreichs unter den Karolingern, 751–918* (Innsbruck, 1908), no. 584 (= D AC 125); Wibod later passed this land on to the possession of his church of S Nicomedes in Fontana Broccola west of Parma, as shown by D BF 26.

[65] D CIII 36. Darmstädter, *Das Reichsgut in der Lombardei*, p. 192.

[66] D L2 45; D Loth2 29. She later gave it to her abbey of S Sisto: D CIII 56.

[67] CDL 286, which shows that the wood was included in the grant D K 27.

[68] As revealed by D BF 36; Darmstädter, *Das Reichsgut in der Lombardei*, pp. 191–2.

Royal politics and regional power in the Late Carolingian Empire

coincidence. Although it was not atypical for aristocratic properties to cluster in the vicinity of royal estates, here we can see this process being deliberately set in motion by a king at the start of his reign.[69] At almost exactly the same time in early 881, the chief adviser of Berengar of Friuli and Wibod, the main power-broker in Emilia, two of the figures who had played crucial political roles after Louis II's death, were granted small properties in the hinterland of one of the new emperor's favourite residences.[70] It was no accident that this was an area in which the empress Engelberga, another such pivotal individual, was also well endowed. These grants reflect Charles's careful use of patronage to cement the political alliances on which his rule depended. Olona was where the emperor relaxed while not conducting business in Pavia.[71] It is probable that these grants to important individuals were intended as country residences for the likes of Wibod and Berengar to use while conferring with the king in similar situations, perhaps to do business in advance of events like the major royal assembly held at Pavia in 886. This was excellent hunting country: Meletto in particular seems to have been something of a game reserve, and other royal forests in the area, such as Battuda near Pavia, fulfilled a similar function.[72] Hunting was a primary aristocratic activity, and one which was used by kings to create a sense of solidarity between them and their nobles.[73] This is a concrete example of how grants of land were used by Charles the Fat to maintain the networks of alliances among the high aristocracy which had been reactivated during his reign after a period of discord in the late 870s.[74]

The function of the estate of Corteolona and the royal monastery of S Cristina as focal points for this set of associations highlights again the potential of royal properties to act as pivots articulating the contours of royal–aristocratic relationships. Did these particular relationships have any measurable effect? We may see them at work already in a charter of March 881, issued at Pavia for Wibod on the intervention of Berengar.[75] It is also demonstrable that Charles's relationship with Engelberga brought him tangible benefits: her stock of former fiscal estates was made available

---

[69] For similar patterns in Lotharingia, see Airlie, 'Political Behaviour of Secular Magnates', p. 198.

[70] See Delogu, 'Vescovi, conti e sovrani' for their political activities at this time.

[71] *AF(B)* s.a. 886, p. 114. D CIII 55 may have been issued on this occasion, despite Kehr's doubts.

[72] Darmstädter, *Das Reichsgut in der Lombardei*, p. 189.

[73] Nelson, 'Carolingian Royal Ritual'; J. Jarnut, 'Die frühmittelalterliche Jagd unter rechts- und sozialgeschichtlichen Aspekten', *Settimane* 31 (1985), 765–808.

[74] For further examples of adjacent holdings of important aristocrats in the area between Pavia and Parma see R. Schumann, *Authority and the Commune. Parma, 833–1133* (Parma, 1973), pp. 92–3, 103–4. Engelberga was the key to these arrangements, given that she had pre-existing associations with Inverno and S Cristina: *Registrum*, ed. Caspar, no. 243; D CIII 166.

[75] D CIII 32.

for use as a source of patronage for imperial agents, and there was also an overlap between the entourages of the emperor and the former empress.[76] Likewise, we have charters which show that Charles was able to intervene directly in Friuli, with Berengar's approval.[77]

The density of imperial authority in the 880s tended to shade out, however, the further south it extended from the traditional royal heartlands of the Po valley. Whereas a king like Louis II had harboured serious (though ultimately fruitless) ambitions in the south of the peninsula, Charles the Fat's influence even in central Italy was only as good as his unstable relationship with the *duces* of Spoleto. Only when Guy of Spoleto was in a state of open rebellion in summer 883 did the emperor experience fleeting success in central Italian affairs, sending in a military force under Berengar and trying to establish relationships with the most influential ecclesiastical institutions in the area.[78] Guy himself was one of the *reguli*, later becoming king of Italy and emperor. His career of opportunistic resistance to Carolingian authority shows that there was indeed scope in the later ninth century for well-placed aristocrats to build up their own power in the absence of a nearby royal presence, at least in semi-detached peripheral regions like Spoleto. Late Carolingian politics was not, therefore, necessarily built on smooth cooperation between centre and locality: such cooperation was always hard-won, constantly renewed and potentially unstable. Guy's successful but turbulent career demonstrates that, while a good political relationship with the king (as in the case of Berengar) was one important route to establishing a platform of local power, it was not the only way. Guy's nurturing of a strong regional network of supporters in Spoleto was built as much on his family's historical influence in the area and their interaction with the papacy and the southern duchies as on his relationship with the kings in the north, and was invaluable in sustaining his bid for royal power in 888–9.[79]

The kind of long-distance political influence attempted in Spoleto was necessarily different, therefore, from the more personal politics constructed by the emperor in the north. In the Carolingian *regnum Italiae* Charles ruled through the deployment of patronage, but backed this up with a regular presence and personal association with the leading men and women of the realm.[80]

---

[76] See MacLean, 'Queenship, Nunneries and Royal Widowhood'. [77] DD CIII 48–9.

[78] *AF(B)* s.a. 883, p. 110; DD CIII 82–4. On the significance of Casauria, one of the churches involved, see L. Feller, 'Aristocratie, monde monastique et pouvoir en Italie centrale au IXe siècle', in Le Jan (ed.), *La Royauté et les élites*, pp. 325–45, at pp. 326–8, 342–3. For the wider context see E. Hlawitschka, 'Die Widonen im Dukat von Spoleto', *QFIAB* 63 (1983), 20–92.

[79] See above all Hlawitschka, 'Die Widonen im Dukat von Spoleto'.

[80] The Olona region represents only one facet of these patronage networks: I intend to publish elsewhere a fuller study of Italian politics in this period.

Royal politics and regional power in the Late Carolingian Empire

FRANCONIA, SAXONY AND BAVARIA

Charles the Fat's progress to assume rule in the remaining parts of the east Frankish kingdom looks almost leisurely in comparison to his usual rapid itineration around the empire. Although his predecessor here, his brother Louis the Younger, died in January 882, Charles did not leave Italy until the end of April and, after passing through Bavaria, did not hold a general assembly with the leading men of his new realms until May in Worms. Worms was a significant choice: along with Mainz and Speyer it formed an urban focus for the important complex of royal estates on the left bank of the middle Rhine, control of which had been one of the main objects of the civil wars of 840–3. The profusion of public cities, rich monasteries and royal estates made it one of the central places of the east Frankish kingdom, along with similarly well-endowed regions of Bavaria. Charles's languid pace in taking the reins in May 882 seems not to have caused him problems: immediately thereafter he set off to fight the Vikings at Asselt accompanied by an army drawn from all over the empire, and co-led by Henry, Louis the Younger's main general.

Louis's reign (876–82) habituated the elites of Franconia and Saxony to nearby kingship, and his presence seems to have had a lasting effect, binding these two *regna* closely together in the mental landscape of the east Frankish political community.[81] It was the configuration of Saxon nobles at Louis's Franconian court which provided the springboard for the emergence of the Ottonian dynasty after 919.[82] These regions were not, however, intensively governed by Charles the Fat, who only visited traditional centres of Carolingian rule like Frankfurt for political set-pieces connected with the succession, when he wished to emphasise particular points to the influential elite of the middle Rhine.[83] The elite, led by the powerful Archbishop Liutbert of Mainz who had been right-hand man to Charles's father and brother, had a strong sense of its own traditional importance in east Frankish politics.[84] These sentiments were, as we saw in chapter 2, reflected in the polemical Mainz continuation of the *Annals of Fulda* produced in Liutbert's circle at this time.[85] However, when the archbishop regained his coveted post of archchaplain in mid-887, the tone of these annals shifted towards approval of the emperor.

---

[81] As debated by the following: J. Semmler, '*Francia Saxoniaque* oder die ostfränkische Reichsteilung von 865/76 und die Folgen', *DA* 46 (1990), 337–74; W. Eggert, '"Franken und Sachsen" bei Notker, Widukind und Anderen. Zu einem Aufsatz von Josef Semmler', in Scharer and Scheibelreiter (eds.), *Historiographie im frühen Mittelalter*, pp. 514–30; Becher, *Rex, Dux und Gens*, pp. 132–58.

[82] Fried, *Ludwig der Jüngere*, pp. 12–13; Becher, *Rex, Dux und Gens*, pp. 66–108.

[83] See below, pp. 151–2.

[84] On the regional significance of the archbishops of Mainz, see Eibl, 'Zur Stellung Bayerns', p. 105.

[85] See also Innes, *State and Society*, pp. 223–4.

Kingship and Politics in the Late Ninth Century

The antagonisms felt by Liutbert's network of allies was not a reflection of Franconian disgruntlement *per se*; the issue was access to court. Up until this point, there is little evidence for Charles's direct intervention in Franconia.[86] Once Liutbert had regained his position at court the problem of Franconia's loss of status under Charles was diminished. This kind of patronage of significant regional leaders could bridge distances between political centre and periphery, siphoning tension out of the system.

Saxony itself was far less intensively governed than Franconia. Throughout the Carolingian period it remained comparatively poor as far as royal properties and churches were concerned.[87] Louis the German's itineration through the region in 852 stands alone as evidence for his direct interference in Saxon affairs.[88] In the reign of Charles the Fat, disputes between members of the Saxon–Thuringian aristocracy appear to have carried on more or less independently.[89] Nevertheless, the military leader Henry, whose family was closely involved in these conflicts, remained a royal stalwart. Charters confirming privileges enjoyed by the monastery of Korvey and the church of Paderborn are the only indications of direct royal intervention in local politics.[90] One of these documents, however, implies that Charles was entitled to expect extraordinary military support from Korvey in times of emergency; and it has been suggested that his association with the house gained him permanent commemoration as one of the figures carved into the church's new westwork.[91] Similarly, we have already met the Saxon Poet, whose work written in the late 880s reveals a sturdy sense of identification with the Carolingian dynasty which had, a century earlier and with some brutality, brought Christianity to the region.[92] Again, although here the contours of royal influence are largely hidden, physical royal presence does not seem to have been an absolute prerequisite of effective political authority.

Charles the Fat loomed larger in Bavaria, which he visited three times during his reign, once as we have seen en route to Worms in 882, and again in 884 and 886, occasions which will be discussed more fully in the next chapter. He pushed the expected royal buttons in the *regnum*, for instance by favouring important churches round Regensburg,

---

[86] DD CIII 65, 66, 70.

[87] C. Carroll, 'The Bishoprics of Saxony in the First Century after Christianization', *EME* 8 (1999), 219–45. See also E. J. Goldberg, 'Popular Revolt, Dynastic Politics and Aristocratic Factionalism in the Early Middle Ages: the Saxon *Stellinga* Reconsidered', *Speculum* 70 (1995), 467–501.

[88] *AF* s.a. 852, pp. 42–3; Reuter, *Germany in the Early Middle Ages*, pp. 84–9.

[89] *AF(B)* s.a. 883, p. 110. See Becher, *Rex, Dux und Gens*, pp. 159–65.

[90] DD CIII 62, 131, 158, 168, 169.

[91] D CIII 158; Fried, *Der Weg in die Geschichte*, pp. 420–1.   [92] See above, p. 63.

Royal politics and regional power in the Late Carolingian Empire

and could count at least one Bavarian among his otherwise exclusively Alemannic entourage. Recent research by Geneviève Bührer-Thierry has drawn attention to the fact that the eleven charters issued by Charles the Fat for Bavarian recipients, a not inconsiderable number in view of the length of his reign there, all share the anomaly of having been promulgated without mention of intercessors.[93] She argues convincingly on the basis of this evidence that Charles dealt directly with Bavaria's high ecclesiastics, who were the charters' chief beneficiaries and who formed a self-contained group which rarely influenced events in other *regna*. The emperor, moreover, proved more than capable of intervening decisively in this episcopal circle, as shown in 884 when he installed the royal notary Waldo in the see of Freising, a position normally monopolised by a powerful local aristocratic family.[94] The distinctiveness of Bavaria's political elite, also evident earlier in the time of Louis the German and later under the Ottonians, was thus recognised by the emperor.[95] Bavaria's traditions as a Carolingian heartland were thus sustained, even if the emperor spent less time there than his predecessors. Bavaria did provide a constituency for the architect of Charles's downfall, Arnulf. However, as we shall see in the next chapter, this event was not a straightforward expression of Bavarian alienation from the centre of power. Rather, it shows us that such sentiments can only be understood when it is appreciated how they interacted with political developments within the configuration of the ruling dynasty.

WEST FRANCIA

The political elites of the west Frankish realm were perhaps those with most to lose from the retreat of royal authority to distant lands across the Rhine. The natural centre of gravity of Carolingian politics had always lain between the Loire and the Meuse, and the aristocracies of these regions had more cause than most to object to the rule of an emperor more likely to spend his time in the Black Forest or Po valley than his family's traditional bases in the north of France and the Low Countries. We have already seen how Charles's relationship with Odo of Paris went some way towards dissipating the resentments to which

---

[93] G. Bührer-Thierry, 'Les évêques de Bavière et d'Alémanie dans l'entourage des derniers rois carolingiens en Germanie (876–911)', *Francia* 16 (1989), 31–52, at 37–40, where she lists only ten charters, omitting D CIII 59 for the monastery of Metten, although this does not negatively affect her argument.

[94] Bührer-Thierry, 'Les évêques de Bavière', pp. 39–40. See also her *Évêques et pouvoir dans le royaume de Germanie. Les Églises de Bavière et de Souabe, 876–973* (Paris, 1997).

[95] Fried, 'The Frankish Kingdoms', pp. 148–9; Hoffmann, 'Grafschaften in Bischofshand', p. 378.

99

Kingship and Politics in the Late Ninth Century

this situation gave birth. Here, on the other hand, we turn to the success or otherwise of the emperor's attempts to associate himself with lesser members of the west Frankish nobility and hence to buy into traditions of west Frankish kingship which would support and legitimise his control of the realm. The emperor was not a total newcomer in the west; his role there in the various toings and froings of the tense dynastic diplomacy of the 870s ensured that he was by no means without contacts west of the Rhine. However, the germane criticism has been made that Charles was 'lacking a personal network of support in western Francia'.[96]

Contemporary authors were somewhat more optimistic than modern historians on the question of Charles's supporters in the west. The St-Vaast annalist said that he was attended at his inaugural assembly in summer 885 at Ponthion by 'all those who were in the kingdom of Carloman [II]'.[97] Across the Channel from the monastery of St-Vaast, the royal biographer Asser, informed as ever on continental affairs, believed that Charles had taken over 'by universal acclamation'.[98] On the face of it, it looks as if the monk of St-Vaast and the bishop of Sherborne probably exaggerated in order to promote an idealised image of a united community of aristocracy and ruler. Although Charles may have had good reasons for the brevity of his stay in the west on the occasion of his accession, it is conspicuous that the range of beneficiaries of imperial charters around this time is limited, confined to recipients in the eastern part of the *regnum Karlomanni*.

On the other hand, the negative opinion of modern historiography is pitched too far towards the other extreme. A remarkable thirty of the sixty-four charters of Charles which survive as originals went to western recipients, a number out of all proportion with the length of his reign there.[99] Even allowing for accidents of survival, this shows that western institutions were eager to obtain and careful to preserve the memory of his favour, and while Charles only travelled west twice, the willingness of west Frankish magnates to visit the court in the east is attested on a number of occasions.[100] The geographical extent of the charters he issued was broad, and they were particularly numerous for recipients in Neustria, Francia proper and Burgundy. Although no recipients from Provence proper are recorded, Charles did grant properties in that *regnum*, and coins bearing his name have been unearthed from mints at Marseille

---

[96] Nelson, *Charles the Bald*, p. 256.   [97] *AV* s.a. 885, p. 56.

[98] Asser, *De Rebus*, chap. 70, p. 52 (as rendered by S. Keynes and M. Lapidge, *Alfred the Great* (London, 1983), p. 87).

[99] K. F. Werner, *Les Origines (avant l'an mil)* (Paris, 1984), p. 420.

[100] E.g. DD CIII 160 and 161, issued at Kirchen for Odo of Paris.

Royal politics and regional power in the Late Carolingian Empire

and Arles.[101] The only area which does not figure in the standard MGH edition of the royal charters is the bulk of Aquitaine, south of a line between the Loire and Nevers, and west of the Rhône. This, however, may be in part due to the vagaries of survival, since we do know from a later charter of Odo that Charles provided a confirmation at some point for the canons of the church of Clermont.[102]

As well as noting that most of the major ecclesiastical institutions of the kingdom benefited in this way from Charles's reign, it is also worth observing that his actual itinerary in west Francia on both visits was very limited, confined to the east (his inauguration) in 885 and the north (the siege of Paris) in 886, showing that church representatives came vast distances to gain access to his ear. This is especially noticeable during the Paris campaign in the second half of 886. The run of charters issued here, which must partly be seen as rewards to those who had brought help, give us a glimpse into the composition of the army. This martial element is reflected in the unusual references to charters being issued 'with the counsel of our *principes* [leading men]'.[103] Contingents from Nevers, Tours, Auxerre, Orléans, Langres and Troyes were certainly present.[104] Certain individual *fideles*, possibly military leaders, were rewarded in Bar, Chartres and Sens.[105] Most far-travelled was the company of Bishop Teotarius of Gerona. He clearly thought it worth the journey to obtain a detailed imperial confirmation, which ordered the people on the church's lands to obey the bishop as if he were a *comes* ('companion') of the emperor.[106]

This evidence shows that Charles did have a political network of support from which, whether or not it can be characterised as 'personal', he was able to benefit on this occasion. The royal court, we can see, was still a pivotal institution for forming and maintaining such networks. In addition to revealing this broad picture, the sources allow us to focus more closely on some of the details of the aristocratic groups of the west in 885–7, how they related to each other and how they operated, and to place them in a context of royal service throughout the 870s and 880s.

---

[101] D CIII 162; 13 of 20 coins found from Arles and Marseille from the period between 840 and 900 were of Charles the Fat (1 of Charles the Bald, 4 of Carloman II, 2 of Louis of Provence): see J.-P. Poly, *La Provence et la société féodale (879–1166). Contribution à l'étude des structures dites féodales dans le Midi* (Paris, 1976), pp. 233–4. D CIII 123 was issued for the church of Lyon, which had been politically connected to Provence proper since Boso's revolt, if not before.

[102] D OP 49.   [103] DD CIII 145, 147. Cf. DD 137a, 138.

[104] DD CIII 138, 139, 143, 145–7.   [105] DD CIII 137, 142, 144.

[106] D CIII 148. The bishops of Gerona had also assisted the Carolingian efforts against Boso: R.-H. Bautier, 'Aux origines du royaume de Provence: de la sédition avortée de Boson à la royauté légitime de Louis', *Provence historique* 23 (1973), 41–68, at 60. Reprinted in R.-H. Bautier, *Recherches sur l'histoire de la France médiévale. Des Mérovingiens aux premier Capétiens* (Aldershot, 1991); D C2 63.

Kingship and Politics in the Late Ninth Century

This will be the subject of the remainder of this chapter, which seeks to establish the nature of Charles's influence in west Francia and to assess its effectiveness. It will become apparent that the answer to this question lies somewhere in between the two polarised opinions of contemporaries (that Charles's support was extensive) and historians (that it was negligible).

THE NORTH FRANKISH CIRCLE

West Frankish royal politics in the 870s and 880s developed at a bewildering rate. The long reign of Charles the Bald ended in 877, but it was the death in 879 of his short-lived son Louis the Stammerer which created greater friction within the kingdom. Two aristocratic factions struggled to control Louis's young sons, one attempting to force through the sole succession of the elder, Louis III, and the other pushing for a division of the realm between Louis and his brother Carloman II. The outcome, after months of tense negotiations which were complicated by the threat of military intervention from yet another Louis (the Younger, of east Francia), was settled in favour of a division, thereby assuring both aristocratic parties of access to *Königsnähe*.[107] From spring 880 until August 882, Louis III served as king of Francia and Neustria, while Carloman II ruled Burgundy and Aquitaine. After the premature death of Louis in that month, Carloman took over as king of the entire western kingdom until December 884, when he too died at an unexpectedly young age. At this point, with the number of available adult male Carolingians having dwindled to one, the west Franks turned east to invite Charles the Fat to take over. The St-Vaast annalist tells us that a Count Theoderic was sent on behalf of the 'Franks' (*Franci*) to find Charles in Italy. In this section we shall attempt to identify these *Franci*, the core of the nobility who supported the emperor's rule in the west. As we shall see, they were a distinct group of magnates based in the Paris region whose political identity was defined by their experience of royal service, especially in defence against the Vikings.

Theoderic, who is often confused in the secondary literature with his namesake 'the Chamberlain', count of Autun, has been convincingly identified by Werner as the count of Vermandois and lay abbot of the monasteries of St-Quentin and Morienval.[108] Some background is necessary in order to put his position in the reign of Charles the Fat

---

[107] Werner, 'Gauzlin von Saint-Denis' is the best exposition of these events.
[108] Werner, 'Untersuchungen v', p. 102 with n. 59; Werner, 'Gauzlin von Saint-Denis', p. 446 with n. 150a. Theoderic the Chamberlain was already dead at this point.

Royal politics and regional power in the Late Carolingian Empire

into context. Theoderic and his associate Abbot Gauzlin of St-Denis were among the most influential men at the court of Louis III, and as such Karl-Ferdinand Werner has discussed this pair as the centre of the most important group of aristocrats in northern France in the early 880s.[109] Their circle had been heavily involved in the succession disputes of 879–80 as leading members of the party which had sought a division of the kingdom. Their opponents, who sought sole rule for Louis III, were led by Hugh 'the Abbot' (of St-Martin in Tours), who eventually became the main adviser of Carloman II. Theoderic, meanwhile, became one of Louis's military commanders against the Vikings. His political position enabled him to intervene in a high-profile dispute between the king and archbishop of Rheims over the episcopal vacancy at Noyon, which was the central place of his county.[110] After Louis died in summer 882, Theoderic maintained a high position at court, since it was on his advice that Carloman reorganised defence of a bridge at Châlons-sur-Marne to help defend the kingdom 'from the infestation of the pagans'.[111] Theoderic may well have been influential in persuading the king to return Gauzlin to the fullness of royal favour after the troubles of 879–80, which he did in 883 as bishop of Paris.[112]

When Carloman died after a hunting accident in winter 884, this same group of aristocrats was at the king's deathbed to take the initiative. Robert-Henri Bautier has shown that Gauzlin was on hand to orchestrate the burial of the young king next to his unfortunate brother at St-Denis, and that it was he who attended to his last wishes.[113] From here it is likely that he and Theoderic gained access to the west Frankish regalia to send out to Charles the Fat.[114] Gauzlin already had some political links to the eastern branch of the Carolingian family. He had been held hostage at the court of Louis the Younger after the battle of Andernach in 876 and had made friendly contacts there.[115] These were doubtless put to good use during the negotiations with Louis preceding the Treaty of Fouron in 878, in which Gauzlin was heavily involved, and during the troubles of 879, when he invited Louis to intervene in the west.[116] Gauzlin's subsequent importance in the reign of Charles the Fat is well attested in the sources. At the siege of Paris he was prominent, and in Abbo's poem it is he who is given the most striking speech concerning the emperor's

---

[109] Werner, 'Gauzlin von Saint-Denis', pp. 441–50.
[110] *AB* s.a. 882, p. 246; D L3 46; Werner, 'Gauzlin von Saint-Denis', pp. 445–6. [111] D C2 76.
[112] D C2 90 shows Theoderic's connections to the bishopric of Paris and the court in general.
[113] Bautier's introduction to DD C2, pp. lv–lvi, lxiv; also D 79 and comments there.
[114] See below, p. 125. [115] *AB* s.a. 879, pp. 235–6.
[116] Note also that these eastern links may have gone back through several decades: in 854, Louis the Younger had been invited to invade by a group, the 'cognatio Gauzberti', who may have been Gauzlin's close relations. *AF* s.a. 854, p. 44; Werner, 'Bedeutende Adelsfamilien', pp. 138–9.

Kingship and Politics in the Late Ninth Century

qualities.[117] The *dux* Ragnoldus who rose to prominence with a short-lived stint as the main military commander in the west after the apparent retirement of Hugh the Abbot may have been a relative of Gauzlin.[118] In addition, just before leaving Paris in 886, Charles issued a charter for the monastery of St-Maur-des-Fossés, which included such extensive privileges as free election of abbots, empire-wide toll freedom for the monks, exemption from military service and confirmation of possession of the cell of Glanfeuil, where the community had been established, where Gauzlin had been an oblate and where its founder Roric, Gauzlin's father, was buried. The charter also requested prayers to be said for Charles, his family and the *stabilitas regni*. This unusually generous imperial privilege to the main monastery of Gauzlin's family (sometimes called the 'Rorgonids' in historiographical shorthand), a proprietary family church *par excellence*, can be seen as a sign of the gratitude which the emperor felt towards the late Gauzlin, who had been one of his chief commanders in the siege of Paris.[119] Theoderic and Gauzlin, therefore, were important figures at all the west Frankish courts of the 870s and 880s.

In his attempt to destroy an older historiographical tradition which ascribed to Hugh the Abbot total dominance of Carolingian politics between 877 and 886, Werner perhaps went too far by suggesting that Hugh was eclipsed by Gauzlin towards the end of his life.[120] One reason for this view is the repeated insistence in the literature that the family to which Hugh belonged (known as the 'Welfs') were implacably opposed to those of Gauzlin (the 'Rorgonids') and Odo (the 'Robertians').[121] However, in the light of more recent research, this now appears to be a potentially misleading method of characterising aristocratic relationships. It is clear, for example, that political circumstances could easily supersede family loyalties, and that the two things were far from identical. An obvious example is the political alliance of the Welf Conrad with Gauzlin in the struggles of 879. There is thus no obstacle to our seeing Hugh, a man with important and extensive political connections in the west, as an ally of Gauzlin and high servant of Charles after 885. If Gauzlin had been on

---

[117] Abbo, *Bella*, I, 48–52, p. 18.

[118] *AV* s.a. 885, p. 57; Werner, 'Bedeutende Adelsfamilien', p. 142; Werner, 'Gauzlin von Saint-Denis', pp. 457–9.

[119] D CIII 149; note that at the same time Charles may have made a concession to St-Germain-des-Prés, another house closely connected to Gauzlin. Gauzlin and other members of his family were also commemorated at Reichenau, with which Charles had close links; see O. G. Oexle, 'Bischof Ebroin von Poitiers und seine Verwandten', *FMSt* 3 (1969), 138–210, esp. 168–81.

[120] E.g. Werner, 'Gauzlin von Saint-Denis', p. 455; Werner, 'Les Robertiens', p. 20.

[121] Werner, 'Bedeutende Adelsfamilien', p. 140; Werner, 'Gauzlin von Saint-Denis', pp. 417–22. I use these clan names advisedly, and purely for convenience.

104

Royal politics and regional power in the Late Carolingian Empire

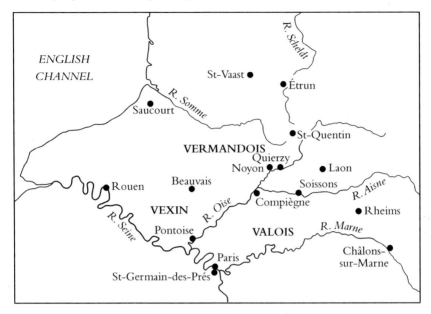

Map 4. Northern Francia

hand at St-Denis to organise the burial of Carloman and the invitation to Charles, it was Hugh who led the negotiations with the Vikings in the meantime.[122] As we have seen, Hugh's nephew Rudolf of Burgundy was an important imperial *marchio* and had been involved in facilitating the journey of Charles to assume the west Frankish crown in 885. Hugh appears posthumously in a number of Charles the Fat's charters, on one occasion even in terms of his gift getting an imperial confirmation, something which cannot be said of Gauzlin.[123] And when they died within weeks of each other in the spring of 886, an east Frankish author described both Hugh and Gauzlin together as 'leading generals of Gaul, in whom lay all hope of the Gauls against the Northmen'.[124] If by the time Carloman was laid to rest the scars of 879 were beginning to heal and some sort of equilibrium had been achieved between the interests of the Gauzlin-Theoderic party and the supporters of Hugh the Abbot,[125] the west Frankish reign of Charles the Fat helped the old antagonisms to be forgotten almost completely.

As well as Gauzlin and Hugh, Theoderic of Vermandois can also be shown to have figured prominently in the active service of the new

---

[122] Regino, *Chronicon*, s.a. 884, p. 122.   [123] DD CIII 143, 145, 161.
[124] *AF(M)* s.a. 886, p. 104.   [125] Werner, 'Gauzlin von Saint-Denis', p. 455.

ruler.[126] We know he was lay abbot of St-Quentin during the reign, since a chronicle fragment records that he improved the monastery walls in 886.[127] This was an important post in Carolingian politics; it had been held by as distinguished a figure as Louis the Pious's brother Hugh, it had been given special consideration in the Treaty of Verdun in being allowed to stay in the west Frankish kingdom, and more recently it (and presumably its abbot, Theoderic) had hosted the definitive negotiations between Gauzlin, Hugh and Louis the Younger in 880.[128] Theoderic also interceded with Carloman II for his proprietary monastery of Morienval: the fact that he did so as 'count and abbot' suggests that he also controlled the county of Valois, in which that monastery lay.[129]

Theoderic also formed a key part of Charles the Fat's defence against the Vikings, as he had Louis III's. In this endeavour he was joined by his brother. Abbo tells us that in the course of the siege of Paris a notable victory was won against the enemy, 3,000 of whom were killed by only 600 defenders: 'And renown had it that the triumphant men had as their leaders two united brothers, Theoderic and Aletramnus.'[130] Aletramnus himself was a man of no mean standing, the count not only of Beauvais but also Laon and Vexin. The battle mentioned by Abbo was not his first participation in the struggle with the Vikings: in 885 he was sent by the emperor to construct a fortification at Pontoise as a first line of defence against the approaching Northmen. The concentration of a sweep of important counties and monasteries in the hands of Theoderic and Aletramnus in a semicircle to the north of Paris made them key players in the region and placed them well to lead the defence of the city.[131] Abbo strongly implies that the 600 soldiers commanded by the brothers were the same 600 imperial troops who had just been sent to Paris by Charles the Fat.[132] The evidence therefore clearly suggests that the two were designated as leaders of the imperial defence of west Francia, and the Seine-Oise area in particular.

These defensive arrangements, that is the setting up of a block of *honores* north of Paris as a means of defending the Seine-Oise area, was picked up and continued in the 890s by Odo, who placed the command in the hands

---

[126] For the following, see Map 4.

[127] *Sermo in tumulatione SS. Quintini, Victorici, Cassiani*, ed. O. Holder-Egger, MGH SS 15 (Hanover, 1887), pp. 271–3.

[128] *AV* s.a. 880, p. 46.

[129] D C2 90; P. Grierson, 'L'origine des comtes d'Amiens, Valois et Vexin', *Le Moyen Age* 10 (3rd series, 1939), 81–125, at 89–91.

[130] Abbo, *Bella*, II, 328–9, p. 90.

[131] *AV* s.a. 885, p. 57. For more detail on the brothers and their *honores* see MacLean, 'Viking Great Army', pp. 86–9.

[132] Abbo, *Bella*, II, 315–29, pp. 88–90.

Royal politics and regional power in the Late Carolingian Empire

of the family of Herbert of Vermandois, a descendant of King Bernard of Italy.[133] They also, however, reach back into the reigns of Louis III and Carloman II. Like Theoderic, Aletramnus had the expected political connections in the Paris region which placed him at the heart of the group around Gauzlin. His brother Theoderic was involved in the dispute over the episcopal vacancy in his county of Beauvais during the reign of Louis III.[134] Aletramnus was a companion of Gauzlin as prisoner in the east following the battle of Andernach, a visit on which, as we saw, Gauzlin is said to have formed useful alliances.[135] Already in 868, Aletramnus is found underwriting a judgement in favour of St-Denis, and in 879, when Gauzlin was abbot, he passed on everything that Louis the Stammerer had just given him in the Laonnois to the same monastery.[136] We have already met Theoderic as a leader of Louis III's field army and advising Carloman on the defence of a bridge over the Marne. Strategically speaking, the *Annals of St-Vaast* suggest that the Oise was already seen as a definitive defensive boundary in the earlier 880s.[137] Moreover, Louis III had endured heavyweight ecclesiastical opposition in order to ensure he got the men he wanted in the vacant sees of Beauvais and Noyon (the central place of Vermandois): the filling of such sees had strategic and political importance as well as implications for church hierarchy.[138] It was Archbishop Fulk of Rheims who famously pointed out to Charles the extreme importance of defending the nodal point of Paris against capture, and his words have been taken by historians to be somewhat prophetic in the light of subsequent events.[139] However, Charles was clearly neither the first nor the last king to ensure that measures were taken to prevent such a defeat. Moreover, despite frequent claims to the contrary by historians, Charles's failure to defeat the Paris Vikings outright is attested nowhere as a factor in his deposition. For all the much-admired bluster of the archbishop of Rheims, it was surely men like Gauzlin, Theoderic, Hugh and Aletramnus who were giving Charles the best advice on how to deal with the Viking menace at the sharp end. Hence we see him

---

[133] Werner, 'Untersuchungen v', pp. 97–8 with n. 40, coining the term 'Oise line', but seeing this as an innovation of Odo rather than the continuation of a late Carolingian pattern.

[134] D L3 46.   [135] *AB* s.a. 876, p. 209.

[136] D CB 314 for 868; for 879, F. Lot, 'Notes historique sur "Aye d'Avignon"', *Romania* 33 (1904), 145–62, at 150.

[137] *AV* s.a. 881, p. 50; 881, p. 51; 882, p. 53; 883, p. 54. Cf. 890, p. 68; 899, p. 81. Charles the Bald also built defensive bridges in the area: see S. Coupland and J. L. Nelson, 'The Vikings on the Continent', *History Today* 38 (1988), 12–19.

[138] D L3 44–7 are the key texts; they are illuminated by Werner, 'Gauzlin von Saint-Denis', pp. 440–9. The politico-military aspects of these disputes are nevertheless usually overlooked in the historiography, which tends to discuss them purely in the context of canon law: e.g. J. Devisse, *Hincmar, Archevêque de Reims 845–882* (Geneva, 1975), pp. 984–9.

[139] Flodoard, *Historia*, 4.5, p. 563.

Kingship and Politics in the Late Ninth Century

coping with exactly the problem he had been invited into the west to contain, and in traditional ways.[140]

We must also briefly consider some other associates of these men. Odo himself is easily located within the group of Charles's stalwarts in the western kingdom. The exact nature of his personal relationship with Charles after 886 has already been discussed. Here it will simply be necessary to point out his connections with other members of the Seine-Oise aristocracy in the 880s. Odo's family was closely connected politically to Gauzlin's, and it is possible that his own wife was a relative of Gauzlin.[141] The latter, by this time returned to the heights of royal favour, and with a number of important *honores* in Paris, including St-Denis, may have been influential in securing Odo's appointment as count there in late 882 or early 883.[142] Gauzlin's closeness to Odo at the siege of Paris is apparent from the report of Abbo, whose evidence is particularly noteworthy since he was related to the former and wrote for the latter.[143] His work casts them together as defenders of Paris, one as 'consul', the other as 'praesul' of the city.[144] Theoderic also had influential connections in Paris, and if he mediated the return of Gauzlin he may also have influenced the appointment of Odo.[145] Finally Hucbald, count of Senlis and another notable figure in the Seine-Oise area, was a close political ally of Odo.[146]

Odo's political links with Gauzlin and Theoderic are enough to suggest that he too was one of the 'Franci' who sent out the invitation to Charles the Fat in December 884. Like Gauzlin's, his family were well connected in east Carolingian political circles, and Odo himself had been at the east Frankish royal monastery of Lorsch in 876.[147] His brother Robert was already a count in Namur on the line splitting Lotharingia, and had been at Metz in 884 to seek the emperor's patronage. The esteem in which Charles held Robert is emphasised both by the terms used by the charter

[140] As Werner, 'Untersuchungen v' shows, Theoderic and Aletramnus may have been related to Herbert of Vermandois, who also began his steep rise to prominence in the reign of Charles the Fat. The general link allows us to make sense of Herbert's succession to the brothers in their *honores* north of Paris.

[141] Favre, *Eudes*, p. 13; Werner, 'Bedeutende Adelsfamilien', p. 140, n. 15.

[142] Werner, 'Les Robertiens', p. 20. The appointment may have been smoothed by Odo's familial links to another kin who had traditionally controlled Paris earlier in the ninth century: G. P. A. Brown, 'Politics and Patronage at the Abbey of St-Denis (814–98): the Rise of a Royal Patron Saint', D.Phil. thesis, University of Oxford (1989), esp. pp. 163–7, 177–203; 200–1 for Odo's relationship.

[143] On Abbo and the Rorgonids see Oexle, 'Ebroin von Poitiers', p. 207, n. 354.

[144] Abbo, *Bella*, I, 40–59, pp. 16–18 for the sense of joint responsibility. The key offices of Gauzlin and Theoderic later ended up in Odo's hands. They may thus have been related: Werner, 'Gauzlin von Saint-Denis', p. 461 and n. 220.

[145] D C2 76 shows Theoderic's association with Bishop Ingelwin.

[146] Bischoff (ed.), *Anecdota Novissima*, pp. 131–2.

[147] D Lor 1835. Werner, 'Les Robertiens', pp. 15–8 on the family's east Frankish origins.

Royal politics and regional power in the Late Carolingian Empire

to describe him, 'noble man and most faithful count', and his success in getting a valuable estate handed over to his *fidelis* Sanctio, the father of the tenth-century monastic reformer St Gerard of Brogne.[148] Indeed, Odo himself occupies an unusually prominent position in imperial charters even *before* being put in charge of Neustria, further evidence of his close relationship with Charles.[149]

Another member of this group of imperial supporters who was of special political significance is Askericus, who became bishop of Paris in autumn 886 after Gauzlin's death on 16 April. He was already well-connected in the Paris area, since his brother Tetbert was the count of Meaux killed fighting the Vikings in 888, and they probably also belonged to an extended family group which included Herbert of Vermandois.[150] Askericus also leads us back to the first appearance of the emperor on west Frankish soil in May 885; in Charles's first west Frankish diploma, issued at Grand in Burgundy, he intervened along with the *marchio* Rudolf and his son Pippin for the emperor's *fidelis* Dodo.[151] Those named as petitioners for third parties in royal charters may be regarded as 'in' at court. Askericus's association with the *marchio* Rudolf, another key supporter of the emperor, highlights his closeness to the throne.[152]

Both his position in the May 885 charter and his connections to the Paris area and its main comital families suggest that Askericus was intimately involved in Theoderic's mission to receive the new king. He certainly figures prominently in Charles's entourage. Abbo gives us to believe that his appointment as bishop was among Charles's first acts upon entering Paris in 886, and it is possible that the bishopric had been held open for him since Gauzlin's death in April: Charles evidently retained control of appointments in the west, a point perhaps underrated by Werner.[153] The bishop-elect himself presumably arrived there in the imperial entourage, as there is no reference to him during the siege itself, and he may have spent the previous eighteen months attached to the court. Askericus clearly remained in favour. In 887 it was he who went to the imperial court at Kirchen to collect the ransom owed to the Paris Vikings.[154]

---

[148] D CIII 105; see J. Wollasch, 'Gerard von Brogne und seine Klostergründung', *Revue Bénédictine* 70 (1960), 62–82, at 63. 'Most faithful' is an unusual superlative; cf. DD CIII 2, 57, 89, 102.

[149] DD CIII 139, 143, 146. On Charles and Odo see above, pp. 49–55.

[150] Abbo, *Bella*, II, 456, p. 100; *AV* s.a. 888, p. 66; Werner, 'Untersuchungen v', pp. 96–7.

[151] D CIII 116.   [152] DD CIII 116 and 137.

[153] Abbo, *Bella*, II, 335–7, p. 90; also *AV* s.a. 886, p. 62. He is called 'vocatus episcopus' on his first charter appearance. Werner, 'Untersuchungen v', p. 95; 'Gauzlin von Saint-Denis', pp. 454–5.

[154] *AV* s.a. 887, p. 63.

Kingship and Politics in the Late Ninth Century

GEILO OF LANGRES

If Askericus helps give more depth to the group of north Frankish aristocrats standing behind the simple reference of the annalist of St-Vaast to the mission of count Theoderic, he also brings us further south into Burgundy and introduces us to Geilo, the bishop of Langres: the charter issued for the *fidelis* Dodo at the request of Askericus, Rudolf and Pippin was composed by scribes from the Langres scriptorium. Shortly afterwards Dodo concluded a precarial agreement with Geilo, ensuring that his properties would go to the church of Langres after his death.[155] Askericus and Geilo certainly knew each other personally, as they must have met at court on several occasions. However, if Askericus had spent some time travelling round with the imperial entourage, it is Geilo who emerges most spectacularly as a court figure after 885.

Bautier has studied his career and his church's privileges in great detail, and so only one or two points need be made here.[156] Bautier sees Geilo as a sinister figure, and casts his rise in terms of a progressive and sustained attempt to acquire as many temporal rights as possible from the Carolingians in order to increase his authority in northern Burgundy. He appears first as abbot of Tournus in the later years of Charles the Bald's reign before moving on to participate at Boso's king-making ceremony at Mantaille in 879, an act which won him the diocese of Langres. Then he joined the flood of erstwhile Boso partisans rushing to defect to the Carolingians in 880, and became one of Carloman II's steadiest supporters, retaining his ill-gotten diocese and remaining with the new king during the protracted siege of Vienne. As will be seen in the next chapter, he was involved in orchestrating the inception of Charles the Fat's west Frankish rule, and he was unusually prominent in the surviving records of Charles's patronage.[157] After the emperor's death he switched to the party of Guy of Spoleto, whom he crowned in 888 before his own death later that year.

This fast-changing career under several masters, and the fact that the great number of his gifts allow him to be characterised as the grasping aristocrat, a classic historiographical villain, seems to have been what led Bautier to see in Geilo something of a chancer, a man 'of debatable personal morals', who displayed 'a total lack of scruples'.[158] This judgement of his actions (his actual personality is, of course, obscure) seems rather

---

[155] D CIII 154.

[156] R.-H. Bautier, 'Les diplômes royaux carolingiens pour l'église de Langres et l'origine des droits comtaux de l'évêque', in R.-H. Bautier, *Chartes, sceaux et chancelleries. Études de diplomatique et de sigillographie médiévales* (vol. I, Paris, 1990) pp. 209–42, esp. pp. 216–30.

[157] DD CIII 117, 118, 129, 147, 152–4, 155a, 162. His scribes connect him to DD 116, 137, 155.

[158] Bautier, 'Les diplômes royaux', pp. 223 and 216 respectively.

Royal politics and regional power in the Late Carolingian Empire

anachronistic. Geilo's service of several masters in turn was far from unusual; the unusual thing is that we are able to chart it so closely. Aristocrats had to think on their feet when the configuration of power in the ruling house altered, and when a king turned up at one's doorstep, as they did on Geilo's in 879, 880, 885 and 888, the choice was not really a free one. Likewise, it cannot be simply assumed that any magnate who was conspicuously successful in obtaining royal patronage was a malignant leech. Consideration of Geilo's career is thus valuable not only for the light it casts on the west Frankish dimension of Charles's rule. His unusually well-documented activities also serve to exemplify the positions of powerful bishops more generally, figures often seen as inimical to the effectiveness of royal authority in this period.

In reality, there is no good evidence that Geilo's relationship with Charles the Fat was anything but cooperative. Charles had already had some dealings with the church of Langres before 885; in 882 he confirmed a precarial deal agreed between Guy of Spoleto and the *praepositus* Otbert.[159] Langres was also endowed with properties in Transjurane Burgundy, where Charles the Fat had had influence since the early 870s.[160] Geilo's church was a focus for commemoration of the emperor, and the bishop was present with the court in the east on a number of occasions, notably at Lorsch on 28 August 885, where a ceremony was held to commemorate the death of Louis the German, who had died on the same day nine years earlier and whose body lay in that monastery.[161]

Geilo really came to the fore during the crucial events of 887. The most important point came when the bishop received several charters on the same day, 15 January 887, at the royal *palatium* of Sélestat (Schlettstadt) in Alsace.[162] These documents reveal a classic instance of the temporal empowerment of bishops in the heart of the empire at this time, a trend usually discussed as an aspect of declining royal power. Accordingly, Bautier, this time citing with admiration Geilo's political sagacity, claims that having exacted these grants the bishop realised that the tide was turning against the ailing Charles, and that he now sidled off to Chalon-sur-Saône to a meeting with the most important of the Provençal ecclesiastical nobility. The text of the meeting, which took place on 18 May in the church of St-Marcel-lès-Chalon, reveals only discussion about the peace of the church and the confirmation of various property transactions, but it is reasonable to suppose that political matters were also on the agenda.[163]

---

[159] D CIII 61.   [160] D L2 12.   [161] D CIII 129; see below, pp. 132–3.

[162] DD CIII 152–4, probably D 155a.

[163] A. Roserot, 'Chartes inédites des IXe et Xe siècles', in *Bulletin de la Société des Sciences historiques et naturelles de l'Yonne* (1898), 161–207.

111

Kingship and Politics in the Late Ninth Century

Bautier suggests that these matters were an expression of intent to persuade the weak-willed and dying Charles to adopt as his successor his young cousin Louis of Provence, son of Boso and Irmingarde; and that the gifts made at Sélestat were a (clearly ill-judged) sign of gratitude from the happy king that Geilo was remaining loyal as others considered jumping ship.[164] There is no sign, however, that anyone else *was* thinking about deserting the king in January 887, and in fact some of the men who supported Guy of Spoleto in 888 are found at exactly this time still in favour with Charles, and even accepting a diminution of their comital holdings.[165] Bautier also presents the assembly at Chalon as a sinister double of Mantaille, significantly coming shortly after Boso's death in January. In fact, the attendance at the 887 synod was rather less impressive than at the 879 one, and confined mostly to representatives from the northern part of Provence. There is no *de facto* reason to be suspicious about such a group of ecclesiastics getting together to discuss matters of mutual concern.[166] Admittedly, these were men who knew all about raising non-Carolingians to the throne[167]; but they also knew all about the consequences. Many of them had been among the first to realise the futility of the situation in 880 as the armies of Charles the Fat and his cousins and brother closed in on Vienne.

An alternative reconstruction of events can be put forward. The timing of the gifts to Geilo in early 887 is significant, as they were issued exactly four days after the death of the usurper Boso on 11 January. As will be argued in chapter 6, it was at this point, as the news reached Sélestat, that Charles the Fat and his advisers decided to make some sort of accommodation with Boso's young son Louis, to expunge from the record the usurping activities of his father, and hence to neutralise any threat he might pose, by reincorporating him into the legitimate Carolingian family.[168] Geilo was present when the news arrived, and he knew exactly what the emperor planned. The empress Engelberga, Louis's grandmother, became involved in negotiations in early February, which shows how quickly Charles must have moved after hearing of Boso's death, and the young prince was received at Kirchen in the summer. The bishop can thus be seen as a royal agent at Chalon, sent to explain and negotiate the new status of Louis with the leading ecclesiastical power-brokers of his father's former kingdom, and hence to keep them involved at the centre of imperial politics. Geilo was there not to conspire to force Louis on the emperor, but rather to mediate the imperial decision to adopt Louis

---

[164] Bautier, 'Les diplômes royaux', pp. 221–2.
[165] D CIII 155. As Bautier acknowledges; 'Les diplômes royaux', p. 222 and n. 52.
[166] D CIII 155a; Bautier, 'Les diplômes royaux', p. 221.
[167] As observed by Airlie, '*Semper fideles?*', p. 142.   [168] See below, pp. 161–9.

112

Royal politics and regional power in the Late Carolingian Empire

with the nobles of Provence, who would thus obtain a secure link to the political centre. The council at Chalon was held on 18 May. This fits comfortably with the timing of the Kirchen assembly, which was almost definitely held in June or July.[169] Kirchen must have hosted an elaborate and carefully staged ceremony at which the Carolingian element of Louis's and Charles's relationship was emphasised, and the very highest of the imperial aristocracy were present, including Odo and Berengar. Geilo was also there.[170] Was it perhaps he who had escorted Louis with his mother Irmingarde from Chalon to Kirchen and into the open arms of his benevolent uncle Charles?

The chronology of this hypothesis is strengthened if we reject the supposed incapacity of Charles as the key to understanding these events.[171] The connection between the grants to Geilo and the council of Chalon is strong; one of the items definitely discussed at the synod was exactly the imperial aggrandisement of the position of the bishop of Langres.[172] If, then, it was the news of the death of Boso that inspired Charles and his advisers to begin negotiations with Engelberga and the high churchmen of Provence to bring about a reconciliation with young Louis, and to choose Geilo as the agent for part of these negotiations, why the lavish grants at the same time?

The charters in question amount to a strong confirmation of Geilo's position. The first of them speaks in exalted terms about how he had been entrusted with his *civitas* by God in order to protect its inhabitants and its church. He had, it goes on, built up the walls of his town without the help of any *comes* or *iudex*, thus fulfilling the terms of his trust. He is, therefore, granted all the *ex officio* comital holdings in and around Langres, significant extensions to fiscal rights (including minting), and most of the income from regular markets held in Dijon and Langres.[173] This, although it in part reflects a situation which the charter's *narratio* tells us had already developed, is an imperial approval for the bishop of Langres to become the main secular authority in the diocese, which was one of the principal sees of the kingdom. He was confirmed as the preeminent spiritual and secular power in Langres, Dijon and Tonnerre,[174] and he also held notable churches and properties in Atuyer, Troyes, Lassois and Solignac. By contrast, Charles was happy to diminish the holdings of the local counts on behalf of Geilo's subordinates, like the *praepositus*

---

[169] D CIII 158 issued at Waiblingen on 7 May; DD 159–63 issued at Kirchen, 30 May–23 June; D 164 issued at Lustenau on 24 July.

[170] D CIII 162.   [171] On Charles's illness, see above, pp. 39–41.   [172] D CIII 155a.

[173] D CIII 152; for comments see Bautier, 'Les diplômes royaux', pp. 224–5. DD 153, 154, 155a are similarly impressive enhancements.

[174] See Map 1.

113

Kingship and Politics in the Late Ninth Century

Otbert.[175] This escalation of episcopal power at the expense of comital was not an autonomous process, but was clearly encouraged by kings. Generally speaking, the increase in this type of grant to bishops in the heart of Francia and Burgundy during the 880s must be related to the increase in Viking activity in the region. Bishops based in newly fortified towns provided refuges for threatened communities. The evidence clearly shows this to have been part of a deliberate royally approved policy of episcopal empowerment.[176]

However, the case of the grant to Geilo also suggests more specific royal motives. The preference for delegating authority into the hands of a select group of favoured men was, as we have seen, a policy typically pursued by the Carolingians, and particularly necessary for Charles given the scale of his huge empire. He needed to draw such powerful figures closer to him. To have a man like Geilo, a highly prized *fidelis*, dominating northern Burgundy, in a region which was also on the main road between Italy and west Francia, was not only a benefit for the bishop: it activated the connection between court and locality. Geilo already had political connections with the main players in Provence, forged not least during the days of King Boso. On 15 January 887, though, after Boso was gone once and for all, the bishop was also granted greater material wherewithal to back this up, and a solid position from which to negotiate with the leaders of the Provençal political community on behalf of the emperor.

The fact that the gifts came hot on the heels of Boso's death is rendered even more significant by the fact that the latter had held lands in the diocese of Langres.[177] Were some of these now confirmed by Charles in Geilo's possession? Gaps in the documentation make this impossible to prove. However, a hint that Geilo had in a sense succeeded Boso in parts of his old sphere of influence comes from the bishop's success in persuading Charles to grant the abbey of Donzère in Provence to his old community at Tournus.[178] Almost exactly a decade earlier Donzère had been given to the church of St-Vincent in Viviers by Charles the Bald at the request of Boso.[179] Their relationships with the grant were thus analogous; and in fact it had also been Boso who had intervened with Charles to give Geilo the abbey of Tournus in the first place.[180] The idea

[175] D CIII 155.
[176] This can be inferred from the evidence and conclusions presented by Guyotjeannin, *Episcopus et comes*.
[177] Bautier, 'Les diplômes royaux', p. 219; Bautier, 'Aux origines du royaume de Provence', pp. 52–4.
[178] D CIII 162.
[179] D CB 443. See also D L 107. Might Boso's death explain why the king now felt that the church was back in his gift?
[180] D CB 378. See also D 419 for links between Boso and Dijon.

Royal politics and regional power in the Late Carolingian Empire

that Boso had been 'replaced', like the reconciliation with Louis, would be another way of closing the book on the usurper. The specialness of the emperor's grants to Geilo in early 887 was also acknowledged by the synod of Chalon, whose text distinguishes the general holdings of the church of Langres from the properties 'which [Geilo] in his own time acquired while with his lord the most glorious emperor'.[181] Geilo was a powerful individual. However, his power (and that of others like him) cannot be properly understood without reference to the court and the possibility of specific political motivations for royal concessions of rights and properties.

ROYAL POLITICS AND ARISTOCRATIC IDENTITY IN LATE NINTH-CENTURY WEST FRANCIA

In the men we have been discussing we can see the most conspicuous members of a coherent aristocratic group supporting Charles the Fat in west Francia. Can it be described as a 'personal network'? Charles was a largely absentee ruler of this *regnum*, and these people had not been children with him at the court of Louis the German, nor had they been at his side during his apprenticeship for royal office in Alemannia. Still, there are hints in the evidence at least for Gauzlin, Odo and Geilo of a peculiar trust which could be characterised as personal. Was it a network? This can by no means be simply assumed from the demonstration of the familial links which existed between many of these characters. However, although only some of the very top players are revealed by the evidence, they must represent broad substrata of men and resources,[182] and although the details are often blurry the overall picture is clear. The group based around Paris and Neustria can be linked into a network by our perception of them actually acting together under the authority of the emperor. This was not, or not merely, a 'personal' or a 'familial' network; it was first and foremost a political network. Those who invited Charles in also served him and were rewarded by him; Odo, Gauzlin, Theoderic, Aletramnus and others are seen doing just that. Further south, although the sources are not so revealing, the responsibilities bestowed upon the likes of Geilo of Langres and Bernard Plantevelue show that the Paris group did not represent the entirety of Charles's support. A huge number of western institutions sought out his patronage and took care to preserve its memory. In other words, although his reign in the kingdom of his cousins lasted only two

---

[181] D CIII 155a. Similarly, DD C2 49–55 may reveal, as Bautier, 'Aux origines du royaume de Provence', pp. 58–9 argues, the wholesale confiscation of a block of Boso's properties in Berry.

[182] See Airlie, 'The Aristocracy', pp. 435, 448.

Kingship and Politics in the Late Ninth Century

and a half years, and hence cannot really be 'judged' in comparison to those of some of his longer-lasting forbears, we can see that Charles the Fat had the resources and made the effort not simply to reign there, but also to rule. This renders more intelligible the unmistakable optimism in the power of the new king on the part of Abbo, who wrote at the heart of this network. Charles's rule was respected by his western supporters: they did not break from the eastern kingdom in 885 or even in November 887, but waited until Charles the Fat was dead before choosing a new king.

When they finally did so it was from among their own number, and the opening of Odo's reign shows continuity from that of his predecessor. While he faced more opposition in Aquitaine and Burgundy, in Francia he kept his friends. Most strikingly, the *Annals of St-Vaast* tell us that exactly the same man who had represented the group which invited Charles in winter 884–5 now repeated the favour for Odo in 888. Count Theoderic, whom the annalist describes as predominant in the new king's following, proceeded to negotiate on Odo's behalf with Arnulf of Carinthia.[183] The same political group acted for Odo at the start of 888 as had acted for Charles at the end of 884. Theoderic's son took over from him shortly afterwards before falling foul of the expansionist designs of the count of Flanders.[184] In the meantime, the defence of the Oise and the area north of Paris remained concentrated. Robert became *marchio* of Neustria in the role created for Odo by Charles the Fat in 886. Askericus went on to take charge of the royal chancery. It was an appointee of Charles, Archbishop Walter of Sens, who crowned Odo. It was from this core of support that Odo gradually extended his authority over the *regnum* during the following year or so. Therefore in terms of personnel as well as political structures, the reign of Charles the Fat leads us forward to the start of that of Odo.

Some of these men, like Odo himself or Askericus, were put in place by Charles the Fat. As should be clear, others, like Gauzlin, Theoderic, Aletramnus and Geilo, take us back to the heart of the court circles of Louis III and Carloman II.[185] There are clues, however, which allow us to speculate about the origins of this continuity even further back in time. The Capitulary of Quierzy, in which Charles the Bald spelled out the arrangements for governing the western kingdom when he set off for Italy in 877, reflects a subtle change in the political configuration of the high aristocracy. While the most famous *primores*, namely Hugh the

---

[183] *AV* s.a. 888, pp. 64–5.   [184] *AV* s.a. 895, p. 77.

[185] Note also the Germundus in D CIII 142, perhaps the same man whose daughter had been involved in the bizarre death of Louis III; *AV* s.a. 882, p. 52.

116

Royal politics and regional power in the Late Carolingian Empire

Abbot, Bernard Plantevelue and Boso, were given prominent positions in the kingdom, they had been absent from the key negotiations and were not granted any role at court, probably because Charles hoped to call on them to aid him in Italy should the occasion arise.[186] Those who were given the best access to court were lesser men, from outside the ranks of the 'supermagnates' whom Charles had been building up throughout the 870s, and towards whom the smaller aristocrats may have felt some resentment.[187] Those designated at Quierzy as advisers to Charles's son Louis were connected to each other politically through the court, but also geographically; the core were all, unlike any of the supermagnates, from Francia 'proper'. They were counts Adalelm of Laon, Adalard of the palace, Baldwin of Flanders, Conrad of Sens (later Paris), Theoderic of Vermandois; the bishops of Paris, Tournai, Beauvais and Soissons; and abbots Welf of St-Colombe in Sens (Conrad's brother), Gauzlin of St-Denis and Fulk of St-Bertin. The supermagnates feared that the provisions in Quierzy concerning this group, which Charles bolstered in the latter years of his reign,[188] would become crystallised if the emperor died in Italy, and they broke into revolt in an attempt to draw him back across the Alps. They were too late, and after the absent Charles's death these two groups, the supermagnates and the north Frankish nobles, remained visibly distinct through the reign of Louis the Stammerer.[189] For example, the attempt of Gauzlin, Conrad and their accomplices (including Theoderic, who hosted some of the negotiations at St-Quentin) to force a division of the kingdom in 879–80 was in the main an attempt on behalf of the north Frankish group to wrest influence back from the likes of Hugh, Bernard and Boso, who looked set to benefit exclusively from proximity to the sole kingship of Louis III. This prolonged struggle in particular, with the impending threat of Louis the Younger always looming on the horizon, must have lived long in the memory. The capitulary of 877, then, left a strong imprint on the political alignments of the subsequent years. The document itself even served as a model for the royal *promissiones* of Louis the Stammerer, Carloman and Odo. If by 885 the scars were healing, the distinctiveness of the Frankish magnates we have been discussing was nevertheless informed by this history of political conflict.

While Charles the Bald was building up these men in the last years of his life, we can catch occasional glimpses of how this might have contributed to their formation of a political network. In 870, Charles's

---

[186] *Conventus Carisiacensis*, MGH Capit. vol. 2, nos. 281–2; Nelson, *Charles the Bald*, pp. 246–52.

[187] Airlie, 'Political Behaviour of Secular Magnates', pp. 205–56 is the most detailed account of these developments.

[188] Nelson, *Charles the Bald*, pp. 246–7.   [189] *Ibid.*, p. 255.

117

Kingship and Politics in the Late Ninth Century

negotiating team, prior to the *divisio* of Lothar II's realm agreed with Louis the German at Meersen, was led by Adalelm of Laon, Theoderic of Vermandois and Bishop Odo of Beauvais, along with the chamberlain Engelram and another Adalelm.[190] Adalelm, Engelram, Gauzlin and Conrad were likewise involved together in the rising of Charles the Bald's son Carloman as a letter of Hincmar in 871 shows.[191] Adalelm himself was a relative of Odo of Paris, possibly through marriage to the sister of Robert the Strong.[192] Adalard count of the palace was another who had been taken prisoner at Andernach with Gauzlin and Aletramnus.[193] Of course, such political alliances could change in the blink of an eye. The point of this is simply to show that there is a context for the development of a political network among the members of the north Frankish aristocracy during the 870s, and certainly by 877. Geography here coincided with political and occasionally family interests; Charles the Bald clearly considered them a unit by the time of the assembly at Quierzy. This network was significant in many of the events from 877 to 888 and beyond.

Finally, did what looks from the outside like a political network have such a consciousness of its own position? This is always a difficult question, but there are signs that in this case the answer is yes.[194] A lost set of annals from Theoderic's monastery of St-Quentin recorded in 882: 'after his [i.e. Louis III's] death the *Franci* made Carloman king'.[195] It was, of course, the 'Franci' who were also said to have sent the invitation out to Charles the Fat after Carloman's death.[196] These are views from the inside. An even more telling example is the diploma of Carloman from 884 issued for the church of Châlons-sur-Marne. The charter is unusual because it is dated 'anno II regni Karlomanni regis in Frantia'. This is unique in dating the reign only to Carloman's succession to Louis III in Neustria and Francia, and not in total regnal years back to 879, which was the normal practice of Carloman's chancery.[197] For some people, this implies, it was rule of the north, of Francia proper, which really counted. It is of special interest, then, that the document was drafted

---

[190] *Pactiones Aquenses*, MGH Capit, vol. 2, no. 250.

[191] Flodoard, *Historia*, 3.26, p. 543. Cf. Nelson, *Charles the Bald*, pp. 228–9.

[192] Regino, *Chronicon*, s.a. 892, p. 139; Werner, 'Untersuchungen IV', p. 159.

[193] *AB* s.a. 876, p. 209.   [194] As also argued by Werner, 'Gauzlin von Saint-Denis', p. 453.

[195] *Sermo in tumulatione*, p. 272.

[196] *AV* s.a. 884, p. 56; the use of this word is striking as opposed to the *AV*'s customary use of phrases like 'qui fuerant in regno Karlomanni'. Cf. also *AV* s.a. 886, p. 62 where Charles 'distributed lands among the *Franci*'.

[197] D C2 76. Bautier, introduction to DD C2, pp. xxxvi–xxxix, lxxxi. Carloman's chancery dates are confused, but typically go back either to the death of Louis the Stammerer or the crowning at Ferrières.

Royal politics and regional power in the Late Carolingian Empire

by scribes from outside the chancery, and that one of the men named as intervening for its production is none other than count Theoderic, the representative of the *Franci* in 884 and the lay-abbot of St-Quentin whence came the lost annals.[198] This sort of sentiment fits well with the impression of 'regnal awareness' we get from the literary sources, especially from Gauzlin's relation Abbo, who was given to lambasting the character of Burgundians and Aquitanians while passionately praising the Franks and Neustrians.[199] There was thus a contemporary self-awareness of the significance of the geo-political groupings which had coalesced during the last years of Charles the Bald. The term they used for themselves, 'Franci', was not only geographically appropriate, but also carried connotations of claims to political legitimacy: an extended sense of 'Frankishness' was one of the main ways that Carolingian hegemony was articulated.[200]

The importance of this group based 'in Francia' successively to Charles the Bald, Louis the Stammerer, Louis III, Carloman II, Charles the Fat and Odo must be recognised. Although it is wrong to schematise such ideas too much, there is enough evidence to show a continuum in this network and its main figures from the 870s to the 890s, figures whose political identities were given coherence by their common experience of royal service and defence against the Vikings. This sort of continuity is hardly surprising, but it is rarely if ever stressed, and in fact is often assumed to be absent. In this continuum the reign of Charles the Fat is not to be seen as a 'mere intermezzo'.[201] He used the same tools as had been at the disposal of his predecessors and would be to his successor. Although his reign was in some ways anomalous and was too short to be put to a sustained test of strength it is overly pessimistic to conclude that 877 saw the collapse of west Frankish political institutions.[202] Rather, the reign of Charles the Fat can be seen as a keystone of the bridge connecting the last years of Charles the Bald with the first years of King Odo.

Only thereafter did the situation begin to fragment. As king, Odo enjoyed only moderate success outside Francia proper. One reason for this was that the arrival in the west Frankish kingdom of Guy of Spoleto later in 888 saw the severing of links between the most important Frankish and Burgundian supporters of Charles the Fat: Geilo of

---

[198] Cf. *Karolomanni Capitula Compendii de Rapinis Promulgata*, MGH Capit, vol. 2, no. 286 from 883, also dated 'anno regni sui in Francia primo'.
[199] See above, pp. 60–1.
[200] Fouracre, *Age of Charles Martel*, p. 24 discusses the roots of this concept.
[201] Brühl, *Fodrum, Gistum, Servitium Regis*, pp. 35–6.
[202] As does Nelson, *Charles the Bald*, pp. 258–63.

119

Langres threw in his lot with the new claimant against Odo, and Rudolf had himself proclaimed king in Transjurane Burgundy. Moreover, the rising of Charles the Simple in 893 saw more cracks opening even within the aristocracy of Francia proper itself. The overarching authority of Charles the Fat had provided a focus for the loyalties of these geographically disparate aristocracies, and bound them together into the single political structure of the reunified Carolingian empire. After his death, however, the appearance of several kings competing for legitimacy and support divided the loyalties of these men and forced them to make choices which necessarily pitted them against each other. Now, not even the notional unity which had been articulated by the rule of multiple members of the Carolingian family held sway. The political map of Europe began to metamorphose into its tenth-century shape during the reign of Odo, not during that of Charles: the geographical fragmentation of royal power was a phenomenon of the period after 888, not after 877.

CONCLUSION

The inversion of centre and periphery was an unavoidable fact of late ninth-century politics. Charles the Fat had to embrace the situation. The change was implicitly recognised by a kind of internal *translatio imperii* in 881. In that year, the emperor built a palace at Sélestat in Alsace, the design of which was explicitly based on the architecture of the empire's traditional seat at Aachen. At around the same time, part of the imperial relic collection was brought from Aachen to Alemannia. These acts symbolised the shift in the centre of political gravity which was taking place in the 880s.[203] Charles's access to aristocratic elites in the varied political geography of the restored empire had to rely upon a variety of methods of rule, from personal intervention in Alemannia shading out towards the absentee kingship and political remote control of Saxony. The problems created by physical distance could be short-circuited by the creation of political affinities: important power-brokers like Odo of Paris, Liutbert of Mainz and Geilo of Langres could be made to feel close to the political centre, and to bring their regional influence to bear on behalf of the emperor, by the judicious deployment of patronage. Charles's numerous charters and unusual mobility are testimony to the efforts he put in to maintain these associations. These measures seem to have been more or less effective, in the relatively limited senses that by modern standards we can describe early medieval government as effective.

---

[203] See below, pp. 157–8 and 187–9.

Royal politics and regional power in the Late Carolingian Empire

The empire certainly continued to function as a unit. It is notable that the army sent by Charles against the Vikings at Leuven in 885 was multi-regnal, as had been the one led to Asselt in 882. Similarly in 884, when the Bavarians were sent off to attack the rebellious Guy in Italy, or in 886 at the siege of Paris, we can see the emperor able to deploy men from one part of his empire to go and deal with problems in another.[204] Modern historians typically condemn Charles's reunification of the empire as haphazard, anachronistic and doomed to failure. In the context we have outlined, however, it is understandable that contemporaries were not so pessimistic. Regino saw it as a sign of divine favour, and compared it favourably with the efforts of earlier rulers: 'Charles understood how to take hold of all the kingdoms of the Franks (which his predecessors had acquired only with great bloodshed and effort) easily, quickly and without conflict.'[205]

The bridges built by Charles between centre and locality were supported by over a century of the traditions of Carolingian rule. Aristocrats in the 880s looked instinctively to the dynasty for leadership.[206] They only turned elsewhere once (to Boso, in 879), and that was when Carolingian leadership had become unavailable due to a particularly severe internal power struggle. However, as time passed, the fragility of these bridges became more apparent: after 879, when he began to acquire extra kingdoms, Charles's ability to intervene personally even in Alemannia was noticeably diminished. The pressure of the Viking and Arab raids put extra strain on these relationships and rendered them even more important. The precariousness of the situation was exposed after the emperor fell ill over winter 886–7 and was forced to end his hitherto ceaseless circuits of the empire. Although the likes of Odo, Berengar and Geilo still showed themselves willing to travel long distances to attend court in Alemannia, this arrangement could not continue indefinitely. It interacted dangerously with another problem, namely the chronic shortage of legitimate male Carolingians. Charles did not have any legitimate sons to send out into the *regna* as kings and diffuse access to the dynasty: this, and not newly emergent aristocratic authority, the view that the reunification was 'anachronistic', or the desire of the *regna* to secede, was the crucial difference between his empire and that of Charlemagne and Louis the Pious. The problem was not that the nobility wanted to shake off Carolingian rule: it was that they could not get enough of it. To ease the pressure, the emperor needed above all to resolve the doubts over the imperial succession, and hence find a way to make *Königsnähe* a more readily available

---

[204] *AF(B)* s.a. 884, p. 110; Abbo, *Bella*, II, 330–3, p. 90 for the scope of the Paris army.
[205] Regino, *Chronicon*, s.a. 888, pp. 128–9.   [206] Cf. Fouracre, *Age of Charles Martel*, pp. 23–7.

commodity. The empire *was* too big for one man, but then it always had been. Obedience to the Carolingians was never blind, and the longer Charles's reign continued without such a solution, the more stress would be placed upon his position. The stage was set for Arnulf's coup. The exact nature of the drama that unfolded there is the subject of the following two chapters.

Chapter 5

THE END OF THE EMPIRE I: POLITICS AND IDEOLOGY AT THE EAST FRANKISH COURT

The problems facing Charles the Fat as he approached the crisis of his reign were not, it would seem, purely structural. The 'supervisory' nature of Carolingian government meant that it was indeed possible for one man to rule enormous tracts of territory by forming alliances with influential regional aristocrats. One man could not govern indefinitely, however. In order to understand the causes of the deposition of the emperor and the disintegration of the empire we must reconstruct the chain of events which led up to Arnulf's coup of November 887. These events interacted with aspects of the general political backdrop we have been describing to bring about the final crisis of Carolingian imperial rule. As so often in early medieval politics, the succession was the crucial issue. The fuse was lit in late 884 by the death of Carloman II, which left Charles to rule the whole empire alone and without the immediate prospect of a son to succeed him. From this point on, as Regino pointed out, events moved with bewildering speed to a surprising outcome: 'It was a matter worthy of note, and in the varying evaluation of the outcomes of human affairs astonishing.'[1] The succession came to dominate the politics of the subsequent three years: repeated attempts by Charles to designate his illegitimate son Bernard as heir, moves against the claims of Hugh of Lotharingia and Arnulf himself, the adoption of Louis of Provence, and the divorce of the imperial couple all indicate rapid developments and frantic manoeuvrings within the configuration of the ruling house. In order to understand the nature and significance of these events, in this chapter and the next we will contextualise the changing positions of the main protagonists in the political developments of the 880s. The conventional historiographical version of these developments misleadingly foregrounds the decline of 'state' power and the end of imperial unity as symbols of decline. By reconstructing the political narrative of these critical years afresh, we will seek not only to understand better the causes of the empire's disintegration, but also to suggest some broader

[1] Regino, *Chronicon*, s.a. 887, p. 128.

123

Kingship and Politics in the Late Ninth Century

conclusions about how late Carolingian kingship and politics should be characterised.

THE RESTORATION OF THE EMPIRE, 884–5

On 6 December 884 the king of west Francia Carloman II was killed whilst hunting in the forêt de Lyons. His accidental death (opinion was divided as to whether the fatal injury had been administered by an irate boar or a misplaced sword) at the tender age of 18 was just the latest in a series of grave misfortunes to strike at the top of the Carolingian house.[2] The demises in successive years of the elder statesmen Louis II of Italy (875), Louis the German (876) and Charles the Bald (877) opened the door to what must have seemed to be the start of a new generation of kings at the head of European affairs; this generation, however, was very soon all but wiped out by a bewildering mixture of illness and misadventure. From Louis the Stammerer in 879 to Carloman in 884, five of the six surviving Carolingian kings met premature deaths, and left no legitimate male heirs to succeed them. The intra-family agreement made in 880, which provided for the peaceful succession of these rulers to each other's kingdoms, thus inevitably began to fall apart. The mood of optimism which had inspired the author of the poem *Ludwigslied* to enthuse in 881 about the bellicose qualities of the vigorous Louis III must have turned to disbelief a year later when the heroic king met his doom, a jocular attempt to chase a girl into a house misfiring as he failed to register the potential dangers of riding horses through low doorways.[3] And to anyone who had shared the renewed hope of Hincmar of Rheims in the promise of Carloman II, a hope which inspired the archbishop to revise for him the tract *On the Governance of the Palace*, the outcome of the royal hunt in winter 884 must have been extremely dispiriting. Although no source goes so far as to read the dynasty's bad luck as an expression of divine judgement, the thought must have passed through some minds as the renewed Viking onslaught battered the shores of northern Europe and the descent line of Charles the Bald started grinding to an abrupt and unexpected halt.

Whether or not such gloomy uncertainties were entertained in the minds of contemporaries, at the end of 884 Charles the Fat was, as the only adult male legitimate Carolingian still alive, the only candidate able to succeed Carloman. That the west Franks chose him ahead of one

---

[2] *AV* s.a. 884, p. 55; *AF(M)* s.a. 884, p. 101; Regino, *Chronicon*, s.a. 884, pp. 121–2. Confusion over date and place resolved by Bautier in the introduction to DD C2, pp. liv–lvi.

[3] *AV* s.a. 882, p. 52.

The end of the empire I: politics and ideology at the East Frankish court

of their own number is testimony to the enduring vitality of Carolingian hegemony at this date. Louis the Stammerer's third son Charles the Simple, a five-year-old, was too young to take over a realm beset with Vikings.[4] Although minors had succeeded in such circumstances before and would do so again, the situation was especially serious in 884–5. As the price for their retreat, the Vikings at Amiens had already extracted a phenomenal 12,000 pounds of gold and silver from Carloman, and with an eye to the main chance were now claiming that the king's death released them from their part of the bargain. The new king, whoever he might be, would have to renew the tribute.[5] In the winter of 884–5, then, the uneasy aristocratic communities of the west Frankish kingdom required a leader with the military and political resources to meet this immediate threat, and hoped that Charles the Fat, a man with some experience in such matters, would fit the bill.

By tracing Charles's movements in the first months of 885, we can highlight some important aspects of contemporary political culture and introduce the political circumstances which led to the crisis of his reign. Our best source for the west Frankish reaction to Carloman's death is the contemporary and local annalist of St-Vaast, who tells us that Count Theoderic of Vermandois was sent to Italy to invite Charles to come to Francia. As we saw in the last chapter, Theoderic represented an influential group of magnates from the Paris area (Francia 'proper') which had been close to Carloman II, and had been in a position to orchestrate the dead king's funeral at St-Denis.[6] As a result, they had access to the west Frankish regalia, the clothing, crown, sceptre and sword with which Charles the Bald had passed on the *regnum* to Louis the Stammerer, and which in turn became the property of Louis III and, presumably, Carloman II.[7] This gear had evidently become a necessary accoutrement to legitimate kingship in the western kingdom, and so was probably passed on by Theoderic to Charles the Fat.

On the strength of the report in the *Annals of St-Vaast*, it appears that the invitation was sent out immediately after Carloman's death, and indeed probably before the end of 884. Charles seems, moreover, to have received Theoderic, or at least his message, by February 885 at the latest, for it is on the 15th of that month that we find him issuing an interesting charter in favour of Vodelgis, a *fidelis* of the *marchio* Rudolf.[8] This document was probably issued at Pavia, and can hence be connected with the emperor's preparations to cross the main route over the Mons Iovis pass from Pavia to

---

[4] He was passed over for this reason again in 888: Flodoard, *Historia*, 4.5, p. 563.
[5] Regino, *Chronicon*, s.a. 884, p. 122; *AV* s.a. 884, p. 55; *AF(M)* s.a. 884, pp. 101–2.
[6] *AV* s.a. 884, p. 56; see above, pp. 102–9.   [7] *AB* s.a. 877, pp. 218–19; 879, pp. 234–5.
[8] D CIII 112. Vodelgis later passed on the gift to the church of Lausanne: D RB 7.

125

Kingship and Politics in the Late Ninth Century

Transjurane Burgundy, where Vodelgis and Rudolf were based, and then on to the west. The gift concerns the transfer of considerable properties in the Transjurane area, and it is quite likely that Vodelgis was thus to be in charge of provisioning the imperial entourage as it crossed the Alps and the Jura, and that the properties granted, which were clustered round Yverdon by the main route north-west to Langres via Orbe, were intended to help him do so.[9]

Charles was therefore preparing to make his way west already in February 885. Nevertheless, he did not actually enter the western kingdom itself until mid-June, when he received the submissions of the west Frankish aristocracy at Ponthion.[10] Already prior to this, however, he was issuing charters as 'rex in Gallia'. In other words, the 'constitutive' act of Charles's accession to the west in the eyes of the court was neither his reception of the aristocrats' invitation in early 885, nor his acceptance of their formal submission in June, but rather some other event in between. What might that event have been?

The first charters issued by Charles as 'rex in Gallia' were enacted at Grand in Lotharingia on 20 May 885, and there are no fewer than three of them.[11] This is an unusually high number of charters to be enacted on one day by Charles, or indeed by any Carolingian, and they reveal the presence of several members of the high aristocracy, including Askericus, bishop-elect of Paris, the *marchio* Rudolf, and Wibod, bishop of Parma.[12] A large and important assembly was clearly in progress. The circumstances suggest that it may well have been a consecration ceremony. Consecration, on which Carolingian kingship had always been predicated, was by this time an established component of king-making ceremonies west of the Rhine. Moreover, 20 May 885 was the feast of the Ascension, an eminently appropriate day and quite in keeping with Carolingian use of the sacred calendar to make political statements.[13] Grand itself was also a symbolic venue. It was one of the biggest Roman amphitheatres anywhere in the empire, as well as an important late-Roman religious site.[14] Equally

---

[9] For Charles's speedy journey west across Lombardy, see DD CIII 110–15; *AF(M)* s.a. 884, p. 101; *AF(B)* s.a. 884, 885, p. 113.

[10] *AV* s.a. 885, p. 56. D CIII 122 was issued at Ponthion on 16 June; D 121 at Toul on 12 June.

[11] DD CIII 116–8. For the place, convincingly refuting Kehr's tentative identification of Granges, see Bautier, 'Les diplômes royaux', p. 220 with n. 39.

[12] Askericus: D CIII 116. The presence of Wibod is made probable by his reception of D 115 (issued at Pavia in April) and D 126 (issued at Etrepy in June). Rudolf: D 116. Although Rudolf is not called *marchio* here, the term was used inconsistently in royal charters and often substituted with *comes*, as Ehlers, 'Die Anfänge der französischen Geschichte', pp. 22–3 shows.

[13] M. Sierck, *Festtag und Politik. Studien zur Tagewahl karolingischer Herrscher* (Cologne, Weimar and Vienna, 1995), p. 95.

[14] R. Billoret, 'Grand. Le site gallo-romain. Les nouvelles fouilles 1960–2. La Mosaïque', *Le Pays Lorraine* 44 (1963), 49–80.

The end of the empire I: politics and ideology at the East Frankish court

interesting is the fact that two of the three charters were issued on the intervention of Bishop Geilo of Langres, in whose diocese Grand lay. Intervention formulas are a good indicator of who was 'in' and 'out' at court at any given point: Geilo was, therefore, already enjoying privileged proximity to his new king's ear, and was mediating royal access on this very occasion. The bishop was no stranger to the procedures of king-making: in 879 he had participated in the assembly at Mantaille which had elevated Boso of Vienne to royal status, and in 888 he would consecrate Guy of Spoleto to the west Frankish kingdom, again in the diocese of Langres.[15] Moreover, Charles's consecration was conspicuously commemorated at Langres by order of the emperor.[16] It seems likely, taking all these factors into account, that Geilo anointed Charles as king at Grand on 20 May 885. This would explain why Charles began to style himself 'rex in Gallia' at this point, rather than before or afterwards.

From Charles's point of view Grand was a location chiming with imperial echoes, an ideal forum for the parading of his newly-acquired regalia and for stressing the legitimacy of his rule. However, we must further ask ourselves for whose eyes this performance was intended. The primary audience must have been Lotharingian. The annalist of St-Vaast, when describing the people who came to subject themselves to the new king at Ponthion in June, uses the phrase 'everyone who was in the kingdom of Carloman'.[17] This annalist was very sensitive to what might be called the 'regnality' of the Frankish empire, that is to say that he usually took care to distinguish between different *regna*.[18] In particular he consistently drew a distinction between the 'kingdom of Carloman' (west Francia) and the 'kingdom of Lothar' (Lotharingia), a sensitivity perhaps informed by the peculiar situation of St-Vaast as part of an island of Lotharingian control in the west Frankish kingdom. The political identity of the middle kingdom under Lothar I and his namesake son had solidified at least enough to leave this residue in the language of political geography, and in 885 the 'kingdom of Lothar' was once again united under a single ruler, something the annalist may have wished to emphasise. Indeed, he reports Charles's first command at Ponthion as the new king in exactly these terms: 'he ordered those from the kingdom of the late Lothar and the kingdom of Carloman to set out against the Northmen at Leuven'.[19] But it was only the men of the 'kingdom of Carloman' who had submitted to him at Ponthion. Charles must, on this evidence, have already

[15] *Conventus Mantalensis*, MGH Capit, vol. 2, no. 284, p. 369; *AV* s.a. 888, p. 64.
[16] DD CIII 129, 147 and 153. See below, pp. 148–9. [17] *AV* s.a. 885, p. 56.
[18] Ehlers, 'Die Anfänge der französischen Geschichte', pp. 27–8.
[19] *AV* s.a. 885, p. 56; similar references at 879, p. 45; 882, p. 52; 884, p. 55; 895, p. 75. *AV* s.a. 896, p. 77 for a distinction between 'Francia' and the land 'supra Mosellam'.

Kingship and Politics in the Late Ninth Century

talked to and received the commendations of the representatives of the Lotharingians, and in a different place.[20]

Grand lay right on the line which had divided Lotharingia into east and west since 870, and was hence an ideal place for the gathering of those Lotharingians who mattered. By virtue of this fact, it also emphasised Charles's assumption of direct control of Lotharingia. The emperor had an established claim to the *regnum*'s eastern half, but had delegated control of the western portion to Louis III and then to Carloman II.[21] While he did retain the right to distribute *honores* there, there is no sign that he formally took the magnates of Lotharingia into his commendation, or that he even visited the western region at all before 885. There may therefore have been a degree of ambiguity in the eyes of the aristocracy about the exact nature of his rule in Lotharingia up to this point, an ambiguity which the consecration of 20 May was meant to eradicate. It is possible that even more specific considerations influenced the choice of venue. Hugh, the illegitimate son of Lothar II, had been an intermittent thorn in the Carolingian side since the 870s due to his repeated attempts to acquire his paternal kingdom, and he had proved capable of attracting the support in this venture of a number of significant Lotharingian magnates.[22] In 885, moreover, Hugh's latest revolt was gathering momentum, set off by the new opportunities opened to him by the death of Carloman II.[23] Grand lay in the heartlands of Hugh's support. After his rebellion failed, he himself was captured at Gondreville, the Carolingian palace which lay only about 20 miles from the amphitheatre.[24] The assembly at Grand was therefore surely intended to make a statement about Charles's authority to Hugh's supporters in particular, as well as to the Lotharingian aristocracy as a whole.

The choice of date (the feast of Ascension) suggests that this ceremony was very carefully worked out in advance. The diplomatic evidence backs this up, as it shows that Geilo had the Grand charters drawn up by his scribes before the emperor arrived in his diocese.[25] This hypothesis also helps explain why Charles was keen to make peace with the rebel Guy

---

[20] Regino, *Chronicon*, s.a. 884, p. 122, states that Charles's reception of the magnates took place at Gondreville, near Grand; this backs up the idea that there were two assemblies (Regino is more interested in the one which took place in Lotharingia; the annalist of St-Vaast in the west Frankish one). DD CIII 119 and 120 seem to place Charles at Gondreville shortly after the assembly at Grand, but the documents are probably later forgeries: Bautier, 'Les diplômes royaux', p. 220, n. 39.

[21] MacLean, 'Carolingian Response to the Revolt of Boso', pp. 30–8.

[22] On his supporters see R. Parisot, *Le Royaume de Lorraine sous les carolingiens (843–923)* (Paris, 1899), pp. 478–9; E. Hlawitschka, *Lotharingien und das Reich an der Schwelle der deutschen Geschichte* (Stuttgart, 1968), pp. 164–7.

[23] See below, pp. 149–53. for a full discussion.   [24] Regino, *Chronicon*, s.a. 885, p. 125.

[25] Bautier, 'Les diplômes royaux', p. 220.

The end of the empire I: politics and ideology at the East Frankish court

of Spoleto before leaving the Italian kingdom for the west: Guy had strong political links in the Langres area, and the re-establishment of good relations with him was probably thought to be a wise prelude to the meeting with Geilo.[26] For all that consecration was by this point a more or less necessary ritual to undergo to make good a claim to kingship west of the Rhine, we can appreciate that Charles took great care to achieve the maximum political impact with the ceremony at Grand.

If the proceedings of this assembly were carefully orchestrated to make an impression on the Lotharingian nobility, it would appear that the consecration which took place there was nevertheless intended to apply to Charles's west Frankish kingship in general. The term 'Gallia', which is used in these charters to express the emperor's new position, could be taken in this period to refer to any one of a variety of political units. The fact that Charles issued charters for west Frankish as well as Lotharingian beneficiaries in the weeks before the assembly at Ponthion suggests that it was employed here to mean everything west of the Rhine.[27] What took place at Ponthion itself must therefore have been simply the formal submission of the west Frankish nobles to the new king: the inaugural (or, perhaps slightly anachronistically, 'constitutive') act of his claim to direct rule of everything west of the Rhine was the anointing at Grand.

From here, some of the Lotharingians may have accompanied Charles to Ponthion, whence, as mentioned above, he despatched the two groups to deal with the Vikings encamped at Leuven. It is significant that this should have been the new king's first act, as indeed it had been when he succeeded Louis the Younger in 882 and set off to attack Asselt: the Viking threat, and specifically that posed by these particular Vikings, had been an important reason for the invitation to him to assume the kingship in 885. As 'rex in Gallia', then, Charles's first move was to send the men of Gallia on a joint venture together to defend against invaders who were threatening both their *regna*.

THE ATTEMPTED LEGITIMATION OF BERNARD, AUGUST–OCTOBER 885

Charles's acquisition of the west Frankish throne in 884–5 reunited the empire under a single ruler for the first time since the death of Louis the

---

[26] For the reconciliation see *AF(M)* s.a. 884, p. 101; *AF(B)* s.a. 885, p. 113. For Guy and Langres see D CIII 61. He was made king by Geilo in 888: *AV* s.a. 888, p. 64.

[27] DD CIII 117 and 118 are for monasteries in Dijon. For an analogy, the 848 consecration of Charles the Bald springs to mind: while this ceremony was designed to bolster the king's authority in Aquitaine, it also stood as Charles's anointing to the whole western kingdom; see Nelson, *Charles the Bald*, p. 155.

129

Kingship and Politics in the Late Ninth Century

Pious almost half a century earlier, and marked a high point in his reign. However, the same circumstances which had brought him this dignity with minimal effort, namely the chance deaths of every other adult male legitimate Carolingian, posed anew the problem which had been thought solved by the intra-family agreement made between the Carolingians who had fought Boso in 880: how to settle the succession? After the death of Carloman no legitimate adult male Carolingians remained who could be expected to succeed in the long term, while Charles's own marriage had been barren for over twenty years and hence looked to be an unlikely source of a solution. Bastards were traditionally excluded from kingship by the Carolingians, who sought thus to limit the potential for conflict within the royal house. In these special circumstances, however, the claims of three surviving illegitimate sons of kings, Charles's own son Bernard (born c. 875), Arnulf of Carinthia (son of Karlmann, born c. 850) and Hugh of Lotharingia (son of Lothar II, born c. 855), came seriously into consideration for the first time.

Charles's first attempt at a solution was to have his bastard son legitimised so that he could be designated as an heir. Our only direct narrative source for this is the vitriolic pen of the Mainz annalist, who records that Charles 'wanted, so the rumour went, to depose certain bishops unreasonably and set up Bernard, his son by a concubine, as heir to the kingdom after him, and because he doubted that he could do this himself, he wanted to have it done by the pope, as if by apostolic authority'.[28] The angry reference to the rumour of deposing bishops reflects the opposition to the plan of the annalist's sponsor Liutbert of Mainz, fearful of a perpetuation of his exclusion from court.[29] It is nonetheless also a clear demonstration of how illegitimacy of birth could be used as grounds for opposition to a royal designation. The rhetoric of birth legitimacy, an idea successfully developed by the Carolingians to limit the number of royal claimants, was obviously still alive: it was expected, even in 885, that only a legitimate member of the dynasty could become the next king. However, this discourse became a serious weakness when the pool of potential rulers was already so diminished.

The exact nature of Bernard's papal 'legitimation' will be discussed in the next chapter: the most likely scenario is that Charles was seeking a dissolution of his marriage so that he could marry his son's mother.[30] For

---

[28] *AF(M)* s.a. 885, p. 103.

[29] The attempted deposition of bishops was also the main grounds for Liutbert's opposition to the divorce of Lothar II (and the associated legitimation of Hugh): Carroll, 'Archbishops and Church Councils', pp. 131–5. On Liutbert, see above, chap. 2.

[30] See below, pp. 168–9.

The end of the empire I: politics and ideology at the East Frankish court

present purposes, we will speculate only on what role Charles had in mind for Bernard's immediate future. We know that the meeting with the pope was scheduled for Worms in October, and that, at this assembly, Charles held talks 'with the bishops and counts of Gaul'.[31] It was highly unusual for the emperor to convene such an assembly for a specific group of magnates in a *regnum* outside their own.[32] He must therefore have had a special reason for demanding that they travel to Worms, and given the purpose of the assembly it seems highly likely that this reason was the acquisition of their consent to the legitimation of Bernard prior to his being set up over them as (sub)king. Who exactly were these bishops and counts? The authors of the *Annals of Fulda* and its continuations employ no consistent usage for the geographical term 'Gaul'; sometimes it refers to Charles the Bald's kingdom, sometimes to everything west of the Rhine. However, it was also frequently used in this period to designate Lotharingia alone, especially when it was being referred to as a political unit. Therefore the Mainz annalist reported in 879 that Hugh of Lotharingia was 'playing the tyrant in Gaul' while Zwentibald's Lotharingian kingdom is described by the Bavarian annalist in 900 as 'Gallicanum regnum'.[33] With this in mind it is interesting to note that the only delegation we can definitely say was present at Worms was from the east Lotharingian monastery of St-Maximian at Trier.[34] This foundation was, to judge from the struggles focused on it during the subsequent decade, the main *honor* which had to be controlled by any prospective ruler of Lotharingia.[35] It is, therefore, a plausible conclusion that Charles invited these *primores* to the papal assembly at Worms because he hoped to establish Bernard with the consent of all present as subking of Lotharingia, perhaps when he had come of age. If this was the case it would also explain the cryptic comment of Notker in the *Deeds of Charlemagne* (885–6), a text shot through with observations on Charles the Fat's succession arrangements, when referring to the sacking of Lotharingia's other principal royal monastery, Prüm, by the Vikings: 'I will not tell you of this [Prüm's destruction] until I see your little son Bernard with a sword girt to his thigh.'[36] In this measure, as in the motivations behind the Vienne agreement of 880, we can see

---

[31] *AF(B)* s.a. 885, p. 113 for the assembly; *AF(M)* s.a. 885, p. 103 for the Gauls. The *AF(M)* claim that Charles only sent envoys to the pope from his assembly at Frankfurt in September is implausible, since Hadrian died en route to east Francia in August or September: R. Davis, *The Lives of the Ninth-Century Popes* (Liverpool, 1995), p. 297, n. 3.

[32] Hlawitschka, *Lotharingien und das Reich*, p. 24.

[33] *AF* s.a. 879, p. 93; *AF(B)* s.a. 900, p. 134. See Brühl, *Deutschland-Frankreich*, pp. 137–9.

[34] D CIII 133.   [35] Innes, *State and Society*, pp. 226–7.

[36] Notker, *Gesta*, 2.12, p. 74. Interestingly, Karlmann's sub-regnal authority in Lotharingia around 870 was partly expressed by his petitioning of a charter for Prüm: D LG 141.

131

Kingship and Politics in the Late Ninth Century

again that control of Lotharingia, a *regnum* rich in royal estates and political prestige, was perceived as a key priority by the rulers of the late Carolingian empire.

A further insight into the whole affair is provided by an imperial charter issued on 28 August 885 at the monastery of Lorsch in favour of the church of Langres.[37] Among the conditions of the grant were that the bishop was to hold an annual feast to commemorate the emperor and his consecration, the first charter of an east Frankish king to make such a specification. He was also to ensure the performance of regular prayers for Charles, his wife, his *antecessores*, his offspring ('proles nostra') and the stability of the whole empire. The provision of prayers for the royal progeny was a staple element of Carolingian prayer formulas which helped to make ubiquitous the dynasty's power, emphasising its special relationship with God at churches across the empire. Significantly, however, they were only formally introduced into Charles's charters in the year 885, after the death of Carloman II and the consequent inception of the plan to legitimise Bernard.[38] This particular charter, moreover, was the first one in Charles's reign to link prayers for his *antecessores* to those for his *proles*. It thus has, in common with several charters of the period, a uniquely dynastic feel.[39] This is made even more obvious when one remembers that 28 August was the anniversary of Louis the German's death, and that Lorsch was the site of his tomb. Behind this document, therefore, lies an attempt by the emperor, perhaps articulated through some sort of ceremony, to connect the unquestionable legitimacy of the past generations of his dead family to his son Bernard, emphasising a dynastic continuity.

---

[37] D CIII 129.

[38] DD CIII 111, 117, 123, 129 (all 885), 135, 147, 149 (all 886), 153 (887). 'Proles' provisions do appear in three charters from before 885, DD 28, 35 and 62, but all are literal copies of earlier models from the reigns of Louis the Pious and Karlmann of Bavaria. Their significance is offset by DD 37 and 102, which are also literal copies of earlier charters but which programmatically exclude the word 'proles' which did feature in their models; see E. Ewig, 'Der Gebetsdienst der Kirchen in den Urkunden der späteren Karolinger', in H. Maurer and H. Patze (eds.), *Festschrift für Berent Schwineköper zu seinem siebzigsten Geburtstag* (Sigmaringen, 1982), pp. 45–86, at p. 75. Evidently there was a will in the chancery to keep the word out, even if supervision was not strict enough to stop over-zealous scribes sometimes copying it back in. Equally, after 885, the conscious effort to include the word is clear, as shown by D 135 for the church of Passau. Its formulas were a literal repeat of those in D 134, issued only three days earlier for the same institution, in which the word 'prolis' in the prayer clause was the only new addition: clearly the scribe had mistakenly left it out in the earlier document and smartly corrected himself in the latter.

[39] Cf., for instance, D CIII 27 for Louis II's burial church; D AC 70 for Lorsch; D K 4, which mentions Louis II, Charles the Bald and Louis the German. For comments see Ewig, 'Der Gebetsdienst der Kirchen', pp. 53, 73, 76 and *passim*; R. Schieffer, 'Väter und Söhne im Karolingerhause', in R. Schieffer (ed.), *Beiträge zur Geschichte des Regnum Francorum* (Sigmaringen, 1990), pp. 149–64, at pp. 162–4.

The end of the empire I: politics and ideology at the East Frankish court

The cloisters of Lorsch rang with several other even more recent dynastic associations which enhanced its suitability as the venue for this performance. Louis the Younger had had his father laid to rest there in 876 and it seems he began to promote it as a family mausoleum for the east Frankish line, providing a focus of Carolingian legitimacy in the heart of his own kingdom.[40] He interred his son Hugh (d. 880) there, and constructed a new entrance hall which may have served as a triumphal arch on the procession route to the tombs.[41] In 882 Louis the Younger himself found his final resting place at the monastery.[42] Moreover, the Lorsch calendar records liturgical commemoration of both Louis the German's death and Louis the Younger's subsequent victory over Charles the Bald at the battle of Andernach.[43] Already in June 884 Charles the Fat had begun to tap into this rich seam of east Frankish dynastic legitimacy by ordering an eternal flame to be maintained at the tombs of his father and brother for the good of all their souls.[44]

This promotion of Bernard's (fictive) legitimacy was highlighted further in the 885 charter for Langres by the narrative section's detailing of how the properties involved had been usurped 'by the tyrannical and sacrilegious temerity of certain *principes*'. This phrase provides a direct contrast between the legitimate ruler, restoring the properties to the wronged church in return for dynastic commemoration, and the illegitimate *tyrannus* and his followers, who had removed the lands by force in the first place. The location of Langres on the edge of Lotharingia and the date of late summer 885 make an identification of these 'tyrants' with the recently captured usurper Hugh of Lotharingia and his aristocratic entourage very tempting: the term 'principes' was used only for men of very high status in the ninth century, while 'tyrant' was reserved for usurpers. The chronology of his rebellion, which will be discussed below, allows the suspicion that he may have been forced to attend the Lorsch ceremony prior to his trial at Frankfurt. This charter, and whatever performances lie behind it, may thus stand as witness to an attempt by Charles the Fat not only to assert and emphasise the dynastic legitimacy of his son Bernard, but to contrast it with the tyrannical illegitimacy of his cousin Hugh.

These ideological messages were intended to prime their audience for the formal legitimising of Bernard by the pope at Worms in October.

[40] Fried, *Ludwig der Jüngere*, p. 13; see also Innes, 'Kings, Monks and Patrons', pp. 318–19.
[41] W. Jacobsen, 'Die Lorscher Torhalle. Zum Problem ihrer Datierung und Deutung', *Jahrbuch des Zentralinstituts für Kunstgeschichte* 1 (1985), 9–75.
[42] *AF* s.a. 882, p. 97.
[43] M. McCormick, *Eternal Victory. Triumphal Rulership in Late Antiquity, Byzantium, and the Early Medieval West* (Cambridge, 1986), pp. 361–2.
[44] D CIII 103.

Kingship and Politics in the Late Ninth Century

Every resource was being tapped in support of a move which lacked a better precedent than the inauspicious and indeed scandalous efforts of Lothar II, and was by no means guaranteed to succeed. Unfortunately for him, the effectiveness of Charles's pro-Bernard propaganda did not have a chance to be tested: Pope Hadrian III died on the road before even making it out of Italy.[45] Before considering the consequences of this turn of events for Charles, however, we must examine the positions of the other potential claimants to the throne at this pregnant moment in the politics of the imperial succession, namely Hugh of Lotharingia and, firstly, Arnulf of Carinthia.

THE POSITION OF ARNULF, 876–85

After tracing the descent line of the Carolingian dynasty from 840 down to 881 in his continuation of the chronicle of Erchanbert, Notker the Stammerer cast an approving eye over the Carolingians ruling in his own time. In the west he was glad to see the line of Charles the Bald culminate in the young and vigorous kings Louis III and Carloman II, to whom he referred as 'the hope of Europe'. In his own eastern kingdom, meanwhile, Notker's appreciation of the regal qualities of both Louis the Younger and Charles the Fat was tempered by nagging doubts over their lack of heirs. For the long-term survival of the line of Louis the German, he chose to place his hopes on the shoulders of the late Karlmann's illegitimate son Arnulf: 'O! How I hope he will live, so that the light of the great Louis is not extinguished from the house of the Lord!'[46]

The monk of St-Gall backed up this hope by trying to counteract the memory of Arnulf's illegitimate birth (c. 850) with a heavy stress on the nobility of his mother Liutswind.[47] Indeed, his (fictive) status as an honorary full-born Carolingian may have originally been pushed forward by Karlmann, who lacked other sons and initially hoped that Arnulf would succeed him in Bavaria at least.[48] This intention is reflected in a Regensburg charter from Karlmann's reign, which gives Arnulf the designation 'royal son' (*filius regalis*).[49] This unusual epithet seems to emphasise the son's regality in a more independent way than the customary 'king's son' (*filius regis*). However, Karlmann's plans for his son were hampered by the stroke the king suffered in early 879.[50] Louis the Younger took advantage by trying to extract the allegiance of as many of the Bavarian leading

---

[45] *AF(M)* s.a. 885, p. 103.   [46] Notker, *Continuatio*, p. 330.
[47] *Ibid.*: 'nobilissima femina'. On her, see Schieffer, 'Karl III. und Arnolf', pp. 135–6. Cf. Regino, *Chronicon*, s.a. 880, p. 116, who also appeals to the nobility of Arnulf's mother, along with the resonances of his name, to bridge the legitimacy gap.
[48] Schieffer, 'Karl III. und Arnolf', p. 137.   [49] D Reg 86.   [50] *AF* s.a. 879, p. 92.

The end of the empire I: politics and ideology at the East Frankish court

men as he could, but the situation remained uncertain, as revealed by a Regensburg charter from 879 which is dated by the reigns of all three sons of Louis the German: the drafter clearly had doubts as to who his next king would be.[51] This uneasy situation prevailed after Louis left Bavaria before Easter, when Arnulf seems to have taken over as king in all but name, assuming responsibility for relieving some prominent counts, who were in disagreement with him and his father, of their *honores*. At about the same time, with all parties staking their claims and illness forcing Karlmann to try to regulate his succession definitively, the king started to include Arnulf in the prayer provisions of his charters in an attempt to bolster his son's position further.[52] However, the aggrieved counts appealed to Louis, who duly moved east in November and started to rule by returning their offices. Evidently, there were divisive differences of opinion among the Bavarian nobles as to who should succeed, differences which persisted as long as Karlmann remained as a lame duck ruler. Ultimately these differences were resolved when the latter, too ill to oppose his brother, formally abdicated in Louis's favour, commending Arnulf to him along with the kingdom.[53] The outcome was not, however, inevitable: clearly, Arnulf's succession was feared to be a realistic prospect by his opponents.

Although deprived by Louis of the regnal authority which he had enjoyed in the summer and autumn of 879, Arnulf was allowed to keep the position he had earlier filled under Karlmann: Regino specifies this as control of Carinthia, the modern Austrian region lying to the south-east of Bavaria.[54] We can supplement the abbot of Prüm's report with that of the Bavarian continuator for 884, where it is stated that Arnulf 'held Pannonia' (the south-east frontier of the empire).[55] However, by 884 parts of Pannonia were controlled by the Frankish client *dux* Brazlavo (between the Sava and Drava rivers) and the margrave Arbo (along the Danube), so this evidence requires some refining. A charter dating from between 876 and 880 allows us to be more specific concerning Arnulf's territory. It records a transaction as part of which the deacon Gundbato handed over to the monastery of St-Emmeram in Regensburg his property at

---

[51] D Reg 92.

[52] D K 27 from August; see Ewig, 'Der Gebetsdienst der Kirchen', p. 73 with n. 274.

[53] *AF* s.a. 879, pp. 92–3 for the above events. *AB* s.a. 879, p. 238 and *AS* s.a. 878, p. 742 also record aspects of the fracas. D LY 13 is the proof that Louis was in Regensburg in November.

[54] Regino, *Chronicon*, s.a. 880, p. 117: 'Louis conceded Carinthia to Arnulf, which his father had long ago also given him.'

[55] *AF(B)* s.a. 884, p. 112. K. Bertels, 'Carantania. Beobachtungen zur politisch-geographischen Terminologie und zur Geschichte des Landes und seiner Bevölkerung im frühen Mittelalter', *Carinthia I* 177 (1987), 87–196, at 165–8, speculates that Regino implicitly included Pannonia in his use of the unusual term 'Carantanum'.

Kingship and Politics in the Late Ninth Century

Quartinaha in Pannonia, 'with the permission of his lord the royal off-spring Arnulf, from whom he had received it in possession'.[56] We know from the *Booklet on the Conversion of the Bavarians and Carinthians* (c. 871) that Quartinaha had previously been in the possession of the Slav *dux* (military leader) Kocel (or Chezil).[57] Kocel, and before him his father Pribina, were client princes of the Carolingians whose power base lay in Lower Pannonia, focused on the fortress of Moosburg just west of Lake Balaton, where many of their properties, including Quartinaha, were concentrated.[58] This evidence therefore suggests that Arnulf had been installed in this extended Lower Pannonian realm, which retained both its cohesion and its importance through to the mid-890s at least, in succession to Kocel, who probably died in 875.[59] The immediate bene-fit of this arrangement had been that it provided protection on the east side for Karlmann's expeditions into Italy, some of which were launched from Carinthia.[60] We can also appreciate from the Gundbato charter that Arnulf's authority in Pannonia under Karlmann and probably Louis was quite considerable, and extended to the (royal) prerogative of distribution of significant properties.

A renewal and slight enhancement of Gundbato's charter in the 880s confirms that Arnulf retained control of this strategically important lord-ship under Charles the Fat, whose succession to Bavaria in 882 he does not seem to have challenged.[61] This document was promulgated in Pannonia itself before legates of the bishop of Regensburg and 'in the presence of the *dux* Arnulf'. The use of the designation 'dux' implies a military responsibility which tallies with Arnulf's role as leader of the Bavarians on the Asselt campaign of 882.[62] This military role is commensurate with his control of the south-eastern marches. Therefore, although the charter of confirmation does not, like the original, highlight Arnulf's association

---

[56] D Reg 86.

[57] *De conversione Bagoariorum et Carantanorum Libellus*, ed. G. H. Pertz, MGH SS (vol. 11, Hanover, 1854), p. 14. On the text see now S. Airlie, 'True Teachers and Pious Kings: Salzburg, Louis the German, and Christian Order', in R. Gameson and H. Leyser (eds.), *Belief and Culture in the Middle Ages* (Oxford, 2001).

[58] Moosburg is at modern Zalavár in Hungary, and is not to be confused with the fortress of the same name in Carinthia. On the establishment of Pribina and Kocel's lordship see *De conversione*, pp. 11–14 and Bowlus, *Franks, Moravians and Magyars*, pp. 104–7. For the following see Map 5.

[59] H. Wolfram, *Die Geburt Mitteleuropas. Geschichte Österreichs vor seiner Entstehung, 378–907* (Vienna, 1987), p. 290 with n. 2 for Kocel's death date. The enduring cohesion of the Pannonian command focused on Moosburg is demonstrated by *AF(B)* s.a. 896, p. 130. Arnulf often stayed at Moosburg in the early years of his reign: see Bowlus, 'Arnulf of Carinthia's *Ostpolitik*' for exegesis of his itinerary. D Reg 86 also reveals that Kocel had had properties as far north and west as the Raba river, properties which now came into the hands of Arnulf's man Gundbato: this may have marked the boundary of Kocel/Arnulf's realm, which would explain why it was the terminal point for the ravages of his enemy Zwentibald in their war of 882–4: *AF(B)* s.a. 884, p. 113.

[60] Bowlus, *Franks, Moravians and Magyars*, p. 201.   [61] D Reg 102.   [62] *AF(B)* s.a. 882, p. 107.

136

The end of the empire I: politics and ideology at the East Frankish court

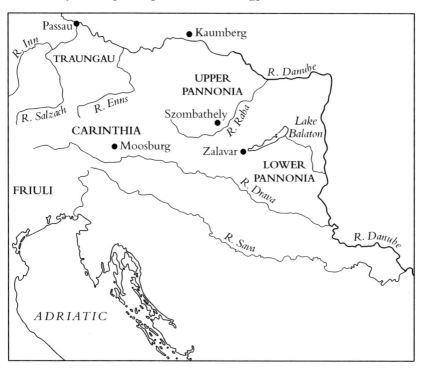

Map 5. Carinthia and Pannonia

with full royal authority with a term like 'royal son', and although he was not necessarily the dominant figure in the politics of the Bavarian kingdom, his initial position under Charles the Fat was powerful and important, at least militarily.[63] The *Annals of Fulda* and its continuations are silent about events on the eastern frontier during the 880s with the sole exception of the Wilhelminer War: this may be a sign that Charles had been happy to delegate management of the region to Arnulf. In fact, the latter's authority even exceeded that enjoyed by his father at a similar age, which was confined largely to military responsibility for Carinthia alone.[64] Because before 884 Louis III and Carloman II remained ahead of him in the queue for the throne, Arnulf, and presumably his admirers like Notker, cannot have been dissatisfied with the role assigned to him by his uncle.

---

[63] G. Tellenbach, 'Zur Geschichte Kaiser Arnulfs', *HZ* 165 (1942), 229–45, at 231–3 argues for Arnulf's domination of Bavaria. Cf. above, p. 99, for the importance of the Bavarian bishoprics.
[64] *AF* s.a. 863, p. 56 says he was 'praelatus Carantanis'.

Kingship and Politics in the Late Ninth Century

The honeymoon period was not to last long. Arnulf's relationship with Charles was irreparably damaged by the so-called Wilhelminer War, a long account of which dominates the Bavarian continuator's annal for 884.[65] The roots of the trouble reached back to 871, when Louis the German appointed a certain Arbo to the command of a key part of the Slavic frontier on the Danube, stretching from the Traungau along to the Vienna basin, then south-east to Szombathely and the Raba river.[66] The sons of the previous incumbents, the celebrated margraves William and Engelschalk, took exception to this state of affairs, and in the reign of Charles the Fat began a campaign to eject Arbo, which met with initial success. Arbo appealed for and received help from both Zwentibald, leader of the Moravian Slavs, and the emperor, who reinstalled the margrave in his command. Zwentibald then escalated the scale of the conflict by invading Pannonia and mutilating one of the sons, revenge, the annalist tells us, both for the harm done to Arbo and for the injuries done to the Moravians by the late margraves William and Engelschalk. This caused the remaining sons to withdraw from the authority of Charles the Fat in order to become the men of Arnulf. Arnulf refused to swear oaths of peace with Zwentibald, or to hand over the sons, to which the Moravians responded with further invasions. Finally, after the conflict had taken up the best part of two and a half years, the emperor himself turned up in late 884 and received Zwentibald as his man at the Kaumberg near Tulln, receiving promises of peace and fidelity.[67] The Slavic *dux* Brazlavo was also received as Charles's man on this occasion.[68] Peace was not sealed between Arnulf and the Moravians until the latter part of the following year.[69]

Some important points concerning Charles's relationship with Arnulf emerge from this protracted feud. Firstly, the emperor's will concerning eastern frontier comital appointments prevailed: Arnulf had no rights as far as redistributing *honores* went. Admittedly, the cost was unusually high, but then dispossessing the scions of an established margrave family was an unusually bold decision, considering that standard Carolingian tactics would have been to rubber-stamp the status quo. Moreover, despite his obvious distress at the whole affair, and his particular hatred for the Moravians, who acted on behalf of Arbo and eventually Charles, the Bavarian annalist ultimately blamed the sons, stating that the tragedy had

---

[65] *AF(B)* s.a. 884, pp. 110–13. For commentary see Bowlus, *Franks, Moravians and Magyars*, pp. 208–16.

[66] Bowlus, *Franks, Moravians and Magyars*, p. 208; Wolfram, *Die Geburt Mitteleuropas*, p. 289.

[67] *AF(B)* s.a. 884, p. 113.

[68] See Wolfram, *Die Geburt Mitteleuropas*, pp. 355–7 on him.   [69] *AF(B)* s.a. 885, p. 114.

The end of the empire I: politics and ideology at the East Frankish court

come about 'as a result of the actions of the said children'.[70] Secondly, it is clear that Arnulf made a conscious decision to stand against Charles when he received the sons as his men after they withdrew from the emperor's commendation. Opposition to the appointment of Arbo and all that stemmed from it was an act of rebellion, a situation which was publicly recognised when Charles formally acknowledged Zwentibald's fidelity in 884 at the Kaumberg, which, pointedly, was a key stronghold in Arbo's lordship.[71] The Moravian *dux* was (politically and geographically) a natural ally for the emperor against Arnulf, who posed the additional threat of being a potential usurper: the meeting at the Kaumberg did not humble Zwentibald, but rather established him as a Frankish client.[72] As he and Arnulf were still at war, this act implicitly gave imperial sanction for the continuation of the conflict. This display of force and unity must not only have demoralised Arnulf, but also set the seal on the major territorial gains which Zwentibald had made and retained in Lower Pannonia.[73] The course of the Wilhelminer War is a classic example of the interplay between aristocratic rivalries, royal authority and external peoples which frequently determined the course of events on the Carolingian frontiers.[74] That it happened at all is not a symbol of declining Carolingian prestige. No western European dynasty of the early medieval period controlled a monopoly of the means of legitimate force. Moreover, the war's outcome was not, as has been claimed, damaging to Charles the Fat's authority; rather, his positive intervention ensured that it was ultimately a major political setback for his nephew.[75] The point was emphatically driven home by the route of the emperor's subsequent journey to Italy, on

---

[70] *AF(B)* s.a. 884, p. 112. This could also be rendered: 'through the puerile plan made beforehand', but the general point still stands.

[71] A clue to Arnulf's motives in his vehement opposition to Arbo may be given by the latter's close family links to Pribina and Kocel: Bowlus, *Franks, Moravians and Magyars*, pp. 202–8. This may have given him a claim to influence in the Lower Pannonian lordship which threatened Arnulf.

[72] As Bowlus, *Franks, Moravians and Magyars*, p. 214 rightly stresses.

[73] *Ibid.*, p. 292; Wolfram, *Die Geburt Mitteleuropas*, p. 292; Notker, *Gesta*, 2.14, p. 78 refers to Arnulf's lands as 'diminished'. The location of Moravia and of the main engagements of this war are matters of debate, but there is agreement that Arnulf's Pannonian losses were big: see M. Eggers, *Das Grossmährische Reich. Realität oder Fiktion. Eine Neuinterpretation der Quellen zur Geschichte des mittleren Donauraumes im 9. Jahrhundert* (Stuttgart, 1995), pp. 256–7, 263–8.

[74] Reuter, *Germany in the Early Middle Ages*, pp. 124–5.

[75] For instance, J. M. H. Smith, '*Fines imperii*: the Marches', in *NCMH2*, pp. 169–89, at p. 182; cf. Reuter, *Germany in the Early Middle Ages*, p. 116. We should also note here that by turning against Zwentibald, Arnulf saw a decline in the influence over the Moravian church of his ally Bishop Wiching of Nitra, and a consonant increase in the authority of Wiching's rival Methodius, who was supported by Charles: Bowlus, *Franks, Moravians and Magyars*, pp. 214–15; A. Róna-Tás, *Hungarians and Europe in the Early Middle Ages* (Budapest and New York, 1999), p. 286. This severing of ecclesiastical links between Arnulf and Zwentibald must have isolated him even more.

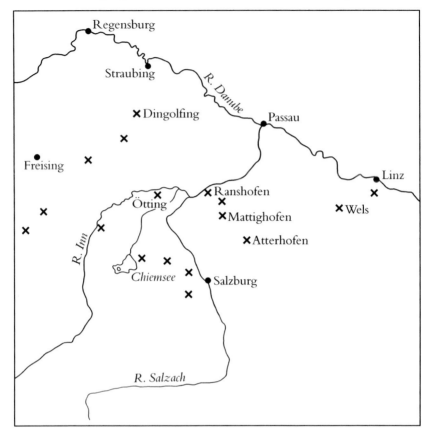

Map 6. Fiscal rights granted to Ötting in D CIII 128

which he pointedly conducted his army through Arnulf's heartland in Carinthia.[76]

The whole episode demonstrated to Arnulf the practical limits of his authority, much as had the resolutions of similar conflicts between Louis the German and his sons. Arnulf was able to intervene for the rebels as an alternative point of authority with a semi-autonomous power base. As with Louis the German's sons, however, such activities would always bring royal anger down on the rebels' heads: as a Carolingian himself, the potential for Arnulf's rebellion to become a usurpation was too great to ignore. On the other side of the coin, Arnulf was not the ruler's son, nor was he of legitimate birth, and hence he could have no automatic

---

[76] *AF(B)* s.a. 884, p. 113; Bowlus, 'Arnulf of Carinthia's *Ostpolitik*', p. 561 with n. 22.

The end of the empire I: politics and ideology at the East Frankish court

expectation of a share in royal power. Failure to remain in the emperor's good books was potentially very damaging to any hopes he might have had of succeeding to a throne, and there are some indications that, once the Wilhelminer War brought him to his knees, Charles wanted to keep him there. The evidence comes in the form of a charter issued by the emperor in favour of the church of Ötting on 25 August 885.[77] This document records a rather substantial gift of fiscal rights in no fewer than nineteen royal *curtes*, in addition to a share of the tolls at two. The estates named are all in eastern Bavaria and Upper Austria, primarily in the complex of royal properties in the region of the Inn and Salzach river valleys. This area had been the springboard for many a campaign into Carinthia and Pannonia in the reigns of Louis the German and, especially, Karlmann, and some of these very estates were regularly involved in provisioning such excursions.[78] Three of the first four centres named in the charter, Ranshofen, Mattighofen and Atterhofen, were absolutely essential to Carolingian logistical structures on the way to Salzburg and the middle Enns passes.[79] Others, such as Dingolfing and Loiching on the Isar, were used as staging points on the way from Regensburg down to the Inn–Salzach complex. In the ninth century, grants such as these often indicated the preparation of a campaign route for the arrival of an army.[80] By giving these rights to the royal chapel attached to the important royal palace of Ötting, the tomb of King Karlmann, Charles was reinforcing this extensive royal logistical network and securing its readiness to support a royal army passing through the region.

What makes this gift even more striking is that throughout the previous part of his reign Charles had shown absolutely no interest in the Inn–Salzach area, preferring instead to bolster the properties and privileges of churches on the other major route east, from Regensburg downstream along the Danube and through Arbo's lordship.[81] This was the path he had taken on his only previous visit to the marches as king, en route to meet Zwentibald in 884 at the Kaumberg, which itself lay on property administered by the church of Regensburg.[82] The Ötting charter also stands out among Charles's Bavarian diplomas by having been

[77] D CIII 128 enacted at Waiblingen. See Map 6.
[78] Bowlus, *Franks, Moravians and Magyars*, pp. 197–201 offers observations on the region under Karlmann.
[79] *Ibid.*, p. 84. The other one of the four, Wels, was connected to Mattighofen by road, and was also a key supply point on the route to Carinthia; *ibid.*, p. 231.
[80] Bowlus, *Franks, Moravians and Magyars*, pp. 30–2 is the most accessible discussion of the methodology.
[81] DD CIII 59, 72–5, 107, 113, 127, 134–5.
[82] DD CIII 107–9 were issued at Regensburg in September 884 on the way to this meeting. D LG 96 for Regensburg's rights in the area. Charles had earlier visited the marches on campaign in 869: *AF* s.a. 869, pp. 68–9.

141

issued in Alemannia: he normally patronised Bavarian institutions only when in that *regnum*.[83] We may assume, therefore, that his sudden interest in the Ötting network as he passed through Alemannia in August 885 had a particular reason, and the most likely explanation is that he was planning a campaign of some sort across the passes into Carinthia.[84]

Two circumstances allow us to furnish Charles with a motive for deciding at this point to impress Arnulf with another show of force. Firstly, in August 885, Arnulf had still not made peace with the Moravians, and so remained the one volatile element in the configuration of the south-eastern marches: Arbo to his north, Brazlavo to his south, and Zwentibald to his east (now in possession of the area between Lake Balaton and the Danube) all stood in confirmed loyalty to the emperor. Secondly, the Ötting charter was enacted only three days before the ceremony held at Lorsch which was designed, as we have seen, to pave the way for the designation of Bernard as the emperor's heir.[85] The projected campaign which lies behind the Ötting document was thus a product of a time in which Charles's thinking was dominated by the resolution of the imperial succession. It was surely intended to pre-empt any resistance Arnulf may have mounted to Bernard's designation, which threatened his own hopes of a crown. Such resistance was all the more likely to be forthcoming because, with the death of the logical and intended successor Carloman II in December 884, the claims of illegitimate Carolingians acquired a new credibility. Since Arnulf had already shown himself willing to rebel over matters of considerably less import, another visit to his heartland from the emperor and his army was a timely measure to take in support of the controversial plan to designate Bernard, and was justified by the fact that Arnulf was still in a state of war with confirmed imperial allies in the south-east.

We know that Charles had already arranged to meet Hadrian III at Worms in early October to legitimise Bernard, so any campaign could not have proceeded until after that date. Charles eventually spent Christmas and part of January at Regensburg and, given the timescale and the general inaccessibility of Alpine passes in the winter, it seems likely that this pause had been his intention from the beginning.[86] Here was a built-in

---

[83] Bührer-Thierry, 'Les évêques de Bavière', pp. 38–9. This is largely true of all Charles's charters, which were only in unusual circumstances issued outside the kingdom they concerned.

[84] D CIII 127 reveals that Engilmar, abbot of Regensburg and bishop of Passau, was also present at Waiblingen. This is a unique example in Charles's reign of a Bavarian churchman travelling outside his home *regnum* to obtain a charter, and is presumably to be explained by his participation in the planning of this campaign. Both churches had substantial interests in Carinthia.

[85] See above, pp. 132–4.

[86] For itinerary details see *AF(M)* s.a. 885, p. 103; *AF(B)* s.a. 886, p. 114; DD CIII 134–5.

The end of the empire I: politics and ideology at the East Frankish court

opportunity for Arnulf to come to terms with the situation: he took it, making peace with Zwentibald under the watchful eyes of the Bavarian nobles.[87] The Bavarian continuator, our source for this agreement, places it at the very end of his annal for 885, after the blinding of Hugh, which probably took place in September.[88] It is therefore quite likely that Arnulf instigated the peace after hearing that Charles was planning to head east. Ultimately, the emperor never made the crossing into Carinthia, travelling instead to Italy to meet the new pope. We may assume that this was because, after ending his quarrel with the Moravians, Arnulf appeared in Regensburg himself over the festive season and gave satisfaction to his uncle.[89] He would have been all the readier to do so after the death of the pope, a setback for Bernard which rekindled his own hopes of receiving some sort of royal designation.

To summarise, it is clear that Arnulf's position changed over time. Having tasted actual royal power as his father's regent in the middle months of 879, he failed to secure the succession but retained his position under Louis the Younger. Initially well placed under Charles the Fat's authority in a military role analogous to (but more extensive than) that which had been enjoyed by Karlmann in his younger days, his part in the Wilhelminer War of 882–4 lost him the favour of the emperor as well as large stretches of territory in Lower Pannonia. His fall from grace had, by an unlucky twist of fate, coincided with the deaths of the last legitimate Carolingian rulers: he hit his political nadir just as his claim to share in the imperial succession might have acquired new plausibility. Accordingly, Charles decided to put all his eggs into Bernard's basket, not merely passing over Arnulf but taking active measures to keep him in his place.

That the swift failure of Bernard's planned legitimation gave Arnulf new hopes of a return to high favour is probable, but Charles showed himself little inclined to satisfy them. By the time Notker the Stammerer came to write his *Deeds of Charlemagne* (885–6) for Charles the Fat, he had lost the cautious optimism he had expressed in 881 for Arnulf's chances of succeeding the heirless Charles the Fat. Now it seemed to him that even Arnulf's military responsibilities had been criminally reduced: 'May your own sword, tempered already in the gore of the Northmen, stand in their way, and may the sword of your brother Karlmann, which is stained in their blood too, be joined to yours', he told the emperor, with an obvious reference to Charles and Arnulf's cooperation at Asselt:

---

[87] *AF(B)* s.a. 885, p. 114. [88] See below, pp. 149–51.

[89] The Bavarian annalist's reference to the presence of the Bavarian nobles suggests that Arnulf made this peace at court in Regensburg. See pp. 156–8 for more on this hypothetical encounter.

143

Kingship and Politics in the Late Ninth Century

But Karlmann's sword is now rusting away, not through cowardice, but through want of funds and because the lands of your most faithful Arnulf are so diminished. If you in your mighty power only have the will to ordain this, it should not be a difficult matter for this sword to be made sharp and bright once more. This one small bough, together with the tiny twig which is Bernard, is all that is left to burgeon on the once-prolific stock of Louis, and it is under the branch of your own protection, which alone remains, that it is free to form its leaf.[90]

Not only was Arnulf's military involvement now limited, but Notker's words imply a perception on his part that Arnulf's chances of succession had been ruled out by the emperor; he exhorted Charles to remember that Arnulf was just as much of the line of Louis the Pious as was Bernard. This point had also been implicit in his *Continuation of the Chronicle of Erchanbert*, which drew a line through the descent of the Carolingians from Louis the Pious down to Louis the Younger, Charles the Fat and Arnulf. Charles's determined preference for the 'tiny twig' (Bernard) over the 'small bough' (Arnulf) at a time when the options were so limited exasperated the monk of St-Gall and filled him with great trepidation for the line's continuance.[91] Notker astutely saw, to continue with his felicitous arboreal metaphor, that the Carolingian family tree was in danger of withering unless all of its branches were tended. As will become clear, Charles's failure to listen to Notker's advice was his ultimate undoing. In the end, it was his stubborn refusal to consider Arnulf's claims after 885 which would drive his nephew back into rebellion and inspire the fateful coup of November 887.

THE REVOLT OF HUGH, SEPTEMBER 885, AND THE ORIGINS OF 'GERMAN' ROYAL CONSECRATION

The earlier analysis of the Lorsch charter of August 885 as a weapon in the ideological armoury deployed by Charles in support of his plan to legitimise Bernard illustrated how royal diplomas can give us valuable evidence for the political agenda of the Carolingian court at particular moments. The prayer clauses by which the Carolingians sought to harness the intercessory power of the church and its martyrs to their own worldly success could also contain coded political messages. The Lorsch charter, as well as providing a clear example of this, also introduces us to another type of formula which, if anything, was even more obviously political, namely that which demanded the celebration of significant anniversaries in the lifetime of a ruler. This type of provision, which was founded on late Roman antecedents, achieved its greatest

[90] Notker, *Gesta*, 2.14, p. 78.   [91] See below, pp. 218–22.

The end of the empire I: politics and ideology at the East Frankish court

Carolingian currency in west Francia between the reigns of Charles the Bald and Charles the Simple.[92] Its most striking form was the request for the annual liturgical commemoration of a king's consecration, to be subsequently replaced with that of his death day. The memory of the king's acquisition of his earthly kingdom, and later his entrance to its heavenly counterpart, was thus preserved at major royal churches, and often celebrated with a large-scale banquet provided for by the income from specially designated estates.[93] Such gestures reinforced the relationship between rulers and their ecclesiastical allies and made a conspicuous statement about the political resources of kings. In addition, they drew attention to the anointed character of Carolingian kingship: the ritual itself, based on biblical precedent and the ceremonies for the anointing of bishops, and also thought of as analogous to baptismal unction, was one of the fundamental characteristics of Carolingian rule, giving substance to the dynasty's political theology of a special relationship with God. These developments in commemoration practice represent an escalation in the intensity of political praying in the later ninth century, powered by the Carolingians' desire to imprint a heavier reminder of their presence and authority on the sacred calendar.

Despite the importance of consecration to Carolingian rule, the first solid evidence for the consecration of an east Frankish/German ruler does not appear until the inauguration of Conrad I in 911. The fact that four of Charles the Fat's surviving charters make allusion to such arrangements has therefore often puzzled scholars. These documents, all of which date from 885 or later and which provide further insights into the succession situation, merit renewed investigation. Three were drawn up by and issued for the west Frankish church of Langres, while the other was a chancery product for the east Frankish royal monastery of Fulda.[94] All four demand the celebration of the anniversary of Charles's *consecratio* (and then death) with prayers and feasts, with the exception of the middle Langres one which omits the feast. A fifth charter, also datable to 885, details the establishment of a similar commemoration and *refectio* at the monastery of Reichenau, with Charles's approval, by

---

[92] For the background see E. Kantorowicz, *Laudes Regiae. A Study in Liturgical Acclamation and Medieval Ruler Worship* (Berkeley and Los Angeles, 1958), pp. 65–9; A. Stoclet, 'Dies unctionis. A Note on the Anniversaries of Royal Inaugurations in the Carolingian Period', *FMSt* 20 (1986), 541–8. Charles the Bald is the most analysed anniversary celebrator; see for example J. M. Wallace-Hadrill, 'A Carolingian Renaissance Prince: the Emperor Charles the Bald', *Proceedings of the British Academy* 64 (1978), 155–84, at 166.

[93] On feasts see Nelson, 'Carolingian Royal Ritual', p. 126. A vivid literary description of an episcopal feast is provided by Notker, *Gesta*, 1.18, pp. 23–4.

[94] Langres: DD CIII 129 (28 August 885), 147 (29 October 886), 153 (15 January 887). Fulda: D CIII 132 (23 September 885).

145

Kingship and Politics in the Late Ninth Century

Bishop Chadolt of Novara.[95] It should be pointed out that this charter was explicitly connected to an imperial confirmation, and that the annual feast it specified was to be provided for from a donated royal estate. It can therefore be read as the by-product of a fifth, now lost, imperial diploma concerned with commemoration. This is entirely consistent with what we know about Chadolt, who had been in the entourage of Charles since the early 870s, and who was the brother of the archchancellor Liutward of Vercelli: he was just the kind of man we would expect to be entrusted with the setting up of an anniversary celebration at a key monastery in the emperor's heartlands.[96] Taken together, these five documents, all of which survive as originals, constitute the earliest evidence both for the anointing of an east Frankish king and for its commemoration. They are, therefore, of considerable significance in any assessment of the character of east Frankish kingship, conventionally conceived of as ideologically unsophisticated.[97]

Only two of the five charters, those from Fulda and Reichenau, furnish us with a date for this celebration: 'that is, the Lord's epiphany'.[98] The question of exactly which of Charles's accessions took place on the feast of Epiphany (6 January) has exerted and divided scholars for decades.[99] The only plausible candidates are 877 (for the kingdom of Alemannia) and 880 (for the kingdom of Italy): all of Charles's other successions can be shown to have taken place definitely not on this date. Neither possibility, however, is altogether satisfactory. The existence of an east Frankish consecration tradition in which to place the postulated 877 event, which is purely hypothetical, is disputable.[100] In any case, since Louis the German's sons were not crowned or anointed as kings during

[95] Mabillon, *Vetera Analecta*, p. 427; see further above, pp. 88–9. For the 885 dating see E. Hlawitschka, 'Die Diptychen von Novara und die Chronologie der Bischöfe dieser Stadt vom 9.–11. Jahrhundert', *QFIAB* 52 (1972), 767–80, at 777. C. Erdmann, 'Der ungesalbte König', *DA* 2 (1938), 311–40, at 316, placed it in 883, presumably on the basis of D AC 65, in which Charles's confirmation of the Reichenau charter (now lost) is associated with another imperial confirmation issued in 883 for Chadolt's brother Liutward (D CIII 92). Nothing in Arnulf's charter forces us, however, to assume that the lost confirmation was also enacted in 883. The similarities between the Reichenau charter and D CIII 132 for Fulda are more persuasive as evidence that it too belongs in 885, and this dating fits better with the context outlined below.

[96] For Chadolt in the young Charles's entourage see *Liber Memorialis Romaricensis*, fol. 9r; Fleckenstein, *Die Hofkapelle der deutschen Könige*, p. 195; cf. A. Zettler, *Die frühen Klosterbauten der Reichenau. Ausgrabungen-Schriftquellen-st. galler Klosterplan* (Sigmaringen, 1988), p. 106.

[97] Although see now E. J. Goldberg, ' "More Devoted to the Equipment of Battle than the Splendor of Banquets": Frontier Kingship, Military Ritual, and Early Knighthood at the Court of Louis the German', *Viator* 30 (1999), 41–78.

[98] D CIII 132. The Reichenau text says 'id est Epiphaniarum die'.

[99] C. Brühl, 'Fränkischer Krönungsbrauch und das Problem der "Festkrönungen" ', *HZ* 194 (1962), 265–326 is still important, and discusses the prior historiography at 298–9.

[100] *Ibid.*, esp. pp. 299–303 is a clear discussion of the evidence, ultimately coming down cautiously against.

The end of the empire I: politics and ideology at the East Frankish court

his lifetime, it would be difficult to explain why Charles would wait over four months after his father's death to have himself elevated to full royal status, and why this event left no trace in the sources. The more popular choice of 880 has a slightly stronger case, but one which is still anything but conclusive.[101] The only major narrative source to directly mention Charles's assumption of the Italian kingdom is a brief chronicle penned by Notker the Stammerer, which does not provide a date, but does tell us that he was made king by the massed bishops and *primores*, including the pope, at Ravenna.[102] There is no reason to doubt Notker, who wrote only a year after the event and had an eyewitness report from his friend and regular correspondent, the imperial notary Waldo.[103] However, we cannot definitely place Charles at Ravenna before 11 January, when he renewed a treaty with the Doge of Venice, and the immediately preceding diplomas show he was still at Pavia on 8 January.[104] On the face of it, Charles was not at Ravenna on Epiphany. Scholars have tried to resolve this inconvenient problem by claiming that the earlier diplomas were drawn up at Pavia before 8 January, and then enacted in Ravenna on that date.[105] However, this conjecture of so-called 'ununified dating' (an old standby of the puzzled Carolingianist) can be played more than one way, and in any case seems only to have been deemed necessary on the prior assumption that the later Epiphany references must refer to the Italian coronation of 880. The reasoning is circular: we only doubt the dating clauses of the charters because we 'know' Charles was at Ravenna on 6 January 880, but we can only place him there on that day if the dating clauses are wrong. Even then, we cannot be absolutely sure that Charles *was* consecrated king of Italy, although this would not have been out of keeping with Italian practice. Notker only says that 'he was made king [*rex constituitur*] by them [i.e. the pope, bishops and *primores*]', whereas in the very next breath he does explicitly mention consecration when Charles became emperor in February 881.[106]

Both 6 January 877 and 6 January 880 therefore look at best dubious as the anniversary referred to in the later royal charters. An alternative approach to this otherwise intractable problem is to change the question, and focus our attention instead on the nature and purpose of the commemoration charters themselves. One obvious question to ask, regardless of whether 877 or 880 is one's preferred date, is why it was not

---

[101] Sierck, *Festtag und Politik*, pp. 72–3 is the latest proponent of the 880 theory.
[102] Notker, *Continuatio*, p. 329.
[103] W. von den Steinen, *Notker der Dichter und seine geistige Welt. Darstellungsband* (Berne, 1948), p. 492.
[104] DD CIII 15–17.   [105] See Kehr's preambles to DD CIII 16, 17 and 132.
[106] The dating practices of Charles's chancery do not help, because his reign in Italy is habitually dated back to Karlmann's abdication in November 879: Sierck, *Festtag und Politik*, pp. 93–4.

Kingship and Politics in the Late Ninth Century

until 885 that the anniversary provisions made their first appearance in royal diplomas. The answer usually given is that the custom was directly imported after Charles became king of west Francia in the early months of that year.[107] However, it would be wrong to assume that ideas about rulership travelled around the Carolingian empire in such a determinedly mechanical fashion. Charles had, after all, been to the court of the arch-anniversary celebrator Charles the Bald himself.[108] If the east Frankish court wanted to celebrate the king's consecration in Alemannia or Italy, we must surely credit its members with enough intelligence to do so without waiting several years for their king to annex west Francia. We should look instead for a political explanation for this development in the form of documents which, as we have seen, were designed to deliver pointed ideological messages.[109]

To decode these documents, we must look in detail at the circumstances which produced them. The first three charters show some interesting peculiarities. The first we have already encountered: it was issued at Lorsch for the church of Langres on 28 August 885. By its terms, the monks and congregation of Langres were to offer prayers and enjoy a feast [*refectio*] laid on by the bishop, in the first instance on Charles's 'day of consecration', for which no date was specified, and then on the anniversary of his death. This document was drawn up by the scribes of Bishop Geilo. The second charter was made within the royal chancery, issued in September 885 for the monastery of Fulda, and specified Epiphany as the anniversary date of the emperor's consecration. Our third diploma is a restoration of properties to the canons of Langres made by Charles during the siege of Paris in October 886. In return, in addition to their habitual constant intercession on Charles's behalf, the canons would offer up special prayers to commemorate 'the day of our consecration, which is . . . [blank space]'. This blank space is very surprising, and requires explanation. Geilo, who was the grant's petitioner and who had the charter drafted by his staff in advance, was, as discussed in the last chapter, a close confidant of Charles in the later years of his reign, and cannot have been ignorant of the date of the emperor's consecration. The missing word must imply, therefore, that Geilo did not know *which* consecration the emperor wanted celebrated, and had his scribes leave a gap to be filled in when he brought the parchment to Charles outside Paris a few weeks later. This makes sense if

---

[107] E.g. Ewig, 'Der Gebetsdienst der Kirchen', p. 76; Sierck, *Festtag und Politik*, p. 79.

[108] *AB* s.a. 871, p. 181.

[109] On this subject in general see also H. Wolfram, 'Political Theory and Narrative in Charters', *Viator* 26 (1995), 39–51, and B. Merta, 'Recht und Propaganda in Narrationes karolingischer Herrscherurkunden', in Scharer and Scheibelreiter (eds.), *Historiographie im frühen Mittelalter*, pp. 141–57.

The end of the empire I: politics and ideology at the East Frankish court

we consider the possibility that the commemoration provisions specified in the earlier two charters, those from August and September 885, were in fact concerned with two *different* anniversaries.

The September document explicitly concerned Epiphany. If the drafters of the August Langres charter did not therefore have Epiphany in mind, they nevertheless seem to have thought that the commemoration date, which was not specified, was self-evident. The most likely explanation is that Geilo was here referring to Charles's Lotharingian/west Frankish anointing on 20 May 885. Not only, as argued earlier, had Geilo presided over this occasion himself; but Charles's charters for Langres were also authenticated with a special west Frankish imperial seal, a fact which further highlights Geilo's investment in creating a specifically west Frankish image for the emperor.[110] By establishing the annual commemoration of Charles's west Frankish inauguration event at Langres, Geilo not only exalted the emperor's position there, but he also sought to re-emphasise the role of himself and his church in Charles's elevation to the Lotharingian/west Frankish kingship and to bask in the reflected glory. The August 885 diploma most probably represents a reference to this ceremony. Here at least we can admit an infiltration of west Frankish practice into the court customs of the emperor, not by some automatic process of induction, but in a specific reference to a recent event made by one of its orchestrators.[111] However, the charter issued for Fulda a month later in September 885 reveals that Charles himself had different ideas about the date on which his consecration should be celebrated. The inauguration in this document of a different commemoration on the feast of Epiphany shows the court taking a new lead in such matters, and provides the alternative date which confused (or affronted) Geilo and forced him to leave a blank space in composing the subsequent charter for the Langres canons in 886.

If, then, the Langres charters do not refer to the Epiphany commemoration, the appearance of this celebration in a grant to Fulda requires further explanation. To help us with this, the timing and progress of the revolt of the Lotharingian pretender Hugh is a crucial factor. Hugh, the illegitimate son of Lothar II, had agitated for his paternal kingdom sporadically during the late 870s and early 880s, but since 882 had been at peace with the ruling Carolingians.[112] He chose to revolt again in 885, it

---

[110] Kehr's introduction to the MGH edition, pp. lxiii–lxiv. See above, pp. 126–9.

[111] D CIII 153, enacted 15 January 887, copies the formulas of D 129 literally, and so offers no further evidence on the establishment of imperial commemorations at Langres.

[112] Parisot, *Le Royaume de Lorraine*, pp. 442–77 and G. Tellenbach, 'Die geistigen und politischen Grundlagen der karolingischen Thronfolge. Zugleich eine Studie über kollektive Willensbildung

Kingship and Politics in the Late Ninth Century

would seem, because of the succession situation. With Charles now the only adult male legitimate Carolingian, Hugh's claim to a share of the succession was in theory at least as strong as those of his bastard cousins Arnulf and Bernard. Moreover, his hopes were in imminent danger if Charles intended to hand Lotharingia, the *regnum* desired by Hugh and the source of his support, to Bernard.[113] This not only gave Hugh an immediate reason to rebel, but by the same token also gave Charles a motive to dispose of him on a permanent basis. Hugh was captured, brought into the presence of the emperor, blinded and then confined to a monastery.[114] Two aspects of the widely reported affair demonstrate Charles's particular anxiety to deal decisively with Hugh. One is that, although the *dux* Henry had the main role in the capture of both Hugh and his collaborator Godafrid, only the latter received summary punishment (execution), while the former was brought alive to the emperor for judgement. The other is that Hugh was blinded and confined to a monastery, a penalty designed to exclude its victim definitively from the chance of succession.[115] It is significant that this punishment had not been inflicted on him after his previous rebellions, but that it *was* in 885, at this pregnant moment in the configuration of the politics of succession.

The sources are not explicit concerning the venue for the judicial proceedings against Hugh, and offer varying information on the location of his imprisonment. Regino states that Hugh was captured by Henry at Gondreville before being blinded, imprisoned in St-Gall and then moved, during the reign of Zwentibald (895–900), to Prüm. He does not say where the blinding was carried out. The only other authority to offer geographical details is the Mainz annalist, who tells us that Hugh was blinded in the emperor's presence before being confined to the monastery of St-Boniface at Fulda. These accounts, which, by no accident, come from those authors best placed to know, are not mutually exclusive. Regino, who met and tonsured Hugh when he was at Prüm, plays up the Lotharingian context of his capture and exile, adding only that St-Gall was where he was immediately prior to travelling to Prüm in the late 890s. This does not gainsay the information that immediately after his blinding he had been sent to Fulda, a detail which we would

---

und kollektives Handeln im neunten Jahrhundert', *FMSt* 13 (1979), 184–302, at 286–8 offer discussions of Hugh's career.

[113] Above, pp. 131–2. Regino, *Chronicon*, s.a. 885, p. 123 is clear that Hugh was after the 'regnum paternum'. See Parisot, *Le Royaume de Lorraine*, p. 478 on his supporters.

[114] References in what follows will be to: Regino, *Chronicon*, s.a. 885, pp. 123–5; *AF(M)* s.a. 885, p. 103; *AF(B)* s.a. 885, p. 114; *AV* s.a. 885, p. 57, all of which provide reports of these events.

[115] G. Bührer-Thierry, '"Just Anger" or "Vengeful Anger"? The Punishment of Blinding in the Early Medieval West', in B. Rosenwein (ed.), *Anger's Past. The Social Uses of an Emotion in the Middle Ages* (Ithaca, 1998), pp. 75–91.

The end of the empire I: politics and ideology at the East Frankish court

expect the Mainz annalist, a member of the entourage of the prelate in whose geographical and jurisdictional hinterland that abbey lay, to know. We can also reach a firm conclusion as to the venue for the trial. Justice of this kind had to be seen to be done: the first general assembly convened after Hugh's capture and the emperor's return from the west was held at Frankfurt in September. The royal palace at Frankfurt provided the necessary context for a public display of just and legitimate rulership to be mobilised against the recalcitrant usurping bastard.[116] It was a Carolingian site *par excellence*, with an unbroken tradition as one of the key centres, along with Regensburg, of legitimate east Frankish rulership stretching back through the reign of Louis the German and beyond. The Mainz continuator implies a connection between the trial of Hugh and this royal assembly by placing them adjacent in his annal, although he writes them up for literary effect as two separate set-pieces.[117] The same annalist was presumably in attendance as part of the entourage of Archbishop Liutbert, which would explain why he is the sole narrative source for both the assembly and for the details of Hugh's trial. The annalist provides unique details, including the fact that Hugh's uncle was also blinded, and that the rest of their supporters 'were stripped of their horses, arms and clothing, and scarcely escaped naked'. This punishment was perhaps intended as a humiliating negation of their badges of nobility.[118] All this points to the conclusion that Hugh was dealt with at the Frankfurt assembly, then sent to Fulda.

In other words, the Fulda diploma, the first east Frankish royal charter to establish the commemoration of a king's consecration, was issued on the occasion of Hugh's trial and in favour of the monastery where he would be imprisoned. It ought, therefore, to be read at least in part as an ideological statement about royal legitimacy, designed, ultimately, to boost the succession claims of Bernard. The charter's audience was the trial's audience. Hugh's very person was a bad precedent, a living reminder of the failure of Lothar II to carry out a plan almost identical to the one Charles was undertaking. This would not have gone unnoticed

---

[116] *AF(M)* s.a. 885, p. 103 mentions the assembly, where DD CIII 130–2 were issued between 6 and 23 September. *AV* s.a. 885, p. 57 implies Hugh was captured just before 25 July. D CIII 127, issued at Waiblingen on 23 August, is the first evidence for Charles's return to the east.

[117] *AF(M)* s.a. 885, p. 103. The section on Hugh is a self-contained story, the only one in the *AF(M)* truly favourable to Charles, of the fitting fate of the rebellious bastard; by contrast, the Frankfurt paragraph forms part of the story of divine scorn for Charles's plan to legitimise Bernard. The stories' differing intentions, and indeed the desire of the author to set up a contrast making an implicit point about the correct and wrong way to treat illegitimate Carolingians, is what forces their separation.

[118] On which see J. L. Nelson, 'Ninth-Century Knighthood: the Evidence of Nithard', in C. Harper-Bill, C. Holdsworth and J. L. Nelson (eds.), *Studies in Medieval History Presented to R. Allen Brown* (Woodbridge, 1989), pp. 255–66. Reprinted in Nelson, *The Frankish World*.

Kingship and Politics in the Late Ninth Century

by contemporaries, especially those who, like Liutbert, were inclined to oppose the prospect of Bernard's designation. Hugh had to be dealt with decisively, before an audience of such people, in a location and manner that stressed the emperor's legitimacy and his own lack of it. The charter must also be considered in association with the ceremony which had taken place at Lorsch on 28 August. It is possible that, as argued above, the leader of the 'tyrannical princes' mentioned in the charter issued on that day were in fact Hugh and his supporters, taken to Lorsch to help emphasise Bernard's legitimacy and the pretender's lack of it, before being hauled off to Frankfurt and his fate a few days later.[119]

Some form of court ceremonial must have taken place on these occasions, although the precise nature of this is now irretrievable. However, the point could hardly have been emphasised any more clearly to the *primores* gathered at Lorsch and Frankfurt, to whom the charter's provisions would have been made known: Bernard was to be considered a legitimate Carolingian, Hugh was not. It was certainly understood by the Mainz annalist, who said that, with Hugh's imprisonment in Fulda, 'there was an end to his tyranny [i.e. illegitimate claim to rule]'.[120] Nor would it have been missed by Notker the Stammerer, who in 881 had ended his *Continuatio*, a text detailing the descent of Carolingian legitimacy through the generations after 840, with an anxious admonitory reference to the 'tyrants' (meaning usurpers) Hugh and Boso: 'They, meanwhile, reflecting on human shame, we cover in silence until, either, changed into princes of the earth they attain a reward for their folly; or, so that the disturbers of the *res publica* suffer fittingly by being burned to cinders and scattered to the winds, they are condemned in name or rather ignominy and their memory damned in this world.'[121] Notker would have been pleased when the prayers and celebrations of the monks of Fulda on the anniversary of Charles the Fat's consecration drowned out the pleas for recognition of their unwilling guest, the mutilated 'tyrant' Hugh. His illegitimacy, and Charles's rightful divinely ordained authority, were thus constantly reaffirmed. This is a classic case of the clinical brutality which the Carolingians were occasionally given to inflict on their opponents, justifying their actions with high-minded religious and political rhetoric.[122]

---

[119] See above, pp. 133–4.   [120] *AF(M)* s.a. 885, p. 103.   [121] Notker, *Continuatio*, p. 330.

[122] A comparable instance would be the show-trial of Tassilo of Bavaria in 788: see now Airlie, 'Narratives of Triumph'. Cf. also D. A. Warner, 'Ideals and Action in the Reign of Otto III', *JMH* 25 (1999), 1–18, at 15–17. These examples all highlight the fact that very often ideological statements about authority were made to impress specific audiences in quite specific circumstances: cf. F.-R. Erkens, '*Sicut Esther Regina*. Die westfränkische Königin als *consors regni*', *Francia* 20 (1993), 15–38, at 35; M. McCormick, 'Analyzing Imperial Ceremonies', *Jahrbuch der österreichischen Byzantinistik* 35 (1985), 1–20.

The end of the empire I: politics and ideology at the East Frankish court

The court, therefore, decided to establish celebrations on the feast of Epiphany at this time for very specific reasons, as an adjunct to the public punishment of Hugh and to make a clear statement about authority and legitimacy to a particular audience. However, we may deduce from the Reichenau charter, whose issuer Chadolt was also very close to the court, as well as from the ambivalent Langres one, that these provisions were then intended to be propagated around other important ecclesiastical foundations in the empire; Fulda was not to be the only place where Charles's kingship was exalted. If this is so, one question remains: why Epiphany? If 6 January does not correspond to any actual consecration of Charles the Fat, then it must represent a symbolic celebration invoked for ideological or ceremonial reasons.[123]

By the ninth century, 6 January was firmly established in the west as the festival of three key events from the life of Christ: his reception of the Magi, his baptism, and his first miracle at Cana.[124] The Magi had some interesting associations in contemporary eyes which will detain us here. Since the fifth century they had been interpreted in western thought as kings, and accordingly Jesus, to whom they humbled themselves, was seen as a king over kings. This reading obviously lent itself to ideological uses in connection with imperial aspirations and ideas about Christological kingship; ideas which, as is well known, achieved their fullest expression in Ottonian art. They were nonetheless already present in the Carolingian period: images of empire and triumph associated with Christ and the Magi are visible in the Utrecht Psalter (c. 820s), the Stuttgart Psalter (c. 830) and in Charles the Bald's *Codex Aureus* (870), while the implicit identification between Christ and the earthly king also emerges from works like Thegan's biography of Louis the Pious and the text of many a royal *adventus* ceremony: the Old Testament may well have dominated the Carolingian Renaissance, but its architects frequently drew on the New as well.[125]

---

[123] Kehr, in his preamble to D CIII 132, was forced to a similar conclusion. Even if Charles's celebration does refer to an Italian consecration, which, if it took place, was very near to Epiphany, and was Charles's first anointing, we still need to explain the appearance of the commemoration in 885, and why it was chosen in preference to, say, the west Frankish consecration.

[124] F. L. Cross and E. A. Livingstone, *The Oxford Dictionary of the Christian Church*, 3rd edn (Oxford, 1997), pp. 554, 1020. On the feast's earlier history see also K. Holl, 'Der Ursprung des Epiphanienfestes', *Sitzungsberichte der königlichen preussischen Akademie der Wissenschaften* 29 (1917), 402–38.

[125] H. Mayr-Harting, *Ottonian Book Illumination: an Historical Study*, 2nd edn (London, 1999), p. 68; R. Deshman, '*Christus rex et magi reges*: Kingship and Christology in Ottonian and Anglo-Saxon Art', *FMSt* 10 (1976), 367–406, at 375–7; R. Deshman, 'The Exalted Servant: the Ruler Theology of the Prayerbook of Charles the Bald', *Viator* 11 (1980), 385–417, at 393, 414; R. C. Trexler, *The Journey of the Magi. Meanings in History of a Christian Story* (Princeton, 1997), p. 54; Innes, 'Politics of Humour'; E. Kantorowicz, 'The "King's Advent"' and the Enigmatic Panels in

153

Kingship and Politics in the Late Ninth Century

Given these imperial associations, Epiphany had specific relevance to Charles the Fat in 885 as a symbol of, and a seal upon, his succession to a new position: sole ruler of the entire territory of the empire of Charlemagne, a physical confirmation and fulfilment of the imperial title he had acquired in 881. After all, Epiphany was not merely a feast of Christ's regality, but also had a confirmatory character with connotations of renewal, celebrating the Messiah's reappearance (to the Gentiles) in a new and divinely exalted form. How exactly might these ideas have been intended to be read? In that he had plans to insert Bernard as a subking in Lotharingia, and that he had established client relationships with foreign leaders like Zwentibald of Moravia and Alan of Brittany, Charles may have claimed quite literally to be a king over kings (although admittedly the Carolingans did not usually like to acknowledge the royal status of such rulers).[126] There is good evidence, however, that his imperial ideology went further than this. Notker the Stammerer's *Deeds of Charlemagne*, written for Charles in St-Gall at exactly this time (885–6), elaborates a theory of Carolingian power based on the Book of Daniel, in which the dynasty is interpreted as the head of a new world empire, securely anchored to the masterplan of sacred history. The dynasty's divinely ordained superiority extended over Byzantium, Africa and the rest of the known world, and it is clear that Notker expected Charles the Fat to identify himself as the incumbent ruler of this notional 'empire' in succession to Charlemagne. Charles, who commissioned the work and may well have influenced its content, is elided with Charlemagne by Notker, and hence designated as head of the world; there is evidence here, then, that the events of 885 inspired the court to pursue a new imperial rhetoric.[127] Notker also ascribed God, or Christ-like qualities to the Charlemagne he depicted in this work.[128] A further product of the St-Gall scriptorium, the so-called Golden Psalter, may have been presented to Charles the Fat at exactly this time. Its imperial imagery and depiction of a Carolingian ruler as the Old Testament King David,

---

the Doors of Santa Sabina', *The Art Bulletin* 26 (1944), 207–31, at 210–11; Kantorowicz, *Laudes Regiae*, pp. 58, 92. See in general also B. Schwineköper, 'Christus-Reliquien-Verehrung und Politik', *Blätter für deutsche Landesgeschichte* 117 (1981), 183–281, which concentrates on a slightly later period; C. Chazelle, *The Crucified God in the Carolingian Era. Theology and Art of Christ's Passion* (Cambridge, 2001).

[126] See above, pp. 76, 131–2, 139, 142.

[127] On Notker's view of the Carolingian world empire, see especially T. Siegrist, *Herrscherbild und Weltsicht bei Notker Balbulus. Untersuchungen zu den Gesta Karoli* (Zurich, 1963), pp. 109–44. It is interesting in this context that the *Deeds* referred to consecration as an ancient practice which, in east Frankish terms, it certainly was not: Notker, *Gesta*, 1.10, p. 13; Goetz, *Strukturen der spätkarolingischen Epoche*, p. 23, n. 65

[128] Siegrist, *Herrscherbild und Weltsicht*, pp. 79–89.

The end of the empire I: politics and ideology at the East Frankish court

a typological forerunner of Christ, would also have resonated with the set of ideas about imperial authority being expounded by Charles's court in 885.[129]

There is also a context in which to place Charles's attempt to crystallise these abstract ideas into the court ceremonial which must lie behind our charters' Epiphany references.[130] An indirect influence came from the east, where Byzantine imperial ritual accorded prominence to Epiphany at this time: it was one of the major feasts of the Byzantine liturgical year and was celebrated in Constantinople (according to the *Book of Ceremonies*) with imperial processions and acclamations.[131] We know that Byzantine ceremonial was not only understood but indeed imitated at the court of Louis the German after his diplomatic contact with Basil I in the early 870s.[132] However, Epiphany was not only the feast of the Magi, it was also the feast of Christ's baptism: to ninth-century western minds he was not only revealed as a king over kings on that day, he was also consecrated.[133] A source for this idea lay much closer to home than Constantinople, at the Alemannic monastery of St-Gall, home to Notker the Stammerer. In late 884 he had sent his famous sequence book, known as the *Liber Ymnorum*, to Charles's archchaplain Liutward so that it could be used at court to celebrate the liturgy on the high feast days of the church.[134] In the hymn to be sung on Epiphany, the section on the baptism of Christ echoes the language used in contemporary discussions

[129] C. Eggenberger, *Psalterium Aureum Sancti Galli. Mittelalterliche Psalterillustration im Kloster St. Gallen* (Sigmaringen, 1987). I develop these points below, pp. 225–6.

[130] Kantorowicz discusses the feast as an important focus for court ceremonial from the late Roman Empire up to the late Middle Ages in two articles, 'Oriens Augusti – Lever du Roi', *Dumbarton Oaks Papers* 17 (1963), 117–77 and 'Dante's "Two Suns"', in his *Selected Studies* (New York, 1965), pp. 325–38, but states that it fell into disuse in the early medieval west.

[131] Kantorowicz, 'Oriens Augusti', pp. 149–62; A. Kazhdan et al., *The Oxford Dictionary of Byzantium* (New York and Oxford, 1991), p. 715. The *Book of Ceremonies*, although a tenth-century text, reveals much about ninth-century practice: see A. Cameron, 'The Construction of Court Ritual: the Byzantine *Book of Ceremonies*', in D. Cannadine and S. Price (eds.), *Rituals of Royalty. Power and Ceremonial in Traditional Societies* (Cambridge, 1987), pp. 106–36. In Byzantium, however, the reception of the Magi was celebrated on 25 December rather than Epiphany.

[132] Notker, *Gesta*, 2.11, pp. 68–70; Goldberg, 'Frontier Kingship, Military Ritual, and Early Knighthood', pp. 71–2.

[133] The links between baptism and consecration in Carolingian political and eschatological thought are illuminated by D. Alibert, '*Semen eius in aeternum manebit* . . . Remarques sur l'engendrement royal à l'époque carolingienne', in M. Rouche (ed.), *Mariage et sexualité au Moyen Age. Accord ou crise?* (Paris, 2000), pp. 135–45.

[134] That the book was intended for use in this way is suggested by the fact that Notker sent it to the archchaplain, and by what seem to be quite practical directions for use in the text: e.g. Notker, *Liber Ymnorum*, in von den Steinen (ed.), *Notker der Dichter. Editionsband*, pp. 8–91, at p. 10. Von den Steinen, *Notker der Dichter. Darstellungsband*, pp. 504–7 for the work's date. See also J. Duft, 'Der Impetus für Notkers Sequenzen', in his *Die Abtei St Gallen*, (3 vols., Sigmaringen, 1990–4), vol. 2, pp. 136–47.

Kingship and Politics in the Late Ninth Century

of royal consecration: he is 'consecrating baptism for us' and is 'to be anointed over all the saints'.[135] The use of these words is striking. Notker was among the first western writers to lay particularly heavy stress on the importance of the feast of Epiphany: only three other hymns on Epiphany and its octave survive from east of the Rhine in the earlier Middle Ages, and all come from a circle influenced by the Stammerer.[136] It is therefore significant that in his *Liber Ymnorum,* ideas about Christ as king of kings and the association with the baptism on Epiphany as consecration come together and can be placed at the heart of the imperial court in the mid-880s.[137] Notker did not here provide a coherent programme for imperial ideology, but his work nevertheless contained the full range of associations which clustered around the 'imperial interpretation' of Epiphany. The charters which we have been investigating in this section reveal, therefore, not a reference to an actual consecration, but an ideological statement about Charles's Christological authority inspired by the circumstances of 885, and using ideas current at court.[138] Epiphany was imperial, and Charles was a special kind of emperor.

It is hence significant that Charles chose Regensburg, where he over-wintered in 885–6, as the first venue for whatever court ceremonies or celebrations may have accompanied the feast.[139] It has already been argued that Arnulf, still on shaky ground as far as his relationship with Charles went, was probably present at this court to make good his faith with the emperor and ward off a potential imperial invasion of Carinthia.[140] Having marshalled the ideological and ceremonial trappings of rulership to support his legitimation of Bernard's claim and his destruction of Hugh's, we ought not to be surprised if Charles now sought to aim such resources in the direction of Arnulf, the third would-be king.

Interestingly, we know from one of the chronicles describing Arnulf's successful coup against Charles in November 887 that Arnulf had previously sworn fidelity to the emperor on a relic of the True Cross, an item which Charles now sent back to his nephew in a last-ditch effort to

---

[135] Notker, *Liber Ymnorum,* pp. 22–3.

[136] Von den Steinen, *Notker der Dichter. Darstellungsband,* pp. 286–90. For an example see the anonymous *In Octava Theophaniae* edited by von den Steinen, *Notker der Dichter. Editionsband,* p. 103.

[137] For Christ as 'regnator' and 'rex regum', see also Notker, *Liber Ymnorum,* pp. 42, 46, 88–9.

[138] McCormick, 'Analyzing Imperial Ceremonies', pp. 9–10 discusses analogous examples from Late Antiquity in which depictions of political rituals were 'meant to symbolise a conception of imperial victoriousness' rather than refer to actual events. Charles's situation in 885 also bears some comparison with the English king Edgar's 'imperial' consecration of 973: see J. L. Nelson, 'Inauguration Rituals', in her *Politics and Ritual in Early Medieval Europe* (London, 1986), pp. 283–307, at pp. 297–303.

[139] *AF(M)* s.a. 885, p. 103; *AF(B)* s.a. 886, p. 114 for Charles's Christmas 885 stay in Bavaria. He issued D CIII 134 at Regensburg on 7 January 886.

[140] See above, pp. 142–3.

The end of the empire I: politics and ideology at the East Frankish court

remind him of his obligations.[141] This relic had been at the east Frankish court since it was brought to Louis the German at Regensburg by Byzantine ambassadors on Epiphany in 872.[142] Charles the Fat inherited the fragment, and kept it in a most unusual reliquary of which the eleventh-century St-Gall house historian Ekkehard IV provides a detailed description (he had seen it because Arnulf donated the reliquary to the monastery after Charles's death). It was a container of pure gold, decorated with precious stones and fashioned in the shape of a chapel. It was inscribed with the words: 'See the casket of the cross and of holy Mary with the saints. This Charles chose to have [as] his highest chapel.'[143] 'Summa capella' (highest chapel) was a term characteristically used to describe the royal chapels of the Carolingian empire, located at Aachen, Regensburg and Frankfurt, and dedicated to the Virgin Mary.[144] The ur-chapel, Charlemagne's palace chapel at Aachen, was sacked by Vikings in the early 880s (they used it as a stable), and we have a subsequent charter relating how its relic collection was rescued by the monks of nearby Stavelot-Malmedy and brought to the court of Charles the Fat, who rewarded the industrious brethren with a generous gift of land.[145] Might not this reliquary, shaped like a chapel, called 'summa capella' and inscribed with a dedication to the Mother of God, have been created to house the Aachen chapel relics along with the fragment of the True Cross?[146] Charles never visited the old seat of the empire: this reliquary looks as if it were intended as a miniature substitute Aachen, quite literally Carolingian legitimacy in a box.

This artefact, and its contents, represented a kind of internal *translatio imperii*, a symbolic manifestation of the relocation of the political centre of the empire from Aachen to the backwaters of Alemannia. The identification of the Alemannic elite with the Carolingian charisma of Aachen was made explicit in the works of Notker, and Charles himself deliberately fostered connections with the chapels at Regensburg and Aachen.[147] The

---

[141] *AF(M)* s.a. 887, p. 106.   [142] *AF* s.a. 872, p. 75.

[143] Ekkehard, *Casus S. Galli*, chap. 10, p. 34: 'En crucis atque piae cum sanctis capsa Mariae, Hanc Karolus summam delegit habere capellam'. Alternative translations of this phrase are possible for instance: 'Charles chose for his chapel to have this [highest] thing.' However, the general point would stand: I am grateful to Mary Garrison for discussion of this problem. The casket was described in similar terms by a later interpolator of Notker's *Gesta Karoli* who (wrongly) attributed it to Charlemagne: Notker, *Gesta*, p. 15, n. r.

[144] As in the etymology given by Notker, *Gesta*, 1.4, p. 15.

[145] *AF* s.a. 881, p. 97; D CIII 64. The relics are described as 'pignora sanctorum'. Kehr's doubts over the relevant section of this charter are unjustified: see also L. Falkenstein, *Karl der Grosse und die Entstehung des Aachener Marienstiftes* (Paderborn, 1981), n. 357.

[146] On portable chapels in general, see P. E. Schramm and F. Mütherich, *Denkmale der deutschen Könige und Kaiser*, 2nd edn (Munich, 1981), p. 32.

[147] J. L. Nelson, 'Aachen as a Place of Power', in M. de Jong and F. Theuws (eds.), *Topographies of Power in the Early Middle Ages* (Leiden, Boston and Cologne, 2001), pp. 217–41, at pp. 234–6.

Kingship and Politics in the Late Ninth Century

transfer of the relics was not part of a fragmentation of Frankish power. Rather, it reflects the dynamic nature of early medieval politics, which were engaged in a continuous dialogue with the past, driven by the needs of the present. As so often, the broad motivations lying behind this act also found a specific audience: it was on this casket that Arnulf, seeking to stave off the planned imperial invasion of Carinthia, swore fealty to his uncle in Regensburg, probably on Epiphany 886. The ideological connotations of this are clear: the event highlighted Charles's legitimacy and his nephew's lack of it, sending a clear message to the magnates of Bavaria and Carinthia who formed Arnulf's potential constituency and who were no doubt gathered for the occasion.[148] In other words, the pro-pagandistic trappings to the ordering of the imperial succession which were concocted in late 885 were targeted at belittling the claims of Arnulf of Carinthia and his supporters as well as those of Hugh of Lotharingia and his; and hence were ultimately designed to bolster the position of Bernard in the eyes of the aristocratic community.[149]

In conclusion to this section, it is worth stressing two points and registering a caveat. Firstly, if the 885–6 royal charters referring to the supposed consecration of Charles the Fat are to be understood properly, they must be read in the context of the very specific political circumstances which produced them and gave them meaning: they are intricately bound up with the question of the imperial succession. Secondly, this should be taken as evidence for a lively interest in political ideas at Charles's court, at least at this one point in time. Neither he nor any other east Frankish king exercised their authority unthinkingly or in the blinkered fashion which has sometimes been assumed.[150] In a sense, this *did* represent the importing of a west Frankish tradition into east Frankish politics, but also a reinterpretation and reuse of this tradition in a quite different context. Here we have evidence for east Frankish engagement with the symbolism of consecration well before the famous anointing of Conrad I in 911, which highlights some fundamental similarities as well as differences in the political cultures either side of the Rhine. The absence of an east Frankish Hincmar, a prolific annalist who was also closely involved in

---

D CIII 109, Charles's only charter for the Aachen chapel was, significantly, issued while he was at the chapel in Regensburg. During the same visit Charles began to foster his connections with Regensburg itself as a centre of legitimate power, having an eternal flame lit for his own soul in the royal chapel: D 107.

[148] Schwineköper, 'Christus-Reliquien-Verehrung', p. 205 suggests that this oath of loyalty on the True Cross was an imitation of Byzantine practice.

[149] I am not convinced that the implicit references to the three Magi in these ideas were to be directly paralleled to the three competitors for the throne.

[150] Goldberg, 'Frontier Kingship, Military Ritual, and Early Knighthood' also develops this theme, although it will be evident that I part company from him on his view of Charles the Fat at p. 73.

158

The end of the empire I: politics and ideology at the East Frankish court

actually orchestrating political rituals, is very significant. To some extent, the unusually high 'ritual profile' of Charles the Bald's reign is down to Hincmar: writers chronicling other reigns, from Charles the Great to Charles the Fat, were simply not so interested.

One good reason for this lack of interest, and this is the caveat, is the fact that rhetoric of this kind, whatever its claims, is not necessarily translated into real authority.[151] Often ideology was used to fill a gap in 'real' authority, and this, in the final reckoning, is how it was with Charles the Fat. The events of 885, especially the accession to the western kingdom, the plan to get the pope to help legitimise Bernard and the clinical elimination of Hugh reveal a high point in the reign, and a great confidence in the conception and exercise of Charles's kingship. In this context, the self-association with the Christological feast of Epiphany and the imperial claims reflected in Notker's *Deeds* make perfect sense. However, Charles's balloon was very quickly punctured by the unexpected death of Pope Hadrian III in September as he made his way north towards his appointment with the emperor and his son. Bernard's position was thus seriously weakened. The succession issue was once again thrown into doubt, and the more time that passed without a credible solution, the greater the anxiety that would worm its way into the minds of the aristocratic political community, priming them for Arnulf's bid for power. However highly he may have conceptualised his own emperorship, and however much effort he may have put into transmitting these ideological messages about legitimacy to the aristocratic audiences at Lorsch, Frankfurt and Regensburg, all the rhetoric came to look like so much empty bluster as long as this fundamental problem remained. Indeed, to some hostile observers the death of Hadrian III was a divine judgement on the unrighteousness of Charles's intentions, an opinion which would surely have gained ground as time passed.[152] Moreover, Arnulf may only have been so willing to come to heel in 886 because Bernard's legitimation had already failed and he envisaged new possibilities for himself. The atmosphere of unease is nowhere better illustrated than in book 2 of Notker's *Deeds of Charlemagne*, which is full of portentous warnings about the future of the Carolingian line.[153]

Charles and his advisers must, of course, have realised all this. Accordingly, the ideas about dynastic legitimacy which had accompanied the great optimism and bold plans of summer and autumn 885 were discarded. Notker's *Gesta* was never finished, and as quickly as they had developed, the circumstances which had produced the first east Frankish

---

[151] As extensively argued by Buc, *Dangers of Ritual*.
[152] *AF(M)* s.a. 885, p. 103.   [153] On which see below, pp. 218–22.

159

royal anniversary celebrations disappeared. Lacking the impetus of the court, the commemorations slid into dormancy almost immediately after they had been introduced, except at Langres, where Bishop Geilo still occasionally took the opportunity to remind the emperor and his own entourage of the part he had played in consecrating Charles to the western kingdom in 885. However, the fact that the blank space left by Geilo for the consecration date in the October 886 charter for the canons of Langres was never filled in stands as testimony to Charles's lapse of interest and change of fortunes. The dynastic propaganda which had been invoked to support the development of an exalted conception of the imperial role in summer 885 was partly a means to an end; it was of limited use, and even counter-productive, as long as the serious political problems surrounding the imperial succession remained unresolved. These remnants of one of the most impressive expressions of political thought east of the Rhine in the ninth century are, ultimately, witness to a politics of desperation. The emperor's attempts to overcome these problems, and the reasons for his ultimate failure, will be the subject of the following chapter.

Chapter 6

THE END OF THE EMPIRE II:
RESPONSE AND FAILURE

CAROLINGIAN UNITY AND THE ADOPTION OF LOUIS OF
PROVENCE, APRIL–JUNE 887

Hadrian III probably met his unexpected end in September 885 and, seemingly due to his unpopularity in Rome, was buried in the north Italian monastery of Nonantola rather than being taken back to the Holy See.[1] His successor Stephen V was appointed quickly and without direct consultation with the emperor, whose attempt to have him deposed on this technicality failed because the election had taken place with the co-operation of the imperial legate in Rome.[2] Charles was still preoccupied with the stalled plan to legitimate Bernard, who remained in the prayer clauses of imperial charters in 886 and early 887, and had doubtless hoped to influence the election to ensure that the new pontiff was sympathetic to its resuscitation. With Stephen's accession a *fait accompli* by the end of 885, the emperor had no choice but to travel to Italy at the start of 886 and negotiate with him directly. The specific outcome of the talks held during Charles's five- or six-month stay south of the Alps is not known beyond the fact that he extracted papal permission to translate bishops from devastated sees. However, our source for this information, the Bavarian annalist, cryptically adds that 'many matters were arranged as he [Charles] wished'.[3] With the succession situation the way it was, and given the events of the preceding few months, it is very likely that the emperor was still pursuing papal sanction for the designation of his illegitimate son.

Whatever general approval for the scheme may have been agreed by Stephen V in early 886, Charles's attention for the second half of that year was fully occupied by the siege of Paris, precluding any opportunity

---

[1] *AF(M)* s.a. 885, p. 103; Davis, *Lives of the Ninth-Century Popes*, pp. 297, n. 3, 298, n. 8.

[2] *AF(M)* s.a. 885, pp. 103–4; *Liber Pontificalis*, ed. L. Duchesne (Paris, 1955–7), chap. 112, pp. 191–2. Reuter, *Annals of Fulda*, p. 99, n. 11, and Davis, *Lives of the Ninth-Century Popes*, p. 299, n. 9 for commentary.

[3] *AF(B)* s.a. 886. p. 114.

161

Kingship and Politics in the Late Ninth Century

to convene an assembly north of the Alps which the pope might attend. The next developments did not take place until the first few months of 887, when Charles decided to adopt his seven-year-old cousin Louis of Provence ('the Blind', future king of Provence and Italy, and emperor). Louis's heritage was, from a dynastic point of view, an equal mix of the good and the bad: although his father was the usurper Boso, from his mother Irmingarde, daughter of the emperor Louis II, he inherited *bona fide* Carolingianness.

Our main source for this event is the Bavarian continuator's comment in his annal for 887, immediately after reporting Boso's death: 'the emperor came to meet him [Louis] at the *villa* of Kirchen on the Rhine, and received him with honour to be his man, as if he were his adopted son'.[4] The adoption is often seen as a battleground in a wider dispute about the nature of the empire. It is nearly always glossed by historians as a move planned by the archchancellor Liutward, supposedly acting as the representative of a faction with a principled belief in the divisibility of the empire. His subsequent ejection from court and replacement by Liutbert of Mainz is thus thought to represent the victory of a 'unity' party bent on retaining the territorial integrity of the realm. On the strength of the Mainz annalist's invective against Liutward in his 887 report, where the fallen archchancellor is said to have conspired with Arnulf to bring down Charles, this ideological disagreement is brought to bear as a key factor in the deposition of the emperor.[5] However, it would not be an exaggeration to say that the principle of imperial unity here identified has been more appealing to historians of the twentieth century than it was to people living in the ninth.[6] The high-water mark of Carolingian imperial history is seen as coinciding with the period when the empire was united, from 771 until 840. However, division of the realm between all the king's sons was in fact the norm in Frankish tradition, only prevented in the late eighth and early ninth centuries by dynastic accident. The idea of unity was never really a fixed principle in Carolingian government, despite the best efforts of Louis the Pious in the 810s and 820s to make it so, efforts which ended in disaster. Rather, unity was a rhetorical position which could be adopted in response to rather more specific political

---

[4] *AF(B)* s.a. 887, p. 115: 'obviam [Hludovicum] imperator ad Hrenum villa Chirihheim veniens honorifice ad hominem sibi quasi adoptivum filium eum iniunxit.'

[5] Keller, 'Zum Sturz Karls III.', pp. 379–84; Tellenbach, 'Die geistigen und politischen Grundlagen', p. 230; Bührer-Thierry, 'Le conseiller du roi', p. 112; Fried, *Der Weg in die Geschichte*, pp. 428–9.

[6] It is a particularly strong theme in L. Halphen, *Charlemagne and the Carolingian Empire*, trans. G. de Nie (Amsterdam, New York and Oxford, 1977), which was written as Europe fell into conflict in the 1930s and 1940s.

The end of the empire II: response and failure

circumstances.[7] For example, Florus of Lyon's lament on the division of the empire, the *locus classicus* of Carolingian unity theory, is often read by historians as representative of a general clerical reaction against the projected *divisio* of 843. In reality, as Janet Nelson has argued, Florus was a partisan author, and his work had the specific aim of re-emphasising the imperial claims of Lothar in the run-up to the Verdun negotiations.[8] There is no source to back up this supposed ideological divide as an explanation for Charles's deposition. What we know of the thoughts of Liutbert of Mainz gives no clue that he believed unchangingly in the maintenance of Frankish territorial coherence, and we know nothing reliable about the personality or views of Liutward beyond what we choose to deduce from his actions; the circularity of that approach is obvious.[9] In other words, historians have sometimes interpreted the key political events of the year 887 as the result of a clash between factions representing two momentous ideologies; ideologies which we cannot prove to have even existed, never mind to have been at the forefront of the minds of the protagonists.[10] If the 'unity' explanation thus fails to convince, it remains to be established what the adoption actually did signify.

The most developed statement of the view that Louis was intended to inherit the entire empire was made by Eduard Hlawitschka in his 1968 book on Lotharingia, subsequently criticised by Ursula Penndorf and Heinz Löwe, then defended and elaborated by Hlawitschka in an article in 1978, since when it has been more or less accepted by historians.[11] A

---

[7] U. Penndorf, *Das Problem der "Reichseinheitsidee" nach der Teilung von Verdun (843). Untersuchungen zu den späten Karolingern* (Munich, 1974) generally succeeds in demystifying the concept of Carolingian *Reichseinheitsidee*, but is often ignored. See now F.-R. Erkens, '*Divisio legitima* und *unitas imperii*. Teilungspraxis und Einheitsstreben bei der Thronfolge im Frankenreich', *DA* 52 (1996), 423–85.

[8] J. L. Nelson, 'The Search for Peace in a Time of War: the Carolingian *Brüderkrieg*, 840–843', in J. Fried (ed.), *Träger und Instrumentarien des Friedens im hohen und späten Mittelalter* (Sigmaringen, 1996), pp. 87–114, at pp. 101–2; cf. the discussion of the *Visio Karoli* below, p. 166.

[9] For some of what we do know about Liutbert see H. Büttner, 'Erzbischof Liutbert von Mainz und die Rechtstellung der Klöster', in G. Droege et al. (eds.), *Landschaft und Geschichte. Festschrift für Franz Petri zu seinem 65. Geburtstag* (Bonn, 1970), pp. 104–15; W. Hartmann, *Das Konzil von Worms 868* (Göttingen, 1977), pp. 56, 68, 93–9, 105–6.

[10] It is telling that some historians (such as R. Schieffer, 'Karl III. und Arnolf', p. 148) swap the positions supposedly held by Liutbert and Liutward: the 'unity' hypothesis is not being proven here, but simply used as a convenient explanation for obscure events.

[11] Respectively Hlawitschka, *Lotharingien und das Reich*, pp. 32–8; Penndorf, *Das Problem der "Reichseinheitsidee"*, pp. 133–4; H. Löwe, 'Das Karlsbuch Notkers von St. Gallen und sein zeitgeschichtlicher Hintergrund', in his *Von Cassiodor zu Dante. Ausgewählte Aufsätze zur Geschichtschreibung und politischen Ideenwelt des Mittelalters* (Berlin and New York, 1973), pp. 123–48, at p. 144; E. Hlawitschka, 'Nachfolgeprojekt aus der Spätzeit Kaiser Karls III.', *DA* 46 (1978), 19–50. Hlawitschka's arguments as represented in what follows can be found in these places; references will be given for direct quotes. It will be evident that my argument differs from those of Penndorf and Löwe.

Kingship and Politics in the Late Ninth Century

brief survey of the arguments and evidence is therefore necessary here to show that Hlawitschka's case remains flawed.

The fact that Louis was adopted by Charles in some sense is not disputed: adoption was a well-established political ritual in several early medieval kingdoms. What is at stake is the significance which one reads into this fact. Hlawitschka supports his central assertion, that inheritance 'was the logical consequence of adoption', by reference to other adoptions, from the Roman, Merovingian, Byzantine, Carolingian and central medieval periods.[12] However, apart from the chronological and geographical remoteness of many of these examples, which makes them of questionable relevance, almost all of them can in fact be used to prove the contrary case: while adoption was sometimes associated with inheritance, when it was it had to be spelled out explicitly. Spiritual kinship ties were conceived of quite loosely before the twelfth century, and did not have identical status to biological ties: the two bonds were complementary, not equivalent.[13] More often, spiritual adoption established a patron–client relationship than a father–son one.[14] A concrete contemporary example of this is given by the report in the *Annals of Fulda* of an eternal peace made in 873 between the Saxons and Danes which was sponsored by Louis the German. The Danish legates asked 'that he should deign to treat their lords, the aforementioned kings, as if they were his sons, while they for their part would venerate him as a father all the days of their life'.[15] The language of politics and peace thus frequently overlapped with the language of kinship. At least in part, therefore, the adoption of 887 must be seen in these terms, as symbolising the reconciliation of the line of Lothar to the Carolingian fold after the aberration of the *tyrannus* Boso.[16]

The record of Louis's election to kingship in 890 as recorded in the Capitulary of Valence also supports the counter-case that the adoption was really about reconciliation.[17] The relevant section tells us (rather awkwardly): 'The most excellent Emperor Charles previously conceded [to Louis] the royal dignity, and Arnulf, his successor, through his sceptre and his most sagacious legates, was confirmed in everything to be the authoriser and supporter of the kingdom.' Arnulf was Charles's successor,

---

[12] Hlawitschka, 'Nachfolgeprojekt', p. 26.

[13] J. H. Lynch, *Godparents and Kinship in Early Medieval Europe* (Princeton, 1986), pp. 179, 190–1.

[14] *Ibid.*, p. 191; see also J. Fried, 'Boso von Vienne oder Ludwig der Stammler? Der Kaiserkandidat Johanns VIII.', *DA* 32 (1976), 193–208, at 194, n. 6, and 197–204.

[15] *AF* s.a. 873, p. 78–9.

[16] Reuter, *Annals of Fulda*, p. 113, n. 6. In general see now P. J. E. Kershaw, '*Rex Pacificus*: Studies in Royal Peacemaking and the Image of Peacemaking in the Early Medieval West', PhD thesis, University of London (1998), a published version of which is forthcoming.

[17] *Hludowicus Regis Arelatensis Electio*, MGH Capit, vol. 2, no. 289.

164

The end of the empire II: response and failure

and established himself as a supporter of the 'dignitas' which Charles's act had 'previously conceded'. In other words, the conjunction made by the text between Arnulf's and Charles's support for Louis implies that they were of like kind, that one confirmed the other. Arnulf, of course, did not name Louis as his heir. Rather, he recognised his right to be considered royal, and granted him 'licence of authority'; by implication, this was also what Charles did. Nowhere does the text of Valence say that Louis was considered as Charles's heir. By contrast, his relationships to King Boso ('son of the most excellent King Boso') and to the middle Carolingian line ('descendant of the most glorious emperor the late Louis', 'of the imperial lineage') are both heavily stressed, as Louis and his supporters called on all possible sources of legitimacy to boost his claims. In other words, Louis's supporters conceived of what took place at Kirchen in 887 not as a royal designation, but rather as a readmission to the royal family, a recognition that he shared in the charisma of the Carolingians.

We also have a post-Kirchen charter issued by Charles for Louis's mother Irmingarde, Louis himself and his sisters. This document, which survives in the original from August 887, records a request made by Irmingarde to Charles to confirm in charter form what he had granted them at Kirchen; this turns out to be a general confirmation of Louis II's holdings and grants to his family, and no mention at all is made of the adoption.[18] Moreover, while Irmingarde's daughters are referred to in the penalty clause as Charles's 'most beloved daughters', a not unusual recasting of family ties in the spiritual-Christian language of Carolingian political dialogue, Louis is named twice, both times as 'Irmingarde's son, and our nephew [nepos]'.[19] This charter, together with another issued for the empress Engelberga on the same day, read like a *magna carta* of general confirmations for the family of Louis II. Although Charles had issued confirmations for Louis II's family before, these ones are marked out by the naming of Louis's grandchildren, and by the fine in the penalty clause of Engelberga's charter, which was double any previous threatened amount.[20] They thus fit in well with the view that the reception at Kirchen was primarily intended to make a definitive peace with the whole Lotharingian branch of the family after the death of Boso, backed by general confirmations of the rights and properties which had accrued to all its surviving members.

[18] D CIII 165; Hlawitschka, 'Nachfolgeprojekt', pp. 38–9.
[19] D CIII 165. Note also that the text itself was probably composed by a scribe of Irmingarde's, which makes it doubly significant that the adoption is not mentioned. Cf. references to Engelberga as Charles's 'sister'; DD CIII 22, 56, 156, 166.
[20] D CIII 166.

165

Kingship and Politics in the Late Ninth Century

It should be noted that the confirmations apply to whatever Louis II passed on to his family 'by the law of heredity': again, the context of Louis's Lotharingian descent is paramount. The same appeal to Lotharingian heredity is made by the *Vision of Charles the Fat*, a text purportedly narrated by the eponymous emperor himself.[21] Despite the various theories in existence about the dating of this text, Hlawitschka's own arguments for associating it with Louis's election to kingship in 890 are, to my mind, by far the most convincing.[22] The text, composed at the episcopal church of Rheims, was designed to enhance Louis's royal claims by emphasising his place in a Lotharingian imperial dynastic continuity, and to tempt him into a northwards expansion into the kingdom of Odo, with whom Archbishop Fulk of Rheims was at loggerheads. As such it is a work of propaganda produced in the specific circumstances of Rheims in 890 and cannot, as Hlawitschka also claims, be used to prove that Louis's adoption in 887 (to which it does not even allude) was intended by Charles to be an imperial designation. If the adoption really was the basis for an imperial claim, it is inexplicable that these pro-Louis texts did not mention it.

All things considered, therefore, the evidence points towards the conclusion that the adoption was intended as a ritual of peacemaking between Charles and the Lotharingian Carolingian line whose last male representative Louis was. Again, the outlines of the rituals performed are lost. A trace may, however, be detectable in a list of names in the Reichenau memorial book, headed by Lothar I, whose name is written in large red letters, with Engelberga, Irmingarde and Louis below. The list has a very dynastic feel and may well have been entered as part of the ceremonial surrounding the adoption at nearby Kirchen.[23] The fact that the Bavarian annalist reports the adoption of Louis in association with his reference to the death of his 'tyrant' father Boso (11 January 887) strongly suggests that it was this event, rather than developments in the succession situation, which inspired Charles to make peace with Louis. Moreover, the idea that the plans for the reconciliation were conceived when the news of Boso's death reached court in January would also explain why the empress Engelberga was in Alemannia in February of that year.[24] Her presence at court should be seen as part of the preparatory negotiations

---

[21] *Visio Karoli*, ed. G. Waitz, MGH SS 10 (Hanover, 1852), p. 458.

[22] Hlawitschka, *Lotharingien und das Reich*, pp. 98–106. Space does not permit discussion of the different cases. The latest discussion is P. Dutton, *The Politics of Dreaming in the Carolingian Empire* (Lincoln and London, 1994), pp. 233–51.

[23] See D. Geuenich, 'Zurzach- ein frühmittelalterliche Doppelkloster?', in Maurer and Patze (eds.), *Festschrift für Berent Schwineköper*, pp. 29–43, at p. 42 with n. 95.

[24] D CIII 156.

The end of the empire II: response and failure

for the imperial adoption of her grandson and the restoration to favour of the whole Lotharingian branch of the Carolingian family.[25]

If the adoption of Louis fits best into a context of reconciliation after the death of Boso, another piece of evidence has a more direct bearing on the state of the succession issue in the first half of 887. A letter of apology sent by Stephen V to Charles the Fat reveals that the emperor had requested the pope's presence at an assembly in Alemannia on 30 April 887, a request which Stephen now turned down.[26] Hlawitschka reckoned that Stephen had been summoned to oversee the adoption of Louis by Charles.[27] However, the fact that the April assembly was held at Waiblingen, while Louis was received at Kirchen no earlier than the end of May, renders this improbable: there were two separate assemblies.[28] Almost certainly, Stephen had been asked to come and legitimise Bernard to permit his designation as heir, perhaps something to which he had been willing to agree in principle during his negotiations with Charles in early 886.

This aborted meeting helps us put the adoption of Louis into perspective. Both assemblies were long-planned: Louis's had been in the offing since his father's death in January, while the pope stated he had received the emperor's invitation on 30 March, which was just about as early in the year as was possible after the Alpine passes had cleared. The reception of Louis cannot therefore simply have been a reaction to the failure of Stephen to appear at Waiblingen: he was not made heir in Bernard's place. What part, then, might the adoption have been intended to play in the resolution of the succession crisis? There are two ways in which the reception could have helped Charles. Firstly, it ought to be stressed that Louis's formidable mother and grandmother, both political heavyweights in the Carolingian middle kingdom, were closely involved in the negotiations leading up to the Kirchen assembly. Peace and reconciliation with Louis was actually a sign of reconciliation with, and a revival of, the whole Lotharingian branch of the Carolingian dynasty. Their cooperation was desirable if, as argued earlier, Charles's plan was to install Bernard as subking in Lotharingia.[29] Secondly, even if the emperor did not regard Louis as an immediate heir in June 887, or consider granting him a subkingdom, making peace with him at least provided the safety net of another potential successor.[30] Louis was still a minor

---

[25] Boso's death probably also motivated Charles to involve Geilo of Langres in these proceedings as his go-between with the Provençal bishops: see above, pp. 112–15.

[26] *Fragmenta Registri Stephani V. Papae*, ed. E. Caspar, MGH Epp, vol. 7, no. 14.

[27] Hlawitschka, 'Nachfolgeprojekt', p. 25; Tellenbach, 'Die geistigen und politischen Grundlagen', p. 296.

[28] *AF(B)* s.a. 887, p. 115 for the Waiblingen assembly.   [29] See above, pp. 131–2.

[30] Cf. Poupardin, *Le Royaume de Provence*, p. 147.

Kingship and Politics in the Late Ninth Century

(born c. 880) but Charles was in no position to worry about hedging his bets.

The highly significant political nature of these assemblies at Waiblingen and Kirchen accounts for the attendance of imperial aristocrats like Berengar of Friuli, Odo of Paris and Geilo of Langres.[31] Their consent, and that of their peers, would be required to guarantee the designation of Bernard and the recognition of Louis. We do not need to resort to the view (based entirely on the benefit of hindsight) that their presence was part of an imperial plan to designate members of the high aristocracy as heirs in May–June 887.[32] Hincmar's *On the Governance of the Palace* gives a firm context for the appearance of such magnates at royal courts and assemblies to discuss, among other things, royal policy for the forthcoming year.[33] One other clear reason for the presence of Odo in particular was to accompany Bishop Askericus of Paris to collect the ransom which had been promised to the Seine Vikings as the price for lifting the siege of Paris in the previous year.[34] That Viking matters were on the agenda of these assemblies is also suggested by the privileges issued at the same time to delegations from Tournus and Soissons, both of which provided for their defence in case of attack.[35] The fact that these men were prepared to travel such a long way from west Francia to imperial assemblies in the east is another sign that the emperor's favour was still seen as important, and that the political connections between centre and locality remained activated.

However, whatever the exact role envisaged for Louis by Charles, it was aired in the wake of yet another failure on the Bernard front. Stephen V's letter to the emperor is largely a list of vague and somewhat unlikely apologies excusing him from attendance at Waiblingen, including the vileness of one of the legates and a lack of time to get ready. He professed confusion over exactly what he was being asked to do, yet his reference to Charles's 'necessitas' suggests that he was well aware of the general purpose of his projected journey. His confusion may reflect the vagueness and naïvety of Charles's request, and of the overall conception of the plan to legitimate Bernard: exactly what did the emperor expect the pope to do? In all probability, we must assume that he wanted approval for a

---

[31] *AF(B)* s.a. 887, p. 115 for Berengar at Waiblingen; DD CIII 160–2 for Odo and Geilo at Kirchen.

[32] Keller, 'Zum Sturz Karls III.', pp. 379–84; Fried, *Der Weg in die Geschichte*, pp. 428–9.

[33] Hincmar, *De Ordine Palatii*, eds. T. Gross and R. Schieffer, MGH Fontes (Hanover, 1980), chap. 30, pp. 84–6.

[34] *AV* s.a. 887, pp. 63–4. Since Odo had already received a general confirmation of the privileges and properties of his abbey of St-Martin in Tours (D CIII 139), the comparatively minor charters he received in 887 (DD 160–1) were unlikely to have been the main reason for his journey to east Francia; they should be seen as by-products of his attendance at court.

[35] DD CIII 162–3.

The end of the empire II: response and failure

dissolution of his barren marriage which would leave him free to wed Bernard's mother. Such tactics were known to work in the early Middle Ages: there is some evidence for the retrospective legitimation of bastards along these lines in tenth-century Normandy.[36] More pertinently, the dower charter of Louis II for his wife Engelberga, drawn up in 860, was later tampered with to backdate their marriage to 851. The aim of this must have been to retrospectively legitimise the couple's union and the status of their children at a time when such issues were under scrutiny due to the ongoing divorce case of Lothar II.[37] This move has some analogies with the situation of Charles the Fat, were he seeking to marry Bernard's mother. However, there was no specific Frankish or papal ceremony which could be performed on Bernard himself to decisively remove the stain on his legitimacy with which he had been born. The precedents were not good. Whereas the issue at stake in the tumultuous case of Lothar II was whether or not his first marriage (and the legitimacy of Hugh, his son by it) should be canonically recognised, Bernard had incontestably been born to a concubine outside marriage. The emperor and the pope were improvising. Loose ends would inevitably remain, and Stephen's mind cannot but have been drawn to reflect on the political mess caused by the divorce politics of the 860s, into a repeat performance of which he was presumably keen to avoid being sucked. Another consideration was an unwillingness to turn his back on the fluid and dangerous factional politics of the late ninth-century Vatican.[38] Whatever the exact line of the pope's reasoning, from Charles's point of view this was another serious political setback and threat to his credibility. Bernard remained illegitimate and unapproved, Arnulf remained out in the cold, and Charles remained unable to resolve the pressing problem of the succession. With doors slamming in his face at every turn, the emperor decided to try a new angle. As we shall see, however, even with his options diminishing, he was still determined to keep his increasingly frustrated nephew out of the picture.

THE ROYAL DIVORCE, SUMMER 887

The failure of the second attempt to get Bernard legitimised was a severe setback for Charles. Although Boso was now dead, and Louis of Provence was back in the circle of potential heirs, Arnulf was recovering his balance

---

[36] E. van Houts, 'Countess Gunnor of Normandy (c. 950–1031)', *Collegium Medievale* 12 (1999), 7–24, at 12–14.
[37] D L2 30.
[38] For references to the often-deadly factional fighting in Rome, see *AF(M)* s.a. 882, p. 99; *AF(B)* s.a. 883, p. 109; Reuter, *Annals of Fulda*, p. 94, n. 17 provides commentary.

Kingship and Politics in the Late Ninth Century

after the humiliation of 885–6 and, as we have seen, it was becoming increasingly worrying to people like Notker that the succession issue was still not settled. To lose one pope from the support of his plans may have been unlucky, but two looked careless: Stephen V's thinly veiled rebuttal of Charles's request to come to Waiblingen to legitimise Bernard showed that this possible solution was a dead end for the foreseeable future. A new approach was most assuredly called for. This brings us to Charles's divorce of the empress Richgard and the expulsion from court of the archchancellor Liutward in summer 887. Our only narrative source for this story is Regino's *Chronicon*, and its description of the emperor's actions are here worth repeating in full:

Charles expelled from his side in disgrace a certain Liutward, the bishop of Vercelli, a man who was very dear to him and his only adviser in the administration of affairs of state, accused of the crime of adultery because he had been inappropriately familiar with the queen in secret. After a few days he called his wife Richgard (for that was the empress's name) before a judicial assembly [*contio*] concerning the same matter and, amazingly, he testified in public that he had never joined with her sexually, although she had been his consort for more than ten years of legitimate marriage. She for her part declared that she remained untouched not only by him, but by all male union, and that she gloried in her virginity. She confidently asserted that if it pleased her husband she would prove herself by the judgement of almighty God, either through trial by combat or hot ploughshares, for she was a pious woman. After the divorce was completed [*facto discidio*] she retired to the monastery which she had constructed on her own land [Andlau] in order to serve God.[39]

Historians have by and large been happy to accept Regino's allegation of adultery at face value, reading it as yet another case in the catalogue of disasters which are presumed to pepper Charles's reign, revealing his loss of control over events.[40] However, there is a discrepancy in Regino's account. If Richgard was a virgin, which is presented as the grounds for divorce, how could Liutward have been guilty of adultery with her, the reason given for his expulsion from court? At least one of these two elements in the story must be false. Hlawitschka noticed this and concluded that Regino invented the story of the imperial couple's chastity in order to depict Charles as a perfect model of Christian virtue, taking his material from the episode in 873 when the king had reportedly tried to renounce the trappings of the world, including intercourse with his

[39] Regino, *Chronicon*, s.a. 887, p. 127.
[40] E.g. Löwe, 'Das Karlsbuch Notkers', p. 142; P. Stafford, *Queens, Concubines and Dowagers: the King's Wife in the Early Middle Ages* (Athens, 1983), p. 95.

The end of the empire II: response and failure

wife.[41] But Regino did not necessarily intend to portray Charles as a paragon of virtue; the point of his version of the pious and stoical emperor's deposition was more a lesson about how even the most conspicuous worldly success was reliant on God-given *fortuna* and could be suddenly snatched away by the shortcomings of human frailty.[42] Moreover, and in keeping with this viewpoint, the abbot of Prüm was not beyond criticising Charles's actions as unworthy, as in his negative judgement of the outcome of the siege of Paris, and in his accusation that Boso had been wrongly persecuted by the Carolingians, who thus showed themselves to be perjurers.[43]

A more important element in Regino's story is his use of precise canonical language to describe the divorce. The phrase 'facto discidio', for instance, is also used in the same author's famous compilation of canon law, *De Synodalibus Causis*.[44] One would further note the judicial term 'contio' used to describe the hearing, the mutual declarations of innocence and the ordeal used as proof.[45] The apparent reference to Charles's outburst of 873 (implied by the otherwise mysterious mentioning of a ten-year period of marriage) can be read as a device used by Regino (or perhaps an unconscious elision) to emphasise the validity of the grounds for divorce by referring back to another well-known point in the emperor's life when he had openly announced a desire to withdraw from the world. All this suggests that whether or not Richgard was actually a virgin, this was the claim made publicly by the emperor in order to ensure that the divorce, or more properly annulment, could proceed canonically without descending into the legal and political shambles experienced in the 860s by the similarly intentioned Lothar II.

This interpretation is supported by the evidence of the *Life of St. Verena*, a short hagiographical text surviving in manuscripts from Reichenau, St-Gall and Einsiedeln and thought to have been written

---

[41] Hlawitschka, 'Nachfolgeprojekt', pp. 44–6. The 873 reference comes from the claim that the marriage had lasted 'for more than ten years', which would be an odd thing to say in 887 when the couple had been married in 862. The 873 incident was widely reported: *AF* s.a. 873, pp. 77–8; *AB* s.a. 873, pp. 190–2; *AX* s.a. 873, pp. 31–2. On this see Nelson, 'Monks, Secular Men and Masculinity'.

[42] Cf. now H.-H. Körtum, 'Weltgeschichte am Ausgang der Karolingerzeit: Regino von Prüm', in Scharer and Scheibelreiter (eds.), *Historiographie im frühen Mittelalter*, pp. 499–513.

[43] Regino, *Chronicon*, s.a. 887, p. 127; 879, p. 114 respectively. On Regino and Boso see F. Staab, 'Jugement moral et propagande. Boson de Vienne vu par les élites du royaume de l'est', in Le Jan (ed.), *La Royauté et les élites*, pp. 365–82.

[44] Regino, *De Synodalibus Causis*, ed. F. G. A. Wasserschleben (Leipzig, 1840), book II, chaps. 244–5, p. 309; cf. chap. 243, pp. 308–9.

[45] Löwe, 'Das Karlsbuch Notkers', pp. 142–3; G. Bührer-Thierry, 'La Reine adultère', *Cahiers de civilisation médiévale Xe–XIIe siècles* 35 (1992), 299–312, at 307–9.

Kingship and Politics in the Late Ninth Century

by Hatto, archbishop of Mainz and abbot of Reichenau, for Richgard following her retirement to her proprietary convent at Andlau.[46] With this in mind, it is significant that the *Life* is expressly intended as an *exemplum* for a virginal life, and that its subject may well have been married, perhaps chastely, before retiring to fulfil her monastic vocation.[47] We know that Hatto was a member of Charles the Fat's entourage while he himself was a mere monk at Reichenau.[48] It is therefore not entirely out of the question that the emperor commissioned him to write the *Life* on the occasion of his wife's retreat in 887, rather than, as is usually supposed, Hatto composing it spontaneously sometime after 888.[49] This possibility is strengthened by the fact that Richgard's monastery of Zurzach, where Verena's cult was celebrated, was intended to be removed from the empress's control once her husband died so that it could be transferred to whichever church he was buried in.[50] Her links with the cult of Verena would thus have been severed after January 888, a fact which argues for an early date for the *Life* and hence the involvement of Charles in the propagation of the story that his marriage had been chaste. Contemporary acceptance of this story may be reflected in the fact that unusual stories circulated at the time of Charles's death describing his holiness and ascent to heaven.[51]

Was Richgard really a virgin? Although we cannot know, this seems unlikely. Charles, who had a son, was not, and his anxious and repeated attempts to solve his succession problems throughout the 880s make it improbable that he would have tolerated a chaste marriage for over twenty-five years. Bernard was apparently still a minor when Notker wrote the *Deeds of Charlemagne* in the mid-880s, and so is likely to have been born *after* 873, the year when Charles claimed a desire to renounce sexual intercourse.[52] Although probably not privy to the secrets of the imperial bedchamber, Notker expressed the belief in 881, and again in 885–6, that there was yet a chance of Richgard and Charles conceiving.[53]

---

[46] See A. Reinle, *Die heilige Verena von Zurzach. Legende-Kult-Denkmäler* (Basel, 1948), pp. 26–31 for the text. On authorship and audience see *ibid.*, pp. 21–2; Geuenich, 'Zurzach', pp. 38–9; T. Klüppel, *Reichenauer Hagiographie zwischen Walahfrid und Berno* (Sigmaringen, 1980), pp. 60–4.

[47] Reinle, *Die heilige Verena*, chap. 2, p. 26 (*exemplum*), chap. 5, p. 27 (reference to a marriage); cf. Reinle's comments at p. 36.

[48] *Liber Memorialis Romaricensis*, fol. 9r.

[49] It is suggestive, though no more than that, that the divorce was carried out in June 887, shortly before Verena's feast day on 1 September, which would have provided a suitable occasion for a presentation of the *Vita*.

[50] D CIII 43.

[51] Regino, *Chronicon*, s.a. 888, pp. 128–9; *AV* s.a. 887, p. 64; *AF(B)* s.a. 887, p. 116.

[52] Notker, *Gesta*, 2.12, p. 74; 2.14, p. 78 describes him in diminutive terms.

[53] Notker, *Continuatio*, p. 330; Notker, *Gesta*, 2.14, p. 78.

The end of the empire II: response and failure

If the divorce was not therefore the result of a genuine inclination for renunciation on the part of the royal couple, it was probably political. Why would Charles have wanted to orchestrate the expulsion of his wife?[54] Clearly, exactly because they had failed to produce children together, and canonical separation on the grounds of chastity cleared the way for a new marriage. Indeed, ninth-century efforts to streamline Frankish marriage practices made a claim of chastity essential for this purpose.[55] Why now and not before? Because previous succession plans, namely the Vienne succession agreement made in 880 and the two attempts to legitimise Bernard, had proved fruitless, and so a new tactic was necessary. After the failure of his partnerships with Hadrian III and Stephen V, Charles decided (or was forced by circumstances) to abandon papal sponsorship as the legitimating device for his plans, and to replace it with a public ordeal.[56]

Another change of tack is also identifiable: it is unlikely that the plan this time round was for Charles to legitimise Bernard retrospectively by marrying his mother, who, given that we have no information about her, seems not to have been of noble stock. For the likes of Notker, who in his *Continuatio* made a point of approvingly stressing the nobility of the mothers of Arnulf and Louis the Younger's illegitimate son Hugh, while neglecting to mention Bernard at all, this may have been seen as a barrier to this solution.[57] As well as this, the problem of Bernard's illegitimate birth was thornier even than that of Lothar II's son Hugh in the disputes of the 860s. Whereas Lothar had been able to argue that Hugh had been born within wedlock, Bernard's birth was incontrovertibly extra-marital. This meant that his legitimacy would always remain contestable. While Charles may have believed that papal endorsement would be enough to counteract this argument, he appears not to have been confident that he could succeed on his own authority. It is surely no coincidence that Bernard was dropped from imperial charter prayer clauses in late 887 for the first time since 885.[58]

---

[54] It is worth stressing that Richgard seems to have been a willing participant in her own fate. Keller, 'Zum Sturz Karls III.', p. 354, n. 63 presumes that her expulsion led her relatives to join Arnulf's coup in outrage; I know of no evidence to support this assertion.

[55] See P. Toubert, 'The Carolingian Moment (Eighth–Tenth Century)', in A. Burguière et al. (eds.), *A History of the Family* (Cambridge, 1996), pp. 379–406; J. Gaudemet, *Le Marriage en occident. Les moeurs et le droit* (Paris, 1987), pp. 109–32.

[56] See R. Bartlett, *Trial by Fire and Water. The Medieval Judicial Ordeal* (Oxford, 1986), esp. pp. 16–20 on the link between allegations of sexual misconduct and ordeals by hot iron.

[57] Notker, *Continuatio*, p. 330. Assuming he had reached majority by 890–1, when he led revolts against Arnulf, Bernard must have been born before Notker wrote this text, in 881.

[58] One telling example: D CIII 168 from September 887, in which there is no mention of *proles*, although the textual model, which the charter otherwise followed faithfully, did include such a reference. See Ewig, 'Der Gebetsdienst der Kirchen', p. 75.

Kingship and Politics in the Late Ninth Century

There were presumably plenty of promising noble candidates for the position of queen, well capable of bearing 'a little Louis or Charles' to the emperor.[59] Either way, the divorce and remarriage scheme was yet another clear sign that Arnulf of Carinthia was to have no part in the succession plans of Charles the Fat. Since 885 Arnulf had been the second most senior Carolingian, both in closeness to the main bloodline (outranking Bernard in age) and in practical support. With the blinding of Hugh in late 885, and the second failure of Bernard's designation in early 887, he was the only realistic successor (Louis of Provence and Charles the Simple being too young). The fact that despite these circumstances Charles was now very publicly turning in a different direction must have convinced Arnulf that the door was closing on him forever unless he acted swiftly. The divorce made obvious to him the emperor's intransigence on the identity of his heir, and alerted him to the fact that the remarriage which was surely imminent might strengthen Charles and weaken his own position still further. Bernard may no longer have posed Arnulf a threat: but in the divorce, finally, was a succession scheme which had some potential to succeed. Even though it would be years before any new son would be old enough to take over as king, things were finally moving forward for Charles the Fat. This may have been the decisive factor which set in motion the chain of events which culminated in Charles's deposition in November.

This hypothesis leaves certain loose ends to be tidied up. What, for instance, can be said of the role of Liutward of Vercelli in all this? If he had actually committed adultery, which would be inconsistent with Charles's claim that Richgard was a virgin, it is very striking that this was not mentioned by the Mainz annalist in his litany of biblically-inspired accusations against the archchancellor in his annal for 887.[60] The language of sexual impropriety was particularly well suited to this author's purpose and he had a ready-made biblical parallel available to him in the Book of Esther, which he utilised extensively to compose this annal.[61] His silence is therefore deafening.

If, then, Liutward was not really an adulterer, why was he expelled from court? A charter of late 887 refers back to the dispossession of the archchancellor, relating that it had taken place 'on the occasion of certain risings'.[62] This vague clue is probably to be placed in the context of factionalism surrounding the succession issue. That factions had formed around this point is clear. As we have seen, Charles had tried to remove

---

[59] Notker, *Gesta*, 2.11, p. 68.   [60] On which see above, pp. 28–30.
[61] Bührer-Thierry, 'Le conseiller du roi', p. 122. Bührer-Thierry's proposed solution is that the adultery did take place but was somehow too sensitive to mention.
[62] D CIII 170.

The end of the empire II: response and failure

'certain bishops' from office after objections had been made to the 885 plan to legitimise Bernard.[63] Two years later in 887 the two continuators of the *Annals of Fulda* attributed Liutward's ejection to Charles's discussions with 'his men' and 'the Alemans'.[64] Both these latter reports imply friction between parties at the court itself, although, since almost all of the men in Charles's entourage were Alemans (including Liutward and Liutbert), we can say little more about their makeup. Most historians see the turning point of this dispute as being concerned with the adoption of Louis of Provence and a consequent argument over the principle of imperial unity, but, as argued earlier, this explanation is methodologically unsatisfactory. Moreover, the plan to adopt Louis was conceived by Charles upon hearing of the death of Boso in January 887, and was certainly well underway by the time the empress Engelberga made representations at the court in February.[65] If Liutward opposed the plan, it is inexplicable that he should have remained in favour until at least the end of May that year, and indeed quite possibly until after the adoption was effected.[66]

If the connection between the adoption and the fall of the archchancellor is severed, and actual adultery is ruled out, then the relatively overlooked fact, recorded by Regino, that Liutward was deposed in connection with the beginning of the divorce proceedings takes on much greater significance. The particular functions of the queen within the Carolingian court made her a potential crystallising point for the formation of factions and her arrival or departure could easily lead to the rise and fall of groups of prominent royal advisers; certainly, the crises of Louis the Pious's reign had come to a head in large part over court politics focused on the influence of his second wife Judith.[67] Similarly,

---

[63] *AF(M)* s.a. 885, p. 103. It may be more than chance that this event coincided with the withdrawal of Salomon, future bishop of Constance and abbot of St-Gall, from the imperial court. Cf. U. Zeller, *Bischof Salomo III. von Konstanz, Abt von St. Gallen* (Leipzig and Berlin, 1910), pp. 42–3.

[64] *AF(M)* s.a. 887, p. 105; *AF(B)* s.a. 887, p. 115.   [65] See above, pp. 161–9.

[66] *AF(B)* s.a. 887, p. 115 shows him still in favour in May. The last charter he subscribed as archchancellor was D CIII 159, dated 30 May, while Liutbert's first appearance was in D 160, dated 16 June. Both of these were enacted at Kirchen, which is also where Louis was adopted. However, we do not know the exact date on which this took place; it is entirely possible that it was done while Liutward was still in place and, given his preeminence at court, the ceremony could well have been orchestrated by him. With this in mind, it is interesting to note that the feast of Ascension, which offered a striking parallel of the reception of a son to emphasise the significance of the adoption, fell on May 25. For this suggestion and others about the sacred significance of dates in May 887 for this assembly, and about Charles the Fat's penchant for associating the feast of Ascension with important political statements, see Sierck, *Festtag und Politik*, pp. 95, 103, 157.

[67] Bührer-Thierry, 'La reine adultère', pp. 299–301, 311–12 offers apposite general comments. See also E. Ward, 'Agobard of Lyons and Paschasius Radbertus as Critics of the Empress Judith',

175

the fall of Liutward is most likely, in the circumstances outlined above, to have been due to his close association with the empress at the court of Charles the Fat. If it can be shown that his political position was closely linked to hers, then we can understand why he might have tried to oppose the divorce–succession plan and ended up out on his ear. The next two sections of this chapter will attempt to substantiate this assertion.

Before that, however, some further discrepancies remain. Firstly, we have to explain why Regino accused Liutward and Richgard of illicit extra-marital activities if, as argued, the establishment of the empress's virginity was the real issue at stake in the divorce. A possible answer lies in the fact that by the late ninth century the rhetoric of sexual impropriety was firmly established as an effective weapon of political attack. The close relationship between a queen and an adviser was liable to be transformed by accusation or rumour into a case of adultery. Such rumour would be plausible to someone like Regino, writing two decades after the event from the perspective of an outsider and as someone with little regard for the bishop of Vercelli, whom he depicted as an archetypal despiser of Christ's command.[68] Elsewhere Regino lamented that the fall of the Carolingians was down to the 'sterility of their wives', a statement which hints that, despite his allegations about Liutward, he knew what had really been at stake in the events of 887.[69]

Secondly, the question arises of why the two continuations of the *Annals of Fulda* fail to mention the divorce at all. For the Mainz annalist this is not hard to explain. His polemical and calculated deployment of facts to create an image of bad kingship (or, as in the 887 annal, bad archchancellorship) necessitated, as we saw most clearly in his account of the siege of Asselt, a tendency to pass over actual circumstances in silence if they did not fit his purpose. In 887 this author, now with a favourable attitude towards the emperor after the restoration to favour of Liutbert, chose to ignore various events connected to the succession (such as the death of Boso, the adoption of Louis, the invitation to Pope Stephen and the divorce of Richgard) which, had he still been hostile to Charles, he might have used in an invective against court policy. The divorce, if adultery was not involved, had no real value as a weapon with which to criticise his main target, Liutward. On the other hand, the

---

Studies in Church History 27 (1990), 15–25; E. Ward, 'Caesar's Wife: the Career of the Empress Judith, 819–29', in Godman and Collins (eds.), *Charlemagne's Heir*, pp. 205–27.

[68] Regino, *Chronicon*, s.a. 901, p. 148; Sierck, *Festtag und Politik*, pp. 240–1. I intend to publish fuller thoughts on Regino elsewhere.

[69] Regino, *Chronicon*, s.a. 880, p. 117, cited, naturally, without wishing to endorse the sexist implications of the remark.

The end of the empire II: response and failure

general theme of this annal, Liutward's pride and consequent attempts to usurp royal rights, could imply his opposition to the emperor's decision to divorce his wife. Moreover, Carolingian political and historical texts were steeped in the world of the Old Testament. The explicit parallel made by the Mainz annalist between Charles and King Ahasuerus from the Book of Esther in his account of the year 887 may also have served as a sidelong reference to the matter. Ahasuerus had, like Charles, decided to divorce his first wife, something which may have influenced the annalist's choice of biblical reference: the criticism of the archchancellor which was the text's primary purpose would otherwise have been better served by the selection of Jeroboam from the book of Kings.[70] Moreover, the Esther model was not chosen for its depiction of queenly adultery. However, the argument could be played more than one way, and it is probably wise not to push the significance of the parallel too far. The perspective of the Bavarian continuator had also shifted: from his previous position as a provincial chronicler generally favourable to Charles, in his 887 entry he wrote as an apologist for Arnulf, casting his rise in terms of a realm-wide aristocratic *conspiratio* against an inactive and mortally ill emperor.[71] If this change in attitude is explained, as seems likely, by the fact that the author wrote this account up retrospectively, after Charles's death in January 888, to which he refers in his 887 annal, then it was clearly not in keeping with his representation of events to include the emperor's divorce of Richgard. His Charles the Fat was inactive, ill and at the mercy of others, while his Arnulf was responding to a general call for his firm leadership, not to a new twist in the succession politics of the royal house. The idea, which would be implied by the mention of the divorce, that Arnulf had rebelled in response to a quite legitimate exclusion from power, hardly cast him in a flattering light.

In any case, the evidence does not therefore allow us to accept that the divorce was simply some scandal which was foisted from nowhere upon the startled emperor, nor that Liutward and Richgard were engaged in a sinister conspiracy against Charles.[72] Likewise, ideological (imperial unity) and sexual motivations have been ruled out. What remains is actually quite a clever move by the emperor to make a virtue out of a necessity. The declaration of the chastity of his marriage was designed not only to get him out of a barren union with the opportunity to find a new wife, but to sanctify the situation and eliminate grounds for opposition. Clearly, Charles and his advisers had absorbed the lessons to be learned

---

[70] Bührer-Thierry, 'Le conseiller du roi', pp. 114–15.
[71] Bowlus, 'Arnulf of Carinthia's *Ostpolitik*', p. 557.
[72] Thus Tellenbach, 'Die geistigen und politischen Grundlagen', p. 248; Löwe, 'Das Karlsbuch Notkers', p. 142.

Kingship and Politics in the Late Ninth Century

from the problems of some of his predecessors, notably Lothar II. Unfortunately, the details of what actually went on in June 887 are obscure, despite the existence of several sources. The case for the archchancellor's opposition to the divorce for factional reasons has so far been made largely by a process of elimination. The best way to add substance to the presumed close political relationship between Richgard and Liutward is hence to contextualise their respective positions in the politics of the empire.

THE CAREER OF LIUTWARD

A column in the memorial book of the monastery of Remiremont, very probably entered before 876 and possibly connected with Charles the Fat's journey to visit Charles the Bald in 872, shows that Liutward, at this time only a Reichenau monk, was in the future ruler's entourage before he was raised to kingship.[73] If 872 is indeed the correct date, this demonstrates Liutward's readiness to follow his lord even into rebellion against Louis the German. Moreover, it appears on palaeographical grounds that both this and a similar record left in the *liber memorialis* of Pfäffers in Rhaetia were actually written by Liutward himself, a further indication of his importance to Charles even at this early stage.[74] This evidence also adds weight to Paul Kehr's suggestion that Charles had been developing a chancery and diplomatic style for some time before 876, accounting for the individualistic series of charters issued during his early years as king.[75] After Charles had assumed full power in Alemannia, Liutward was involved in the chancery's development both as scribe and, from 878 at the latest, archchancellor.[76] On the occasion of his Italian coronation at Ravenna in early 880, the king intervened in a jurisdictional dispute between the churches of Rome and Milan to impose Liutward on the see of Vercelli.[77] Sometime between then and November 882 he added the title of archchaplain to his list of dignities. Finally, at some point before 884 Liutward also seems to have become abbot or proprietor of the prestigious Italian monastery of Bobbio.[78]

---

[73] *Liber Memorialis Romaricensis*, fol. 9r. The naming of Charles as *rex* rather than *imperator* rules out the date of 885 often ascribed to this entry.

[74] *Libri Confraternitatum Sancti Galli, Augiensis, Fabariensis*, ed. P. Piper, MGH (Berlin, 1884), p. 361; Tellenbach, 'Liturgische Gedenkbücher', pp. 396–9.

[75] Kehr, *Die Kanzlei Karls III.*, p. 6.

[76] *Ibid.*, p. 7, noting also that the use of the term *archicancellarius* was hitherto unknown in the east; perhaps this denotes a more hierarchic organisation in Charles's chancery; pp. 14–17 for the personal connections between Liutward and individual notaries such as Inquirinus, who was also present in the royal entourage at Remiremont.

[77] Schmid, 'Liutbert von Mainz', p. 53.

[78] Notker, *Liber Ymnorum*, p. 8; von den Steinen, *Notker der Dichter. Darstellungsband*, p. 505.

The end of the empire II: response and failure

There is no doubting, therefore, the fact that the rise to power of Charles was very much in tandem with that of his long-term associate Liutward. However, historians, in keeping with the view of Charles as a sickly and weak personality, have credited the bishop of Vercelli with having an overwhelming control of the politics of the reign at the king's expense; Bund's view that Liutward was 'the director of imperial policy' is not atypical.[79] There are three main pieces of evidence which are taken to support this view. The first and second are the accounts of the Mainz annalist and of Regino of Prüm, both of which characterise Liutward in such terms. However, it has already been argued that both these authorities were hostile to the archchancellor for other reasons, and deployed the image of the unique counsellor as a polemical motif to discredit him as an obstacle to *consensus* and *consilium*.[80] Their opinions are therefore not to be accepted at face value. We have already encountered several other individuals who figured prominently among the close advisers of the emperor, men such as Odo of Paris, Geilo of Langres, Theoderic of Vermandois and the unnamed 'Alemans' consulted about the downfall of Liutward.[81] The profile of these men gives the lie to the assertion that the latter enjoyed exclusive access to the throne. The Bavarian annalist probably comes closest to characterising the archchancellor's position accurately when he refers to Liutward as 'the most important counsellor of the royal palace'; this is by no means an unusual or sinister way of defining the power of the archchancellor at any Carolingian court of the ninth century.[82]

The third piece of evidence for Liutward's alleged supremacy is the great number of times he is mentioned as intercessor in royal diplomas of Charles the Fat; according to Fleckenstein, this 'demonstrates that it was he who actually shared out governmental favour'.[83] Certainly, Liutward was named as intervener considerably more often than any other individual, and it is valid to use this sort of evidence as an indication of

---

[79] K. Bund, *Thronsturz und Herrscherabsetzung im Frühmittelalter* (Bonn, 1979), p. 478. Cf. Borgolte, 'Karl III. und Neudingen', p. 21; cf. Keller, 'Zum Sturz Karls III.', p. 338 on the bishop's 'ruling influence over the emperor'; A. Angenendt, *Kaiserherrschaft und Königstaufe. Kaiser, Könige und Päpste als geistliche Patrone in der abendländischen Missiongeschichte* (Berlin and New York, 1984), p. 261 describes him as 'all-powerful'.

[80] See above, pp. 28–30; 176. On this rhetorical device see Bührer-Thierry, 'Le conseiller du roi', pp. 115–17, 119–21.

[81] Note that as well as Liutward, Odo and Hugh the Abbot are also granted the rare privilege of featuring in the prayer clauses of an imperial charter, a provision normally reserved for members of the royal family; DD CIII 92, 145, 160. All three are, strictly speaking, confirmations of prayer provisions originally made by the charters' recipients.

[82] *AF(B)* s.a. 887, p. 115. Cf. Hincmar, *De Ordine Palatii*, chap. 12, p. 54 on Adalhard as 'first among the emperor's chief counsellors'; chap. 16, pp. 62–4 on the co-supremacy of the archchancellor in the palace.

[83] Fleckenstein, *Die Hofkapelle der deutschen Könige*, p. 191; also stressed by Keller, 'Zum Sturz Karls III.', pp. 338–40.

Kingship and Politics in the Late Ninth Century

who was 'in' and 'out' of favour at court.[84] However, closer analysis of these documents casts some doubt on the standard interpretation. Of the thirty-four known interventions for third parties which he made between February 880 and February 887 (our first and last examples), no fewer than twenty-five concerned Italian affairs. Of the rest, four were for the western kingdom, three for Lotharingia and only two for Alemannia.[85] The well-known diversity of style in Charles the Fat's charters, due to the fact that many of them were drafted by scribes of the beneficiaries, does not account for this bias in the figures, as the main formulas were standardised and supervised by an imperial notary and the archchancellor before being enacted.[86] That this supervision included the formulas for intercession, which became fairly standard from the reign of Charles onwards, is indicated by the fact that they appeared for the first time in different *regna* (with different chancery traditions) more or less simultaneously.[87] The implication, therefore, is that Liutward's influence was limited primarily to Italy.[88]

Even here, however, his power was not omnipresent. The geographical spread of beneficiaries on whose behalf the bishop is known to have petitioned the emperor is essentially confined to the western half of northern Italy, stretching in a loop west from Brescia through Bergamo and Milan to Asti, and then back east as far as Reggio by way of Pavia and Piacenza.[89] There are four exceptions to this observation. Three charters from June 883, which were intended to strengthen the relationship between the emperor and the churches of Casauria, Farfa and Fermo in and around the duchy of Spoleto, were issued at the request of Liutward.[90] These documents stand alone as diplomatic evidence for Charles's intervention in the affairs of the duchy, and presumably represent an opportunistic attempt to establish control while the *dux* Guy was out of royal favour in summer 883.[91] The fourth exception is the intervention of Liutward in

---

[84] For a literary depiction of intervention at court, see Notker, *Gesta*, 1.4, pp. 5–6; Goetz, *Strukturen der spätkarolingischen Epoche*, p. 26.

[85] Italy: DD CIII 18, 21, 23, 26–9, 33, 36, 39, 44–8, 78, 82–4, 87, 111, 114–15, 126, 156. West: DD 123, 129, 151, 153. Lotharingia: DD 94, 104, 121. Alemannia: DD 38, 99. DD 54 (for the church of Vercelli) and 92 (for Liutward and Reichenau) are disqualified as the bishop was also a recipient.

[86] Kehr, *Die Kanzlei Karls III.*, pp. 36–7, 43, 49.

[87] D CIII 18 of February 880 for the Italian priest Leo is the first true example, while DD 24 and 38 from July 880 and May 881 respectively, are early examples from Alsace and Alemannia.

[88] See Bührer-Thierry, 'Les évêques de Bavière', p. 35, where she reaches slightly different figures for Liutward's interventions.

[89] See Map 7.   [90] DD CIII 82–4.

[91] *AF(M)* s.a. 883, p. 100; *AF(B)* s.a. 883, pp. 109–10 states that Guy was accused of treason, presumably in absentia, at Nonantola, where these two charters were issued. Note that D CIII 83 mentions Guy, but tellingly without his title *dux*. Lechner, 'Verlorene Urkunden', no. 539 for the

The end of the empire II: response and failure

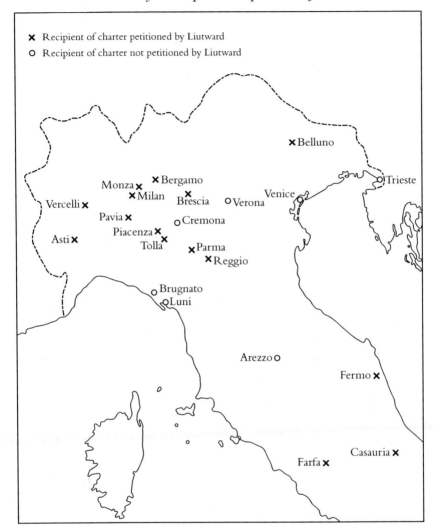

Map 7. Liutward's Italian interventions

February 882 for the church of Belluno in Friuli. Here, the archchancellor was named only as the grant's co-petitioner, in the illustrious company of the *marchio* Berengar.[92] It is striking that Liutward, despite his obvious

---

church of Teramo in Spoleto probably also belongs in 883. The other known lost Italian charters of Charles are all for recipients no further south or south-east than Florence.
[92] D CIII 48.

Kingship and Politics in the Late Ninth Century

influence in the west of the *regnum Italiae*, was not involved in the distribution of royal favour in Friuli and eastern Lombardy on any other occasion.[93] This suggests that from Verona eastwards the shots were being called by Berengar and his allies, whom we have already encountered as vigorous royal representatives in this important region, and explains why Liutward could not intercede alone in Belluno.[94] Berengar and his close associate Count Waltfred of Verona, conversely, were on at least one occasion involved in the securing of royal patronage for a west Lombard recipient while they were at court.[95] We might add the prominent participation of these men in royal judicial hearings, something which cannot be said of Liutward.[96] It is also worth remembering that even Liutward's involvement in the attempt to secure imperial influence in Spoleto could only be accomplished in the wake of an initially successful military invasion led by Berengar.[97] These observations are paralleled by the fact that of the nine times Liutward is known to have intervened for beneficiaries north of the Alps, four were in conjunction with other powerful figures from the relevant area, while two others make mention of associated, though less significant, petitions.[98] From the intervention evidence, therefore, the archchancellor's influence over the distribution of imperial patronage appears to have been comparatively weak outside north-west Italy.

There is a further case to be made that Liutward's power differed from Berengar's qualitatively, and not just in its sphere of influence. Six men are given the title *consiliarius* (counsellor) in the charters of Charles the Fat, of whom Liutward is easily the most frequently mentioned.[99] The meaning of this word, which (in charters) is largely confined to Italian sources and at all times denoted a magnate or official of unusual proximity to the throne, was argued in an influential article by Hagen Keller to have undergone a subtle transformation in Italy in the course of the

---

[93] DD CIII 37, 49, 76, 80, 110.

[94] See above, pp. 70–2. Friuli and the north-east had a strong political identity strengthened by the factional struggles of the 870s: see Delogu, 'Vescovi, conti e sovrani'; and in general H. Krahwinkler, *Friaul im Frühmittelalter. Geschichte einer Region vom Ende des fünften bis zum Ende des zehnten Jahrhunderts* (Vienna, Cologne and Weimar, 1992).

[95] D CIII 32, issued at Pavia for Bishop Wibod and the church of Parma.

[96] DD CIII 25 and 31, concerning rights and properties in Novalese, Sienna and Arezzo.

[97] *AF(B)* s.a. 883, p. 110.

[98] D CIII 38 in Alemannia with Richgard; DD 94 and 104 in Lotharingia with Hugh of Lotharingia and Richgard; D 123 in Lyon with the *marchio* Bernard Plantevelue. DD 99 and 153 refer to approaches made by Abbot Rothoh of Reichenau and Geilo of Langres respectively. Of Liutward's twenty-five Italian intercessions, only four were co-petitioned.

[99] DD CIII 21, 23, 29, 33, 36, 47, 78, 111, 114, 115, 126 (Liutward); D 16 (Waltfred of Verona and Berthold, count of the palace); D 32 (Berengar of Friuli and Waltfred of Verona); D 47 (Wibod of Parma); D 86 (Otulf).

The end of the empire II: response and failure

ninth century. At first a simple auxiliary epithet to describe a magnate high in royal favour, under Louis II it came to refer more specifically to men in court positions who were sent out by the king to represent him in different roles in the localities while remaining outside the ranks of the entrenched local aristocracy. After 875, claimed Keller, the bearers of the title were in fact these very entrenched aristocrats, men without whom kings could not do, and who had an unavoidably high share in royal government, a role institutionalised by the carrying of the name *consiliarius*.[100] Of the six *consiliarii* of Charles the Fat, three, Wibod, Berengar and Waltfred, seem to fit Keller's post-875 model most approximately. Wibod, bishop of Parma since before 860, was a major player in Italian politics under all the late Carolingian kings, acting for example as ambassador for both Louis II and the empress Engelberga.[101] The landed power of the church under his control was monumental, comprising key properties throughout northern Italy, partly thanks to the heavy patronage he attracted from the Carolingians.[102] Charles the Fat continued this patronage, referred to Wibod as his 'highest counsellor', and brought him along to attend his west Frankish coronation in 885.[103] Berengar and Waltfred also fit the Keller scheme. Their position as well-established magnates in the eastern half of Lombardy meant that they too had a pre-existing practical authority which was recognised and institutionalised by Charles the Fat, manifest in his conferment on them of titles like *consiliarius* and *marchio*. The circumstances of men like these meant that they had to be considered in the running of the Italian kingdom; but Charles the Fat, like every other king of the early Middle Ages (and not just those after 875), ruled with and through such people, not in spite of them.

The same was not true, however, for the other three *consiliarii*. Liutward was not from a family with deep roots in Italy. Rather, as we have seen, he was an Aleman who had been parachuted into the see of Vercelli by the new king in 880. His position was achieved thanks to a longstanding personal association with Charles the Fat. He was not a major beneficiary of royal largesse. The gift of a decent array of estates to the church of

---

[100] H. Keller, 'Zur Struktur der Königsherrshaft im karolingischen und nachkarolingischen Italien. Der "consiliarius regis" in den italienischen Königsdiplomen des 9. und 10. Jahrhunderts', *QFIAB* 47 (1967), 123–223. Kasten, *Königssöhne und Königsherrschaft*, pp. 410–15 is a recent supporter of Keller's arguments.

[101] *AB* s.a. 870, p. 175; 872, p. 188.

[102] See Keller, 'Zur Struktur der Königsherrshaft', p. 221; U. Benassi (ed.) *Codice diplomatico Parmense* (vol. 1, Parma, 1910), nos. 25 and 25bis. For his influence see P. Delogu, 'Vescovi, conti e sovrani'.

[103] DD CIII 15, 32, 33, 36, 115, 126, 171. D 47 for Wibod as 'highest counsellor', when he intervened for the church of Reggio along with Liutward. D 126, issued at Etrepy in June 885, for Wibod in west Francia.

183

Kingship and Politics in the Late Ninth Century

Vercelli in March 882 looks like an attempt to create a more solid base for the bishopric out of imperial properties in the area.[104] Even so, it was nothing compared to the far-reaching properties under the control of men such as Wibod and Berengar. The archchancellor's lack of deep roots in Lombardy is well illustrated by his conflict with Berengar in 886–7, when Liutward was accused of forcibly removing the *marchio*'s niece from a nunnery in Brescia in order to marry her off to a member of his family, and suffered a retaliatory raid on Vercelli for his trouble.[105] This looks like a clear case of the parvenu seeking to establish his kin by engineering a marriage into a local family with a more prestigious pedigree which, in this case, contained a strain of imperial blood.[106] Berengar was held to be the aggressor by the emperor, lending some weight to Karl Schmid's suggestion that Charles and Engelberga, the convent's proprietor, may actually have consented to Liutward's actions.[107] Ultimately, however, the *marchio*'s opposition to the union seems to have prevailed, backed by his undeniably significant military following. To advance his relatives step by step was thus a painstaking business for the archchancellor, who had to rely on *Königsnähe* rather than any great political presence in Italy.[108] He is always encountered in the sources at the emperor's side or on imperial business. He travelled with the court, and did not depend on his position as bishop of Vercelli to further his career in any independent way.[109] He certainly did not somehow rule Italy as regent when the king was north of the Alps. This almost constant attendance at the side of the emperor must help explain why Liutward is found intervening in charters so much more often than the likes of Berengar and Wibod, who were more liable to stay in their own centres of power: the archchancellor was more often at court. To some extent, in other words, his great prominence in clauses of intercession has been misread by historians; it cannot be translated directly into a proportionately superior role in the actual governance of the realm.[110]

---

[104] D CIII 54. D CIII 323 mentions further gifts by Charles to the church, but may well be suspect; see Kehr's preface to D 54.

[105] *AF(M)* s.a. 887, pp. 105–6; *AF(B)* s.a. 886, p. 114; 887, p. 115.

[106] See Schmid, 'Liutbert von Mainz', pp. 45–8 for discussion of the feud. Berengar was a descendant of Louis the Pious. It is worth noting that, as in 883, he was seemingly the main military power in northern Italy.

[107] *AF(B)* s.a. 887, p.115; Schmid, 'Liutbert von Mainz', p. 47.

[108] Other members of his family did find some success in this regard; his brother Chadolt became bishop of Novara in August 882 but he, as another of the Reichenau monks who had been in Charles's entourage before 876, had access to *Königsnähe* independent of Liutward. For Chadolt's dates see Hlawitschka, 'Die Diptychen von Novara'. Another Liutward, probably a relative of the pair, was subsequently bishop of Como; Keller, 'Zur Struktur der Königsherrshaft', p. 215.

[109] Although episcopal rank may have been considered a prerequisite for the post of archchaplain.

[110] See Bougard, 'La cour et le gouvernement', pp. 257–9 for similar criticisms of the Keller model.

The end of the empire II: response and failure

Liutward's position in Italy, therefore, conforms better to Keller's model of the role of the *consiliarius* during the reign of Louis II than to that which he proposes for the period after 875. He was a man without top-rank landed credentials but with great influence based primarily on a prestigious court job and privileged access to the king, and used as a sort of general royal representative sent into the localities to undertake a variety of tasks. Hence we encounter him as a conspicuous mediator of royal patronage in western Lombardy, as an agent of the attempt to intervene in Spoleto, and also as an occasional ambassador of Charles at the papal curia.[111] We might say that while a man like Wibod became a *consiliarius* because he was bishop of Parma, Liutward became bishop of Vercelli because he was a *consiliarius*. Similar conclusions apply to the other two Alemans entitled *consiliarii* during the reign, whose power likewise relied on court positions; Berthold as count of the palace and Otulf as royal chaplain.[112] Men like these tend to loom large in our sources as a result, and must be seen, especially in the case of Liutward, as particularly enjoying the confidence of the king. However, we should not let their prominence obscure the authority undeniably wielded by the bishops and *marchiones* who resided away from court. The two types of aristocrat identified by Keller thus coexisted in post-875 Italy, just as they always had done in Carolingian politics: it is tidy but overly schematic to postulate a simple 'rise' of the territorial aristocracy to eclipse those whose positions relied more on royal favour. Nevertheless, while *Königsnähe* could be a spectacular maker of men, as the archchancellor was eventually to find out it could also be dangerously ephemeral.

THE EMPRESS AND THE ARCHCHANCELLOR

The archchancellor's career was, then, closely linked to his personal association with the emperor and his position at court. We now need to query where Richgard entered into this equation. Two sets of sources imply close links between Liutward and the empress.[113] Firstly, the letters of John VIII reveal that the pope, when particularly keen to exert influence over the emperor, would write exhortatory missives to both empress and archchancellor: significantly, Richgard only appears in John VIII's letters in association with Liutward.[114] Secondly, the pair intervened together

---

[111] For the latter, *Registrum*, ed. Caspar, no. 263; *AB* s.a. 882, p. 249; *AF(M)* s.a. 885, pp. 103–4.
[112] Fleckenstein, *Die Hofkapelle der deutschen Könige*, p. 194; Keller, 'Zur Struktur der Königsherrshaft', p. 217.
[113] Bührer-Thierry, 'Les évêques de Bavière', p. 36 states the pair were related, but it is not clear on what evidence.
[114] *Registrum*, ed. Caspar, nos. 291, 309.

three times in Charles's charters.[115] The importance of this is highlighted by the facts that they are the only major duo which appears more than once in the diplomas, and that the empress only interceded for third parties without Liutward on two occasions.[116] When she appeared in these documents, more often than not she was associated with the archchancellor. The geographical and institutional variety in these three grants, for the priest Ruodbert in Alemannia, the canons of St-John in Monza, and the episcopal church of Liège, further highlights the unusual importance of the role that the two played together in mediating access to the royal throne while they resided at court. Moreover, in Alemannia, we have already met Richgard and Liutward at the hub of a set of political arrangements established by Charles to deal with places of special importance in his home *regnum*.[117]

Richgard also possessed an independent power base as *rectrix* (proprietor) of a series of wealthy and prestigious nunneries and monasteries: namely the convents Säckingen, SS Felix and Regula in Zurich, S Marino in Pavia and her own foundation of Andlau in Alsace, as well as the male monastery of Zurzach.[118] She also seems to have spent an unknown length of time as abbess of St-Stephen in Strasbourg, probably before marrying Charles.[119] While Carolingian women often controlled such religious institutions, Richgard's holdings are distinguished by their number and scale.

Enough evidence survives to uncover some of her strategies for managing these houses.[120] Many of the properties they controlled formed part of the heritage of Richgard's natal family, traditionally one of the most dominant in Alsace, which had fallen on hard times during a period of political turbulence in the late 860s. As well as serving her family interests, the empress, in tandem with her husband, used the resources of her convents to facilitate royal patronage and alliance-building in the area. In the most spectacular example of these political moves, which represent a clear

---

[115] DD CIII 38, 46 and 104.
[116] DD CIII 109 (for the *Marienkapelle* at Aachen, with Liutbert of Mainz as co-petitioner) and 154 (for the royal *fidelis* Dodo and the church of Langres). DD 116 and 137 both mention as interveners Rudolf and his son Pippin, but they seem to be counted as a single 'unit', Pippin presumably being a minor.
[117] See above, pp. 87, 90.
[118] See Map 8. DD CIII 7 (February 878, Säckingen and Zurich), 42 (October 881, Pavia), 96 (February 884, Andlau), 43 (October 881, Zurzach) are the key charters. On the status of Zurzach see Geuenich, 'Zurzach- ein frühmittelalterliche Doppelkloster?'
[119] D. Geuenich, '*Richkart, ancilla dei de caenobio Sancti Stephani*. Zeugnisse zur Geschichte des straßburger Frauenklosters St. Stephan in der Karolingerzeit', in Schnith and Pauler (eds.), *Festschrift für Eduard Hlawitschka*, pp. 97–109.
[120] For full discussion of Richgard's nunneries and their significance, see MacLean, 'Queenship, Nunneries and Royal Widowhood'. For the following see Map 8.

The end of the empire II: response and failure

Map 8. Richgard's monastic empire

example of how the interests of a king could be made to coincide with those of his wife, we find her again closely associated with the archchancellor Liutward. In January 881, while en route to receive his imperial coronation, Charles engineered a swap of lands between Liutward and the episcopal church of Chur in Rhaetia. Liutward handed over a selection of churches in Vorarlberg and south Tirol, which he held as life benefices from the king, and received in return an enormous grant of 150 manses in Alsace, in the estates of Sélestat (Schlettstadt), Kinzheim, Breitenheim and Winzenheim.[121] Thomas Zotz has convincingly placed this document into the context of royal palace policy: Sélestat was Charles's only *palatium* in Alsace, the prime focus of his authority there, and Zotz shows

---

[121] D CIII 30; cf. D *Bünd* 75.

Kingship and Politics in the Late Ninth Century

that his reign is the most likely time for the construction of an Aachen-style rotunda, 22 metres in diameter, the foundations of which were discovered at the turn of the last century under the church of St George. This gift of land to Liutward can thus be seen as a measure taken by the king to reclaim the royal centre and church of Sélestat and allow the creation of a palace reminiscent of Aachen.[122] The very deliberate nature of this project is highlighted by the unusual nature of the charter concerned: rather than taking the form of a royal confirmation of a swap already agreed, the king, probably taking advantage of an episcopal vacancy, simply stated that he wished the swap to take place.[123] In a fashion similar to that which we saw with regard to the royal estate of Neudingen, Charles included Liutward in the close control of specific areas which were of special importance to him.

But Richgard must also have played a part here, as she had done in Neudingen. Sélestat and Kinzheim at least were estates with which she had intimate connections through both family and institutional relationships. They had long been associated with her family's power, and she retained a personal stake in them due to her control of the nunneries in Zurich and Andlau, to which they belonged. By strengthening his links with northern Alsace, and especially the area around Sélestat, through the agency of both his wife and his chief counsellor, Charles sought to turn an aristocratic landscape into a royal one. The gift to Liutward consolidated him and Richgard together as a force to be reckoned with in the region; in a sense it added more pieces to the jigsaw of royal presence in northern Alsace and Carolingianised its topography. The grant was made as the royal couple journeyed to Italy to receive the imperial dignity, an occasion on which Andlau's position would be sealed by being placed in the protection of St Peter.[124] The timing thus implies a connection between these events and the gift of lands to Liutward. The grant ensured king, queen and archchancellor would stand together at the centre of a web of property and power relations which articulated itself in the construction of the imperial palace at Sélestat.

The palace was of special importance in 881 because Aachen itself was in the kingdom of Louis the Younger (as was Lorsch, another key site of Carolingian legitimacy), and Alsace was on the frontier of Charles's kingdom. However, the region's importance did not diminish once these

---

[122] T. Zotz, 'Carolingian Tradition and Ottonian-Salian Innovation: Comparative Observations on Palatine Policy in the Empire', in Duggan (ed.), *Kings and Kingship* pp. 69–100, at pp. 81–4.

[123] D CIII 30 is, unfortunately, a late cartulary copy. However, the confirmation charter D AC 9 refers to the original document in exactly these terms, stressing the agency of Charles in engineering the swap.

[124] D CIII 96 gives some details.

The end of the empire II: response and failure

circumstances changed. Charles never visited Aachen: Sélestat, whose architecture it echoed, remained the main physical focus of his power in the middle kingdom throughout his reign, sustaining his entourage there while he was present, and standing as a monument to his authority when he was not. In the bigger picture, we may interpret this as part of an attempt to make manifest the late ninth-century shift of imperial gravity to the east Frankish kingdom.[125] The new emperor needed a new Aachen. The palace and its hinterland, founded on properties controlled by the king through his wife and archchancellor, articulated Charles's rule in Alsace and symbolised the imperial prestige which he had inherited and remodelled.[126]

These arrangements were not destroyed by the events of summer 887, when both empress and archchancellor left court. For her part, Richgard retained control of Andlau, the centre of her network of influence in Alsace. In the case of Liutward, we can infer from an imperial charter of 887 issued for his nephew that the disgraced archchancellor had lost lands in the wake of his deposition: the nephew had lost out as well and was now being compensated.[127] Probably included among the bishop's losses were the Alsatian possessions which he had swapped with the church of Chur in 881. These may have reverted to the direct control of the emperor himself: this measure would have been fairly simple if the see were still vacant at this time.[128] The properties were certainly part of the royal fisc when Otto the Great decided to return them to Chur in 952.[129]

The blunt nature of the sources can be a hindrance to the study of the politics of late Carolingian east Francia, and forces us to infer scraps of information from the course of events. From such fragments it emerges that both Richgard and Liutward were extremely important in the patronage

---

[125] See above, pp. 120 and 157–8 and below, pp. 222–7. There is an obvious analogy with Charles the Bald, who built a 'new Aachen' in his kingdom at Compiègne.

[126] On palaces as mediators of royal authority, see Airlie, 'Palace of Memory'; on the political importance of Alsace, see T. Zotz, 'Das Elsaß- ein Teil des Zwischenreiches?' in H.-W. Herrmann and R. Schneider (eds.), *Lotharingia. Eine europäische Kernlandschaft um das Jahr 1000* (Saarbrücken, 1995), pp. 49–70, esp. pp. 57–64. On spiritual and cultural bonds between Alemannia and Alsace in Charles's reign see D. Geuenich, 'Elsaßbeziehungen in den St. Galler Verbrüderungsbüchern', in P. Ochsenbein and E. Ziegler (eds.), *Codices Sangallenses. Festschrift für Johannes Duft zum 80. Geburtstag* (Sigmaringen, 1995), pp. 105–16.

[127] D CIII 170.

[128] As it had been in 881. Unfortunately the evidence does not allow certainty on this question, beyond the fact that there was a bishop of Chur installed by early 888: see the commentary in DD *Bünd*, p. 498.

[129] D OG 157. D 167 from 953 confirms the restoration and adds to the list another set of properties in the Strasbourg and Sélestat areas which were therefore perhaps also included in the original transfer of Chur lands to Liutward. D AC 9 from 888 confirms the Rhaetian lands of Chur but is tellingly silent on the Alsace properties, which had clearly not reverted to the bishopric in the meantime.

politics of Charles the Fat, and that frequently they acted together. The emperor, the empress and the archchancellor can be said to have sat together at the centre of a kind of network of personal politics reaching out in various directions to carry out projects closely related to the court and the maintenance of royal power. This conclusion provides us with a context for accepting the connection made by Regino between Liutward's expulsion from court and the royal divorce in summer 887, even after we have ruled out adultery. We have seen that the archchancellor's influence was built more or less exclusively on his position at court and his personal relationship with the imperial couple. He was no vice-regent of Italy, but rather a man without any deep roots who was sent out to represent Charles in various different contexts. While he enjoyed the ruler's favour, his position was secure; as soon as he lost it, he had nothing to fall back on. It is evidently untrue to say, as some have, that Charles could not do without him. Rather, it was Liutward who could not do without Charles. The emperor had agency in these events, they were not simply foisted upon him.

So, although the details escape us, the evidence permits us to conclude that somehow Liutward's influence at court, which was indeed privileged, had by 887 become closely linked to the position of the empress. When Charles hatched a plan to divorce his wife and remarry in the hope of producing a legitimate heir, a plan to which Richgard seems to have acquiesced, Liutward saw his position threatened and opposed him. Charles, who had little time for such politicking when issues of much greater import, like the continuation of the Carolingian line, were at stake, proceeded to relieve him of his duties and hand them over to the obvious replacement, Liutbert of Mainz. The Mainz annalist, clearly not one to be gracious in victory, attempted to blacken Liutward's name further by claiming that he fled to Arnulf and helped plot Charles's downfall.[130] This seems, on the whole, to be more invective than fact.[131] The fallen archchancellor does not figure prominently in Arnulf's reign as a man of distinction, and presumably retired to Vercelli: certainly, he was later killed in Lombardy during a Magyar attack.[132] There is therefore no justification for seeing the removal of Liutward as the spur for the coup. He did not engineer it, nor was he so important that his fall rendered the emperor vulnerable. We must look elsewhere to explain where the impetus came from. Charles, and not his fallen archchancellor, was the key figure in the events of 887.

---

[130] *AF(M)* s.a. 887, p. 106. [131] Bührer-Thierry, 'Le conseiller du roi', p. 121.
[132] Regino, *Chronicon*, s.a. 901, p. 148; cf. Sierck, *Festtag und Politik*, pp. 240–1. He was, however, present at the Council of Mainz in 888.

The end of the empire II: response and failure

The contrasting fates of the empress and the archchancellor are instructive. An indication of how Charles sought to remove all trace of his wife from court is given by the fact that she was henceforth purged from the prayer provisions of imperial charters, a measure designed to reinforce the annulling of the marriage.[133] Nevertheless, her retreat was seen, on the evidence of the *Life of Verena*, as honourable and virtuous. Liutward, on the other hand, was subjected to a much more virulent form of *damnatio memoriae*. While Richgard was buried (c. 900) in her own church at Andlau, and was recognised as a saint by Pope Leo IX in 1049, Liutward's obituary was not even entered into the memorial book of Reichenau, the monastery where he had been brought up and where other members of his family were commemorated along with the Carolingians and their deceased *fideles*. His long career in service to Charles the Fat ended abruptly and bitterly, and stands as eloquent testimony to the precarious position of those aristocrats whose power depended too much on the changeable favour of Carolingian kings.

THE DEPOSITION OF CHARLES THE FAT, NOVEMBER 887

Historians have long differed over the nature of the deposition of Charles the Fat: was it an impromptu coup inspired by the self-interest of Arnulf, or the work of a wide-reaching magnate conspiracy dissatisfied with Carolingian rule?[134] Those who take the former line invoke the Bavarian continuator who, writing retrospectively in Arnulf's power base and hence anxious to justify the new king's actions, implied general approval for the usurpation. Conversely, the Mainz annalist, now back on Charles's side after the restoration of his patron Archbishop Liutbert to court, presented Arnulf as a rebel, seizing power by (implicitly illegitimate) force alone.[135] The historiographical problem was that proponents of both points of view, by leaning on alternative continuations of the *Annals of Fulda*, were able to reach equally well-documented conclusions without attempting to resolve the sources' mutual incompatibility. Neither side took much notice of the thoughts of Regino of Prüm who, reflecting several years later on the course of events, was arguably more measured and less polemical on this point. He could still hardly believe how quickly power had slithered from the hands of Charles the Fat: 'It was a matter worthy of note, and in the varying evaluation of the outcomes of

---

[133] D CIII 168 is especially interesting since the charter from which it was almost totally copied *did* include the king's *coniunx* in the prayer clause; see Ewig, 'Der Gebetsdienst der Kirchen', p. 75.
[134] See above, pp. 6–7. [135] Bowlus, 'Arnulf of Carinthia's *Ostpolitik*', p. 557.

human affairs astonishing.'[136] For Regino there was a moral to the story: it served as a demonstration of how God-given *fortuna* could be all too easily lost thanks to the tragic intervention of human frailty. However, his assessment of the wide-reaching outcome of the strife of 887–8 was essentially a political one. Events had brought it about: during an assembly at Tribur in November 887 the magnates had decided that Charles was too ill to rule and summoned Arnulf, and, even more importantly for Regino, Charles had then died. In this sense, the argument of the last two chapters has been essentially sympathetic to that of Regino: by ignoring modern preoccupations about the 'constitutional' significance of the rebellion in the grand narrative of medieval German history, we can understand it instead as the outcome of a very specific set of political circumstances and decisions, and see quite clearly that things could indeed have been different.

The key circumstance was the unravelling of the Carolingian family settlement of 880 due to the unpredictable deaths of the heirless Louis the Younger, Louis III and, finally, Carloman II. The consequent shortage of access to the dynasty and the increasing remoteness of the court from the traditional heartlands of the empire made a successful resolution of Charles the Fat's succession plans even more vital then they might otherwise have been. Political uncertainty, as so often, was the prelude to political crisis. This time, the future of the Carolingian royal monopoly hung on Charles's success. The emperor's crucial mistake was his determined obstruction of Arnulf's hopes of sharing in the succession after his acts of rebellion during the Wilhelminer War: the emperor's obduracy and unwillingness to compromise led ultimately to his deposition. Of course, Arnulf was still not a legitimate Carolingian but, had he taken over as an approved imperial heir rather than as a usurper, would the 'kinglets' have had the same justification and confidence in ascending their own thrones? At a stage prior to this, if Hadrian III had not died in 885 and Bernard had been publicly designated as an heir, would Arnulf have had the same justification in revolting? What if the emperor had turned to the minor Charles the Simple? We cannot answer any of these questions, but simply posing them highlights the fact that the outcome was not inevitable. Chance and the course of events played their part in bringing about the end of the Carolingian empire.

It was the divorce and remarriage plan, as the first of Charles's schemes to show any signs of success, which must have finally convinced Arnulf that an open rebellion was his best realistic chance of acquiring a throne.

---

[136] Regino, *Chronicon*, s.a. 887, p. 128.

The end of the empire II: response and failure

His stock had risen in the years after 885 as the other contenders fell by the wayside, but if the emperor could watch his plan to designate Bernard fail twice and still leave his nephew out in the cold, his chances were definitely receding. With Charles showing signs of serious illness, the possibility of permanent exclusion must have seemed very real to Arnulf. Motive coincided with opportunity. Two years of peace with Zwentibald of Moravia had allowed Arnulf to recover his strength after the setbacks of the Wilhelminer War. The Moravians, moreover, were always fickle friends of Carolingian rulers, and alliances on and across the eastern frontier characteristically shifted with great speed. In the same way that a coincidence of interests had made Zwentibald a natural ally of Charles against Arnulf in 884, by late 887 the latter's proximity may have given the ambitious *dux* cause to reassess his priorities: it is significant that a large force of Slavs, presumably including Moravians, figured prominently in the rising against the emperor.[137]

We can surmise that Arnulf's other supporters in his coup likewise came from the south-eastern corner of the empire. Evidence for this comes from the high number of charters, including those to an unprecedented number of individual laymen, which he made in that region during the earliest phase of his reign.[138] Several of these make an explicit connection between Arnulf's accession and the fact that the new king felt himself in such men's debt. For example, a grant to the warrior [*miles*] Engilger was issued 'in recognition of the repeated service done by him for us before we received the name of king'.[139] Arnulf, left by and large to his own devices in the south-east after Christmas 885, had had time to cement his relationship with men like these. They, moreover, stood to suffer the same political exclusion as he did if Bavaria and its marches remained a neglected periphery under the rule of another Alemannic king such as Bernard.[140] The scarcity of *Königsnähe* was an inevitable and temporarily

---

[137] *AF(M)* s.a. 887, p. 106; Bowlus, 'Arnulf of Carinthia's *Ostpolitik*', p. 564.

[138] For example: DD AC 5, 8, 15–17, 20–2, 32, 42–4. See K. Reindel, 'Herzog Arnulf und das Regnum Bavariae', *Zeitschrift für bayerische Landesgeschichte* 17 (1953/4), 187–252, at 205; Bowlus, *Franks, Moravians and Magyars*, pp. 230–2; Schieffer, 'Karl III. und Arnolf', p. 140 (and *passim* on the longer-term process of installation of Arnulf's old allies, like the relatives of William and Engelschalk, into key *honores*). D. Von Gladiß, 'Die Schenkungen der deutschen Könige zu privatem Eigen (800–1137)', *DA* 1 (1937), 80–137, at 84 provides comparative statistics, as does Eibl, 'Zur Stellung Bayerns', pp. 82–99. Arnulf was also supported by Louis the Younger's daughter Hildegard.

[139] D AC 17.

[140] The same consideration, the desire for accessible kingship, also motivated some Alemans to support Bernard in a counter-revolt against Arnulf in 890–1. Eibl, 'Zur Stellung Bayerns', esp. p. 109 shows that Arnulf eventually restored the traditional Franconian-Bavarian axis of the kingdom.

193

Kingship and Politics in the Late Ninth Century

viable aspect of Charles's reign, but the perpetuation of this situation only exacerbated these frustrations. These tensions and circumstances were not unique to the position of Arnulf in 885–7: they are the hallmarks of the classic generational (and geographical) rivalries which had been an endemic feature of Frankish politics since at least the sixth century. Arnulf rebelled for substantially the same reasons as had many excluded junior Carolingians before him, and he found an aristocratic constituency in much the same way as them. He was not, nor did he consider himself to be, the representative of a particular class or the standard bearer of a new age in European history.

As for the actual course of events, our sources are difficult to resolve.[141] Four narratives provide specific dates and places. The Mainz and Hildesheim annalists, along with Regino, place the arrival of Arnulf and the defection of the nobles at a general assembly convened at Tribur around the time of the feast of St Martin (11 November).[142] The Bavarian annalist, on the other hand, states that the deed was done at Frankfurt.[143] Charles's last known imperial charter, although badly corrupted by later forgers, seems to have been issued at Frankfurt on 17 November, while Arnulf issued his first royal diploma ten days later in the same place.[144] Charles subsequently retired to Alemannia, either on a pension generously provided by Arnulf, or to rally his supporters to mount resistance.[145] Either way, the emperor was not long for this world, expiring of unknown natural causes on 13 January 888.[146]

Much scholarly effort has been expended on trying to coax precision from these sources in order to build a clear narrative of events between the key dates of 11 and 27 November. Most attempts, from Keller's meticulous and influential 1966 article 'Zum Sturz Karls III.' onwards, have focused on resolving the apparent doubts in contemporary minds about where, when and how Charles was actually deposed: was it Tribur or Frankfurt, and what transpired there?[147] However, the very fact that equally plausible but mutually contradictory answers to these questions have been suggested by historians leads one to suspect that, as Timothy

---

[141] See BM 1765 for full references to the contemporary and later sources.

[142] *AF(M)* s.a. 887, p. 106; *AH* s.a. 887, p. 19; Regino, *Chronicon*, s.a. 887, pp. 127–8.

[143] *AF(B)* s.a. 887, p. 115.   [144] D CIII 172; D AC 1.

[145] With Arnulf's permission: Regino, *Chronicon*, s.a. 887, p. 128; *AF(B)* s.a. 887, p. 115 (after failing to start a resistance war). *AF(M)* s.a. 887, p. 106 simply says that Charles 'returned to Alemannia'.

[146] *AF(B)* s.a. 887, p. 116 gives the date. Cf. BM 1765d. *AV* s.a. 887, p. 64 mentions a rumour that his own men strangled him.

[147] Keller, 'Zum Sturz Karls III.', pp. 347–73. For criticisms of Keller's arguments, see Hlawitschka, *Lotharingien und das Reich*, pp. 38–48; Bund, *Thronsturz und Herrscherabsetzung*, pp. 477–89; Reuter, *Germany in the Early Middle Ages*, pp. 119–20. P. Kehr, 'Aus den letzten Tagen Karls III.', *DA* 1 (1937), 138–46 is the most significant pre-Keller article.

The end of the empire II: response and failure

Reuter has pointed out, the available sources cannot be made to render definitive answers.[148] Accordingly, only some general points will be made here.

The partisan character of the Mainz and Bavarian annalists has already been stressed. Regino, on the other hand, took a more equivocal line. Although he was writing for members of the court of Arnulf's son Louis the Child, he was also not without sympathy for Charles the Fat. Moreover, he regarded the coup and consequent shattering of the Carolingian hegemony as a tragedy. This willingness to see both sides of the situation lends Regino's testimony an extra credibility. Two things are clear from his version: firstly that the deposition of Charles and the elevation of Arnulf took place at a single assembly, and secondly that the defection of the leading men was spurred by their observation of the gravity of the emperor's illness.[149] Other sources give Regino implicit support. Tellingly, even the Bavarian annals, despite their author's elaboration of a long-term conspiracy theory, back up the single assembly point: 'after the emperor Charles came to Frankfurt, these men [the nobles] invited Arnulf, the son of King Karlmann, to come and chose him for their lord, and without delay decided that he should be made king'.[150] As Regino made out, Arnulf and his retinue must already have been present at the assembly. The abbot of Prüm's emphasis on Charles's illness at this point is also believable: after all, he was dead of natural causes, at the age of only 48 or 49, within two months.[151]

All this backs up Regino's implication of a somewhat on-the-spot decision made by the nobles to invite Arnulf to take over the throne, and jars with the long-term conspiracy depicted by the Bavarian annalist. The general agenda of the latter is further discredited by the charter evidence for Arnulf's supporters discussed earlier: it was not Thuringian, Saxon or even Franconian nobles whose help he rewarded after his succession, but rather men from the south-east and the marches. In the light of this, the Mainz continuator's report of the rising as a sudden coup pushed through by surprise and a display of force begins to look more plausible. A likely reconstruction, taking into account all these elements of the narrative sources, begins with Charles summoning an assembly for magnates from throughout the east Frankish kingdom, perhaps to make a further announcement on the succession issue. Arnulf, ready to press his claims by force since hearing of the emperor's divorce in the summer, turned up unexpectedly with a large armed retinue. Seeing Charles's poor state

---

[148] Reuter, *Annals of Fulda*, p. 103, n. 8.   [149] Regino, *Chronicon*, s.a. 887, p. 127.

[150] *AF(B)* s.a. 887, p. 115.

[151] *AV* s.a. 887, p. 64 supports Regino's interpretation of the single assembly and the emperor's illness.

Kingship and Politics in the Late Ninth Century

of health and considering the uncertain status of the succession, the assembled magnates were mentally primed to be sympathetic to the claims of his nephew, especially given his military backing. An analogy with the Field of Lies in 833 suggests itself, as another occasion on which rival Carolingians had stood face to face with each other while the short-term calculations of aristocratic opinion decided the outcome. Like Louis the Pious's on that occasion, Charles's support melted away almost to nothing, including his closest advisers: 'the Alemans, on whom the king chiefly relied for the conduct of the affairs of his kingdom, were struck with fear, and all straight away defected from him'.[152]

Both continuations of the *Annals of Fulda* tell us that Charles sent Arnulf an embassy: the Bavarian author said it carried gifts symbolic of submission, while the Mainz author stated it bore the fragment of the True Cross on which Arnulf had earlier sworn loyalty to Charles, to persuade him to remember his faith.[153] Either way, there is nothing in any source to suggest a formal deposition ceremony or tonsuring.[154] Even when such a procedure had been attempted, against Louis the Pious in 833, it proved ultimately unsuccessful: Carolingian politics were not governed by such rigid norms and laws, and moments of tension were often resolved with a fair degree of improvisation. As long as Charles lived there was always a chance that the pendulum could swing back in his favour, as it had in Louis's in 834. This ambiguity is highlighted by the fact that Regino refers to Arnulf as *rex* after the coup, yet continues to call Charles *imperator* until his death.[155] The sources disagree as to whether Charles retired to Alemannia on Arnulf's authority or on his own, to raise support. The fact that he went to Neudingen, a place which, as we have seen, had been of particular importance to him since at least 870, may suggest the latter is more likely.[156] However, we may speculate that Charles seemed so ill to Arnulf that the latter was confident his days were numbered, removing

---

[152] *AF(B)* s.a. 887, p. 115. I take this to be a reference to Charles's palace staff, most of whom were Alemans and were taken over en masse by Arnulf; see Fleckenstein, *Die Hofkapelle der deutschen Könige*, pp. 198–202.

[153] *AF(M)* s.a. 887, p. 106; *AF(B)* s.a. 887, p. 115. Regino, *Chronicon*, s.a. 887, p. 128 mentions gifts and the commendation of Bernard to Arnulf. The unspecifed gifts may have included the so-called Ellwangen Casket: see P. E. Schramm, 'Neuentdeckte Bildnisse Karls des Kahlen, seiner Gemahlin und seines Sohnes (876/7). Ein Beleg für die den byzantinern nachgeahmte Krone', in P. E. Schramm, *Kaiser, Könige und Päpste. Gesammelte Aufsätze zur Geschichte des Mittelalters* (vol. 2, Stuttgart, 1969), pp. 110–18, at pp. 114–15 with n. 19a.

[154] Reuter, *Germany in the Early Middle Ages*, p. 120. For the case that there was a formal deposition see E. Jammers, 'Die sog. Ludwigspsalter als geschichtliches Dokument', *ZGO* 103 (1955), 259–71; effectively refuted by Bund, *Thronsturz und Herrscherabsetzung*, pp. 547–9.

[155] Regino, *Chronicon*, s.a. 887, 888, pp. 128–9. *AF(M)* s.a. 887, p. 106 does the same, although it never refers to Arnulf directly as *rex*.

[156] See p. 87. Regino, *Chronicon*, s.a. 887, p. 128 caricatures the emperor's poverty for literary effect, the feast-giver turned into a man who cannot even feed himself.

196

The end of the empire II: response and failure

the need for him to bloody his hands or to engage in proceedings against his sick uncle which might in time come to be seen as dishonourable. The new king also had Bernard commended to him, presumably in order to neutralise his claims.[157] The luckless Bernard's fate was sealed in 891 when he was killed leading a rebellion against Arnulf.[158]

As noted above, any attempt to reconstruct the course of events must remain tentative. The hypothesis just presented, that the deposition came about due to a confluence of Arnulf's motives (resentment at exclusion from royal power) and opportunity (a stand-off with the emperor won by a display of force, and with the nobility swayed by continuing doubts over the succession and Charles's illness), does however make sense as an outcome of the situation created by the course of royal politics since 885. The character of this situation shows how the widely accepted 'strong aristocracy' model is misconceived. The aristocracy had always played a prominent role in determining the resolution of succession struggles and the election of new kings: this was not a novelty in 887. They were only one element in the course of events bringing about the fateful dénouement, along with the respective agendas and priorities of Charles and Arnulf. Arnulf's succession was not necessary or inevitable. The cliché that history is written by the victors is rarely so obviously true as when applied to Carolingian historiography, but this is often overlooked by modern commentators. The 'rise of the aristocracy' model is justified with reference to the Bavarian annalist's account of 887, but this text was written with a propagandistic purpose in mind. It is dangerous to build on it a grand theory of a great historical process inexorably sweeping individuals and events out of their path on the way to 'feudalism', France and Germany. Similarly, explanations based on characterisations of Charles as 'weak' and Arnulf as 'strong', although more rooted in contemporary politics, still pay too little attention to the context of events and the changing positions of the protagonists. The problem is not one of institutional relationships or of necessarily antagonistic individuals holding static positions. Rather, the coup of 887 must be understood in the light of the fluctuating relationships between particular individuals over a relatively short space of time.

Nevertheless, the revolt of 887 was indeed a significant event, due to the fact that no adult male legitimate Carolingians remained: the dynasty's monopoly on royal power which had endured since 751 was shattered. It is this, rather than a shift in the nature of the 'German constitution'

---

[157] Regino, *Chronicon*, s.a. 887, p. 128. Similarly, Hugh of Lotharingia had been commended to Louis the German in 867, and Arnulf to Louis the Younger in 879: *AB* s.a. 867, p. 137; *AF* s.a. 879, p. 93.

[158] *AA* s.a. 890; 891; p. 182.

Kingship and Politics in the Late Ninth Century

for which the deposition of Charles the Fat is truly notable.[159] With royal legitimacy now up for grabs and power vacuums appearing all over the empire, the way was clear for men from outside the legitimate male Carolingian line to stake their claims to kingship. The struggle between Charles and Arnulf had not, however, been fought over these issues. Although the aftermath of Arnulf's coup saw the development of important changes in the shape of Frankish politics, the motivations and actions of its protagonists were not revolutionary, but entirely traditional.

[159] Airlie, '*Semper fideles?*'

Chapter 7

HISTORY, POLITICS AND THE END OF THE EMPIRE IN NOTKER'S *DEEDS OF CHARLEMAGNE*

The events of the mid to late 880s were, as we have seen, crucial for understanding the nature of the crisis of Charles the Fat's reign in particular and of Carolingian political hegemony more generally. In order to find some further reflection of how contemporaries, and in particular members of the imperial court, understood these events, we have at our disposal a text which stands among the major historical works of the whole period, namely the *Deeds of Charlemagne* (*Gesta Karoli* – the title is not contemporary) by Notker the Stammerer, a monk of St-Gall. Earlier generations of historians looked unfavourably upon Notker's anecdotal, humorous, moralising and, by positivist standards, historically inaccurate approach, dismissing it as a laughably gauche imitation of the more stately Carolingian biographies penned by Einhard, Thegan and the Astronomer. Louis Halphen summed up this evaluation when he colourfully pronounced that Notker's *Deeds* was as useful a source for the reign of Charlemagne as was Dumas's *The Three Musketeers* for that of Louis XIII.[1] Recent commentators have been more sympathetic, coming at the *Deeds* from different angles. In particular, David Ganz has shown that the very mangling of historical sources which Halphen saw as the most reprehensible aspect of the *Deeds* is in fact its central structural element. Far from being the naively recorded collection of bizarre anecdotes that it seems to be, Notker's work was actually a carefully constructed exposition of Einhard's *Life of Charlemagne*, designed to invert that work's secular values and place God back at the centre of the reader's understanding of history.[2] The evident distance between Einhard and Notker was, therefore, consciously established. Ganz's favourable assessment of the value of the *Deeds* complements the researches of other scholars, most notably Theodor Siegrist, who traced the influence of Notker's monastic training and outlook on his writings, Hans-Werner Goetz, who read the text as a mirror reflecting manifold aspects of late ninth-century society and

---

[1] L. Halphen, *Études critiques sur l'histoire de Charlemagne* (Paris, 1921), p. 142.
[2] Ganz, 'Humour as History', pp. 171–83.

199

Kingship and Politics in the Late Ninth Century

thought, Matthew Innes, who has deepened our understanding of the monk's sources, and Paul Kershaw, who has illuminated his understanding of language and religious truth.[3]

However, for all that Notker has been vindicated as a major thinker and writer of the Carolingian period, his relevance to the study of contemporary politics has been neglected. Heinz Löwe had just about the first and seemingly also last word on this subject in 1970, in a single article which looks rather isolated when placed next to the numerous works dedicated to the possible political agendas of Einhard.[4] In large part this is because, as this book has repeatedly stressed, while Notker has been rehabilitated, his age has not. Its politics are still seen as self-explanatory and stagnant in contrast to the dynamic intrigues riddling the court circle of Louis the Pious on which Einhard may well have been passing comment. Löwe was also party to these assumptions, and they govern his interpretation of the text.

Accordingly, even the basic question of why the work was written in the first place remains without a satisfactory answer, and seems, remarkably, sometimes to have been regarded as unimportant: Goetz, in the most recent book-length study of the *Deeds*, does not address the issue at all. The most common interpretation of Notker's compendium of idealised vignettes about Charlemagne is, not unreasonably, that they constitute a kind of *Fürstenspiegel*, or 'mirror for a prince', one of the genre of exhortatory texts intended to guide the behaviour of rulers (in this case Charles the Fat) which pepper the literary output of the ninth century.[5] There is much to commend this view, in as much as the *Deeds* consistently stresses some of the classic ideals of Christian kingship (justice, wisdom, prudence), as well as reinforcing the importance of primary monastic virtues such as humility and charity. On the other hand, the work's idiosyncrasies often resist classification, and the characteristics it shares with other mirrors for princes are perhaps outweighed by those it does not. Moreover, certain passages in the text, especially those which address Charles the Fat directly, invite a more specific interpretation. For example, we know from one such section that Charles himself had

---

[3] Siegrist, *Herrscherbild und Weltsicht*; Goetz, *Strukturen der spätkarolingischen Epoche*; M. Innes, 'Memory, Orality and Literacy in an Early Medieval Society', *Past and Present* 158 (1998), 3–36; Innes, 'Politics of Laughter', pp. 147–53; P. Kershaw, 'Laughter After Babel's Fall: Misunderstanding and Miscommunication in the Early Middle Ages', in Halsall (ed.), *Humour, History and Politics*, pp. 179–202, esp. pp. 191–201. This list is not intended to be comprehensive.
[4] Löwe, 'Das Karlsbuch Notkers'.
[5] Siegrist, *Herrscherbild und Weltsicht* is the most comprehensive and influential exponent of this view. On this genre see H. H. Anton, *Fürstenspiegel und Herrscherethos in der Karolingerzeit* (Bonn, 1968). Ganz, 'Humour as History', p. 173 characterises it instead as a kind of school text for Charles the Fat.

Notker's Deeds of Charlemagne

commissioned the work: the so far unanswered question is, why?[6] This chapter will seek to substantiate the assertion that there is more to be made of the contemporary political content of the *Deeds of Charlemagne* than has been hitherto allowed. This will not entail a comprehensive reinterpretation of the entire work, but rather only of parts of it, and only on certain levels, although certain significant implications for the whole text will emerge. The conclusions offered are intended largely to complement, rather than refute, those of previous studies.

THE DATE OF THE *DEEDS OF CHARLEMAGNE*

The *Deeds* as we have it constitutes two books, the first dealing with Charlemagne's care of the church, and the second relating stories about his military exploits and other aspects of secular politics. A planned third book was never written, or has not survived. The date of the work is crucial to establishing its political context. The text is usually dated to between December 883 and November 887, but neither of the termini is entirely satisfactory.[7] To begin at the end, the *terminus ad quem* of November 887 is drawn from the date of Charles's deposition. One factor adduced in support of this date is that the work as we have it is incomplete: the fall of Charles, it follows, caused Notker to abandon his commission. This hypothesis, although plausible, can be refuted. In book 2 of the *Deeds*, as part of a brief digression concerning Louis the German's virtuous character, Notker makes reference to two privileges granted by that king to the impoverished (in his view) community of St-Gall in 873.[8] As the Stammerer pointed out, these had been granted in collaboration with the young Charles the Fat himself, and were clear evidence that Louis was a 'devoted worshipper of God, tireless friend, protector and defender of the servants of Christ'. Notker's aim was to exhort Charles to issue imperial confirmations of these charters, which served to place St-Gall on an equal footing with its near neighbour Reichenau.[9] His point was all the more obvious in that he himself had been instrumental in drafting and cataloguing the original documents, and he echoed their wording in the *Deeds*.[10] Charles did ultimately satisfy Notker's wishes on

---

[6] Notker, *Gesta*, 1.18, p. 22.

[7] For instance, Löwe, 'Das Karlsbuch Notkers', pp. 123, 136; Penndorf, *Problem der "Reichseinheitsidee"*, pp. 150–1; W. Eggert, 'Zu Kaiser- und Reichsgedanken des Notker Balbulus', *Philologus* 115 (1971), 71–80, at 74. See Haefele's introduction, pp. xxiii–xliv, on the manuscript traditions.

[8] Notker, *Gesta*, 2.10, pp. 66–7; DD LG 145–6.

[9] As hinted at in the *Gesta*: St-Gall enjoyed 'none of the privileges of other monasteries'.

[10] H. F. Haefele, 'Studien zu Notkers *Gesta Karoli*', *DA* 15 (1959), 358–93, at 385–9. The reference here to arms and marriage in the same chapter may also be intended to call 873 to Charles's mind: see below, p. 219.

201

Kingship and Politics in the Late Ninth Century

30 May 887.[11] That his charter of this date had not yet been issued when the *Deeds* was written supplies us with a new *terminus ad quem* for the work.[12]

The 883 date, on the other hand, is taken from reports in the St-Gall house histories by Ratpert and Ekkehard IV, which reveal that Charles met and talked with Notker in that year during a three-day visit to the monastery.[13] That this meeting took place is not in doubt, yet there is no compelling reason to ascribe, as historians have tended to do, Charles's commissioning of the *Deeds* to this particular occasion. Charles's presence in the precincts of the monastery at this time receives special prominence in the house chronicles due to the fact that while he was there a change of abbots was effected with imperial confirmation, and ever since then there has been a tendency for historians to attach significant events to the visit.[14] We do not, however, lack for other evidence of very close relations between Charles the Fat and St-Gall. We have already seen that he was probably present there every year during the annual festival of St Otmar until 879, after which he was represented by legates.[15] It is also known that Charles was a keen borrower of books from the monastic library, as were his queen Richgard and his archchancellor Liutward, all at a time when Notker was librarian: it was the Stammerer himself who entered the details of their withdrawals into the library catalogue.[16] Liutward was also the dedicatee of another of Notker's works, the *Liber Ymnorum* of 884.[17] There is every reason, then, to suppose that Charles and other members of his entourage met and had dealings with Notker on other occasions, both before and after late 883. We need not assume that he commissioned the *Deeds* in person, let alone during his famous visit.[18] Therefore, although a reference in the text to the retirement of Abbot

---

[11] D CIII 159. The date was significant as a day of commemoration at St-Gall: Innes, 'Memory, Orality and Literacy', pp. 20–1.

[12] Löwe, 'Das Karlsbuch Notkers', p. 135 acknowledges the significance of this chapter in relation to the 887 charter, but claims that Notker pretended it had not yet been issued to maintain the fiction that he was writing in December 883: why Notker would have wanted to do this is neither obvious nor explained.

[13] Ratpert, *De casibus monasterii S. Galli liber*, PL 126, cols. 1057–80, at cols. 1077–80; Ekkehard, *Casus S. Galli*, chap. 9, p. 32, chap. 38, p. 86.

[14] Schmid, 'Brüderschaften mit den Mönchen', pp. 176–7.   [15] See above, pp. 87–8.

[16] P. Lehmann (ed.), *Mittelalterliche Bibliothekskataloge Deutschlands und der Schweiz. I. Band: Die Bistümer Konstanz und Chur* (Munich, 1918), pp. 72–3, 77, 88. J. Duft, 'Die Handschriften-Katalogisierung in der Stiftsbibliothek St. Gallen vom 9. bis zum 19. Jahrhundert', in Beat M. von Scarpaletti (ed.), *Die Handschriften der Stiftsbibliothek St. Gallen* (St. Gallen, 1983), pp. 9–129, at pp. 12–13; S. Rankin, '*Ego itaque Notker scripsi*', *Revue Bénédictine* 101 (1991), 268–98, at 292–5.

[17] Notker, *Liber Ymnorum*, p. 8; von den Steinen, *Notker der Dichter. Darstellungsband*, pp. 504–7.

[18] Only Siegrist, *Herrscherbild und Weltsicht*, p. 9 entertains the possibility of an epistolary commission.

Notker's Deeds of Charlemagne

Hartmut means we must indeed date it *after* December 883, nothing forces us to date it *in* December 883.[19]

Certain sections of the work appear, moreover, to include references to contemporary events which can help us to pare down this dating frame still further. Firstly, in his discussion of the palace of Aachen, Notker proffers his monastic seclusion as an excuse for not being able to give a physical description of the actual structures, saying that he would leave this task to Charles's 'cancellarii'.[20] This is the only time this word appears in the work to describe imperial representatives, who nonetheless figure frequently under different terms like 'fideles' and 'primores'.[21] Notker, who was himself a redactor of charters at St-Gall, probably therefore used the term 'cancellarii' in its specific sense, to denote members of the royal chancery. Only one charter was issued by Charles the Fat for the royal chapel at Aachen, in the final months of 884.[22] Charles was in Regensburg at the time, and indeed seems, as Notker implied, never to have visited Aachen. Some of his *cancellarii* must therefore either have visited the palace or talked to chapel representatives in 884 to gain the detailed knowledge with which to compose the ensuing document: it was probably this to which Notker was referring in his comment on the description of the palace buildings. Secondly, Notker's account of the raids of the Viking leader Godafrid I (d. 810) displays an interesting anomaly. Although he knew from his readings of Einhard and the *Royal Frankish Annals* that this *dux's* activities had been focused on Frisia, Saxony and the lands of the Slavic Abodrites, Notker places him instead in the Moselle region.[23] This shift strongly suggests that the Stammerer had merged Godafrid I with Godafrid III, who was active in the Moselle just before his death in mid-885.[24] Thirdly, Haefele, following a suggestion of Sabbe, has pointed out that Notker's description of the destruction of the bridge at Mainz in 813 incorporates details which suggest an elision with the fire in the same city in early 886.[25]

We know that book 2 of the *Deeds* was begun on a 30 May.[26] Since the Mainz fire, to which Notker refers at the end of book 1, occurred in March 886, it is likely that book 1 was completed in March, April or May

---

[19] Notker, *Gesta*, 2.10, pp. 66–7. The 883 conversation could, for the sake of argument, have been about church song, a subject in which both men were interested: Ekkehard, *Casus S. Galli*, chap. 46, p. 104. It may be no coincidence that the *Liber Ymnorum* was prepared and sent to court only months later. Ekkehard's wording at chap. 38, p. 86 does not sound like a literary commission: Notker 'Karolo multa querenti pridie quesita resolveret'.

[20] Notker, *Gesta*, 1.30, p. 41.   [21] See Haefele's wordlist for examples.

[22] D CIII 109.   [23] Notker, *Gesta*, 2.13, pp. 75–6. See also below, pp. 213–15.

[24] Regino, *Chronicon*, s.a. 885, p. 123. Haefele's introduction, p. xv.

[25] Notker, *Gesta*, 1.30, pp. 40–1; cf. *AF(M)* s.a. 886, p. 104; Haefele's introduction, pp. xv–xvi.

[26] Notker, *Gesta*, 2.pref., p. 48.

Kingship and Politics in the Late Ninth Century

of that same year. From all this evidence we may conclude that Notker started book 1 no earlier than late 884 (the Aachen charter allusion) and finished it around May 886, and went on to finish book 2 as far as we have it before the end of May 887 (the issuing of the imperial confirmation of St-Gall's privileges). Assuming that he did not stop working on the text for any prolonged period of time (and this was, after all, an imperial commission) it is likely that he began writing closer to the end than to the beginning of the year 885. This hypothetical dating of circa late 885–late 886/early 887 for the *Deeds* is circumstantially supported by another of Notker's works, the so-called *Notatio*.[27] As Siegrist showed, the agenda of this text, which is an annotated bibliography of texts appropriate for a bishop to know, complements one of the fundamental themes of the *Deeds*, namely the exposition, based on the Book of Daniel, of the Carolingian empire as a new world empire.[28] It is reasonable to suppose that Notker composed these works in tandem, so it is significant that the *Notatio* is dated to 885.[29]

The issue of when a text was composed is obviously very closely related to that of why it was written. With the *Deeds of Charlemagne* we are at a disadvantage because of the loss of the preface to book 1, which might well have answered the relevant questions.[30] The following discussion attempts to identify an implicit political agenda in the work which, although masked by Notker's circumspect approach, would nevertheless have been clear to a contemporary audience. This agenda, it will be argued, makes most sense as a commentary on some of the important events of late 885 and 886, and hence supports the evidence for these dates as marking the period of the *Deeds*'s composition.

NOTKER'S BISHOPS

Book 1 of the *Deeds of Charlemagne* is concerned, in its author's own words, 'with the Lord Charlemagne's piety and care of the church'.[31] A brief synopsis of its contents and themes is in order here. Chapters 1–10 are linked together by the broad theme of education and learning, first discussing its Carolingian foundations with Alcuin and the Irish (chapters 1–2), then schools (chapter 3), the worthiness of episcopal candidates (chapters 4–7), and Charlemagne's insistence on strict standards of learning from his clergy (chapters 8–10). The next group of chapters, 11–25, contains the most memorable theme of the whole work, with colourful

---

[27] Edited by E. Raumer in *Mittellateinisches Jahrbuch* 21 (1986).
[28] Siegrist, *Herrscherbild und Weltsicht*, pp. 133–8.
[29] Von den Steinen, *Notker der Dichter. Darstellungsband*, p. 494.
[30] The existence of a preface is mentioned in Notker, *Gesta*, 2.pref., p. 48.   [31] *Ibid.*

Notker's Deeds of Charlemagne

anecdotes about Charlemagne's dealings with both unworthy and virtuous bishops. Chapter 26 is the imperial coronation of 800, while the stories in chapters 27–33 describe the building projects at Aachen and some of the events which took place within its walls. Finally, chapter 34 concerns the emperor's battledress, in preparation for book 2's projected discussion of military matters.

The stories work on a variety of levels. Most of them have individual didactic points to make, the most frequently recurring of which are the humbling of the proud and the rewarding of the humble.[32] Kingly virtues such as constant vigilance and the inspiration of fear are consistently stressed.[33] Stepping back and taking a broader view, however, implicit messages can also be read into Notker's overall structure. For example, the decision to begin his work with Charlemagne's ecclesiastical care contrasts sharply with Einhard's opening discussion of the secular rise of the Carolingians and reinforces Notker's prioritising of the sacred in history.[34] Book I can also be read as a schematisation of the Carolingians' achievement of their world empire, a progression from their acquisition of God's favour and learning, the way this was incorporated into their church, and finally the assumption of empire by Charlemagne.[35] The extent of Notker's artifice cannot be doubted: this was an extremely carefully structured work full of forceful points at first sight concealed but working on a number of different levels.

Our best direct clue to the reason for the involvement of Charles the Fat in the whole procedure comes in a remarkably overlooked group of chapters at the heart of book I. Chapters 16–19 all concern the same bishop, who thus features more prominently in the work than any other protagonist outside the royal family. He was one of Notker's bad bishops, a man of great pride who constantly overreached his position and had to be repeatedly chastised and humbled by Charlemagne. The bishop is described as holding 'the most important see in *Germania*', an unambiguous reference to Mainz.[36] It was very unusual for Notker to come this close to naming an actual bishop in his work; most of his stories give the impression of being purely typological and didactic, and indeed on another occasion he stated explicitly that he preferred not to identify

---

[32] See esp. Siegrist, *Herrscherbild und Weltsicht*, pp. 55–70. This is recorded by Ekkehard, *Casus S. Galli*, chap. 38, pp. 86–8 as one of Notker's main personal concerns.

[33] See Siegrist, *Herrscherbild und Weltsicht*, pp. 71–108; Goetz, *Strukturen der spätkarolingischen Epoche*, pp. 98–113.

[34] This is the argument of Ganz, 'Humour as History'.

[35] Haefele's introduction, pp. xvii–xxi; W. Berschin, *Biographie und Epochenstil im lateinischen Mittellalter* (vol. 3, Stuttgart, 1991), pp. 390–4. Cf. S. Rankin, 'Carolingian Music', in McKitterick (ed.), *Carolingian Culture*, pp. 274–316, at pp. 275–80.

[36] Notker, *Gesta*, 1.17, p. 22.

205

Kingship and Politics in the Late Ninth Century

his subjects.[37] This bishop (who, more correctly, would have been an archbishop) of Mainz was clearly a special case. Notker goes on immediately after naming the man's see to sound a note of caution: 'I am very much afraid, my lord emperor Charles [the Fat], that if I carry out your command, I shall incur the enmity of priests, especially the higher clergy. However, as long as I am assured of your protection, I will not worry too much about these people.'[38] The conjunction of Notker's expression of fear and his extended criticism of the bishop of Mainz lead to the conclusion that these negative stories were intended to have a more contemporary resonance than the focus on Charlemagne seems to suggest: if this was merely an abstract mirror for princes, why would he be worried? Given the other contemporary allusions in the work, the bishop who was so severely criticised in these chapters was surely supposed to be identified with a living figure, Archbishop Liutbert of Mainz, the most important churchman in east Francia from the 860s until the 880s.[39]

It is also evident from Notker's wording that this implicit criticism of Liutbert was incorporated into the text on the orders of Charles the Fat: why would Charles have done this? Liutbert had been a potential thorn in the imperial side ever since 882, when Charles succeeded Louis the Younger and thereby deprived the archbishop of his long-cherished position as archchaplain and main court adviser. The Mainz continuation of the *Annals of Fulda* stands testament to the resentment the excluded Liutbert felt towards Charles and his preferred archchaplain, Liutward of Vercelli.[40] Nevertheless, the offending text does not seem to have become known at court, and the rivalry was not fought out in public. Liutbert's continued high standing (he was, after all, in control of 'the most important see in *Germania*') is reflected by his appearance as petitioner in royal charters before 885.[41] He also led a successful campaign against the Vikings in the Hesbaye in early 885 in the company of the emperor's leading commander Henry, hence presumably with imperial sanction.[42] Open criticism of Liutbert would not have been in Charles's interest up to this point: he may not even have been aware of the extent of the archbishop's resentment towards him.

However, the cordial relations between the two did break down in late 885 over the main political issue of the day, the proposed legitimation of Bernard as the emperor's heir. As we have seen, Charles enlisted the pope

---

[37] *Ibid.*, 1.25, p. 33.   [38] *Ibid.*, 1.18, p. 22.

[39] Löwe, 'Das Karlsbuch Notkers', pp. 140–2 entertained this possibility before eventually identifying the bishop with Liutward of Vercelli, a conclusion which was based on his prior assumption that the latter and the empress were engaged in an anti-imperial conspiracy.

[40] See above, chap. 2.   [41] D CIII 109. See also DD 64–5.

[42] *AF(M)* s.a. 885, p. 102; cf. 883, p. 100.

Notker's Deeds of Charlemagne

to his cause, planning presumably to get him to sanction the annulment of his marriage to the empress Richgard and clear the way for a blessing of his union with Bernard's mother, a concubine whose identity is now unknown. The Mainz annalist added that Charles 'wished, as the rumour went, to depose certain bishops unreasonably' in order to smooth the passage of the plan.[43] The bishops' support for the scheme would have been almost as important as the pope's, as the case of Lothar II had shown, and domestic episcopal opposition would have been a difficult hurdle for Charles to overcome. That our only evidence for such opposition comes in the Mainz annals is very significant: this text served as the mouthpiece of Liutbert himself, expressing his personal views even when they had diverged from the official line of his master Louis the German. We may therefore take it that Liutbert was opposed to the legitimation of Bernard, one potential outcome of which would have been the perpetuation of the primacy of Alemannia in the political geography of the east Frankish kingdom, the very situation which had caused him to lose his court job in the first place.[44] If Charles was thinking of trying to depose his opponents (Liutbert and his nameless associates) or impose other papally enforced ecclesiastical sanctions on them, then he must have become aware of the archbishop's opinions: his opposition must have been public. In addition, this was perhaps the first event of Charles's reign where Liutbert's dormant opposition could be brought into the open and justified with legitimate ecclesiastical arguments, perhaps with the precedent of Lothar II in mind. In the event, the pope's unexpected demise made the whole affair a dead letter, and relations between emperor and archbishop reverted to the uneasy cold war situation which had existed during the preceding years. In late 885, however, in anticipation of, or in the wake of, Liutbert's defiance, Charles had a motive to want to see the archbishop criticised. Notker's fear was justified: Mainz was the metropolitan with jurisdiction over St-Gall, and the Stammerer had already had cautious dealings with him.[45]

Our hypothesis, then, is that Charles the Fat asked Notker to incorporate into the *Deeds of Charlemagne* a thinly-veiled criticism of the behaviour of Archbishop Liutbert in the wake of his opposition to the succession plan of late 885, a commission only carried out by the monk with reluctance and the promise of the emperor's protection. A survey of the criticisms levelled against the offending prelate in the *Deeds* supports this reading. Pride is the sin which dominates the image of the bishop of Mainz in Notker's work. He cuts a ludicrous figure in chapter 16.

---

[43] *AF(M)* s.a. 885, p. 103. See above, pp. 129–31.
[44] Reuter, *Annals of Fulda*, p. 99, n. 7 also infers this from the Mainz annals.
[45] Zeumer (ed.), *Collectio Sangallensis*, no. 43.

207

Kingship and Politics in the Late Ninth Century

Charlemagne, having observed that he was 'greatly fond of vainglory and stupid things' sets a trap for him, persuading a Jewish merchant to stuff and spice a dead mouse and sell it to him as an exotic luxury. The acquisitive churchman naturally falls for this cunning subterfuge and is exposed by the emperor at an assembly in terms which draw the moral of the story. Bishops today, says Charles, are too covetous and prone to indulgence in luxuries, behaviour which is 'in complete contrast' to the charitable pastoral work which they should be doing with the poor instead. The lesson is, it should be noted, couched in the language of ideal and appropriate behaviour.[46]

The kingly aspirations of the man are the subject of the subsequent chapter. While Charlemagne was engaged with war against the Avars, the bishop tried to get the empress to let him borrow the imperial sceptre to use in church processions. The empress stalled him and shared a laugh over the matter with her husband when he returned, before Charlemagne again upbraided the man in public, before a general assembly. This time the contrast between ideal and reality was couched in terms of ambition: where unworldliness was the proper stock of a bishop, this one had tried to seize the sceptre, which 'we are accustomed to carry as a sign of our royal power'.[47] As before, the bishop begged forgiveness and left in humiliation.[48]

Chapter 18 continues the theme of inappropriate royal pretensions at length. Charlemagne decrees that all bishops must deliver a sermon in person in their cathedrals before a set date, on pain of dismissal. This of course greatly worries our episcopal anti-hero, terrified of losing his office and the high living that goes along with it. Forced to mount the pulpit (to the amazement of his congregation, unused to such an event) in the presence of two royal legates, an absurd scene develops in which the incompetent bishop preaches a mighty and lofty sermon against a poor man who has entered the church with a boot on his head, due to his embarrassment at being ginger-haired (thought to be a sign of similarity to Judas Iscariot). This dubious triumph accomplished, he then proceeds to wine and dine the royal legates with great lavishness. With every luxury at his disposal and surrounded by troops of military retainers, 'he lacked nothing [as a pseudo-king] but a sceptre and the name of king'. 'Such a feast was never even laid before the great Charlemagne.' Finally, worried

---

[46] Notker, *Gesta*, 1.16, pp. 19–21.

[47] The transfer of such regalia could signify the transfer of actual authority in Carolingian politics: see now Airlie, 'Narratives of Triumph', pp. 110–11.

[48] Notker, *Gesta*, 1.17, pp. 21–2. Notker's choice of Hildegard as the wife of Charlemagne to figure in his work was in part due to his personal connections: Innes, 'Memory, Orality and Literacy', pp. 24–5.

208

Notker's Deeds of Charlemagne

about the impression he had given the legates, he bribes them with 'gifts worthy of a king'. Unable to lie, they told everything to the emperor, who magnanimously let the bishop off after deciding he had acted ultimately through fear of him, as was proper.[49]

Finally, chapter 19 underlines the bishop's stupidity and arrogance. Charlemagne strikes him to the ground after he rather tactlessly opines that a chorister who was a kinsman of the emperor sings the Alleluja like a country bumpkin ploughing the fields.[50]

Certainly, the points made by Notker about correct episcopal behaviour in these four stories can be read as expressions of timeless Christian ideals. Nonetheless, the fact that they all concern the same bishop should encourage the reader to look for common threads linking the various criticisms. One such theme is the way in which the criticisms are couched in terms of failed ideals. Each time he exhibits an aspect of his sinful nature, the moral is explicitly drawn in terms of how he ought to have behaved: he was worldly and ambitious, for example, where a bishop should have been a humble servant of the poor. This establishment of ideal types was a staple rhetorical strategy for authors wishing to express criticism in the early Middle Ages. We have already seen it at work, for instance, in the Mainz continuation of the *Annals of Fulda*. Notker, moreover, had also expressed firm views on correct episcopal behaviour in his guidebook for Salomon of Constance, the *Notatio*. In some ways, indeed, these four chapters form the centrepiece of everything Notker wrote about bishops. In this bishop's galaxy of sins, notably arrogance, vainglory, worldliness, ambition and stupidity, we find a compendium of everything which the Stammerer found reprehensible in episcopal behaviour. Where previous chapters focused on individual bishops epitomising individual virtues or sins, the bishop of Mainz had a comprehensive set of faults. Whereas the earlier chapters established typologies of right and wrong in Notker's evaluation of the demeanour of prelates in general, in chapters 16–19 he presented an example of a man who personified all the problems he had been discussing. The bishop of Mainz was the climax of the story, the punchline of the joke. This structuring is even made explicit by Notker. Chapters 14 and 15 are positive examples of humble and obedient bishops who are rewarded by Charlemagne with estates. The Stammerer makes clear the contrast between these men and the bishop of Mainz at the beginning of chapter 16: 'Because we have shown how the very wise Charlemagne exalted the

---

[49] Notker, *Gesta*, 1.18, pp. 22–5.

[50] *Ibid.*, 1.19, p. 25. See Haefele, 'Studien zu Notkers *Gesta Karoli*', pp. 381–5 and Kershaw, 'Laughter after Babel's Fall', pp. 191–2 for expositions of this story.

Kingship and Politics in the Late Ninth Century

humble, we will now relate how he humbled the proud.'[51] Their virtuous behaviour serves to throw the actions of the bishop of Mainz into sharper focus. As Siegrist showed, a form of pride designated by the term 'cenodoxia' (literally 'emptiness of doctrine') was for Notker the ultimate sin.[52] His paragons were humble and obedient, the bishop of Mainz was precisely the opposite. He was, as Charlemagne observed, unworthy of the rank of bishop.[53]

This man is, then, revealed by the context of the stories about him in Notker's typology as an anti-ideal, an anti-bishop. Siegrist, in his exposition of the idea of 'cenodoxia' in the *Deeds*, attributed Notker's obsession with this vice to his monastic training and outlook.[54] However this may be, we should also note that there is a distinct theme in Notker's discussion which may also be related to the state of contemporary politics, namely that concerning the need for bishops to be obedient to the king. This is why the good bishops of chapters 14 and 15 are rewarded: their obedience is unquestioning and even causes them distress, but, nevertheless, they obey Charlemagne. In contrast, the bishop of chapters 16–19 deliberately disregards and tries to deceive the royal will. His attempts to go a stage further and actually behave like a king, or even usurp royal powers, are stressed repeatedly by Notker in chapters 17 and 18, as we saw above. This behaviour corresponds neatly to Liutbert of Mainz's opposition to royal policy in late 885. In particular, his attempt to usurp Charlemagne's sceptre, which Notker understands as representing 'a sign of [the king's] royal power', could be read as a fairly direct reference to Liutbert's defiance.

Conversely, the king's right to appoint and depose bishops, one of the issues of contention in 885, is stridently asserted in the *Deeds*.[55] The right to appoint is most clearly expressed in chapter 4, where Charlemagne makes two wise choices of bishop in the face of disapproval and opposition from a variety of sources. The king's decision is seen as the manifestation of divine will, and his authority over appointments is described to him by one of the protagonists as 'the power given to you by God'.[56] Chapter 5 goes even further, ascribing to the ruler the ability to depose bishops as well. Removing an incumbent who had been seduced by the worldly accoutrements of his position, Charlemagne explains his actions thus: 'That proud man, who feared and honoured neither the Lord nor his most special friend [the king]...must forfeit his bishopric, by God's decree and by my own.'[57] Where the haughty bishop wanted to act like a king,

---

[51] Notker, *Gesta*, 1.16, p. 19.   [52] Siegrist, *Herrscherbild und Weltsicht*, pp. 55–70.
[53] Notker, *Gesta*, 1.18, p. 25.   [54] Siegrist, *Herrscherbild und Weltsicht*, pp. 55–70.
[55] See Goetz, *Strukturen der spätkarolingischen Epoche*, pp. 45–51.
[56] Notker, *Gesta*, 1.4, p. 6.   [57] *Ibid.*, 1.5, p. 9.

210

Notker's Deeds of Charlemagne

Charlemagne, 'bishop of bishops', was able effortlessly to exhibit episcopal qualities.[58] The power to appoint and depose was, therefore, the king's by divine approval, while the obligation of obedience fell upon the bishop. The obedience of the episcopate and the potential need to depose some of their number were, as we have seen, issues of great relevance to Charles the Fat as he tried to implement his plan to legitimise Bernard. Notker was telling Charles just what he would have wanted to hear in the autumn of 885, sanctioning his own attempts to assert his authority over the situation by anchoring them to the divinely approved powers enjoyed by his illustrious ancestor Charlemagne.

Notker's portrait of the 'bishop' of Mainz also makes sense in the context of the debate over church hierarchy which was building up in east Francia at precisely this time. The collection of falsified canons known to historians as Pseudo-Isidore found one of its earliest east Frankish outlets in Mainz in the 880s, where Archbishop Liutbert was well aware of its content.[59] Pseudo-Isidore's insistence on the emancipation of prelates from secular power, especially their immunity from lay accusation and punishment, would have bolstered the opposition of Liutbert to Charles in 885, and also provides a firm context for the Mainz annalist's fury at the emperor's attempt to remove his episcopal opponents.[60] The text was also known at St-Gall, where an abbreviated but essentially similar version, known as Pseudo-Remedius, was produced in the early 880s.[61] If, as seems certain given his prominence in the monastery's intellectual activity and book acquisition, Notker was familiar with the collection, then the *Deeds* can also be interpreted on one level as a response to its claims. Notker's attempts to provide a justification for lay (royal) interference in episcopal appointments are no more extreme or one-sided than Pseudo-Isidore/Remedius's attempts to put the opposite case. The consistency and savagery of the *Deeds's* attack on bishops' independence was, in other words, appropriate to the stridency of the counter-assertions which some prelates (notably Hincmar of Rheims) were coming to express at this time.[62] It was appropriate also that a refutation of Pseudo-Isidorean ideas,

---

[58] *Ibid.*, 1.25, p. 33; 1.11, p. 16. This unusual phrase has Constantinian overtones: W. Seston, 'Constantine as Bishop', *Journal of Roman Studies* 37 (1947), 127–31.

[59] H. John, *Collectio Canonum Remedio Curiensi Episcopo Perperam Ascripta*, Monumenta Iuris Canonici, series B (vol. 2, Vatican, 1976), pp. 120–1; H. Fuhrmann, *Einfluß und Verbreitung der pseudoisidorischen Fälschungen* (Stuttgart, 1972), pp. 225–6.

[60] For a convenient summary of Pseuso-Isidore's themes, see John, *Collectio Canonum*, pp. 24–6.

[61] *Ibid.*, pp. 119–24 ascertains the date and place.

[62] See Hincmar, *De Ordine Palatii*, chaps. 5–7, pp. 40–6; J. L. Nelson, 'Kingship, Law and Liturgy in the Political Thought of Hincmar of Rheims', in Nelson, *Politics and Ritual*, pp. 133–71, esp. pp. 139–46. There are some signs that these texts formed part of a wider debate about the authority of kings over bishops and vice versa.

Kingship and Politics in the Late Ninth Century

which were legitimised historically by reference to a series of allegedly authentic papal letters, should be founded on the idealisation of an antithetical historical lay figure (i.e. Charlemagne). More specifically, in the *Deeds*'s attribution of episcopal and even God-like qualities to Charlemagne, 'bishop of bishops', we might read an attempt to shortcircuit the legal collections' claims for bishops' immunity from lay authority.[63] Notker's insistence on the traditional biblical sin of pride as the ultimate vice also provides an antidote to the Pseudo-Remedian claim that this distinction belonged to *sacrilegium*, in the form of usurping the church hierarchy by infringing episcopal independence.[64]

The discussion of bishops which dominates book 1 of the *Deeds* from chapter 4 to chapter 20 thus reaches a climax with the implicit criticism of Liutbert of Mainz incorporated into chapters 16–19.[65] If this was monastic gossip, it was shaped and presented in a very deliberate fashion.[66] The traits elliptically attributed to the archbishop in these stories are not supposed to provide an accurate description of his character. Rather, they make sense as the exposition of a typological scheme: Liutbert is unworthy of his position in every way, and the absolute wrongness of his opposition to the *verbum regis* in the designation of Bernard is shown. More than this, however, the bishop of Mainz cuts a ridiculous figure in these four chapters, clearly intended to be laughed at. It is not surprising that Notker was worried about causing offence. His behaviour is not merely sinful or inappropriate, but indeed completely risible. The purchase of the stuffed mouse, the misdirected 'sermon' against the red-haired man wearing a boot on his head and his attempt at a humorous put-down of the young chorister are all ludicrous, and deliberately portrayed as such. The most laughable action of all is his attempt to usurp the symbols of royalty and to defy the king: Charlemagne and Hildegard themselves find it 'highly amusing' when the bishop tries to lay his hands on the royal sceptre.[67]

---

[63] See for example chaps. 4, 18 and 19 of Pseuso-Remedius which concern obedience to bishops and a forbidding of their removal; John, *Collectio Canonum*, pp. 140, 146–7.

[64] *Ibid.*, chap. 34, p. 155. We do not know if these canon law collections were known at court, but Ekkehard, *Casus S. Galli*, chap. 46, p. 102 does tell us that Liutward of Vercelli gave a collection of 'Greek canons' to St-Gall. The good relationship between Liutward and St-Gall may also have informed Notker's criticism of Liutbert. The issue of canon law merits further investigation.

[65] Chap. 20 (Notker, *Gesta*, pp. 26–7) concerns the criticism of a certain bishop called Recho, the only other named bishop in the work. His significance is not clear: it is possible he was meant to represent one of Liutbert's allies. This ends Notker's main discussion of bishops. Chaps. 21–6, although ostensibly continuing with the same theme, are presented as a digression by the author. Closer examination of these stories reveals that they are more abstract than those preceding, and that they are also distinguished by their principal concern with the actions of the devil in the world and not with the emperor, who does not feature.

[66] Innes, 'Memory, Orality and Literacy', p. 19; J. Fentress and C. Wickham, *Social Memory* (Oxford, 1992), pp. 154–62, esp. p. 155.

[67] Notker, *Gesta*, 1.17, p. 21.

Notker's Deeds of Charlemagne

Ganz and Kershaw have shown how Notker used humour as one of the *Deeds's* central rhetorical devices, designed to help make clear the points contained in his multi-layered anecdotes. If the audience got the joke and smiled 'the smile of understanding', they showed their comprehension of the author's purpose.[68] In chapters 16–19 of book 1, the joke was on Archbishop Liutbert of Mainz.

CONTEMPORARY REFERENCES IN THE *DEEDS OF CHARLEMAGNE*

Notker's text worked, therefore, on a multiplicity of levels. As well as embedding didactic messages in his anecdotes, he also historicised current events in order to please the most important member of his audience, namely the emperor. Elision was a staple literary strategy in many early medieval texts: Einhard himself, Notker's main source, deliberately combined elements from the reigns of Charlemagne and Louis the Pious.[69] The resonance of the section on the bishop of Mainz would not have been missed by a contemporary reader at court conversant with the high political situation of the day. Just as obvious to this audience as the satirising of Liutbert, moreover, would have been the corresponding elision of Charlemagne and Charles the Fat. If Liutbert was equated with the archetypally bad bishop of Mainz, then the king who had bested and humiliated him in those four stories must have been intended, at one level, to be identified with the current ruler. This was, needless to say, a high compliment to pay to Charles the Fat. Several more references to contemporary people and events can be identified in the *Deeds*, some of which continue to flatter the emperor, while others reveal a nervy and fearful Notker, full of concern about the Viking threat and Charles's inability to settle his succession definitively.

Some of these references have already been mentioned in the context of dating the text as a whole. One of them, the story of the invasion of Godafrid I/III in 810/885 is here worth examining in more detail. Notker's version is that Northmen invaded the empire while Charlemagne was away campaigning against the Avars. Receiving a surrender, the emperor returned immediately to invade the Vikings' homeland. However, a cattle disease crippled the army and forced its retreat, perhaps, thought Notker, a sign of God's displeasure at the sins of the Franks. Later, when the emperor was again absent somewhere in the empire, Godafrid invaded and settled the Moselle region. He was then killed by his own son, incensed by his mother's recent repudiation, causing his army to lose

---

[68] Quote from Ganz, 'Humour as History', pp. 181–3; Kershaw, 'Laughter After Babel's Fall'.
[69] Innes and McKitterick, 'The Writing of History', p. 207.

Kingship and Politics in the Late Ninth Century

courage and depart. Charlemagne's victory was thus accomplished without the use of force and was hence a sign of God's favour, although the bellicose emperor did express some regret that he had not had the opportunity to shed any Danish blood.[70] Almost all of these details correspond to what Notker had read in Einhard and the *Royal Frankish Annals*. However, as we mentioned earlier, the historical Godafrid I invaded Frisia, not the Moselle region.[71] The latter had, on the other hand, been the target of the Viking leader Godafrid III in 885 when he launched a raid on centres around the Rhine-Moselle confluence.[72] Notker's 'error' was deliberate: he intended his audience to identify the figure of Godafrid I with that of Godafrid III.[73]

If the two Godafrids were elided by Notker in this chapter, the parallels between the two Charleses were also clear. In 885 Charles the Fat, like Charlemagne in 810, had been absent within the empire when the invaders struck, ordering affairs in his newly acquired western kingdom. Another parallel with 810 was that again the emperor prevailed without having to intervene personally: the *dux* Henry tricked Godafrid into a meeting and slaughtered him and his retainers.[74] Notker's historical inexactitude was, therefore, a symptom neither of incompetence nor of an unquestioning adherence to his sources, oral or written: rather, it was intended to draw the reader's attention to the parallels between the effortless imperial victories of 810 and 885.[75] The Stammerer, moreover, went beyond the laconic reports of the *Royal Frankish Annals* and Einhard in his version of Godafrid's demise by reading into it an expression of divine will.[76] The chapter has an internal balance. The attempt of Charlemagne to invade the homelands of the Northmen fails, a sign of God's disfavour; but this failure is counterpointed by the effortless death of Godafrid, for which Charlemagne acknowledges God's beneficence. The implied comparison, which would have been obvious to a contemporary reader, is a flattering one for the current emperor: while the sins of the Franks had initially obstructed the success of Charlemagne, God was unambiguously

---

[70] Notker, *Gesta*, 2.13, pp. 75–6.

[71] *ARF* s.a. 810, p. 131; Einhard, *Vita Karoli*, chap. 14, p. 77. Saxony and Frisia had always been the focus of Godafrid's ambitions: cf. *ARF* s.a. 804, pp. 118–19; 808, pp. 125–6; 809, pp. 128–9.

[72] Regino, *Chronicon*, s.a. 885, p. 123 identifies Coblenz, Andernach and Sinzig as Godafrid's principal targets.

[73] Haefele accepted this elision in his introduction, p. xv, but thought it was unconscious on Notker's part.

[74] Regino, *Chronicon*, s.a. 885, pp. 123–4.

[75] A similar literary interplay between present and past was incorporated into *AF* s.a. 881, p. 97, where the Vikings are represented using Aachen as a stable. This may have been intended as an exposition of the promise of Godafrid I to sack the palace: Einhard, *Vita Karoli*, chap. 14, p. 77.

[76] This is in keeping with Notker's view of sacred history and his Christian recasting of Einhard as identified by Ganz, 'Humour as History'.

Notker's Deeds of Charlemagne

on the side of Charles the Fat in his easy triumph of 885. Given that Notker was writing for Charles, his expression of this sentiment is not particularly surprising. It echoes the comparison he had expounded more explicitly in his continuation of the chronicle of Erchanbert, another text designed for imperial ears, in 881: 'The most merciful Charles [the Fat] is the equal of the great emperor his great-grandfather Charlemagne in all wisdom, diligence and success in war, and his superior in [maintaining] the tranquility of peace and the prosperity of affairs.'[77] The *Deeds*'s account of Godafrid's invasion thus includes an exposition of this idea, that Charles the Fat was more successful than Charlemagne in achieving peaceful victories.[78]

It is clear, therefore, that one of Notker's historical devices in the *Deeds* was to elide present and past in order to make comments on the course of current events. However, not all of these contemporary references were, like the discussion of Godafrid, intended purely to flatter the emperor. Often the author allowed his own personal interests to take centre stage, most notably in his frequent discussions of and assertions about liturgical chanting and church singing, subjects close to his heart.[79] As was mentioned earlier, he also used the *Deeds* to try to persuade Charles the Fat to confer favours on his monastery: chapter 10 of book 2 contains a clear attempt to persuade the emperor to reissue the privileges his father had conferred on St-Gall in 873.[80] This form of exhortation on specific contemporary issues, rather than on universal ideals of Christian kingship, also underlies the story in chapter 13 of book 1.[81] Here Notker claims to be describing the extraordinary prudence of Charlemagne in not granting more than one county to any individual (other than frontier counts), nor any royal church or abbey to any bishop (except in unusual circumstances). As far as we know Charlemagne followed no such policy of *honor* distribution, and so it seems certain that Notker made these remarks because they were of particular concern to the community of St-Gall in the later ninth century. The holding of multiple counties by a single count was, as we discussed earlier, characteristic of the distribution of power in Alemannia under Louis the German and Charles the Fat, who sought by this measure to streamline their authority.[82] St-Gall itself benefited from the accompanying policy of strengthening selected religious institutions in the area, but the focusing of comital power was

---

[77] Notker, *Continuatio*, pp. 329–30.

[78] The virtue of bloodless success in war and politics is extolled by Regino, *Chronicon*, s.a. 887, p. 128; 888, p. 129 (in reference to Charles the Fat's family politics); and Notker, *Gesta*, 2.17, pp. 81, 85 (Charlemagne's defeat of the Lombards).

[79] E.g. Notker, *Gesta*, 1.10, pp. 12–15.   [80] See above, pp. 201–2.

[81] Notker, *Gesta*, 1.13, p. 17.   [82] See above, pp. 89–91.

Kingship and Politics in the Late Ninth Century

also a potential threat to its autonomy.[83] The most spectacular outbreak of the resulting tension occurred a few years later after Conrad I, following the example set by Charles the Fat, gave property at Stammheim to the monastery, much to the annoyance of the counts Erchangar and Bertold, who had built a fortress on the estate.[84] Likewise, St-Gall was one of the royal abbeys which ended up in episcopal hands at various points in its history, at times coming under the influence or even direct control of the bishop of Constance.[85] In this chapter, therefore, Notker probably hoped to draw Charles's attention to the episcopal and comital threats to St-Gall's independence at a time when the emperor had as yet refrained from confirming its claim to the same extensive freedoms and privileges as nearby Reichenau. It stands as an optimistic attempt to get the emperor to reverse his policies by offering him the incentive of thus emulating Charlemagne, and therefore provides a classic example of an early medieval ecclesiastical author turning a specific complaint into a general rule in order to address a ruler.

Interestingly, however, Notker makes an exception of one man, count Udalrich. He cites 'special reasons' for Charlemagne's decision to allow Udalrich to be the only multiple-county holder in his empire, but does not spell out what they were.[86] It is surely no coincidence, therefore, that the most prominent controller of multiple counties in Notker's own day was also called Udalrich. This Udalrich, known to historians as Udalrich IV, was a descendant of the count of the same name from Charlemagne's reign, and could boast among his *honores* the Linz-, Argen-, Rhein- and Alpgaus, which made him one of the most important royal representatives in the Lake Constance area.[87] He had authority in regions where St-Gall had lands, and he had the emperor's ear. He was clearly not a man to be trifled with, and may indeed have been a political ally of Abbot Bernard of St-Gall.[88] The mention of Udalrich as the exception to the ideals Notker proposed here was thus surely intended to have a contemporary resonance, one which was expedient given the circumstances of St-Gall at the time. He was trying to avoid giving offence to the current count

---

[83] Borgolte, *Geschichte der Grafschaften Alemanniens*, pp. 187–208.

[84] Ekkehard, *Casus S. Galli*, chap. 16, pp. 42–4; see Schmid, 'Brüderschaften mit den Mönchen', pp. 179–81.

[85] Some aspects of this are discussed by H. Maurer, 'St. Gallens Präsenz am Bischofssitz. Zur Rezeption st. gallischer Traditionen im Konstanz der Karolingerzeit', in H. Maurer et.al. (eds.), *Florilegium Sangallense* (St-Gallen, 1980), pp. 199–211.

[86] He mentions that Udalrich was Queen Hildegard's brother, but does not equate this with the 'special reasons'. Udalrich IV was a 'nepos' of Charles the Fat: D LG 124; D CIII 57.

[87] See Borgolte, *Die Grafen Alemanniens*, pp. 255–66; and above, pp. 89–91.

[88] The two men were certainly allies in 890 when they supported the revolt of Charles's son Bernard: Borgolte, *Die Grafen Alemanniens*, p. 263. D LG 71 casts some further light on comital-monastic relations.

Notker's Deeds of Charlemagne

Udalrich, expressing approval at his preeminence. Once again we can see that Notker expected his audience to see themselves in the *Deeds*; and we also appreciate that he envisaged a wider audience than simply the emperor alone, one which included court figures like Udalrich.

This audience would also have been able to derive contemporary significance in Notker's story about Charlemagne's hunting injury in book 2 chapter 8.[89] A certain Isembard killed a beast which had hurt the emperor's leg, bringing its heart back as a trophy for Charlemagne. He had formerly been 'despised and deprived of all his *honores*', and his actions restored his good reputation. As a reward for his actions he received back all the lands he had previously lost, and a cash sum to boot. A version of the story of Isembard's reconciliation was in fact already known to Charles the Fat and formed a central plank of his relationship with St-Gall. The reason for the man's dispossession and exclusion was that he was the son of count Warin, 'the persecutor of your patron [St] Otmar'. The gift to St-Gall of land at Stammheim, whence Warin and his associates had operated in the mid-eighth century, was made by Charles in 879 as an act of symbolic reconciliation with Otmar for the nefarious deeds of his predecessors.[90] The atonement of Charles the Fat was a reinforcement of the atonement of the historical Isembard, which had also taken the form of gifts to the monastery, and hence of a claim to legitimacy which arced back to the dawn of Carolingian influence in Alemannia.[91] Notker's story in this chapter can thus be read as a knowing reference to and affirmation of this aspect of Charles the Fat's relationship with St-Gall, recast and relocated at the centre of the court rituals of Charlemagne. Notker confirmed that the rift between Otmar and the successors of Warin, including Charles, had been completely healed.

Certain stories in the *Deeds* were intended, then, to flatter and exhort Charles the Fat by turns, doing so in allegorical fashion, by taking aspects of the current political situation and overlaying them with resonant events, real or fictive, from the reign of Charlemagne. This elision of time, people and places running through the *Deeds* is entirely in keeping with Notker's conception of history as a flat canvas on which to demonstrate the points he was trying to convey. For authors like him, history was typological, a tool to be used to pass comment on the present, not a question of striving after chronological accuracy or even of faithfulness to his sources.[92] His didactic purpose was furthered if his readers could read themselves represented in the pages of the *Deeds*. Moreover, as we

---

[89] Notker, *Gesta*, 2.8, pp. 60–2.   [90] See above, pp. 87–8.

[91] DD SG 31 and 190; Walther, 'Der Fiskus Bodman', pp. 263–4.

[92] Notker's historical outlook is discussed by Siegrist, *Herrscherbild und Weltsicht*, pp. 109–44 and Ganz, 'Humour as History'.

Kingship and Politics in the Late Ninth Century

saw in the historicising of Liutbert of Mainz, the audience was primed to understand the *Deeds* in some respects as a commentary on current events: Charles the Fat had known this when he commissioned the work. Whether or not the Charlemagne references were based on confirmable facts from sources oral or written, as some were, was not important to the author's view of history. Notker's work ought to be read as a whole, a coherent artifice with a specific audience in mind, an audience which understood the intention of his apparent historical 'errors'.[93]

NOTKER AND THE IMPERIAL SUCCESSION

Alongside these elliptical allusions to events in contemporary politics, the *Deeds of Charlemagne* also contains a number of direct addresses to the emperor expressing Notker's fears about the way his schemes to solve the imperial succession were going. The plan to have Bernard legitimised took shape in the late summer and autumn of 885, and was to have taken the form of a dissolution of the royal marriage and a subsequent papal sanction for the union which had produced the emperor's bastard son. Notker included in the *Deeds* the story of Charlemagne's repudiation of the daughter of the Lombard king Desiderius, which he did 'with the sanction of his most holy priests, because she was bedridden and unable to bear a child'.[94] The course of events confirmed that that the opposition to this act mounted by Desiderius was wrongful and contrary to the will of God as Charlemagne peremptorily crushed him in dramatic fashion. With this story Notker provided an apology by analogy for Charles the Fat's projected annulment of his marriage: it was an acceptable procedure if the union was barren, as was Charles the Fat's, and it had been approved of by Charlemagne himself, not to mention by his devout clergy and the will of God.[95]

However, the projected 885 divorce for which Notker here provided a form of historical justification did not actually take place, prevented by the premature death of the cooperative Pope Hadrian III. As we argued earlier, Charles's response, before his change of tack in mid-887, was to continue trying for a son by Richgard, something which was increasingly unlikely after more than two decades of marriage, and to

---

[93] This conclusion is not necessarily mutually exclusive with those of Innes, 'Memory, Orality and Literacy': Notker's artifice may lie in his deliberate reshaping of oral and written traditions current at St-Gall.

[94] Notker, *Gesta*, 2.17, pp. 81–2. Cf. the story of Godafrid's divorce, 2.13, p. 76.

[95] Löwe, 'Das Karlsbuch Notkers', pp. 143–4 drew a similar conclusion, but thought the passage related to the actual divorce of 887. On that occasion, however, virginity and not barrenness was the justification offered by Charles for his actions; see above, pp. 169–78.

218

Notker's Deeds of Charlemagne

keep open negotiations with the new pope in the hope of obtaining his help for a revival of the Bernard plan.[96] Meanwhile, the claims of the other possible contenders for the throne, principally Arnulf of Carinthia, were persistently disregarded by the emperor.

This policy, which was becoming clear as book 1 of the *Deeds* was completed in early 886, did not meet with the approval of Notker the Stammerer. In his description of Louis the German's character, Notker describes the king's formidable reputation for subduing rebellions quickly and terrifying his heathen enemies beyond the frontiers: 'This reputation was deserved, for he never broke his word in judgement or stained his hands with the shedding of Christian blood except on one occasion, and that was one of final necessity. I dare not tell that story until I see some little Louis or Charles standing at your side.'[97] The story which Notker here recoiled from telling was that of the Battle of Fontenoy (841), a conflict which was still remembered with dread in Carolingian political circles. Fontenoy was the culmination of the bloody civil war which had been fought by Louis the Pious's sons and grandson for the throne and, as such, was hitherto the most infamous succession crisis in Carolingian history.[98] By here juxtaposing it with a reminder of Charles the Fat's lack of a legitimate heir, Notker pointedly expressed to the emperor his fear that this disaster was about to be superseded by one even greater: if Charles died without an heir, the outcome would be the final extinction of the legitimate Carolingian male line. That this heir had to be legitimate (and that, by implication, Bernard would not do) is stressed by Notker's use of the main-line Carolingian names Louis and Charles. As long as such an heir was lacking, the Stammerer also implied that a repeat of the intra-family warfare of Fontenoy was imminent, as the claims of illegitimate Carolingians such as Arnulf, who were at least the sons of kings, reached boiling point. His pessimism about the production of such an heir was palpable.[99]

---

[96] See above, pp. 161–9.   [97] Notker, *Gesta*, 2.11, p. 68.

[98] Hincmar, *Instructio*, col. 986 also demonstrates the enduring impact of Fontenoy.

[99] Notker must have doubted the probability of the marriage producing an heir after such a long barren period: even in the *Continuatio* of 881 he had laid more stress on the wisdom of designating Arnulf; see above, p. 134. Notker, *Gesta*, 2.10, pp. 65–7 also stressed the example of Louis the German, whose saintly lifestyle had been tempered by a realisation that there were 'things without which secular life cannot exist, namely marriage and the use of weapons'. This passage is immediately followed by the section discussed earlier, in which Notker refers to the privileges granted to St-Gall in 873 by Louis and Charles. The issuing of these charters formed part of Charles's reintroduction to secular affairs after the famous episode early in that year when he had attempted to renounce those very things, arms and marriage, which Notker had singled out as important to Louis. His emphasis on these practical aspects of Louis's behaviour may, it follows, show that he feared Charles had not given up the desire for renunciation which he had expressed in 873.

219

Kingship and Politics in the Late Ninth Century

Notker was similarly pessimistic about the chances of Bernard succeeding in the wake of Hadrian III's death. Describing in the very next chapter the destruction by the Vikings in 882 of 'the most noble monastery of that time', in other words Prüm, the monk lamented: 'it is now destroyed, by what cause is only too well known. I will not describe its end until I see your little son Bernard with a sword attached to his thigh.'[100] This is a reference, as argued earlier, to Charles's intention to establish Bernard as subking of Lotharingia when he was old enough.[101] But, and this was Notker's emphasis, Bernard was *not* old enough. His trepidation here and in the previous chapter derived from the fact that at the time he was writing Charles's succession plans remained conditional and unresolved, a situation which could only increase tension in a political community beset by external attack and desperate to know who would replace the ageing emperor.[102]

Notker emphasised this point by referring in the same chapter to an earlier occasion when the lack of a Carolingian boy as tall as a sword had led to the attempt by certain 'giants' to try to seize control of the kingdom. This passage contains no obvious historical reference, and seems to work as another dire warning to Charles the Fat that his succession had to be resolved soon or the Franks would lose God's favour: an heir as tall as a sword (i.e. at the age of majority) was exactly what was missing in 885–6.[103] The identification of the giants with female-line Carolingians, who were by the standards of 'legitimists' like Notker ineligible for kingship, is possibly implied by Notker's description of them as 'like those whom scripture tells us were begotten by the sons of Seth from the daughters of Cain'.[104] It was this kind of man who stood to benefit if Charles did fail to make a viable succession plan. If, Notker implied, Charles died and left the way clear to royal claims based on female-derived Carolingian descent, Pandora's Box would be opened, as the number of candidates would be multiplied exponentially.[105] Arnulf, Bernard, Hugh and Charles the Simple were the only male-line possibilities: female-line descent opened the door to the likes of Berengar, Baldwin of Flanders and numerous others.

---

[100] Notker, *Gesta*, 2.12, p. 74.   [101] See above, pp. 130–2.

[102] *Ibid.*, 2.14, pp. 77–8 is a good example of Notker's warnings about the imminence of the Viking threat.

[103] The reference to divine favour is implied by the allusion to the giants in Genesis 6.4.

[104] Notker's comparison of them to 'those who asked: "what part have we in David and what inheritance in the son of Jesse?"' may imply the same thing, men rejecting the authority of the main Carolingian (Davidic) line. Cf. Alibert, '*Semen eius*', pp. 139–40.

[105] Others have suggested that the giants represented the *reguli* themselves. Cf. Löwe, 'Das Karlsbuch Notkers', p. 146.

Notker's Deeds of Charlemagne

These expressions of unease in chapters 11 and 12 of book 2 were contrasted implicitly by Notker with the precocity of Louis the German described in chapter 10, in which Louis's greatness and royal destiny were revealed as certain while he was still a child at the court of his grandfather. As far as Charlemagne was concerned, Louis guaranteed the future for at least two generations.[106] Charles the Fat had no such assurances. Notker also described Louis's visit to St-Gall in 857 or 859 with two of his sons in such terms of stability. He depicts the sons as two flowers growing from the king's trunk, which 'adorned his head with great glory and protected him'.[107] The idealised family image presented by Charlemagne to Greek envoys is also striking in this context. He stood before them surrounded by his three sons, 'young men who were already made participants in [governing] the kingdom', his daughters and their mother, followed by the hierarchy of the court, all posed in great splendour and dignity.[108] Interestingly, this Greek embassy visited the Frankish court in 812, at a time when Charlemagne had no wife and only one surviving son. Notker would have known this from even a cursory glance at the *Royal Frankish Annals*. Here, as in the other examples, historical accuracy was not the point. The Stammerer sought in these vignettes to create idealised images of family solidarity and continuity, fixing them at points in the Carolingian past which would make clear how sharply they contrasted with the current state of affairs. A resolution of the problem was essential, Notker was saying, to the maintenance of political stability, to close the door on the 'giants'. The urgency of his message would not have been lost on Charles the Fat.

Notker did not, however, stop there: he also proposed a solution to the problems he outlined in chapters 11 and 12 of book 2. In chapter 14, Notker reports a dire prophecy of Charlemagne, moved to tears at the thought of what terrible damage the Vikings might do to his descendants. He continues in the second person:

May your own sword, tempered already in the gore of the Northmen, stand in their way, and may the sword of your brother Karlmann, which is stained in their blood too, be joined to yours. But Karlmann's sword is now rusting away, not through cowardice, but through want of funds and because the lands of your most faithful Arnulf are so diminished. If you in your mighty power only have the will to ordain this, it should not be a difficult matter for this sword to be made sharp and bright once more. This one small bough, together with the tiny splinter which is Bernard, is all that is left to burgeon on the once-prolific stock of Louis, and it is under the branch of your own protection, which alone remains, that it is free to form its leaf.[109]

---

[106] Notker, *Gesta*, 2.10, pp. 65–7. [107] *Ibid.*, 1.34, p. 47.
[108] *Ibid.*, 2.6, pp. 55–7. [109] *Ibid.*, 2.14, p. 78.

221

Kingship and Politics in the Late Ninth Century

For Notker, Arnulf was the answer. Charles had brought his nephew to his knees by the end of 885 as a response to his unwanted interference in the so-called Wilhelminer War.[110] Notker appealed to the emperor's necessity, reminding him of the imminence of the Viking danger and recalling allusively the help Arnulf had given him at the siege of Asselt in 882. The recurring sword metaphor itself is also instructive. Louis the German's interest in swords in preference to gold had marked him out for greatness in Notker's eyes.[111] It was for want of a Carolingian as tall as a sword that the 'giants' had infested the land, and Bernard's minority had been defined in terms of being too young to have a 'sword attached to his thigh'. Arnulf, by contrast, was himself 'the sword of Karlmann', the only potential male-line heir old and experienced enough to be a success. Arnulf was the emperor's best bet for keeping out the claims of the 'giants', the female-line Carolingians, and it was in Charles's power to make his rusty sword new again. To drive the point home, the author described Bernard in the same passage as a 'tiny splinter' 'from the prolific stock of Louis' and reminded Charles again that the 'future little Charles or Louis' which he so desired was yet unborn.

Book 2's depiction of long Carolingian family continuity about to come to an abrupt end culminated in chapter 14. As he had in 881 in his *Continuatio*, Notker urged the admission of Arnulf to the position of official heir (or co-heir, with Bernard) as a man able to combat the forces threatening the empire as he wrote.[112] He combined allusions to an invented 'good old days' of united Carolingian solidarity and continuity with direct pleas to the emperor. That, as we have seen, Notker's fears about Arnulf's reaction to continued exclusion were ultimately realised confirms that the author of the *Deeds* was not merely an important writer and historian, but also an astute political commentator.

CHARLES THE FAT AND CHARLES THE GREAT

The foregoing discussion suggests that the identifiable political concerns expressed in the *Deeds*, as well as the specific contemporary references, support the dates of composition argued for at the start of this chapter. Notker's fears about the state of the imperial succession, with which book 2 is shot through, only became relevant in 885–6, after the death of Carloman II, the fall from favour of Arnulf and the failure of the first attempt to legitimise Bernard. One final aspect of this political situation brings us back to the question of why Charles the Fat might have commissioned Notker's work.

[110] See above, pp. 134–44.   [111] Notker, *Gesta*, 2.18, pp. 88–9.
[112] Notker, *Continuatio*, p. 330.

Notker's Deeds of Charlemagne

We have already seen how Charles wanted to hear stories lampooning the archbishop of Mainz and how, in this as in the other allusive stories discussed above, the emperor was implicitly elided with his great-grandfather Charlemagne. The grandest aspect of this comparison, however, is contained within Notker's historical outlook. The *Deeds* expounds throughout a novel and unique interpretation of the Carolingians' place in world history. St Jerome's commentary on the Book of Daniel had explained the four parts of the dream of Nebuchadnezzar as representing four world empires, the last of which, Rome, would last until the end of history. Notker revised this (in hindsight evidently mistaken) interpretation by putting forward the idea, in the very first chapter of book I, that Charlemagne represented 'the golden head of a second and no less remarkable statue': God had destroyed the statue which symbolised the first four world empires and had created another, with the Carolingians at its head.[113] This was a concept of *renovatio imperii* which pitched its claim neither as a purely Christian nor a Roman empire: the Frankish empire of Charlemagne was universal, and stood at the pinnacle of world and sacred history.[114] Book I then proceeded to expand on this theme by demonstrating the rise of Charlemagne and an empire built on learning and wisdom which became the foundation of its church, finally leading to his assumption of the imperial title.[115]

The more secular aspects of this theme are further developed in book 2, beginning with Rome's loss of God's favour manifest in the death of Julian the Apostate.[116] A series of chapters follow which lampoon the lazy and decadent rulers of previous world empires in Africa, Persia and Byzantium, establishing their moral inferiority to Charlemagne and their new (supposed) status as tribute-paying client princes of the Franks.[117] Significantly, Notker ends this section with a prophetic quotation from Virgil, which he thought was fulfilled by the rise of the Carolingian world empire: 'Either the Parthian shall drink of the Arar or the German of the Tigris.' The Arar, he hastily adds, is to be identified with the Aare (in the east Frankish realm) and not, as some 'ignorant philologists' have it,

---

[113] Notker, *Gesta*, 1.1, p. 1.

[114] H. Löwe, 'Von Theodorich dem Grossen zu Karl dem Grossen. Das Werden des Abendlandes im Geschichtsbild des frühen Mittelalters', in his *Von Cassiodor zu Dante*, pp. 33–74, at pp. 73–4; Siegrist, *Herrscherbild und Weltsicht*, pp. 109–44; Goetz, *Strukturen der spätkarolingischen Epoche*, pp. 69–85.

[115] Haefele's introduction, pp. xvii–xxiii.   [116] Notker, *Gesta*, 2.1, p. 49.

[117] *Ibid.*, 2.6–9, pp. 53–65; see Siegrist, *Herrscherbild und Weltsicht*, pp. 114–27. Cf. C. Wickham, 'Ninth-Century Byzantium through Western Eyes', in L. Brubaker (ed.), *Byzantium in the Ninth Century: Dead or Alive?* (London, 1988), pp. 245–56.

Kingship and Politics in the Late Ninth Century

the west Frankish Saône.[118] The proof of this is that in the reign of Louis the German a tax was raised from land towards the freeing of Christians in the Holy Land: 'In their misery they begged him for it because of the domination once exercised by your great-grandfather Charles and your grandfather Louis.'[119] In other words it was Louis the German and the eastern Carolingians (in whose kingdom, of course, the Aare flowed) who had truly inherited the mantle of world leadership from Charlemagne. Louis, in succession to Charlemagne, was the new 'head of the Franks'.[120]

Notker proceeds immediately, in chapter 10, to discuss Louis the German's personal qualities, his precociousness and his early designation as ruler by Charlemagne.[121] *Therefore* ('itaque') Louis was 'king and emperor of all Germania, Rhaetia, old Francia, as well as of Saxony, Thuringia, Bavaria, the Pannonias and all of the peoples of the north'.[122] The use of the word 'itaque' in this context is significant, as is the phrase 'king and emperor': both usages explicitly identify Louis the German, who was not actually an emperor, as the heir of Charlemagne, marking out his family as the superior Carolingian family branch. This reading of Notker's political ideas is supported by the work of Eggert, who showed that the *Deeds's* focus on the east Frankish line was also reflected in St-Gall's charter formulas. Some of these were penned by Notker himself, and propound a view of history in which Charles the Fat was the *second* Emperor Charles (Charles the Bald was ignored), and in which he, like Louis the German before him, ruled a multi-regnal 'empire' which had east Francia at its centre.[123]

Notker went on to quote Isaiah 51.1: 'Look unto the rock whence ye are hewn.'[124] The message for Charles the Fat was clear: he was a chip off the old block, the heir of Louis as Louis was of Charlemagne, the ruler of a divinely ordained world empire whose centre was, in Notker's eyes, east Francia. The message was also deliberately obvious: the relevant chapters come in sequence, and their overall impact is unmistakable, quite apart from any individual didactic point each might make. Notker also included in book 2 stories about the mystical status of Aachen, whose aura of purity and divinely approved legitimate power had rubbed off

---

[118] Could he have had in mind Thegan, *Gesta Hludowici imperatoris*, chap. 52, p. 244, which cited the same verse in reference to the Saône?

[119] Notker, *Gesta*, 2.9, p. 65.

[120] *Ibid.*, 1.34, p. 47. 'Head' refers to the head of the new symbolic statue and thus of the new world empire: cf. *ibid.*, 1.1, p. 1; 1.24, p. 32; 2.3, p. 52.

[121] *Ibid.*, 2.10, pp. 65–7.   [122] *Ibid.*, 2.11, p. 67.

[123] Eggert, 'Zu Kaiser- und Reichsgedanken'; cf. Eggert, ' "Franken und Sachsen" ', pp. 518–19. Cf. Penndorf, *Problem der "Reichseinheitsidee"*, pp. 149–58.

[124] Notker, *Gesta*, 2.18, p. 89. Louis is described here as 'true emperor'.

Notker's Deeds of Charlemagne

onto Charles's father, Louis the German.[125] These assertions were all the easier to make with the benefit of hindsight, since in 885–6 it had become undeniable that Charles was indeed the heir of Charlemagne, as his only surviving adult male legitimate descendant. One of Notker's aims in the *Deeds* was thus to fix this known outcome in the context of ninth-century history, explaining and legitimising the success of Charles in claiming the mantle of his great-grandfather in terms of the divine masterplan.

The connection between the two rulers was all the clearer given the coincidence that they had the same name, something which is of course much more obvious in Latin than in English translation. The elision of Charles (the Great) and Charles (the Fat) has already been discussed as one of the principal narrative strategies of the *Deeds*; the same implicit point can hardly have been missed by a contemporary court audience reading Notker's explanation of the Carolingian world empire. The link had already occurred to Notker in 881 when he wrote his *Continuatio*, a text which culminated in and celebrated the anointing of Charles as emperor in that same year.[126] It was even more appropriate to the year 885, when Charles's assumption of the west Frankish kingdom reunited the entire Carolingian empire in the hands of one man for the first time since 840 and gave territorial substance to his imperial title. The *Deeds* is, therefore, a product of that same strand of ideology which we have already noted as present in the thinking of Charles the Fat in the year 885, when he began to think of himself as consecrated to the whole empire.[127]

Notker also reveals that it had been Charlemagne whom Charles the Fat was really interested in hearing about, and that his chapters on other kings were digressions.[128] It is therefore eminently possible that Charles himself, who, as we have seen, had been in direct and indirect contact with Notker on several occasions, was involved in the elaboration of these ideas, or at least that he was aware of them before he commissioned them to be written up into a coherent text. This is made more plausible by another famous product of the St-Gall scriptorium which belongs to this period. The so-called *Golden Psalter* contains illustrations accompanying twelve of the psalms which, although they concern scenes from the life of King David, were executed in a style which suggests an iconographic

---

[125] Nelson, 'Aachen as a Place of Power', pp. 234–6. Charles's own familiarity and self-association with the aura of Aachen are clear: see above, pp. 157–8.

[126] Notker, *Continuatio*, pp. 329–30.

[127] See above, pp. 153–8. Notker, *Gesta*, 1.10, p. 13 refers to anointing as an ancient practice, which in late ninth-century east Frankish terms it was not; Goetz, *Strukturen der spätkarolingischen Epoche*, p. 23 and n. 65. This reference to, presumably, the Old Testament, may nevertheless reflect the court's preoccupation with consecration ideas in 885.

[128] Notker, *Gesta*, 2.16, pp. 80–1.

Kingship and Politics in the Late Ninth Century

representation of the Old Testament ruler as a Carolingian, most probably Charles the Fat.[129] The various scenes point in two directions, both back to the Old Testament and to the present day, a common dialectic in Carolingian political thought. David and the current ruler were consciously elided by the artist and installed into the picture cycle as a royal archetype, rising to kingship, defeating enemies and ultimately achieving Christ-like status.[130] Its individual elements, moreover, may refer to actual events in the current king's lifetime; the illustration of Psalm 26 (Samuel anointing David), for instance, may refer to an actual consecration.[131] This particular example was, as has already been explained, especially relevant to the reign of Charles the Fat, in the year 885.[132] Notker and Charles both knew that Charlemagne had had himself compared with David.[133] Notker had also compared himself to Idithun, David's singer, and Charles the Fat to Charlemagne.[134] An elision of Charles the Fat with David (a typical Carolingian conceit) such as that found in the *Golden Psalter* would thus fit this complex of associations and give support to the notion that Charles identified himself with his great-grandfather.[135] The *Golden Psalter* may therefore also have been inspired by the ideological statements of the year 885: it is surely no coincidence that its images have a distinctly imperial, rather than royal, character.[136] That this idea should be reflected in the *Deeds* as well therefore comes as little surprise. In 885 Charles already had the title and the empire: now the *Deeds* provided him with an appropriate ideology, rooting his power in the course of sacred and secular history.

Notker was, however, no mindless mouthpiece of imperial propaganda. His admonitory chapters on the succession situation (11–14) come immediately after his explication of the greatness of the world empire (6–11).

[129] The work is often dated to between 880 and 890: A. Reinle, *Kunstgeschichte der Schweiz* (Frauenfeld, 1968), p. 285. Eggenberger, *Psalterium Aureum*, pp. 13–14 identifies the recipient as either Charles the Fat or Conrad I. The objections of R. Schaab, 'Aus der Hofschule Karls des Kahlen nach St. Gallen. Die Entstehung des Goldenen Psalters', in Ochsenbein and Ziegler (eds.), *Codices Sangallenses*, pp. 57–80, that the codex was conceived and begun at the court school of Charles the Bald, are convincing, but do not negate Eggenberger's argument that it was presented in its existing form as a gift for a later ruler. It was probably at St-Gall, where it was completed and reworked, by Charles the Fat's time.

[130] Eggenberger, *Psalterium Aureum*, esp. pp. 168–77.   [131] *Ibid.*, pp. 82–3.

[132] Other images refer to the king as adulterer, besieger and hunter. The God- or Christ-like king (which makes sense in a Davidic context too) is also a principal theme of the *Gesta Karoli*: Siegrist, *Herrscherbild und Weltsicht*, pp. 79–89.

[133] Notker, *Gesta*, 2.19, p. 89. Cf. 2.6, p. 57; 2.12, p. 71. This came from a reading of Alcuin's letters: Ganz, 'Humour as History', pp. 180–1.

[134] Zeumer (ed.), *Collectio Sangallensis*, additamenta no. 6; Notker, *Continuatio*, pp. 329–30 respectively.

[135] I.e. if Notker = Idithun, then Charles = David. Notker's musical sequences, the *Liber Ymnorum*, had been sent for use at Charles's court in 884.

[136] Eggenberger, *Psalterium Aureum*, pp. 168, 173.

Notker's Deeds of Charlemagne

The implication of this structuring is that, in Notker's eyes, the continuation of Carolingian world domination was conditional, dependent not only on the moral integrity of its people but also on Charles the Fat's successful handling of the succession situation. The dangerous implication of the 'second statue' ideology was that there were, if the Franks lost God's favour, three more world empires to come. Charles was the heir to world power, but its continuation was not yet assured: indeed, Notker feared the worst. He told Charles the Fat what he wanted to hear, but he also told him what he thought he *ought* to hear.

In this circumspection, Notker also reflects the political circumstances of 885–6. We have already seen how the optimistic grand rhetoric of the late summer and autumn of 885 quickly lost its meaning and was dropped as the failure of the Bernard plan and the humbling of Arnulf cast a shadow of doubt into the minds of the Carolingian political community.[137] The *Deeds* was conceived and composed in the midst of this rapidly declining situation. It is no coincidence that the confident assertion of Carolingian world power contained in the structure of book 1, planned in mid–late 885, was infiltrated by the exhortatory digressions and nervous second-person addresses of book 2, written in 886.[138] The change in Notker's outlook reflected the change in the state of the emperor's political situation. Notker feared that Charles's grip on the world empire was becoming ever weaker as time passed. Time ultimately proved the accuracy of Notker's comments, for it was the excluded Arnulf who finally broke that grip in November 887 and inaugurated the age of the *reguli*, in whose number were included some of the very female-line Carolingians against whom the Stammerer had warned.

CONCLUSION

The *Deeds of Charlemagne* may be read, then, as a subtly political document. Under its veneer of general moral and didactic exhortation runs a substratum of contemporary political commentary, by turns allusive and direct, expressed in the contents of the anecdotes and reinforced by their ordering. It may be regarded as a kind of mirror for a prince, but it is also more than simply that. Some loose ends remain to be tidied up. Firstly, if we are to believe that Charles the Fat and members of his entourage understood the implicit points being made by Notker, they would have to have been conversant with events from the actual reign of Charlemagne. For instance, the implied parallel between the two emperors in the story

---

[137] See above, pp. 158–60.
[138] This contrast was noted, but not explained, by Haefele in his introduction, pp. xiv–xv.

Kingship and Politics in the Late Ninth Century

about Godafrid's occupation of the Moselle region only achieves its impact if its readers are familiar with the real actions of Godafrid I in 810, presumably from Einhard and/or the *Royal Frankish Annals*. Fortunately, this familiarity is demonstrable. Einhard's *Life* was one of the bestsellers of the ninth century and copies were present at the court of Louis the German.[139] It was used in the education of the young Charles the Bald, and probably played a similar role in the upbringing of Charles the Fat.[140] In fact, Notker virtually tells us as much in book 2 of the *Deeds* when he refers to 'your great-grandfather Charles, all of whose deeds are well known to you'.[141]

Moreover, Notker's explication of the Carolingian world empire, a theme which runs right through his work, was ultimately reliant on Jerome's commentary on Daniel. We have a St-Gall library catalogue from c. 880 which reveals (in Notker's own hand) that Charles and his associates were accustomed to borrowing some of its volumes.[142] They are not recorded as having consulted the exegesis on Daniel, but the list is only a snapshot of a particular moment in the library's history, so it is entirely plausible that they did just that. We do know that Queen Richgard borrowed a volume of four of Jerome's other commentaries, and that Liutward of Vercelli had read his letters.[143] These interests make their acquaintance with the Daniel text even more likely. In any case, we have already seen that Charles himself had had many opportunities to meet Notker, and that one definite conversation in 883 is recorded. Charles and his court were familiar with Notker's ideas and intentions and would certainly have understood even the most allusive of his comments.

Secondly, what was the intended use of the *Deeds*? Previous commentators have rightly pointed out that it was supposed to amuse the court, the anecdotal form providing an aid to its easy digestion. Whatever their more serious points, the lampoons of idiotic bishops of Mainz, vacuous foreign rulers and ludicrous Vikings must have been designed to elicit laughter. As a text with a small but prestigious court audience it stands along with many of the other works of political theory and commentary produced by the Carolingian Renaissance. The *Deeds* represents a quite

---

[139] B. Bischoff, 'Bücher am Hofe Ludwigs des Deutschen und die Privatbibliothek des Kanzlers Grimalt', in his *Mittelalterliche Studien. Ausgewählte Aufsätze zur Schriftkunde und Literaturgeschichte*, (vol. 3, Stuttgart, 1981), pp. 187–212, at pp. 173, 199.

[140] Wallace-Hadrill, 'Carolingian Renaissance Prince', p. 156; Ganz, 'Humour as History', p. 173.

[141] Notker, *Gesta*, 2.16, p. 80. Löwe, 'Das Karlsbuch Notkers', p. 136 thought that Notker, *Gesta*, 2.17, p. 85 may contain a reference to professional historians at court, from whom Notker is quick to distance himself: 'I leave this for others to write, who follow your highness not for love but in the hope of gain.'

[142] Rankin, 'Ego itaque Notker scripsi', *Revue Bénédicitine* 101 (1991), 292–5.

[143] Lehmann, *Bibliothekskataloge*, p. 73.

Notker's Deeds of Charlemagne

traditional mingling of exaltation of the ruler on the one hand and, on the other, exhortations to better Christian kingship in general as well as to the accomplishment of specific goals.

Ultimately, however, Notker's messages never reached the court. Although there is no way to determine absolutely whether the sudden mid-sentence break in book 2 was the point at which Notker stopped working or is the result of a corruption in the manuscript tradition, the former seems more likely. Evidence for contemporary circulation is totally lacking, interest in the text only picking up in the twelfth century in association with the growth of the cult of Charlemagne.[144] We need not ascribe the breaking off of the text to the deposition of Charles the Fat, as it must have been written *before* the end of May 887.[145] A more likely cause of its non-delivery to its commissioner is the expulsion of Liutward of Vercelli from court and his replacement by Liutbert of Mainz, which took place at exactly this time. The emperor would not have looked favourably on criticism of Liutbert now that he had become his archchancellor, archchaplain and chief adviser. Accordingly, it is at this point that Liutbert's mouthpiece, the Mainz annalist, ended his diatribe against the emperor and shifted to a pro-Charles outlook.

Moreover, the political rhetoric that informed the content and structure of the *Deeds of Charlemagne* had by this time come to seem redundant. The imperial claims and Charlemagne associations which had been appropriate to the political situation at the time of commissioning in 885 were consciously toned down by the emperor in 886.[146] As Notker wrote the second part of the *Deeds* in that year it was becoming increasingly clear that Charles the Fat's persistent failure to solve his succession problem was a major threat to political stability. While Notker's astute political commentary remained relevant, by early 887 the flattering rhetoric was embarrassingly out of date. The gap between ideal and reality had become too wide for the propaganda to be convincing. If Charles the Fat did ever read a version of the *Deeds*, he may well have considered himself appropriately flattered and morally edified. However, he is unlikely to have found its anecdotes terribly amusing as Notker's portentous predictions in book 2 were proved accurate by the sequence of events which brought his reign to a disastrous and premature end.

---

[144] Haefele's introduction, pp. xxiii–xxvii.

[145] Charles did confirm St-Gall's privileges on 30 May 887, a date highlighted by Notker, *Gesta*, 2.pref., p. 48, as reserved by the monks for commemoration of his friend Werinbert: Innes, 'Memory, Orality and Literacy', pp. 20–1. This need not mean that Charles had read the work: he was, it is clear, well-enough acquainted with St-Gall traditions and observances long before 887.

[146] See above, pp. 158–60.

Chapter 8

CONCLUSION

The deposition and death of Charles the Fat marked the end of an era. Contemporaries recognised the event's significance. The fullest verdict was that of Regino of Prüm, writing in 908:

After Charles's death the kingdoms which had obeyed his authority, as if lacking a lawful heir, dissolved into separate parts and, without waiting for their natural lord, each chose a king from within its own innards. This was the origin of great wars; not that the Franks lacked princes who by nobility, courage and wisdom were capable of ruling kingdoms but rather because the equality of descent, authority, and power increased the discord among them: none so outshone the others that the rest deigned to submit to his rule.[1]

The other major author to comment on the events of the year 888 was the Bavarian continuator of the *Annals of Fulda*, who famously stated that after Charles's death 'many kinglets [*reguli*] sprang up in Europe, that is to say in the kingdom of [Arnulf's] uncle Charles'.[2] The importance which these writers laid on the emperor's death was not, of course, objective political analysis. Both of them had axes to grind. Regino's account was coloured by his own experiences: he himself had become a casualty of a particularly murky power-struggle in 890s Lotharingia, during which he was forcibly removed from the abbacy of Prüm, and this informed his bemoaning of the lack of royal authority. The Bavarian annalist, on the other hand, was writing to justify the rise to power of Arnulf. He was quick to claim that the *reguli* had made *themselves* kings, and cast further aspersions on their legitimacy by pointedly listing the names of their non-Carolingian fathers. Arnulf was a *rex*, not a *regulus*, acclaimed by nobles from all over the east Frankish kingdom, and the continuator even implicitly asserted his overlordship over the others by describing how they each came to him to receive his grace.

However, it is important to note that both authors identified the crisis 888 as dynastic in nature. This point is worth dwelling on. Clearly, the

[1] Regino, *Chronicon*, s.a. 888, p. 129; translated by Reuter, *Annals of Fulda*, p. 115, n. 2.
[2] *AF(B)* s.a. 888, p. 116.

230

Conclusion

Carolingian dynasty *per se* did not vanish with the death of Charles the Fat. Arnulf himself was the son of a legitimate Carolingian king, others among the *reguli* were descended from Charlemagne in the female line, and in west Francia direct male-line descendants of Charles the Bald continued to hold royal power intermittently until 987. Carolingian blood still meant something for at least a century after 888. Despite all this, it was extremely significant that Arnulf was illegitimate. As Stuart Airlie has argued, an overlooked achievement and fundamental basis of Carolingian rule up until 888 was the establishment and maintenance of the political myth that its existence was normal and natural.[3] This myth was expressed in the language of legitimacy of birth: only legitimate-born male Carolingians were perceived to be rightful candidates for kingship throughout the ninth century, which is why aristocratic rebellions usually coalesced round a member of the royal house. Even the usurper Boso tried to legitimise his actions by claiming a form of fictive 'full' Carolingianness based on his relationship to the imperial family via his wife.[4] The effect was not to brainwash the aristocracy into blind loyalty towards their kings: indeed, at points of tension alternative allegiances, such as those relating to family or regional identity, could cut across the demands made by rulers and surface as expressions of disloyalty. This is why an opportunist like Boso, reacting to the power-vacuum created by the dispute over the succession to Louis the Stammerer, was able to conceive of seizing a crown for himself in the first place, and why he was able to win over eminent supporters to his cause.

Carolingianness was therefore not the only political discourse available in the ninth century. However, it was the most important discourse for those who, like Boso, wished to be regarded as legitimate kings. 888 necessarily changed this dynastic situation. Arnulf was self-evidently not a legitimate Carolingian, despite the attempts by favourable writers such as the Bavarian continuator to gloss over this fact. As a bastard, he did not have enough credibility to be able to take over control of the whole empire of his uncle, and his direct power was limited to the kingdom east of the Rhine (and, later, south of the Alps). The very fact of his illegitimacy gave a basis for female-line and non-Carolingians to bid for the crowns of the other *regna*. The Carolingian male-line monopoly on kingship was gone, and the field was opened to a myriad of potential claimants, many of whom traded on their more or less distant relationship to the dynasty, but none of whom was the legitimate son of a ruling king. The 'myth'

---

[3] Airlie, '*Semper fideles?*'

[4] Airlie, 'Political Behaviour of Secular Magnates', pp. 275–86, 289–90; MacLean, 'Carolingian Response to the Revolt of Boso', p. 24.

231

Kingship and Politics in the Late Ninth Century

of exclusive Carolingian royal legitimacy could not exist independently of legitimate Carolingians able to lay claim to it.[5] The crucial factor was simply that when Charles the Fat was deposed, there were no adult male legitimate-born Carolingians available to take over, thanks to the high number of premature deaths in the family since the mid-870s. Only Charles the Simple was left, but his minority rendered him unable to push a claim until the damage had been done.

The dynastic crisis of 888 therefore resulted in the definitive breaking up of the Carolingian empire, the last pan-(western) European polity of the Middle Ages, and the appearance of new royal dynasties. However, the roots of this crisis were not deep. Opposition to Carolingian authority *per se* was not the issue. If it had been, why did the west Franks turn to Charles the Fat in 884–5 and not choose a king from among their own number? The end of the Carolingian monopoly on royal legitimacy, and hence of the empire as a territorial unit, was not inevitable, but resulted from a confluence of events and circumstances whose causes lay in recent political history rather than buried deep in the structures of the polity. The aristocracy did not 'rise'. The *reguli* were indeed powerful regional aristocrats. This explains how they were able to make bids for crowns in 887–8; but on its own it does not explain why they tried in the first place.

Clearly, these conclusions have implications for how we should evaluate the reign of Charles the Fat. He was not, even with the best will in the world, a 'great king'. His record against the Vikings was not unequivocally impressive, even if it was no worse than that of other contemporary rulers, while his stubborn attempts at solving the succession problem after 885 were, with the benefit of hindsight, misjudged, and ultimately a major factor in his downfall. Nevertheless, those very attempts were implemented with no small degree of imagination and political ambition, as seen most clearly in the staged ideological claims of late 885 and early 886. Moreover, the situation had only become so critical because of the vagaries of chance which depleted the ranks of the dynasty in the early 880s and caused the unravelling of the Vienne agreement which had been concluded at the end of the war against Boso. Charles's response to the challenges of governing the whole empire, which he had been forced to face because of the way events had transpired, was nothing if not positive. His itinerary reveals him to have been exceptionally mobile, his charters show his vigorous and effective cultivation of local political networks, while his establishment of common interests with the *marchiones* shows practicality and, unsurprisingly, a willingness to adhere to traditional Carolingian methods of ruling through the aristocracy. In

---

[5] Cf. Brühl, *Deutschland-Frankreich*, p. 373.

Conclusion

his reign, Carolingian rule continued to perform its traditional functions as a focal point for the realm and a source of legitimacy for the regional power of important aristocrats. It remained culturally and politically relevant. The problems the emperor faced, and the solutions he tried, were broadly similar to those which characterised every other reign of the period: he was, in short, a typical Carolingian, no more and no less. Charles has been judged on the wrong criteria. He may not have been a great king, but he was by no means a bad or failed one.

In view of this, his reign can no longer be allowed to stand as an emblem for a general decline of Carolingian power in the later ninth century. The teleological models of long-term change which conventionally function as the interpretative keys to this period serve to obscure the more specific contexts of the sources, and to bludgeon off their nuances. When encountered in the late ninth century, the power of members of the high nobility, especially those who we know were soon to become kings, has usually been read as a sign of a glacial process of irresistible historical change in its final stages. However, a strong landed aristocracy, like many of the political phenomena we have observed in the twilight of the Carolingian empire, was in fact an underlying feature of the early medieval world as a whole. When we put the evidence back in the context from which it emerged, it reveals patterns of political power which were entirely appropriate to the circumstances and exigencies of the 870s and 880s. Only when the political narrative for these decades is satisfactorily and critically worked out is it valid to generalise about their place in the overall course of Carolingian history. As it stands at the moment, the accepted grand narrative of decline and fall is not founded on an assimilation of all (or even most of) the available evidence. The historiographical constructs of a 'decline in royal authority' and consonant 'rise of the aristocracy' as generalised phenomena of the period before 888 must be readdressed if they are to retain any validity, but this book has suggested that they may no longer be relevant at all.

If we dispense with the graph of decline which is generally used to plot the trajectory of political power in late ninth-century Europe, then we also need to rethink the implications of this for our understanding of the tenth century, when royal authority is usually thought to have flat-lined. Although the dynastic crisis of 888 did herald the disintegration of the empire as a unit, in terms of the vocabulary, shape and structure of politics there were many continuities. The post-imperial kingdoms, principalities and duchies emerged from units and communities which had been created or endorsed by the Carolingians. Tenth- and even eleventh-century rulers continued to think of themselves as part of a greater Frankish world, not yet 'German' or 'French'. The mechanisms of rule through

Kingship and Politics in the Late Ninth Century

the patronage of regional elites remained crucial: there was no revolution in the nature and patterns of local power.[6] There was certainly disruption, particularly as regional aristocracies jostled for position in the wake of the splintering of the empire in 888. However, the political history of the tenth-century European kingdoms, especially France and Italy, needs further research; and much evidence, particularly charters, awaits full exploitation. Much of the historiography of this period, up to and including the debate over the so-called 'feudal revolution' around the millennium, is informed by the perceived decline of the 'public power' of the Carolingian empire. If we accept that the traditional picture of the late ninth century is in important respects mistaken, then we also have to recalibrate our interpretations and expectations of the succeeding period.

The repercussions of the end of the Carolingian royal monopoly therefore remain to be fully explored. Moreover, many aspects of ninth-century politics themselves deserve reconsideration, especially from the perspective of the localities upwards. The conclusions of this book are not intended to imply that the Carolingian polity was perfectly balanced, that its ever-continuing equilibrium was only disturbed by a chance biological crisis in the main blood line. The Vikings, for example, had certainly placed a premium on the successful maintenance of the links between centre and periphery: who knows how these mechanisms would have held up under the Magyar onslaughts of the 890s and 900s? Or perhaps another Boso, this time more successful, would have appeared to take advantage of some new political crisis or other. By its very nature, the stability of early medieval politics was always vulnerable to the kind of dynastic dispute which shattered the empire in 887–8. However, the fact is that, as long as we bear in mind the comparatively limited scope of early medieval government, the structures of Carolingian authority worked, and kept on working right up until 887. As an overall conclusion, it is therefore important to stress that the political crisis caused by the lack of a satisfactory solution to the succession problems of 884–7 preceded, and hence was not caused by, the disappearance of Carolingian credibility and power. Regino's much-quoted analysis of the equality of the new rulers, with which we began this chapter, was astute: in contrast to 751, no family was strong enough in 888 to take over the Carolingian family business wholesale. What is less frequently stressed is Regino's opening phrase: the rise of the new order took place, he tells us, 'after Charles's death'. The families of the high aristocracy did not 'rise' slowly

[6] Innes, *State and Society*, pp. 222–50.

234

Conclusion

to their royal and ducal positions: they stepped out from the shadow of the Carolingians after the fizzling out of the legitimate male royal line. The death without heir of Charles the Fat caused the definitive end of the Frankish empire and helped to crystallise the political geography of high medieval Europe. In this sense at least, the year 888 can be said to have marked the beginning of a long tenth century.

BIBLIOGRAPHY

1. PRIMARY SOURCES

Abbo, *Bella Parisiacae Urbis*, ed. H. Waquet, *Abbon. Le Siège de Paris par les Normands* (Paris, 1942).

Andreas of Bergamo, *Historia*, ed. G. Waitz, MGH SRL (Hanover, 1878), pp. 220–30.

Annales Alamannici, ed. W. Lendi, *Untersuchungen zur frühalemannischen Annalistik. Die Murbacher Annalen, mit Edition* (Freiburg, 1971).

Annales Bertiniani, eds. F. Grat, J. Vielliard, S. Clémencet and L. Levillain, *Annales de Saint-Bertin* (Paris, 1964).

Annales Fuldenses, ed. F. Kurze, MGH SRG (Hanover, 1891).

Annales Hildesheimenses, ed. G. Waitz, MGH SRG (Hanover, 1878).

Annales Iuvavenses, ed. H. Bresslau, MGH SS 30 (Hanover, 1926), pp. 727–44.

Annales Regni Francorum, ed. F. Kurze, MGH SRG (Hanover, 1895).

Annales Xantenses et Annales Vedastini, ed. B. von Simson, MGH SRG (Hanover, 1909).

Asser, *De Rebus Gestis AElfredi*, ed. W. H. Stevenson (Oxford, 1959).

Bautier, R.-H. (ed.), *Recueil des actes d'Eudes, roi de France (888–898)* (Paris, 1967).

Benassi, U. (ed.), *Codice diplomatico Parmense* (vol. 1, Parma, 1910).

Bischoff, B. (ed.), *Anecdota Novissima: Texte des vierten bis sechzehnten Jahrhunderts* (Stuttgart, 1984).

Bitterauf, T. (ed.), *Die Traditionen des Hochstiftes Freising* (Munich, 1905 and 1909).

Böhmer, J. F. and Mühlbacher, E., *Regesta Imperii. Die Regesten des Kaiserreichs unter den Karolingern, 751–918* (Innsbruck, 1908).

Bruckner, A., *Regesta Alsatiae Aevi Merovingici et Karolini 496–918. I. Quellenband* (Strasbourg and Zurich, 1949).

Capitula Electionis Hludowici Balbi Compendii Facta, ed. A Boretius and V. Krause, MGH Capit (vol. 2, Hanover, 1897), no. 283.

Collectio Sangallensis, ed. K. Zeumer, MGH Formulae Merowingici et Karolini Aevi (Hanover, 1886), pp. 390–437.

Conventus Carisiacensis, ed. A. Boretius and V. Krause, MGH Capit (vol. 2, Hanover, 1897), nos. 281–2.

Conventus Mantalensis, ed. A. Boretius and V. Krause, MGH Capit (vol. 2, Hanover, 1897), no. 284.

De conversione Bagoariorum et Carantanorum Libellus, ed. G.H. Pertz, MGH SS (vol. 11, Hanover, 1854), pp. 1–15.

Dhuoda, *Liber Manualis*, ed. P. Riché (Paris, 1975).

Bibliography

Doniol, H. (ed.), *Cartulaire de Brioude* (Clermont and Paris, 1863).

Einhard, *Vita Karoli*, ed. O. Holder-Egger, MGH SRG (Hanover, 1911).

Ekkehard, *Casus S. Galli*, ed. H. F. Haefele, *St. Galler Klostergeschichten* (vol. 10, Darmstadt, 1980).

Erchempert, *Historia Langobardorum et Beneventanorum*, ed. G. Waitz, MGH SRL, pp. 231–64.

Escher, J. and Schweizer, P. (eds.), *Urkundenbuch der Stadt und Landschaft Zürich* (vol. 1, Zurich, 1888).

Falconi, E. (ed.), *Le Carte Cremonesi dei Secoli VIII–XII* (Cremona, 1979).

Flodoard, *Historia Remensis Ecclesiae*, eds. I. Heller and G. Waitz, MGH SS (vol. 13, Hanover, 1881), pp. 405–599.

Fragmenta Registri Stephani V. Papae, ed. E. Caspar, MGH Epp (vol. 7, Berlin, 1928), pp. 334–53.

Gesta Berengarii imperatoris, ed. P. Winterfeld, MGH Poetae (vol. 4, Berlin, 1899), pp. 354–403.

Gesta Pontificum Autissiodorensium, ed. L. M. Duru, *Bibliothèque historique de l'Yonne* I (1859), pp. 309–509.

Glöckner, K. (ed.), *Codex Laureshamensis* (Darmstadt, 1929–36).

Grat, F., de Font-Réaulx, J., Tessier, G. and Bautier, R.-H. (eds.), *Recueil des actes de Louis II le Bègue, Louis III et Carloman II, rois de France (877–884)* (Paris, 1978).

Hermann of Reichenau, *Chronicon*, ed. G. H. Pertz, MGH SS (vol. 5, Hanover, 1844), pp. 67–133.

Hincmar, *Ad Carolum III imperatorem*, PL 125, cols. 991–2.

De Ordine Palatii, eds. T. Gross and R. Schieffer, MGH Fontes (Hanover, 1980).

Instructio ad Ludowicum Balbum regem, PL 125, cols. 983–90.

Hludowicus Regis Arelatensis Electio, ed. A. Boretius and V. Krause, MGH Capit (vol. 2, Hanover, 1897), no. 289.

John, H., *Collectio Canonum Remedio Curiensi Episcopo Perperam Ascripta*, Monumenta Iuris Canonici, series B (vol. 2, Vatican, 1976).

Karolomanni Capitula Compendii de Rapinis Promulgata, ed. A. Boretius and V. Krause, MGH Capit (vol. 2, Hanover, 1897), no. 286.

Karolomanni Conventus Carisiacensis, ed. A. Boretius and V. Krause, MGH Capit (vol. 2, Hanover, 1897), no. 285.

Kehr, P. (ed.), *Die Urkunden Arnulfs*, MGH Diplomata regum Germaniae ex stirpe Karolinorum (vol. 3, Berlin, 1940).

(ed.), *Die Urkunden Karls III.*, MGH Diplomata regum Germaniae ex stirpe Karolinorum (vol. 2, Berlin, 1936–7).

(ed.), *Die Urkunden Ludwigs des Deutschen, Karlmanns und Ludwigs des Jüngeren*, MGH Diplomata regum Germaniae ex stirpe Karolinorum (vol. 1, Berlin, 1932–4).

Lauer, P. (ed.), *Recueil des actes de Charles III le Simple, roi de France (893–923)* (Paris, 1949).

Lechner, J., 'Verlorene Urkunden', in Böhmer and Mühlbacher, *Regesta Imperii*, pp. 839–73.

Lehmann, P. (ed.), *Mittelalterliche Bibliothekskataloge Deutschlands und der Schweiz. I. Band: Die Bistümer Konstanz und Chur* (Munich, 1918).

Bibliography

Liber Memorialis Romaricensis, ed. E. Hlawitschka, K. Schmid and G. Tellenbach, MGH Libri Memoriales (vol. 1, Dublin and Zurich, 1970).

Liber Pontificalis, ed. L. Duchesne (Paris, 1955–7).

Libri Confraternitatum Sancti Galli, Augiensis, Fabariensis, ed. P. Piper, MGH (Berlin, 1884).

Liudprand of Cremona, *Antapodosis*, ed. J. Becher, MGH SRG (Hanover and Leipzig, 1915).

Ludwigslied, ed. J. K. Bostock, *A Handbook of Old High German Literature* 2nd edn (Oxford, 1976), pp. 239–41.

Mabillon, J., *Vetera Analecta*, 2nd edn (Paris, 1723).

Merlet, R. (ed.), *La Chronique de Nantes*, Collection de textes pour servir à l'Étude et à l'Enseignement de l'Histoire (vol. 19, Paris, 1896).

Meyer-Marthaler, E. and Perret, F. (eds.), *Bündner Urkundenbuch* (vol. 1, Chur, 1947–56).

Miracula S. Opportunae, in Acta Sanctorum Aprilis III (Antwerp, 1675).

Notker, *Erchanberti Breviarium Continuatio*, ed. G. H. Pertz, MGH SS (vol. 2, Hanover, 1829), pp. 329–30.

    Gesta Karoli Magni, ed. H. F. Haefele, *Notker der Stammler, Taten Kaiser Karls des Großen*, MGH SRG NS (Berlin, 1959).

    Liber Ymnorum, ed. W. von den Steinen, *Notker der Dichter und seine geistige Welt. Editionsband* (Bern, 1948), pp. 8–91.

    Notatio, ed. E. Raumer, *Mittellateinisches Jahrbuch* 21 (1986).

Odonis Regis Promissio, ed. A. Boretius and V. Krause, MGH Capit (vol. 2, Hanover, 1897), no. 288.

Önnefors, U., *Abbo von Saint-Germain-des-Prés. 22 Predigten. Kritische Aufgabe und Kommentar* (Frankfurt, Berne, New York and Nancy, 1985).

Pactiones Aquenses, ed. A. Boretius and V. Krause, MGH Capit (vol. 2, Hanover, 1897), no. 250.

Poeta Saxo, *Annalium de Gestis Caroli Magni Imperatoris Libri Quinque*, ed. P. von Winterfeld, MGH Poetae (vol. 4, Hanover, 1899), pp. 1–71.

Poupardin, R. (ed.), *Recueil des actes des Rois de Provence (855–928)* (Paris, 1920).

Pseudo-Cyprian, *De XII abusivis saeculi*, ed. S. Hellmann, *Texte und Untersuchungen zur Geschichte der altchristlichen Literatur*, 3rd series, 4 (1909), 1–60.

Ratpert, *De casibus monasterii S. Galli liber*, PL 126, cols. 1057–80.

Regino, *Chronicon*, ed. F. Kurze, *Reginonis abbatis Prumiensis Chronicon cum continuatione Treverensi*, MGH SRG (Hanover, 1890).

    De Synodalibus Causis, ed. F. G. A. Wasserschleben (Leipzig, 1840).

Registrum Johannes VIII. Papae, ed. E. Caspar, MGH Epp (vol. 7, Berlin, 1928), pp. 1–272.

Roserot, A., 'Chartes inédites des IXe et Xe siècles', in *Bulletin de la Société des Sciences historiques et naturelles de l'Yonne* (1898), 161–207.

Schiaparelli, L. (ed.), *I Diplomi di Berengario I*, Fonti per la Storia d'Italia (vol. 35, Rome, 1903).

Schieffer, T. (ed.), *Die Urkunden Lothars I. und Lothars II.*, MGH Diplomata Karolinorum (vol. 3, Berlin, 1966).

    (ed.), *Die Urkunden Zwentibolds und Ludwigs des Kinds*, MGH Diplomata regum Germaniae ex stirpe Karolinorum (vol. 4, Berlin, 1960).

Bibliography

Schieffer, T. and Mayer, H. E. (eds.), *Die Urkunden der burgundischen Rudolfinger*, MGH Regum Burgundiae e stirpe Rudolfina diplomata et acta (Munich, 1977).

Sedulius Scottus, *Liber de rectoribus christianis, PL* 103, cols. 291–330.

Sermo in tumulatione SS. Quintini, Victorici, Cassiani, ed. O. Holder-Egger, MGH SS (vol. 15, Hanover, 1887), pp. 271–3.

Sickel, T. (ed.), *Die Urkunden Konrad I., Heinrich I. und Otto I.*, MGH Diplomata regum et imperatorem Germaniae (vol. 1, Hanover, 1879–84).

(ed.), *Die Urkunden Ottos des II. und Ottos des III.*, MGH Diplomata regum et imperatorum Germaniae II/i–ii (Berlin, 1888–93).

Tessier, G. et al. (eds.), *Recueil des actes de Charles II le Chauve* (Paris, 1943–55).

Thegan, *Gesta Hludowici imperatoris*, ed. E. Tremp, MGH SRG (Hanover, 1995).

Visio Karoli, ed. G. Waitz, MGH SS (vol. 10, Hanover, 1852), p. 458.

Vita Verenae, in Reinle, *Die heilige Verena*, pp. 26–31.

Von den Steinen, W. (ed.), *Notker der Dichter und seine geistige Welt. Editionsband* (Bern, 1948).

Wartmann, H. (ed.), *Urkundenbuch der Abtei St.Gallen* (Zurich, 1863–6).

Widemann, J. (ed.), *Die Traditionen des Hochstifts Regensburg und des Klosters St. Emmeram* (Munich, 1943).

2. SECONDARY SOURCES

Abels, R., *Lordship and Military Obligation in Anglo-Saxon England* (London, 1988).

Airlie, S., 'After Empire: Recent Work on the Emergence of Post-Carolingian Kingdoms', *EME* 2 (1993), 153–61.

'Narratives of Triumph and Rituals of Submission: Charlemagne's Mastering of Bavaria', *TRHS*, 6th series, 9 (1999), 93–119.

'Private Bodies and the Body Politic in the Divorce Case of Lothar II', *Past and Present* 161 (1998), 3–38.

'*Semper fideles?* Loyauté envers les carolingiens comme constituant de l'identité aristocratique', in Le Jan (ed.), *La Royauté et les élites*, pp. 129–43.

'The Aristocracy', in *NCMH2*, pp. 431–50.

'The Nearly Men: Boso of Vienne and Arnulf of Bavaria', in A. Duggan (ed.), *Nobles and Nobility in Medieval Europe* (Woodbridge, 2000), pp. 25–41.

'The Palace of Memory: the Carolingian Court as Political Centre', in S. Rees-Jones, R. Marks and A. Minnis (eds.), *Courts and Regions in Medieval Europe* (Woodbridge, 2000), pp. 1–20.

'The Political Behaviour of Secular Magnates in Francia, 829–79', D.Phil. thesis, University of Oxford (1985).

'True Teachers and Pious Kings: Salzburg, Louis the German, and Christian Order', in R. Gameson and H. Leyser (eds.), *Belief and Culture in the Middle Ages* (Oxford, 2001).

Carolingian Politics (forthcoming).

Alibert, D., '*Semen eius in aeternum manebit*... Remarques sur l'engendrement royal à l'époque carolingienne', in M. Rouche (ed.), *Mariage et sexualité au Moyen Age. Accord ou crise?* (Paris, 2000), pp. 135–45.

Bibliography

Althoff, G., 'Breisach- ein Refugium für Rebellen im frühen Mittelalter?', in Nuber et al. (eds.), *Archäologie und Geschichte*, pp. 457–72.

'Gandersheim und Quedlinburg. Ottonische Frauenklöster als Herrschafts- und Überlieferungszentren', *FMSt* 25 (1991), 123–44.

Angenendt, A., *Kaiserherrschaft und Königstaufe. Kaiser, Könige und Päpste als geistliche Patrone in der abendländischen Missiongeschichte* (Berlin and New York, 1984).

Anton, H. H., 'Pseudo-Cyprian. De duodecim abusivis saeculi und sein Einfluß auf den Kontinent, insbesondere auf die karolingischen Fürstenspiegel', in H. Löwe (ed.), *Die Iren und Europa im früheren Mittelalter* (Stuttgart, 1982), pp. 568–617.

Fürstenspiegel und Herrscherethos in der Karolingerzeit (Bonn, 1968).

Arnaldi, G., 'Pavia e il *Regnum Italiae* dal 774 al 1024', *Atti del 4 congresso internazionale di studi sull'alto medioevo* (Spoleto, 1969), pp. 175–87.

Arnold, B., *Medieval Germany, 500–1300. A Political Interpretation* (London, 1997).

Princes and Territories in Medieval Germany (Cambridge, 1991).

Atsma, H. (ed.), *La Neustrie. Les pays au nord de la Loire de 650 à 850* (2 vols., Sigmaringen, 1989).

Auzias, L., *L'Aquitaine carolingienne (778–987)* (Toulouse and Paris, 1937).

Barthélemy, D., 'Debate: the "Feudal Revolution" I', *Past and Present* 152 (1996), 196–205.

'La chevalerie carolingienne: prélude su XIe siècle', in Le Jan (ed.), *La Royauté et les élites*, pp. 159–75.

Bartlett, R., *The Making of Europe. Conquest, Colonization and Cultural Change 950–1350* (London, 1993).

Trial by Fire and Water. The Medieval Judicial Ordeal (Oxford, 1986).

Bauduin, P., 'La frontière normande aux Xe–XIe siècles: origine et maitrise politique de la frontière sur les confins de la haute Normandie (911–1087)', Thèse de doctorat, University of Caen (1998).

Bautier, R.-H., 'Aux origines du royaume de Provence: de la sédition avortée de Boson à la royauté légitime de Louis', *Provence historique* 23 (1973), 41–68. Repr. in Bautier, *Recherches sur l'histoire de la France médiévale.*

'Le règne d'Eudes (888–898) à la lumière des diplômes expédiés par sa chancellerie', *Comptes rendus de l'académie des inscriptions et belles-lettres* (1961), 140–57.

'Les diplômes royaux carolingiens pour l'église de Langres et l'origine des droits comtaux de l'éveque', in Bautier, *Chartes, sceaux et chancelleries. Études de diplomatique et de sigillographie médiévales* (vol. 1, Paris, 1990), pp. 209–42.

'Les Poids de la Neustrie ou de la France du nord-ouest dans la monarchie carolingienne unitair d'après les diplômes de la chancellerie royale (751–840)', in Atsma (ed.), *La Neustrie*, vol. 2, pp. 535–63. Repr. in Bautier, *Recherches sur l'histoire de la France Médiévale.*

Recherches sur l'histoire de la France médiévale. Des Mérovingiens aux premier Capétiens (Aldershot, 1991).

Becher, H., 'Das königliche Frauenkloster San Salvatore/Santa Giulia in Brescia im Spiegel seiner Memorialüberlieferung', *FMSt* 17 (1983), 299–392.

Becher, M., *Rex, Dux und Gens. Untersuchungen zur Entstehung des sächsischen Herzogtums im 9. und 10. Jahrhundert* (Husum, 1996).

Bentley, M. (ed.), *Companion to Historiography* (London and New York, 1997).

Bibliography

Berner, H. (ed.), *Bodman. Dorf, Kaiserpfalz, Adel* (Sigmaringen, 1977).

Berschin, W., *Biographie und Epochenstil im lateinischen Mittelalter* (Stuttgart, 1991).

Bertels, K., 'Carantania. Beobachtungen zur politisch-geographischen Terminologie und zur Geschichte des Landes und seiner Bevölkerung im frühen Mittelalter', *Carinthia I* 177 (1987), 87–196.

Billoret, R., 'Grand. Le site gallo-romain. Les nouvelles fouilles 1960–2. La Mosaïque', *Le Pays Lorraine* 44 (1963), 49–80.

Bischoff, B., 'Bücher am Hofe Ludwigs des Deutschen und die Privatbibliothek des Kanzlers Grimalt', in Bischoff, *Mittelalterliche Studien. Ausgewählte Aufsätze zur Schriftkunde und Literaturgeschichte* (vol. 3, Stuttgart, 1981), pp. 187–212.

Borgolte, M., 'Die Geschichte der Grafengewalt im Elsaß von Dagobert I. bis Otto dem Großen', *ZGO* 131 (1983), 3–54.

'Karl III. und Neudingen. Zum Problem der Nachfolgeregelung Ludwigs des Deutschen', *ZGO* 125 (1977), 21–55.

Die Grafen Alemanniens im merowingischer und karolingischer Zeit. Eine Prosopographie (Sigmaringen, 1986).

Geschichte der Grafschaften Alemanniens in fränkischer Zeit (Sigmaringen, 1984).

Borst, A., 'Die Pfalz Bodman', in Berner (ed.), *Bodman*, pp. 169–230.

Bougard, F., 'La cour et le gouvernement de Louis II (840–875)', in Le Jan (ed.), *La Royauté et les élites*, pp. 249–67.

'Palais princiers, royaux et imperiaux de l'Italie carolingienne et ottonienne', in Renoux (ed.), *Palais royaux et princiers*, pp. 181–94.

La Justice dans le royaume d'Italie de la fin du VIIIe siècle au début du XIe siècle (Rome, 1995).

review of K. Wanner, *Die Urkunden Ludwigs II*, *Francia* 24 (1997), 211–13.

Bowlus, C. R., 'Imre Boba's Reconstructions of Moravia's Early History and Arnulf of Carinthia's *Ostpolitik* (887–892)', *Speculum* 62 (1987), 552–74.

Franks, Moravians and Magyars. The Struggle for the Middle Danube, 788–907 (Philadelphia, 1995).

Braunfels, W. (ed.), *Karl der Grosse. Lebenswerk und Nachleben* (5 vols., Düsseldorf, 1965–7).

Brown, G. P. A., 'Politics and Patronage at the Abbey of St-Denis (814–98): the Rise of a Royal Patron Saint', D.Phil. thesis, University of Oxford (1989).

Brühl, C., 'Das Palatium von Pavia und die *Honorantiae civitatis Papiae*', *Atti del 4 congresso*, pp. 189–220.

'Fränkischer Krönungsbrauch und das Problem der "Festkrönungen"', *HZ* 194 (1962), 265–326.

Deutschland-Frankreich: Die Geburt zweier Völker (Cologne and Vienna, 1990).

Fodrum, Gistum, Servitium Regis. Studien zu den wirtschaftlichen Grundlagen des Königtums im Frankenreich und in der fränkischen Nachfolgestaaten Deutschland, Frankreich und Italien vom 6. bis zur Mitte des 14. Jahrhunderts (Cologne, 1968).

Palatium und Civitas. Studien zur Profantopographie spätantiker Civitates vom 3. bis 13. Jahrhundert (Cologne and Vienna, 1975).

Brunner, K., 'Der fränkische Fürstentitel im neunten und zehnten Jahrhundert', in Wolfram (ed.), *Intitulatio II.*, pp. 179–340.

Oppositionelle Gruppen im Karolingerreich (Vienna, Cologne and Graz, 1979).

Bibliography

Brunold, U. and Deplazes, L. (eds.), *Geschichte und Kultur Churrätiens. Festschrift für Pater Iso Müller OSB zu seinem 85. Geburtstag* (Disentis, 1986).

Brunterc'h, J. P., 'Naissance et affirmation des principautés au temps du roi Eudes: l'exemple de l'Aquitaine', in Guillot and Favreau (eds.), *Pays de Loire*, pp. 69–116.

Buc, P., 'Ritual and Interpretation: the Early Medieval Case', *EME* 9 (2000), 183–210.

The Dangers of Ritual. Between Early Medieval Texts and Social Scientific Theory (Princeton and Oxford, 2001).

Bührer-Thierry, G., ' "Just Anger" or "Vengeful Anger"? The Punishment of Blinding in the Early Medieval West', in B. Rosenwein (ed.), *Anger's Past. The Social Uses of an Emotion in the Middle Ages* (Ithaca, 1998), pp. 75–91.

'La reine adultère', *Cahiers de civilisation médiévale Xe–XIIe siècles* 35 (1992), 299–312.

'Le conseiller du roi: les écrivains carolingiens et la tradition biblique', *Médiévales* 12 (1987), 111–23.

'Les évêques de Bavière et d'Alémanie dans l'entourage des derniers rois carolingiens en Germanie (876–911)', *Francia* 16 (1989), 31–52.

Évêques et pouvoir dans le royaume de Germanie. Les Églises de Bavière et de Souabe, 876–973 (Paris, 1997).

Bulst, W., '*Susceptacula regum*. Zur Kunde deutscher Reichsaltertümer', in Bulst, *Lateinisches Mittelalter: Gesammelte Beiträge* (Heidelberg, 1984), pp. 130–68.

Bund, K., *Thronsturz und Herrscherabsetzung im Frühmittelalter* (Bonn, 1979).

Büttner, H., 'Erzbischof Liutbert von Mainz und die Rechtstellung der Klöster', in G. Droege et al. (eds.), *Landschaft und Geschichte. Festschrift für Franz Petri zu seinem 65. Geburtstag* (Bonn, 1970), pp. 104–15.

Geschichte des Elsaß I. Politische Geschichte des Landes von der Landnahmezeit bis zum Tod Ottos III. und ausgewählte Beiträge zur Geschichte des Elsaß im Früh- und Hochmittelalter (Sigmaringen, 1991).

Cameron, A., 'The Construction of Court Ritual: the Byzantine *Book of Ceremonies*', in D. Cannadine and S. Price (eds.), *Rituals of Royalty. Power and Ceremonial in Traditional Societies* (Cambridge, 1987), pp. 106–36.

Campbell, J. (ed.), *The Anglo-Saxons* (London, 1982).

Carroll, C. J., 'The Bishoprics of Saxony in the First Century after Christianization', *EME* 8 (1999), 219–45.

'The Archbishops and Church Councils of Mainz and Cologne During the Carolingian Period, 751–911', PhD thesis, University of Cambridge (1998).

Castagnetti, A., 'Arimanni e signori dall'età postcarolingia alla prima età communale', in G. Dilcher and C. Violante (eds.), *Strutture e transformazioni della signoria rurale nei secoli X–XII* (Bologna, 1996), pp. 169–285.

Cavadini, J., *The Last Christology of the West. Adoptionism in Spain and Gaul, 785–820* (Philadelphia, 1993).

Chazelle, C., *The Crucified God in the Carolingian Era. Theology and Art of Christ's Passion* (Cambridge, 2001).

Claussen, M. A., 'God and Man in Dhuoda's *Liber Manualis*', *Studies in Church History* 27 (1990), 43–52.

Collins, R., 'The Carolingians and the Ottonians in an Anglophone World', *JMH* 22 (1996), 97–114.

Bibliography

Early Medieval Europe, 300–1000 (London, 1991).

Corradini, R., *Die Wiener Handschrift Cvp 430. Ein Beitrag zur Historiographie in Fulda im frühen 9. Jahrhundert* (Frankfurt, 2000).

Coulson, C., 'Fortresses and Social Responsibility in Late Carolingian France', *Zeitschrift für Archäologie des Mittelalters* 4 (1976), 29–36.

Coupland, S., 'From Poachers to Gamekeepers: Scandinavian Warlords and Carolingian Kings', *EME* 7 (1998), 85–114.

'The Frankish Tribute Payments to the Vikings and their Consequences', *Francia* 26 (1999), 57–75.

'The Rod of God's Wrath or the People of God's Wrath? The Carolingians' Theology of the Viking Invasions', *Journal of Ecclesiastical History* 42 (1991), 535–54.

'The Vikings in Francia and Anglo-Saxon England to 911', in *NCMH2*, pp. 190–201.

Coupland, S. and Nelson, J. L., 'The Vikings on the Continent', *History Today* 38 (1988), 12–19.

Cross, F. L. and Livingstone, E. A., *The Oxford Dictionary of the Christian Church* 3rd edn (Oxford, 1997).

Darmstädter, P., *Das Reichsgut in der Lombardei und Piemont (568–1250)* (Strasbourg, 1896).

Davies, W. and Fouracre, P. (eds.), *Property and Power in the Early Middle Ages* (Cambridge, 1995).

Davis, R., *The Lives of the Ninth-Century Popes* (Liverpool, 1995).

de Jong, M., *In Samuel's Image: Child Oblation in the Early Medieval West* (Leiden, New York and Cologne, 1996).

Delogu, P., 'Vescovi, conti e sovrani nella crisi del regno Italico (ricerche sull'aristocrazia Carolingia in Italia III)', *Annali della scuola speciale per archivisti e bibliotecari dell'Università di Roma* 8 (1968), 3–72.

Deshman, R., '*Christus rex et magi reges:* Kingship and Christology in Ottonian and Anglo-Saxon Art', *FMSt* 10 (1976), 367–406.

'The Exalted Servant: the Ruler Theology of the Prayerbook of Charles the Bald', *Viator* 11 (1980), 385–417.

Devisse, J., *Hincmar, Archevêque de Reims 845–882* (Geneva, 1975).

Devroey, J. P., 'The Economy', in R. McKitterick (ed.), *The Early Middle Ages* (Oxford, 2001), pp. 97–129.

Études sur le grand domaine carolingien (Aldershot, 1993).

Dhondt, J., *Études sur la naissance des principautés territoriales en France (IXe–Xe siècle)* (Bruges, 1948).

Dopsch, A., *Die Wirtschaftsentwicklung der Karolingerzeit*, 2nd edn (Weimar, 1921–2).

Duft, J., 'Der Impetus für Notkers Sequenzen', in J. Duft, *Die Abtei St. Gallen* (3 vols., Sigmaringen, 1990–4), vol. 2, pp. 136–47.

'Die Handschriften-Katalogisierung in der Stiftsbibliothek St. Gallen vom 9. bis zum 19. Jahrhundert', in Beat M. von Scarpaletti (ed.), *Die Handschriften der Stiftsbibliothek St. Gallen* (St. Gallen, 1983), pp. 9–129.

Duggan, A., *Kings and Kingship in Medieval Europe* (London, 1993).

Dümmler, E., *Geschichte des ostfränkischen Reiches*, 2nd edn (3 vols., Leipzig, 1887–8).

Dunbabin, J., *France in the Making, 843–1180* (Oxford, 1985).

Bibliography

Dutton, P. E., *Carolingian Civilization: A Reader* (Ontario, 1993).

The Politics of Dreaming in the Carolingian Empire (Lincoln and London, 1994).

Eggenberger, C., *Psalterium Aureum Sancti Galli. Mittelalterliche Psalterillustration im Kloster St. Gallen* (Sigmaringen, 1987).

Eggers, M., *Das Grossmährische Reich. Realität oder Fiktion. Eine Neuinterpretation der Quellen zur Geschichte des mittleren Donauraumes im 9. Jahrhundert* (Stuttgart, 1995).

Eggert, W., ' "Franken und Sachsen" bei Notker, Widukind und Anderen. Zu einem Aufsatz von Josef Semmler', in Scharer and Scheibelreiter (eds.), *Historiographie im frühen Mittelalter*, pp. 514–30.

'Zu Kaiser- und Reichsgedanken des Notker Balbulus', *Philologus* 115 (1971), 71–80.

Ehlers, J., 'Die Anfänge der französischen Geschichte', *HZ* 240 (1985), 1–44.

Eibl, E. M., 'Zur Stellung Bayerns und Rheinfrankens im Reiche Arnulfs von Kärnten', *Jahrbuch für Geschichte des Feudalismus* 8 (1984), 73–113.

Endemann, T., *Markturkunde und Markt in Frankreich und Burgund vom 9. bis 11. Jahrhundert* (Constance and Stuttgart, 1964).

Erdmann, C., 'Der ungesalbte König', *DA* 2 (1938), 311–40.

Erkens, F.-R., '*Divisio legitima* und *unitas imperii*. Teilungspraxis und Einheitsstreben bei der Thronfolge im Frankenreich', *DA* 52 (1996), 423–85.

'*Sicut Esther Regina*. Die westfränkische Königin als *consors regni*', *Francia* 20 (1993), 15–38.

Ewig, E., 'Der Gebetsdienst der Kirchen in den Urkunden der späteren Karolinger', in Maurer and Patze (eds.), *Festschrift*, pp. 45–86.

Falkenstein, L., *Karl der Grosse und die Entstehung des Aachener Marienstiftes* (Paderborn, 1981).

Favre, E., *Eudes. Comte de Paris et roi de France (882–898)* (Paris, 1893).

Feller, L., 'Aristocratie, monde monastique et pouvoir en Italie centrale au IXe siècle', in Le Jan (ed.), *La Royauté et les élites*, pp. 325–45.

Felten, F. J., *Äbte und Laienäbte im Frankenreich. Studien zum Verhältnis von Staat und Kirche im frühen Mittelalter* (Stuttgart, 1980).

Fentress, J., and Wickham, C., *Social Memory* (Oxford, 1992).

Fleckenstein, J., 'Über die Herkunft der Welfen und ihre Anfänge in Süddeutschen Raum' in Tellenbach (ed.), *Studien und Vorarbeiten*, pp. 71–136.

Die Hofkapelle der deutschen Könige. I. Teil: Grundlegung. Die karolingische Hofkapelle (Stuttgart, 1959).

Fossier, R., 'Les tendances de l'économie: stagnation ou croissance?', *Settimane* 27 (1981), 261–74.

Fouracre, P., 'Carolingian Justice: the Rhetoric of Improvement and Contexts of Abuse', *Settimane* 42 (1995), 771–803.

'Eternal Light and Earthly Needs: Practical Aspects of the Development of Frankish Immunities', in Davies and Fouracre (eds.), *Property and Power*, pp. 53–81.

'The Context of the OHG *Ludwigslied*', *Medium Aevum* 54 (1985), 87–103.

The Age of Charles Martel (Harlow, 2000).

Freed, J., 'Reflections on the Medieval German Nobility', *American Historical Review* 91 (1986), 553–75.

Bibliography

Fried, J., 'Boso von Vienne oder Ludwig der Stammler? Der Kaiserkandidat Johanns VIII.', *DA* 32 (1976), 193–208.

'The Frankish Kingdoms, 817–911: the East and Middle Kingdoms', in *NCMH2*, pp. 142–68.

Der Weg in die Geschichte. Die Ursprünge Deutschlands bis 1024 (Berlin, 1994).

Könige Ludwig der Jüngere in seiner Zeit (Lorsch, 1984).

Fuhrmann, H., *Einfluß und Verbreitung der pseudoisidorischen Fälschungen* (Stuttgart, 1972).

Ganshof, F. L., *Frankish Institutions Under Charlemagne* (Providence, 1968).

The Carolingians and the Frankish Monarchy (London, 1971).

Ganz, D., 'Humour as History in Notker's *Gesta Karoli Magni*', in E. King, J. Schaefer and W. Wadley (eds.), *Monks, Nuns and Friars in Mediaeval Society* (Sewanee, 1989), pp. 171–83.

Gaudemet, J., *Le Marriage en occident. Les moeurs et le droit* (Paris, 1987).

Geary, P., *The Myth of Nations: the Medieval Origins of Europe* (Princeton, 2002).

Geuenich, D., 'Aus den Anfängen der Fraumünsterabtei in Zürich', in Brunold and Deplazes (eds.), *Geschichte und Kultur*, pp. 211–31.

'Elsaßbeziehungen in den St. Galler Verbrüderungsbüchern', in Ochsenbein and Ziegler (eds.), *Codices Sangallenses*, pp. 105–16.

'*Richkart, ancilla dei de caenobio Sancti Stephani.* Zeugnisse zur Geschichte des straßburger Frauenklosters St. Stephan in der Karolingerzeit', in Schnith and Pauler (eds.), *Festschrift für Eduard Hlawitschka*, pp. 97–109.

'Zurzach- ein frühmittelalterliche Doppelkloster?', in Maurer and Patze (eds.), *Festschrift für Berent Schwineköper*, pp. 29–43.

Gibbon, E., *History of the Decline and Fall of the Roman Empire*, new edn. (2 vols., Chicago, 1990).

Gibson, M. T. and Nelson, J. L. (eds.), *Charles the Bald, Court and Kingdom*, 2nd edn. (Aldershot, 1990).

Gillmor, C., 'War on the Rivers: Viking Numbers and Mobility on the Seine and Loire, 841–886', *Viator* 19 (1988), 79–109.

Godman, P. and Collins, R. (eds.), *Charlemagne's Heir: New Perspectives on the Reign of Louis the Pious, 814–840* (Oxford, 1990).

Goetz, H.-W., 'Der letzte "Karolinger"? Die Regierung Konrads I. im Spiegel seiner Urkunden', *Archiv für Diplomatik* 26 (1980), 56–125.

'*Regnum*: zum politischen Denken der Karolingerzeit', *ZSRG GA* 104 (1987), 110–89.

'Typus einer Adelsherrschaft im späteren 9. Jahrhundert: der Linzgaugraf Udalrich', *St. Galler Kultur und Geschichte* 11 (1981), 131–73.

Dux und Ducatus. Begriffs- und verfassungsgeschichtliche Untersuchungen zur Entstehung des sogenannten 'jüngeren' Stammesherzogtums an der Wende vom neunten zum zehnten Jahrhundert (Bochum, 1977).

Strukturen der spätkarolingischen Epoche im Spiegel der Vorstellungen eines zeitgenössischen Mönchs. Ein Interpretation der Gesta Karoli Notkers von Sankt Gallen (Bonn, 1981).

Goffart, W., 'Zosimus, the First Historian of Rome's Fall', in Goffart, *Rome's Fall and After* (London and Ronceverte, 1989), pp. 81–110.

Bibliography

Goldberg, E. J., 'Creating a Medieval Kingdom: Carolingian Kingship, Court Culture and Aristocratic Society under Louis of East Francia (840–76)', PhD thesis, University of Virginia (1998).

'"More Devoted to the Equipment of Battle than the Splendor of Banquets": Frontier Kingship, Military Ritual, and Early Knighthood at the Court of Louis the German', *Viator* 30 (1999), 41–78.

'Popular Revolt, Dynastic Politics and Aristocratic Factionalism in the Early Middle Ages: the Saxon *Stellinga* Reconsidered', *Speculum* 70 (1995), 467–501.

Grierson, P., 'L'origine des comtes d'Amiens, Valois et Vexin', *Le Moyen Age* 10 (3rd series, 1939), 81–125.

Guillot, O., 'Formes, fondements et limites de l'organisation en France au Xe siècle', *Settimane* 38 (1991), 57–124.

'Les étapes de l'accession d'Eudes au pouvoir royal', in *Media in Francia. Recueil de mélanges offert à Karl Ferdinand Werner* (Maulévrier, 1989), pp. 199–223.

Guillot, O. and Favreau, R. (eds.), *Pays de Loire et Aquitaine de Robert le Fort aux premiers Capétiens* (Poitiers, 1997).

Guyotjeannin, O., *Episcopus et comes. Affirmation et déclin de la seigneurie épiscopale au nord du royaume de France* (Geneva, 1987).

Haefele, H. F., 'Studien zu Notkers *Gesta Karoli*', *DA* 15 (1959), 358–93.

Halphen, L., *Charlemagne and the Carolingian Empire*, trans. G. de Nie (Amsterdam, New York and Oxford, 1977).

Études critiques sur l'histoire de Charlemagne (Paris, 1921).

Halsall, G., *Warfare and Society in the Barbarian West* (London, forthcoming).

Halsall, G. (ed.), *Humour, History and Politics in Late Antiquity and the Early Middle Ages* (Cambridge, 2002).

Hannig, J., 'Zentralle Kontrolle und regionale Machtbalance. Beobachtungen zum System der karolingischen Königsboten am Beispiel des Mittelrheingebietes', *Archiv für Kulturgeschichte* 66 (1984), 1–46.

'Zur Funktion der karolingischen *missi dominici* in Bayern und in den südöstlichen Grenzgebieten', *ZSRG GA* 101 (1984), 256–300.

Hardt-Friedrichs, F., 'Markt, Münze und Zoll im ostfränkischen Reich bis zum End der Ottonen', *Blätter für deutsche Landesgeschichte* 116 (1980), 1–31.

Hartmann, W., *Das Konzil von Worms 868* (Göttingen, 1977).

Ludwig der Deutsche (Darmstadt, 2002).

Heather, P., 'State Formation in Europe in the First Millennium AD', in B. Crawford (ed.), *Scotland in Dark Age Europe* (St Andrews, 1994), pp. 47–70.

Helvétius, A.-M., *Abbayes, évêques et laïques. Une politique du pouvoir en Hainaut au Moyen Âge (VIIe–XIe siècle)* (Brussels, 1994).

Hen, Y., and Innes, M. (eds.), *The Uses of the Past in the Early Middle Ages* (Cambridge, 2000).

Hirsch, P. (ed.), *Die Erhebung Berengars von Friaul zum König in Italien* (Strasbourg, 1910).

Hlawitschka, E., 'Die Diptychen von Novara und die Chronologie der Bischöfe dieser Stadt vom 9.-11. Jahrhundert', *QFIAB* 52 (1972), 767–80.

'Die Widonen im Dukat von Spoleto', *QFIAB* 63 (1983), 20–92.

'Nachfolgeprojekt aus der Spätzeit Kaiser Karls III.', *DA* 46 (1978), 19–50.

Bibliography

Franken, Alemannen, Bayern und Burgunder in Oberitalien (774–962). Zum Verständnis der fränkischen Königsherrschaft in Italien (Freiburg, 1960).

Lotharingien und das Reich an der Schwelle der deutschen Geschichte (Stuttgart, 1968).

(ed.), *Königswahl und Thronfolge in fränkisch-karolingischer Zeit* (Darmstadt, 1975).

Hodges, R., *Dark Age Economics*, 2nd edn (London, 1989).

Towns and Trade in the Age of Charlemagne (London, 2000).

Hodges, R. and Whitehouse, D., *Mohammed, Charlemagne and the Origins of Europe. Archaeology and the Pirenne Thesis* (London, 1983).

Hoffmann, H., 'Grafschaften in Bischofshand', *DA* 46 (1990), 374–480.

Holl, K., 'Der Ursprung des Epiphanienfestes', *Sitzungsberichte der königlichen preussischen Akademie der Wissenschaften* 29 (1917), 402–38.

Innes, M., '*A Place of Discipline*: Aristocratic Youth and Carolingian Courts', in C. Cubitt (ed.), *Court Culture in the Early Middle Ages* (forthcoming).

' "He never even allowed his white teeth to be bared in laughter." The Politics of Laughter in the Carolingian Renaissance', in Halsall (ed.), *Humour, History and Politics*, pp. 131–56.

'Kings, Monks and Patrons: Political Identities and the Abbey of Lorsch', in Le Jan (ed.), *La Royauté et les élites*, pp. 301–24.

'Memory, Orality and Literacy in an Early Medieval Society', *Past and Present* 158 (1998), 3–36.

'Teutons or Trojans? The Carolingians and the Germanic Past', in Hen and Innes (eds.), *Uses of the Past*, pp. 227–49.

State and Society in the Early Middle Ages (Cambridge, 2000).

Innes, M., and McKitterick, R., 'The Writing of History', in McKitterick (ed.), *Carolingian Culture*, pp. 193–220.

Jackman, D., 'Rorgonid Right: Two Scenarios', *Francia* 28 (1999), 129–53.

Jacobsen, W., 'Die Lorscher Torhalle. Zum Problem ihrer Datierung und Deutung', *Jahrbuch des Zentralinstituts für Kunstgeschichte* 1 (1985), 9–75.

Jammers, E., 'Die sog. Ludwigspsalter als geschichtliches Dokument', *ZGO* 103 (1955), 259–71.

Janin, P., 'Heiric d'Auxerre et les *Gesta Pontificum Autissiodorensium*', *Francia* 4 (1976), 89–105.

Jarnut, J., 'Die frühmittelalterliche Jagd unter rechts- und sozialgeschichtlichen Aspekten', *Settimane* 31 (1985), 765–808.

Johanek, P., 'Der fränkische Handel der Karolingerzeit im Spiegel der Schriftquellen', in K. Düwel et al. (eds.), *Der Handel der Karolinger- und Wikingerzeit* (Göttingen, 1987), pp. 7–68.

Kaiser, R., 'Les évêques neustriens du Xe siècle dans l'exercise de leur pouvoir temporel d'après l'historiographie médiévale', in Guillot and Favreau (eds.), *Pays de Loire*, pp. 117–43.

'Münzpriviligien und bischöfliche Münzprägung in Frankreich, Deutschland und Burgund im 9.–12. Jahrhundert', *Vierteljahrschrift für Sozial- und Wirtschaftsgeschichte* 63 (1976), 289–338.

'*Teloneum Episcopi*. Du tonlieu royal au tonlieu épiscopal dans les *civitates* de la Gaule (VIe–XIIe siècle)', in W. Paravicini and K. F. Werner (eds.), *Histoire comparée de l'administration (IVe–XVIIIe siècles)* (Munich, 1980), pp. 469–85.

Bibliography

Kämpf, H. (ed.), *Die Entstehung des deutschen Reiches (Deutschland um 900)* (Darmstadt, 1956).

Kantorowicz, E., 'Dante's "Two Suns"', in Kantorowicz, *Selected Studies* pp. 325–38.

'Oriens Augusti - Lever du Roi', *Dumbarton Oaks Papers* 17 (1963), 117–77.

'The "King's Advent" and the Enigmatic Panels in the Doors of Santa Sabina', *The Art Bulletin* 26 (1944), 207–31.

Laudes Regiae. A Study in Liturgical Acclamation and Medieval Ruler Worship (Berkeley and Los Angeles, 1958).

Selected Studies (New York, 1965).

Kasten, B., *Königssöhne und Königsherrschaft. Untersuchungen zur Teilhabe am Reich in der Merowinger- und Karolingerzeit* (Hanover, 1997).

Kazhdan, A. P. et al., *The Oxford Dictionary of Byzantium* (New York and Oxford, 1991).

Kehr, P., 'Aus den letzten Tagen Karls III.', *DA* 1 (1937), 138–46.

Die Kanzlei Karls III. (Berlin, 1936).

Keller, H., 'Zum Sturz Karls III. Uber die Rolle Liutwards von Vercelli und Liutberts von Mainz, Arnulfs von Kärnten und der ostfränkischen Großen bei der Absetzung des Kaisers', *DA* 34 (1966), 333–84.

'Zur Struktur der Königsherrshaft im karolingischen und nachkarolingischen Italien. Der "consiliarius regis" in den italienischen Königsdiplomen des 9. und 10. Jahrhunderts', *QFIAB* 47 (1967), 123–223.

Kershaw, P., 'Laughter After Babel's Fall: Misunderstanding and Miscommunication in the Early Middle Ages', in Halsall (ed.), *Humour, History and Politics*, pp. 179–202.

'*Rex Pacificus*: Studies in Royal Peacemaking and the Image of Peacemaking in the Early Medieval West', PhD thesis, University of London (1998).

Keynes, S., 'A Tale of Two Kings: Alfred the Great and Aethelred the Unready', *TRHS* 36 (1986), pp. 195–217.

Keynes, S. and Lapidge, M., *Alfred the Great* (London, 1983).

Kienast, W., *Der Herzogstitel in Frankreich und Deutschland (9. bis 12. Jahrhundert)* (Munich and Vienna, 1968).

Studien über die französischen Volksstämme des Frühmittelalters (Stuttgart, 1968).

Klüppel, T., *Reichenauer Hagiographie zwischen Walahfrid und Berno* (Sigmaringen, 1980).

Körtum, H.-H., 'Weltgeschichte am Ausgang der Karolingerzeit: Regino von Prüm', in Scharer and Scheibelreiter (eds.), *Historiographie im frühen Mittelalter*, pp. 499–513.

Koziol, G., *Begging Pardon and Favour. Ritual and Political Order in Early Medieval France* (Ithaca and London, 1992).

Krah, A., *Absetzungsverfahren als Spiegelbild von Königsmacht. Untersuchungen zum Kräfteverhältnis zwischen Königtum und Adel im Karolingerreich und seinen Nachfolgestaaten* (Aalen, 1987).

Krahwinkler, H., *Friaul im Frühmittelalter. Geschichte einer Region vom Ende des fünften bis zum Ende des zehnten Jahrhunderts* (Vienna, Cologne and Weimar, 1992).

La Rocca, C., 'Les cadeaux nuptiaux de la famille royale en Italie' (forthcoming).

La Rocca, C. and Provero, L., 'The Dead and their Gifts. The Will of Eberhard, Count of Friuli, and his Wife Gisela, Daughter of Louis the Pious (863–864)',

Bibliography

in F. Theuws and J. L. Nelson (eds.), *Rituals of Power from Late Antiquity to the Early Middle Ages* (Leiden, Boston and Cologne, 2000), pp. 225–80.

Lapidge, M., 'The Hermeneutic Style in Tenth-Century Anglo-Latin Literature', *Anglo-Saxon England* 4 (1975), 67–111.

Lauranson-Rosaz, C., 'Le Roi et les grands dans l'Aquitaine carolingienne', in Le Jan (ed.), *La Royauté et les élites*, pp. 409–36.

L'Auvergne et ses marges (Velay, Gévaudan) du VIIIe au XIe siècle. La fin du monde antique? (Le Puy-en-Velay, 1987).

Le Jan, R., 'Continuity and Change in the Tenth-Century Nobility', in A. Duggan (ed.), *Nobles and Nobility in Medieval Europe* (Woodbridge, 2000), pp. 53–68.

'*Domnus, illuster, nobilis.* Les mutations du pouvoir au Xe siècle', in M. Sot (ed.), *Haut Moyen-Age. Culture, education et société. Études offertes à Pierre Riché* (Paris, 1990), pp. 439–48.

Famille et pouvoir dans le monde franc (VIIe–Xe siècle). Essai d'anthropologie sociale (Paris, 1995).

Le Jan, R. (ed.), *La Royauté et les élites dans l'Europe carolingienne (début IXe siècle aux environs de 920)* (Lille, 1998).

Lendinara P., 'The Third Book of the *Bella Parisiacae Urbis* by Abbo of Saint-Germain-des-Prés and its Old English Gloss', *Anglo-Saxon England* 15 (1986), 73–89.

Leyser, K., 'Early Medieval Canon Law and the Beginnings of Knighthood', in L. Fenske et al. (eds.), *Institutionen, Kultur und Gesellschaft im Mittelalter. Festschrift J. Fleckenstein* (Sigmaringen, 1984), pp. 549–66.

Rule and Conflict in an Early Medieval Society: Ottonian Saxony (London, 1979).

Lot, F., 'Notes historique sur "Aye d'Avignon"', *Romania* 33 (1904), 145–62.

Löwe, H., 'Das Karlsbuch Notkers von St. Gallen und sein zeitgeschichtlicher Hintergrund', in Löwe, *Von Cassiodor zu Dante*, pp. 123–48.

'Geschichtschreibung der ausgehenden Karolingerzeit', *DA* 23 (1967), pp. 1–30. Repr. in Löwe, *Von Cassiodor zu Dante*, pp. 180–205.

'Von Theodorich dem Grossen zu Karl dem Grossen. Das Werden des Abendlandes im Geschichtsbild des frühen Mittelalters', in Löwe, *Von Cassiodor zu Dante*, pp. 33–74.

Von Cassiodor zu Dante. Ausgewählte Aufsätze zur Geschichtschreibung und politischen Ideenwelt des Mittelalters (Berlin and New York, 1973).

Lugge, M., *"Gallia" und "Francia" im Mittelalter. Untersuchungen über den Zusammenhang zwischen geographischer-historischer Terminologie und politischem Denken vom 6.–15. Jahrhundert* (Bonn, 1960).

Lund, N., 'Allies of God or Man? The Viking Expansion in a European Perspective', *Viator* 20 (1989), 45–59.

Lynch, J. H., *Godparents and Kinship in Early Medieval Europe* (Princeton, 1986).

MacLean, S., 'Charles the Fat and the Viking Great Army: the Military Explanation for the End of the Carolingian Empire', *War Studies Journal* 3 (1998), 74–95.

'Queenship, Nunneries and Royal Widowhood in Carolingian Europe', *Past and Present* (forthcoming).

'The Carolingian Response to the Revolt of Boso, 879–87', *EME* 10 (2001), 21–48.

Martindale, J., 'The Kingdom of Aquitaine and the Dissolution of the Carolingian Fisc', *Francia* 11 (1985), pp. 131–91.

Bibliography

Maurer, H., 'St. Gallens Präsenz am Bischofssitz. Zur Rezeption st. gallischer Traditionen im Konstanz der Karolingerzeit', in H. Maurer et al. (eds.), *Florilegium Sangallense* (St-Gallen, 1980), pp. 199–211.

Maurer, H. and Patze, H. (eds.), *Festschrift für Berent Schwineköper zu seinem siebzigsten Geburtstag* (Sigmaringen, 1982).

Mayr-Harting, H., *Ottonian Book Illumination: An Historical Study*, 2nd edn (London, 1999).

McCormick, M., 'Analyzing Imperial Ceremonies', *Jahrbuch der österreichischen Byzantinistik* 35 (1985), 1–20.

   Eternal Victory. Triumphal Rulership in Late Antiquity, Byzantium, and the Early Medieval West (Cambridge, 1986).

   Origins of the European Economy. Communications and Commerce, AD 300–900 (Cambridge, 2001).

McKitterick, R., 'Constructing the Past in the Early Middle Ages: the Case of the Royal Frankish Annals', *TRHS* 6th series, 7 (1997), 101–30.

   'Gibbon and the Early Middle Ages in Eighteenth-Century Europe', in McKitterick and Quinault (eds.), *Edward Gibbon and Empire*, pp. 162–89.

   'Political Ideology in Carolingian Historiography', in Hen and Innes (eds.), *The Uses of the Past*, pp. 162–74.

   'The Audience for Carolingian Historiography', in Scharer and Scheibelreiter (eds.), *Historiographie im frühen Mittelalter*, pp. 96–114.

   'The Illusion of Royal Power in the Carolingian Annals', *English Historical Review* 105 (2000), 1–20.

   'Zur Herstellung von Kapitularien: Die Arbeit des Leges-Skriptoriums', *Mitteilungen des Instituts für Österreichische Geschichtsforschung* 101 (1993), 3–16.

   The Frankish Kingdoms under the Carolingians, 751–987 (London and New York, 1983).

   (ed.), *Carolingian Culture: Emulation and Innovation* (Cambridge, 1994).

   (ed.), *The New Cambridge Medieval History, Volume II c.700–c.900* (Cambridge, 1995).

McKitterick, R. and Quinault, R. (eds.), *Edward Gibbon and Empire* (Cambridge, 1997).

Meens, R., 'Politics, Mirrors of Princes and the Bible: Sins, Kings and the Well-Being of the Realm', *EME* 7 (1998), 345–57.

Merta, B., 'Recht und Propaganda in Narrationes karolingischer Herrscherurkunden', in Scharer and Scheibelreiter (eds.), *Historiographie im frühen Mittelalter*, pp. 141–57.

Mordek, H., 'Karolingische Kapitularien', in H. Mordek (ed.), *Überlieferung und Geltung normativer Texte des frühen und hohen Mittelalters* (Sigmaringen, 1986), pp. 25–50.

Müller-Mertens, E., *Die Reichsstruktur im Spiegel der Herrschaftspraxis Ottos der Großen* (Berlin, 1980).

Musset, L., *Les Invasions. Le Second Assaut contre l'Europe chrétienne (VIIe–XIe siècles)* (Paris, 1965).

Nass, K., *Die Reichskronik des Annalista Saxo und die sächsische Geschichtsschreibung im 12. Jahrhundert* (Hanover, 1996).

Bibliography

Nelson, J. L., 'Aachen as a Place of Power', in M. de Jong and F. Theuws (eds.), *Topographies of Power in the Early Middle Ages* (Leiden, Boston and Cologne, 2001), pp. 217–41.

'Bad Kingship in the Earlier Middle Ages', *Haskins Society Journal* 8 (1996), 1–26.

'Charles le Chauve et les utilisations du savoir', in D. Iogna-Prat et al. (eds.), *L'École carolingienne d'Auxerre* (Paris, 1991), pp. 37–54. Repr. in Nelson, *Rulers and Ruling Families*.

'History-Writing at the Courts of Louis the Pious and Charles the Bald', in Scharer and Scheibelreiter (eds.), *Historiographie im frühen Mittelalter*, pp. 435–42.

'Inauguration Rituals', in Nelson, *Politics and Ritual*, pp. 283–307.

'Kingship and Empire in the Carolingian World', in McKitterick (ed.), *Carolingian Culture*, pp. 52–87.

'Monks, Secular Men and Masculinity, c.900', in D. M. Hadley (ed.), *Masculinity in Medieval Europe* (Harlow, 1999), pp. 121–42.

'Ninth-Century Knighthood: the Evidence of Nithard', in C. Harper-Bill, C. Holdsworth and J. L. Nelson (eds.), *Studies in Medieval History Presented to R. Allen Brown* (Woodbridge, 1989), pp. 255–66. Repr. in Nelson, *The Frankish World*.

'Public *Histories* and Private History in the Work of Nithard', *Speculum* 60 (1985), 251–93. Repr. in Nelson, *Politics and Ritual*.

'The *Annals of St-Bertin*', in Gibson and Nelson (eds.), *Charles the Bald*, pp. 23–40.

'The Franks and the English in the Ninth Century Reconsidered', in P. E. Szarmach and J. T. Rosenthal (eds.), *The Preservation and Transmission of Anglo-Saxon Culture* (Kalamazoo, 1997), pp. 141–58. Repr. in Nelson, *Rulers and Ruling Families*.

'The Intellectual in Politics: Context, Content and Authorship in the Capitulary of Coulaines, November 843', in Nelson, *The Frankish World*, pp. 155–68.

'The Lord's Anointed and the People's Choice: Carolingian Royal Ritual', in Nelson, *The Frankish World*, pp. 99–130.

'The Problematic in the Private', *Social History* 15 (1990), 355–64.

'The Search for Peace in a Time of War: the Carolingian Brüderkrieg, 840–843', in J. Fried (ed.), *Träger und Instrumentarien des Friedens im hohen un späten Mittelalter* (Sigmaringen, 1996), pp. 87–114.

Charles the Bald (London and New York, 1992).

Politics and Ritual in Early Medieval Europe (London, 1986).

Rulers and Ruling Families in Early Medieval Europe: Alfred, Charles the Bald and Others (Aldershot, 1999).

The Annals of St-Bertin: Ninth-Century Histories (vol. 1, Manchester and New York, 1991).

The Frankish World, 750–900 (London and Rio Grande, 1996).

Niermeyer, J., *Mediae Latinitatis Lexicon Minus* (Leiden, 1976).

Nuber, H., Schmid, K., Steuer, H. and Zotz, T. (eds.), *Archäologie und Geschichte des ersten Jahrtausends in Südwestdeutschland* (Sigmaringen, 1990).

Ochsenbein, P., and Ziegler, E. (eds.), *Codices Sangallenses. Festschrift für Johannes Duft zum 80. Geburtstag* (Sigmaringen, 1995).

Bibliography

Oesterle, H. J., 'Die sogenannte Kopfoperation Karls III. 887', *Archiv für Kulturgeschichte* 61 (1979), 445–51.

Oexle, O. G., 'Bischof Ebroin von Poitiers und seine Verwandten', *FMSt* 3 (1969), 138–210.

Parisot, R., *Le Royaume de Lorraine sous les carolingiens (843–923)* (Paris, 1899).

Penndorf, U., *Das Problem der "Reichseinheitsidee" nach der Teilung von Verdun (843). Untersuchungen zu den späten Karolingern* (Munich, 1974).

Pirenne, H., *Medieval Cities* (New York, 1925).

Mohammed and Charlemagne (London, 1939).

Pohl, W., 'History in Fragments: Motecassino's Politics of Memory', *EME* 10 (2001), 343–74.

Poly, J.-P., *La Provence et la société féodale (879–1166). Contribution à l'étude des structures dites féodales dans le Midi* (Paris, 1976).

Poupardin, R., *Le Royaume de Bourgogne (888–1038). Étude sur les origines du royaume d'Arles* (Paris, 1907).

Le Royaume de Provence sous les carolingiens (855–933?) (Paris, 1901).

Rankin, S., 'Carolingian Music', in McKitterick (ed.), *Carolingian Culture*, pp. 274–316.

'*Ego itaque Notker scripsi*', *Revue Bénédicitine* 101 (1991), 268–98.

Reimitz, H., 'Ein fränkisches Geschichtsbuch aus Saint-Amand', in C. Egger and H. Weigl (eds.), *Text-Schrift-Codex. Quellenkundliche Arbeiten aus dem Institut für österreichische Geschichtsforschung* (Vienna, 1999), pp. 34–90.

Reindel, K., 'Herzog Arnulf und das Regnum Bavariae', *Zeitschrift für bayerische Landesgeschichte* 17 (1953/4), 187–252.

Reinle, A., *Die heilige Verena von Zurzach. Legende-Kult-Denkmäler* (Basel, 1948).

Kunstgeschichte der Schweiz (Frauenfeld, 1968).

Renoux, A. (ed.), *Palais médiévaux (France-Belgique)* (Le Mans, 1994).

(ed.), *Palais royaux et princiers au Moyen Age* (Le Mans, 1996).

Reuter, T., 'Plunder and Tribute in the Carolingian Empire', *TRHS*, 5th series, 35 (1985), 75–94.

'The End of Carolingian Military Expansion', in Godman and Collins (eds.), *Charlemagne's Heir*, pp. 391–405.

'The Medieval Nobility in Twentieth-Century Historiography', in Bentley (ed.), *Companion to Historiography*, pp. 177–202.

'The Origins of the German *Sonderweg*? The Empire and its Rulers in the High Middle Ages', in Duggan (ed.), *Kings and Kingship*, pp. 179–211.

Germany in the Early Middle Ages, c. 800–1056 (London and New York, 1991).

The Annals of Fulda: Ninth-Century Histories (vol. 2, Manchester and New York, 1992).

Reuter, T. (ed.) *The Medieval Nobility. Studies on the Ruling Classes of France and Germany from the Sixth to the Twelfth Century* (Amsterdam, New York and Oxford, 1979).

Reynolds, S., 'The Historiography of the Medieval State', in Bentley (ed.), *Companion to Historiography*, pp. 117–38.

Fiefs and Vassals. The Medieval Evidence Reinterpreted (Oxford, 1994).

Riché, P., *The Carolingians: A Family Who Forged Europe* (Philadelphia, 1993).

Bibliography

Róna-Tás, A., *Hungarians and Europe in the Early Middle Ages* (Budapest and New York, 1999).

Rosenwein, B. H., 'The Family Politics of Berengar I, King of Italy (888–924)', *Speculum* 71 (1996), 247–89.

Negotiating Space: Power, Restraint and Privileges of Immunity in Early Medieval Europe (Manchester, 1999).

Sassier, Y., *Recherches sur le pouvoir comtal en Auxerrois du Xe au début du XIIIe siècle* (Auxerre, 1980).

Schaab, R., 'Aus der Hofschule Karls des Kahlen nach St. Gallen. Die Entstehung des Goldenen Psalters', in Ochsenbein and Ziegler (eds.), *Codices Sangallenses*, pp. 57–80.

Scharer, A. and Scheibelreiter, G. (eds.), *Historiographie im frühen Mittelalter* (Vienna and Munich, 1994).

Schieffer, R., 'Karl III. und Arnolf', in Schnith and Pauler (eds.), *Festschrift für Eduard Hlawitschka*, pp. 133–49.

'Väter und Söhne im Karolingerhause', in Schieffer (ed.), *Beiträge zur Geschichte des Regnum Francorum* (Sigmaringen, 1990), pp. 149–64.

Die Karolinger (Stuttgart, Berlin and Cologne, 1992).

Schlesinger, W., 'Die Auflösung des Karlsreiches', in Braunfels (ed.), *Karl der Grosse*, vol. 1, pp. 792–857.

Schmid, K., 'Brüderschaften mit den Mönchen aus der Sicht des Kaiserbesuchs im Galluskloster vom Jahre 883', in H. Maurer (ed.), *Churrätisches und st. gallisches Mittelalter. Festschrift für Otto P. Clavadetscher zu seinem fünfundsechzigsten Geburtstag* (Sigmaringen, 1984), pp. 173–94.

'Königtum, Adel und Klöster zwischen Bodensee und Schwarzwald (8.–12. Jahrhundert)', in Tellenbach (ed.), *Studien und Vorarbeiten*, pp. 225–334.

'Liutbert von Mainz und Liutward von Vercelli im Winter 879/80 in Italien. Zur Erschließung bisher unbeachteter Gedenkbucheinträge aus S. Giulia in Brescia', in E. Hassinger, J. H. Müller and H. Ott (eds.), *Geschichte, Wirtschaft, Gesellschaft. Festschrift Clemens Bauer zum 75. Geburtstag* (Berlin, 1974), pp. 41–60.

'Von den "Fratres conscripti" in Ekkeharts st. galler Klostergeschichten', *FMSt* 25 (1991), 109–22.

Schneider, G., *Erzbischof Fulco von Reims (883–900) und das Frankenreich* (Munich, 1973).

Schneidmüller, B., 'Regnum und Ducatus. Identität und Integration in der lothringischen Geschichte des 9. bis 11. Jahrhunderts', *Rheinische Viertel-jahrsblätter* 51 (1987), 81–114.

Karolingische Tradition und frühes französisches Königtum. Untersuchungen zur Herrschaftslegitimation der westfränkisch-französischen Monarchie im 10. Jahrhundert (Wiesbaden, 1979).

Schnith, K. R. and Pauler, R. (eds.), *Festschrift für Eduard Hlawitschka zum 65. Geburtstag* (Kallmünz, 1993).

Schramm, P. E., 'Neuentdeckte Bildnisse Karls des Kahlen, seiner Gemahlin und seines Sohnes (876/7). Ein Beleg für die den byzantinern nachgeahmte Krone', in Schramm, *Kaiser, Könige und Päpste*, vol. 2, pp. 110–18.

Kaiser, Könige und Päpste. Gesammelte Aufsätze zur Geschichte des Mittelalters (Stuttgart, 1969).

Bibliography

Schramm, P. E. and Mütherich, F., *Denkmale der deutschen Könige und Kaiser*, 2nd edn (Munich, 1981).

Schumann, R., *Authority and the Commune. Parma, 833–1133* (Parma, 1973).

Schwineköper, B., 'Christus-Reliquien-Verehrung und Politik', *Blätter für deutsche Landesgeschichte* 117 (1981), 183–281.

Semmler, J., '*Francia Saxoniaque* oder die ostfränkische Reichsteilung von 865/76 und die Folgen', *DA* 46 (1990), 337–74.

Sergi, G., 'Anscarici, Arduinici, Aleramici: elementi per una comparazione fra dinastie marchionali', in G. Andenna et al. (eds.), *Formazione e strutture dei ceti dominanti nel medioevo: marchesi, conti e visconti nel regno italico (secc. IX–XII)* (Rome, 1988), pp. 11–28.

'L'Europa carolingia e la sua dissoluzione', in N. Tranfaglia and M. Firpo (eds.), *La Storia. I grandi problemi dal Medioevo all'Età contemporanea* (10 vols., Turin, 1986), vol. 2, pp. 231–62.

Seston, W., 'Constantine as Bishop', *Journal of Roman Studies* 37 (1947), 127–31.

Siegrist, T., *Herrscherbild und Weltsicht bei Notker Balbulus. Untersuchungen zu den Gesta Karoli* (Zurich, 1963).

Sierck, M., *Festtag und Politik. Studien zur Tagewahl karolingischer Herrscher* (Cologne, Weimar and Vienna, 1995).

Smith, J. M. H., '*Fines imperii*: the Marches', in *NCMH2*, pp. 169–89.

Province and Empire. Brittany and the Carolingians (Cambridge, 1992).

Staab, F., 'Jugement moral et propagande. Boson de Vienne vu par les élites du royaume de l'est', in Le Jan (ed.), *La Royauté et les élites*, pp. 365–82.

Stafford, P., *Queens, Concubines and Dowagers: the King's Wife in the Early Middle Ages* (Athens, 1983)

Stoclet, A., '*Dies unctionis*. A Note on the Anniversaries of Royal Inaugurations in the Carolingian Period', *FMSt* 20 (1986), 541–8.

Stubbs, W., *Germany in the Early Middle Ages 476–1250* (London, 1908).

Sullivan, R., 'The Carolingian Age: Reflections on its Place in the History of the Middle Ages', *Speculum* 64 (1989), 267–306.

Swanton, M. (trans.), *The Anglo-Saxon Chronicle* (London, 1996).

Szarmach, P., 'The (Sub-) Genre of the Battle of Maldon', in J. Cooper (ed.), *The Battle of Maldon. Fiction and Fact* (London and Rio Grande, 1993), pp. 43–61.

Tabacco, G., *I Liberi del re nell'Italia carolingia e postcarolingia* (Spoleto, 1966).

The Struggle for Power in Medieval Italy (Cambridge, 1989).

Tellenbach, G., 'Die geistigen und politischen Grundlagen der karolingischen Thronfolge. Zugleich eine Studie über kollektive Willensbildung und kollektives Handeln im neunten Jahrhundert', *FMSt* 13 (1979), 184–302.

'From the Carolingian Imperial Nobility to the German Estate of Imperial Princes', in Reuter (ed.), *The Medieval Nobility*, pp. 203–42.

'Liturgische Gedenkbücher als historische Quellen', in *Mélanges Eugène Tisserant* (vol. 5, Vatican, 1964), pp. 389–400.

'Zur Geschichte Kaiser Arnulfs', *HZ* 165 (1942), 229–45.

Königtum und Stamme in der Werdezeit des Deutschen Reiches (Weimar, 1939).

(ed.), *Studien und Vorarbeiten zur Geschichte des grossfränkischen und frühdeutschen Adels* (Freiburg, 1957).

Bibliography

Thompson, J. W., *The Dissolution of the Carolingian Fisc in the Ninth Century* (Berkeley, 1935).

Thorpe, L., *Two Lives of Charlemagne* (London, 1969).

Toubert, P., 'The Carolingian Moment (Eighth-Tenth Century)', in A. Burguière et al. (eds.), *A History of the Family* (Cambridge, 1996), pp. 379–406.

Trexler, R. C., *The Journey of the Magi. Meanings in History of a Christian Story* (Princeton, 1997).

Van Houts, E., 'Countess Gunnor of Normandy (c. 950–1031)', *Collegium Medievale* 12 (1999), 7–24.

Vercauteren, F., 'Comment s'est-on défendu, au IXe siècle dans l'empire Franc contre les invasions normandes', in *XXXe congrès de la Fédération Archéologique de Belgique* (Brussels, 1936), 117–32.

Verhulst, A., *The Carolingian Economy* (Cambridge, 2002).

The Rise of Cities in North-West Europe (Cambridge, 1999).

Vogel, W., *Die Normannen und das fränkische Reich bis zur Gründung der Normandie (799–911)* (Heidelberg, 1906).

Vollmer, F., 'Die Etichonen. Ein Beitrag zur Frage der Kontinuität früher Adelsfamilien', in Tellenbach (ed.), *Studien und Vorarbeiten*, pp. 137–84.

Von den Steinen, W., *Notker der Dichter und seine geistige Welt. Darstellungsband* (Berne, 1948).

Von Gladiß, D., 'Die Schenkungen der deutschen Könige zu privatem Eigen (800–1137)', *DA* 1 (1937), 80–137.

Waitz, G., *Deutsche Verfassungsgeschichte* (8 vols., Berlin, 1876–96).

Wallace-Hadrill, J. M., 'A Carolingian Renaissance Prince: the Emperor Charles the Bald', *Proceedings of the British Academy* 64 (1978), 155–84.

'The Franks and the English in the Ninth Century: Some Common Historical Interests', in Wallace-Hadrill, *Early Medieval History* (London, 1975), pp. 201–16.

The Frankish Church (Oxford, 1983).

Walther, H. G., 'Der Fiskus Bodman', in Berner (ed.), *Bodman*, pp. 231–75.

Ward, E., 'Agobard of Lyons and Paschasius Radbertus as Critics of the Empress Judith', *Studies in Church History* 27 (1990), 15–25.

'Caesar's Wife: the Career of the Empress Judith, 819–29', in Godman and Collins (eds.), *Charlemagne's Heir*, pp. 205–27.

Warner, D. A., 'Ideals and Action in the Reign of Otto III', *JMH* 25 (1999), 1–18.

Wattenbach, W., Levison, W., and Löwe, H., *Deutschlands Geschichtsquellen im Mittelalter* (vol. 5, Weimar, 1973).

Werner, K. F., 'Bedeutende Adelsfamilien im Reich Karls des Grossen. Ein personengeschichtlicher Beitrag zum Verhältnis von Königtum und Adel im frühen Mittelalter', in Braunfels (ed.), *Karl der Grosse*, vol. 1, pp. 83–142.

'Die Nachkommen Karls des Großen bis um das Jahr 1000 (1.–8. Generation)', in Braunfels (ed.), *Karl der Grosse*, vol. 4, pp. 403–84.

'Gauzlin von Saint-Denis und die westfränkische Reichsteilung von Amiens (März 880). Ein Beitrag zur Vorgeschichte von Odos Königtum', *DA* 35 (1979), 395–462. Repr. in Werner, *Vom Frankenreich*.

'Gott, Herrscher und Historiograph. Der Geschichtsschreiber als Interpret des Wirken Gottes in der Welt und Ratgeber der Könige (4. bis 12. Jahrhundert)',

Bibliography

in E.-D. Hehl et al., *Deus qui mutat tempora. Menschen und Institutionen im Wandel des Mittelalters* (Sigmaringen, 1987), pp. 1–31.

'Important Noble Families in the Kingdom of Charlemagne – a Prosopographical Study of the Relationship Between King and Nobility in the Early Middle Ages', in Reuter (ed.), *The Medieval Nobility*, pp. 137–202.

'Kingdom and Principality in Twelfth-Century France', in Reuter (ed.), *Medieval Nobility*, pp. 243–90.

'La genèse des duchés en France et en Allemagne', *Settimane* 27 (1981), 175–207. Repr. in Werner, *Vom Frankenreich*.

'Les duchés "nationaux" d'Allemagne au IXe at au Xe siècle', in *Les Principautés au moyen-âge. Actes du congrès de la Société des historiens médiévistes de l'enseignement supérieur public, Bordeaux 1973* (Bordeaux, 1979), pp. 29–46. Repr. in Werner, *Vom Frankenreich*.

'Les premiers Robertiens et les premiers Anjou (IXe–Xe siècle)', in Guillot and Favreau (eds.), *Pays de Loire*, pp. 9–67.

'Les Robertiens', in M. Parisse and X. Barral I Altet (eds.), *Le Roi de France et son royaume autour de l'an mil* (Paris, 1992), pp. 15–26.

'Missus-Marchio-Comes. Entre l'administration centrale et l'administration locale de l'empire carolingien', in W. Paravicini and K. F. Werner (eds.), *Histoire comparée de l'administration (IVe–XVIIIe sièles)* (Munich and Zurich, 1980), pp. 191–239. Repr. in Werner, *Vom Frankenreich*.

'Untersuchungen zur Frühzeit des französischen Fürstentums (9.–10. Jahrhundert)', *Die Welt als Geschichte* 18 (1958), 256–89 (parts I–III); 19 (1959), 146–93 (part IV); 20 (1960), 87–119 (parts V–VI).

'Völker und Regna', in C. Brühl and B. Schneidmüller (eds.), *Beiträge zur mittelalterlichen Reichs- und Nationsbildung in Deutschland und Frankreich* (Munich, 1997), pp. 15–43.

'Westfranken-Frankreich unter den Spätkarolinger und frühen Kapetingern (888–1060)', in Werner, *Vom Frankenreich*.

Les Origines (avant l'an mil) (Paris, 1984).

Structures politiques du monde franc (VIe–XIIe siècles) (London, 1979).

Vom Frankenreich zur Entfaltung Deutschlands und Frankreichs. Ursprünge-Strukturen-Beziehungen. Ausgewählte Beiträge. Festgabe zu seinem sechzigsten Geburtstag (Sigmaringen, 1984).

West, G., 'Charlemagne's Involvement in Central and Southern Italy: Power and the Limits of Authority', *EME* 8 (1999), 341–67.

Wickham, C., 'Ninth-Century Byzantium through Western Eyes', in L. Brubaker (ed.), *Byzantium in the Ninth Century: Dead or Alive?* (London, 1988), pp. 245–56.

Wickham, C. and Reuter, T., 'Introduction', in Davies and Fouracre (eds.), *Property and Power*, pp. 1–16.

Wolfram, H., 'Lateinische Herrschertitel im neunten und zehnten Jahrhundert', in Wolfram (ed.), *Intitulatio II.*, pp. 19–178.

'Political Theory and Narrative in Charters', *Viator* 26 (1995), 39–51.

Die Geburt Mitteleuropas. Geschichte Österreichs vor seiner Entstehung, 378–907 (Vienna, 1987).

(ed.), *Intitulatio II. Lateinische Herrscher- und Fürstentitel im neunten und zehnten Jahrhundert* (Vienna, Cologne and Graz, 1973).

Bibliography

und seine Klostergründung', *Revue Bénédictine* 70

Whence and Whither?', in R. T. Farrell (ed.), *The*
ester, 1982), pp. 128–53.
Konstanz, Abt von St. Gallen*, (Leipzig and Berlin,

en der Reichenau. Ausgrabungen- Schriftquellen-st. galler
988).
and Ottonian-Salian Innovation: Comparative Ob-
y in the Empire', in Duggan (ed.), *Kings and Kingship*,

chenreiches?' in H.-W. Herrmann and R. Schneider
ropäische Kernlandschaft um das Jahr 1000 (Saarbrücken,

der Königsherrschaft im deutschen Südwesten in
scher Zeit', in Nuber, Schmid, Steuer and Zotz (eds.),
, pp. 275–93.
e la terminologie palatiale au moyen age', in Renoux
iciers, pp. 7–15.

INDEX

Aachen, 81, 120, 157, 188–9, 203, 224; *see also* relics
Abbo of St-Germain, poet, 27, 36, 55–64, 82, 103, 106, 108
Adalald, archbishop of Tours, 67
Adalard, count of the palace, 117–18
Adalbert, count in Alemannia, 89–90
Adalelm, count of Laon, 117–18
Adalgisus, count of Piacenza, 71, 72
Adalroch, *missus*, 71
Ahab, 33
Alan of Brittany, 154
Aletramnus, count in west Francia, 106, 116
Andernach, Battle of (876), 103, 133
Andlau, 172, 186, 188, 189, 191
Andreas of Bergamo, historian, 62–3
Annals of Fulda, 23–47, 86, 97–8, 130, 131, 138, 151, 174, 176–7, 190, 191, 195, 230
Annals of St-Bertin, 46
Annals of St-Vaast, 36, 62, 100, 102, 125, 127
anointing, *see* consecration
Aquitaine, 60–1, 101
Arbo, margrave, 135, 137–8, 139, 141, 142
aristocracy, 3, 8, 12–14, 15–16, 17–18, 19, 48–80, 83–90, 122, 191; *see also* Berengar of Friuli; Bernard Plantevelue of the Auvergne; Gauzlin of St-Denis; Hugh the Abbot; Odo of Paris; Udalrich
armies, 16–17, 32, 34, 58, 121; *see also* Vikings
Arnulf of Carinthia, king and emperor, 2, 26, 34, 61, 89, 99, 116, 122, 123, 130, 134–44, 156–8, 159, 162, 164–5, 173–4, 177, 190, 191–8, 219, 220, 221–2, 227, 230–1
Askericus of Paris, bishop, 57, 109, 116, 126, 168
Asselt, siege of (882), 30–7, 97
Asser, biographer, 100
Atuyer, 113
Auvergne, the, *see* Bernard Plantevelue of the Auvergne
Auxerre, 51–3

Baldwin of Flanders, 117–18, 220
Bautier, Robert-Henri, 103, 110–11
Bavarian annalist, the, *see Annals of Fu*
Beauvais, 107–8
Belluno, *see* Haimo of Belluno
Berardus, Italian count, 70
Berengar of Friuli, *marchio*, later king a emperor, 28, 70–9, 92, 94–6, 113, 181–2, 184, 220
Bernard, son of Charles the Fat, 123, 142, 143, 151, 152, 154, 159, 161, 172, 173–4, 182–3, 192–3, 197, 2(212, 218–22, 227
Bernard Plantevelue of the Auvergne, 69–70, 72–9, 115, 117
Berthold, count of the palace, 185
bishops, 204–13; *see also* Frotar of Bourg Gauzlin of St-Denis; Geilo of Lang Haimo of Belluno; Liutbert of Ma Liutward of Vercelli; Raino of Ang Walter of Orléans; Walter of Sens; of Parma
Bobbio, 178
Bodman, 40, 83, 86, 89
Book of Ceremonies, The, 155
Boso of Vienne, 21–2, 68, 69, 110, 112– 114–15, 117, 121, 127, 152, 162, 16 166, 169–71, 231; *see also* Mantaille, Assembly of (879); Vienne, Oaths o (880)
Brazlavo, Slavic *dux*, 135, 138, 142
Breitenheim, 187
Bührer-Thierry, Geneviève, 30, 99
Burgundians, 60–1

capitularies, 15, 19–20
Caput Pariol, 94
Carinthia, 135–40; *see also* Arnulf of Carin
Carloman II, 66, 69, 76, 102–3, 107–8, 11 117, 118, 123, 124–6, 128, 132, 137, 192
Chadolt of Novara, bishop, 88, 146, 153

258

Index

Chalon, *see* St-Marcel-lès-Chalon, synod of (887)

Châlons-sur-Marne, 103

Charlemagne, king and emperor, 33, 64, 77, 121, 199–229

Charles the Bald, king and emperor, 8, 17, 21, 65–6, 74, 75, 77, 83, 91, 114, 116–17, 124, 148, 159, 178, 224, 228

Charles the Fat, king and emperor
  and aristocracy, *passim*
  deposition and death, 2, 6, 56, 191–8
  early years, 83–6
  illness, 39–41
  imperial coronation, 188
  itinerary, 37–42, 82, 97, 100–1, 125–6, 147
  kingship of, *passim*
  nickname, 1
  personality, 46
  sources for, 10

Charles the Simple, king, 77, 120, 125, 192, 220, 232

charters, 20, 53–4, 82, 99, 100, 111, 120, 126–7, 132–3, 141–2, 144–53, 165, 169, 178, 179–84, 186

Chezil, *see* Kocel

Chur, 187, 189

Conrad I, king, 145, 158

Conrad of Paris, count, 104, 117–18

Conrad of Transjurane Burgundy, count, 67, 68

consecration, royal/imperial, 18, 110, 126–7, 144–60

consiliarius (title), 182–5

Corteolona, 93–5

counts, *see honores*

Daniel, book of, 221–3, 228

David, king, 225–6

Desiderius, Lombard king, 218

Dhondt, Jan, 3–4, 12, 79

Dijon, 113

Dodo, royal *fidelis*, 109, 110

Donzère, 114

Dorestad, 11

duchies, 4–5, 49, 59–64, 65; *see also* principalities

Eberhard of Friuli, *marchio*, 71

Ebo of Rheims, archbishop, 29

Ebolus of St-Denis, abbot, 57

economy, 11–12

Einhard, biographer, 33, 57, 59, 199, 205, 213, 214, 228

Ekkehard IV of St-Gall, historian, 88, 157, 202

Engelberga, empress, 92, 94–6, 112–13, 166, 169–70, 171, 183

Engelschalk, margrave, 137–8

Engilger, Bavarian warrior, 193

Epiphany, 146–56

Erardus, Italian count, 71

Erchempert of Monte Cassino, historian, 63, 74

Erchingen, 88

Esther, Book of, 30, 174, 177

Field of Lies, the (833), 196

fisc, royal, 12–14, 94–6, 97

Florus of Lyon, 163

Fontenoy, battle of (841), 219

Fouron, Treaty of (878), 103

Frankfurt, 97, 151, 194

Frotar of Bourges, archbishop, 74

Fulda, 145, 148, 149, 150, 151, 152

Fulk of Rheims, archbishop, 56, 107, 117–18, 166

Gauzlin of St-Denis, abbot and bishop, 39, 57, 58, 103–6, 107–8, 115–16

Geilo of Langres, bishop, 110–16, 119, 120, 126–7, 128, 148–9, 160, 168

Gerold, *marchio* in Bavaria, 77

Gibbon, Edward, 1, 8

Glanfeuil, 104

Godafrid I, Viking leader, 203, 213–15

Godafrid III, Viking leader, 31, 32, 150, 203, 213–15

Golden Psalter of St-Gall, 154, 225–6

Gondreville, 150

Grand, Lotharingia, 126–9

Gundbato, deacon, 135, 136

Guy of Spoleto, *dux* and king, 70, 96, 111, 112, 119, 121, 127, 128, 180

Hadrian III, pope, 134, 142, 159, 161, 173, 192

Haimo of Belluno, bishop, 71–2, 181

Halphen, Louis, 199

Hartmut of St-Gall, abbot, 203

Hatto of Mainz, archbishop, 171–2

Henry, royal general, 34, 38–9, 61, 97, 98, 150, 214

Herbert of Vermandois, count, 107, 109

Herifridus, bishop of Auxerre, 51–3

Hildebold, count in Alemannia, 89–90

Hildegard, queen, 212

Hincmar of Rheims, archbishop, 36, 37, 43, 124, 158, 159, 168, 211

Hlawitschka, Eduard, 163, 166

honores (offices), 14–16, 51, 67, 72, 73–5, 76–7, 183; *see also* aristocracy

Hucbald of Senlis, count, 108

259

Index

Hugh of Lotharingia, son of Lothar II, 26, 123, 128, 130, 133, 143, 149–53, 220
Hugh of St-Quentin, 106
Hugh, son of Louis the Younger, 133
Hugh the Abbot, 39, 51, 65–6, 67, 103, 104–5, 116, 117
hunting, 19, 39, 95, 103, 124, 217

identities, *see* national/regional identities
Inverno, 94
Irmingarde, princess, 113, 162, 165, 166
Isembard, nobleman, 217

Jerome, St, 221–3, 228
John VIII, pope, 185
Judith, empress, 175
Julian the Apostate, 223

Karlmann of Bavaria, king, 83–6, 91–2, 94, 134–5, 141, 221–3
Kaumberg, 138
Keller, Hagen, 182–3, 194
Kienast, Walther, 49, 61, 64
Kinzheim, 187, 188
Kirchen, assembly of (887), 109, 112–13, 162, 167–8
Kocel, Slavic *dux*, 136
Korvey, 98

land, *see* aristocracy; fisc, royal; *honores*
Langres, 132–3, 145; *see also* Geilo of Langres
Lassois, 113
Lausanne, 68, 85
lay abbacies, 72–3; *see also* Morienval; St-Julien; St-Martin; St-Maurice d'Agaune
Leuven, 129
Life of St Verena, see Verena, St
Liutbert of Mainz, archbishop, 24–6, 28–30, 33, 38–9, 44–5, 46, 86, 97–8, 120, 130, 151, 152, 162–3, 190, 205–13, 229
Liutfrid, count and *fidelis* of Rudolf, 68
Liutswind, Arnulf's mother, 134
Liutward of Vercelli, archchancellor, 25–6, 28–30, 31, 33, 35, 44–5, 46, 53, 70, 87, 91, 155, 162–3, 169, 178–86, 187–91, 202, 228, 229
lordship, territorial, 73–5
Lorsch, 111, 132–3, 142, 152
Lothar I, emperor, 127, 163, 164, 166
Lothar II, king, 25, 85, 134, 151, 169–71, 178
Lotharingia, 48, 82, 126–9, 131–2, 166–8; *see also* Hugh of Lotharingia
Louis II of Italy, emperor, 70, 72, 91, 96, 124, 165, 169, 178, 182–3

Louis III of west Francia, king, 37, 102–3, 107–8, 117, 118, 124, 128, 137, 192
Louis of Provence, king and emperor, 112–13, 123, 162–8
Louis the German, king, 25, 38, 83–6, 89, 98, 99, 111, 124, 132, 140, 141, 157, 164, 178, 207, 221, 224–5
Louis the Pious, emperor, 8, 19, 21, 77, 83, 121, 162, 175, 196
Louis the Stammerer, king, 17, 65, 102, 117, 124, 231
Louis the Younger, king, 25, 38, 83–6, 97, 102, 117, 132–3, 134–6, 192
Löwe, Heinz, 200
Ludwigslied, the, 124

Magi, the, 153
Mainz annalist, the, *see Annals of Fulda*
Manasses, Burgundian count, 68
Mantaille, Assembly of (879), 68, 110, 112, 127; *see also* Boso of Vienne
marchio (as a title), 67, 70, 183
Meletto, 94
Moosburg, 136
Moravia, 85; *see also* Zwentibald of Moravia
Morienval, 106
Moutier-Grandval, 68

national/regional identities, 4–5, 59–64, 82, 115–20; *see also* duchies; principalities
Neudingen, 87, 196
Neustria, 49–61, 65–6, 67, 76–7, 79; *see also* Hugh the Abbot; Odo of Paris; Robert the Strong
Notker the Stammerer, historian, 27, 63, 85, 88, 131, 134, 143–4, 147, 152, 154–6, 159, 172, 199–229
Noyon, 107

Odo of Paris, count and king, 49–67, 72–9, 101, 104, 106, 108–9, 111, 115–16, 117, 119–20, 166, 168
offices, *see honores*
Orléans, 50–1
Otbert, *praepositus* of Langres, 111
Ötting, 141–2
Otto I, king and emperor, 189
Otulf, royal chaplain, 185

Paderborn, 98
palaces, royal, 93; *see also* Aachen; Bodman; Corteolona; Frankfurt; Kirchen, assembly of (887); Moosburg; Ötting; Ponthion; Ravenna; Regensburg; Sélestat; Ulm
Palding, 89

260

Index

Pannonia, 135–40

Paris, siege of (885–6), 35, 55–64, 103, 106, 121; *see also* Abbo of St-Germain

Pavia, 93, 94–6, 125, 147

Peter, Berengar's chaplain, 94

Pfäffers, 178

Pîtres, Edict of (864), 18

Ponthion, 126, 127, 129

Pontoise, 106

Pribina, Slavic *dux*, 136

principalities, 4–5, 49, 59–64

Prüm, 131, 150

Pseudo-Cyprian, 43

Pseudo-Isidore, 211–12

Pseudo-Remedius, 211–12

Quartinaha, 136

queens, queenship, *see* Engleberga; Irmingarde; Judith; Richgard

Quierzy, Capitulary of (877), 15, 116–17

Ragnoldus, military leader, 104

Raino of Angers, bishop, 67

Ratpert of St-Gall, historian, 202

Ravenna, 93, 147, 178

rebellions, 20–2, 64, 178; *see also* Boso of Vienne; Hugh of Lotharingia

regalia, 125, 127, 208

Regensburg, 98, 157

Regino of Prüm, historian, 27, 36, 79, 121, 123, 150, 169–70, 171, 176, 190, 191–2, 195, 230

Reginold, *fidelis* of Rudolf, 68

regional identities, *see* national/regional identities

Reichenau, 28, 83, 87–9, 145, 166, 191, 201, 216

relics, 87, 120, 156–8

Remiremont, 178

Richgard, empress, 85, 90, 91, 169, 178, 185–91, 202, 207, 228

Robert, Odo's brother and count, 108, 116

Robert the Strong, count, 49, 53, 54, 65–6, 75

Roric, father of Gauzlin, 104

Royal Frankish Annals, 26, 45, 214, 221

Rudolf of Transjurane Burgundy, *marchio* and king, 67–9, 72–9, 109, 120, 125, 126

Ruodbert, custodian of the royal chapel, 87, 186

S Cristina, Olona, 93–5

S Marino, Pavia, 186

S Sisto, Piacenza, 94

Säckingen, 186

Salluciolas, 94

Salomon of Constance, bishop, 89, 209

Sanctio, royal *fidelis*, 109

Saucourt, Battle of (881), 37

Saxon Poet, 63, 98

Schlesinger, Walter, 6, 7

Schlettstadt, *see* Sélestat

Sélestat (Schlettstadt), 90, 111, 120, 187–9

Solignac, 113

Spoleto, 96, 180; *see also* Guy of Spoleto

SS Feliz and Regula, Zurich, 83, 186, 188

Stammheim, 87–9, 90, 216, 217

St-Boniface, Fulda, *see* Fulda

St-Denis, 103, 107, 125

Stephen V, pope, 161, 167, 168–9, 173

St-Gall, 63, 83, 86, 87–9, 150, 201–3, 215–16, 217; *see also* Ekkehard IV; Notker the Stammerer; Ratpert of St-Gall

St-Julien, Brioude, 69, 72, 74

St-Marcel-lès-Chalon, synod of (887), 111, 112–13, 115

St-Martin, Tours, 50, 53, 65, 72–3

St-Maur-des-Fossés, 104

St-Maurice d'Agaune, 72–3

St-Quentin, 106, 117, 118; *see also* Theoderic of Vermandois; Hugh of St-Quentin

Strasbourg, 89

St-Vincent, Viviers, 114

subkingship, 48, 78, 121, 131–2, 143, 167–8

Suppo, Italian count, 71

Susinate, 94

Tellenbach, Gerd, 6

Teotarius of Gerona, bishop, 101

Tetbert of Meaux, count, 109

Teutbertus, episcopal candidate in Auxerre, 51–3

Thegan, biographer, 29

Theoderic of Vermandois, count, 102–3, 104, 105–8, 115–16, 118–19, 125

Tonnerre, 113

Toulouse, counts of, 76–7

Tournus, 114

trade, 11–12

Tribur, 192, 194

Troyes, 113

True Cross, the, *see* relics

Turimbert, Burgundian count, 68

Udalrich, count in Alemannia, 89–90, 91, 216–17

Ulm, 83

Valence, Capitulary of (890), 164–5

Verdun, Treaty of (843), 4, 106, 163

Verena, St, 171–2, 191

261

Index

Vienne, Oaths of (880), 21–2, 48, 124, 173, 192, 232
Vigonzone, 94
Vikings, 17–18, 20, 30–7, 55–64, 97, 102, 106, 114, 124–5, 129, 164, 168, 206, 221–2, 234; *see also* Asselt, siege of; Godafrid I; Godafrid III; Paris, siege of
Virgil, 223
viscounts, 73
Vision of Charles the Fat, The, 166
Vodelgis, *fidelis* of Rudolf, 68, 125

Waiblingen, 167–8
Wala, Charlemagne's cousin, 77
Walter of Orléans, bishop, 50–3
Walter of Sens, archbishop, 50, 51–3, 116
Waltfred of Verona, count, 71, 182–3
warfare, *see* armies; Vikings; Wilhelminer War
Wars of the City of Paris (poem), *see* Abbo of St-Germain

Weißenburg, 26
Welf of St-Colombe, abbot, 117–18
Werner, Karl-Ferdinand, 5, 103
Wibaldus of Auxerre, bishop, 51–3
Wibod of Parma, bishop, 92, 94–6, 126, 182–3, 184
Wido of Spoleto, *see* Guy of Spoleto
Wigbert, count, 31, 33
Wilhelminer War (882–4), 137–8, 139, 192
William, margrave, 137–8
Winzenheim, 187
Worms, 97, 131–2

Yverdon, 126

Zurzach, 171–2, 186
Zwentibald of Lotharingia, king, 150
Zwentibald of Moravia, Slavic *dux*, 137–8, 139, 142, 143, 154, 192–3

Cambridge Studies in Medieval Life and Thought
Fourth Series

Titles in series

1 The Beaumont Twins: The Roots and Branches of Power in the Twelfth Century
D. B. CROUCH

2 The Thought of Gregory the Great*
G. R. EVANS

3 The Government of England Under Henry I*
JUDITH A. GREEN

4 Charity and Community in Medieval Cambridge*
MIRI RUBIN

5 Autonomy and Community: The Royal Manor of Havering, 1200–1500*
MARJORIE KENISTON MCINTOSH

6 The Political Thought of Baldus de Ubaldis*
JOSEPH CANNING

7 Land and Power in Late Medieval Ferrara: The Rule of the Este, 1350–1450*
TREVOR DEAN

8 William of Tyre: Historian of the Latin East*
PETER W. EDBURY AND JOHN GORDON ROWE

9 The Royal Saints of Anglo-Saxon England: A Study of West Saxon and East Anglian Cults
SUSAN J. RIDYARD

10 John of Wales: A Study of the Works and Ideas of a Thirteenth-Century Friar*
JENNY SWANSON

11 Richard III: A Study of Service*
ROSEMARY HORROX

12 A Marginal Economy? East Anglian Breckland in the Later Middle Ages
MARK BAILEY

13 Clement VI: The Pontificate and Ideas of an Avignon Pope*
DIANA WOOD

14 Hagiography and the Cult of Saints: The Diocese of Orléans, 800–1200
THOMAS HEAD

15 Kings and Lords in Conquest England*
ROBIN FLEMING

16 Council and Hierarchy: The Political Thought of William Durant the Younger*
CONSTANTIN FASOLT

17 Warfare in the Latin East, 1192–1291*
CHRISTOPHER MARSHALL

18 Province and Empire: Brittany and the Carolingians
JULIA M. H. SMITH

19 A Gentry Community: Leicestershire in the Fifteenth Century, c. 1422–c. 1485*
ERIC ACHESON

20 Baptism and Change in the Early Middle Ages, c. 200–1150*
PETER CRAMER

21 Itinerant Kingship and Royal Monasteries in Early Medieval Germany, c. 936–1075*
JOHN W. BERNHARDT

22 Caesarius of Arles: The Making of a Christian Community in Late Antique Gaul*
WILLIAM E. KLINGSHIRN

23 Bishop and Chapter in Twelfth-Century England: A Study of the *Mensa Episcopalis**
EVERETT U. CROSBY

24 Trade and Traders in Muslim Spain: The Commercial Realignment of the Iberian Peninsula, 900–1500*
OLIVIA REMIE CONSTABLE

25 Lithuania Ascending: A Pagan Empire Within East-Central Europe, 1295–1345
S. C. ROWELL

26 Barcelona and Its Rulers, 1100–1291*
STEPHEN P. BENSCH

27 Conquest, Anarchy and Lordship: Yorkshire, 1066–1154*
PAUL DALTON

28 Preaching the Crusades: Mendicant Friars and the Cross in the Thirteenth Century*
CHRISTOPH T. MAIER

29 Family Power in Southern Italy: The Duchy of Gaeta and Its Neighbours, 850–1139*
PATRICIA SKINNER

30 The Papacy, Scotland and Northern England, 1342–1378*
A. D. M. BARRELL

31 Peter des Roches: An Alien in English Politics, 1205–1238*
NICHOLAS VINCENT

32 Runaway Religious in Medieval England, c. 1240–1540*
F. DONALD LOGAN

33 People and Identity in Ostrogothic Italy, 489–554*
PATRICK AMORY

34 The Aristocracy in Twelfth-Century León and Castile*
SIMON BARTON

35 Economy and Nature in the Fourteenth Century: Money, Market Exchange and the Emergence of Scientific Thought*
JOEL KAYE

36 Clement V*
SOPHIA MENACHE

37 England's Jewish Solution, 1262–1290: Experiment and Expulsion*
ROBIN R. MUNDILL

38 Medieval Merchants: York, Beverley and Hull in the Later Middle Ages*
JENNY KERMODE

39 Family, Commerce and Religion in London and Cologne: A Comparative Social History of Anglo-German Emigrants, c. 1000–c. 1300*
JOSEPH P. HUFFMAN

40 The Monastic Order in Yorkshire, 1069–1215
JANET BURTON

41 Parisian Scholars in the Early Fourteenth Century: A Social Portrait
WILLIAM J. COURTENAY

42 Colonisation and Conquest in Medieval Ireland: The English in Louth, 1170–1330
BRENDAN SMITH

43 The Early Humiliati
FRANCES ANDREWS

44 The Household Knights of King John
S. D. CHURCH

45 The English in Rome, 1362–1420: Portrait of an Expatriate Community
MARGARET HARVEY

46 Restoration and Reform: Recovery from Civil War in England, 1153–1165
GRAEME J. WHITE

47 State and Society in the Early Middle Ages: The Middle Rhine Valley, 400–1000
MATTHEW INNES

48 Brittany and the Angevins: Province and Empire, 1157–1203
JUDITH EVERARD

49 The Making of Gratian's *Decretum*
ANDERS WINROTH

50 At the Gate of Christendom: Jews, Muslims and 'Pagans' in Medieval Hungary, *c.* 1000–*c.* 1300
NORA BEREND

51 Making Agreements in Medieval Catalonia: Power, Order, and the Written Word, 1000–1200
ADAM J. KOSTO

52 The Making of the Slavs: History and Archaeology of the Lower Danube Region, *c.* 500–700
FLORIN CURTA

53 Literacy in Lombard Italy, *c.* 568–774
NICHOLAS EVERETT

54 Metaphysics and Politics in the Thought of John Wyclif
STEPHEN E. LAHEY

55 Envoys and Political Communication in the Late Antique West, 411–533
ANDREW GILLETT

56 Kings, Barons and Justices: The Making and Enforcement of Legislation in Thirteenth-Century England
PAUL BRAND

57 Kingship and Politics in the Late Ninth Century: Charles the Fat and the End of the Carolingian Empire
SIMON MACLEAN

Also published as a paperback